Get the eBook FREE!

(PDF, ePub, Kindle, and liveBook all included)

We believe that once you buy a book from us, you should be able to read it in any format we have available. To get electronic versions of this book at no additional cost to you, purchase and then register this book at the Manning website.

Go to https://www.manning.com/freebook and follow the instructions to complete your pBook registration.

That's it!
Thanks from Manning!

Good Code, Bad Code

Think Like a Software Engineer

Good Code, Bad Code

Think Like a Software Engineer

TOM LONG

MANNING
SHELTER ISLAND

For online information and ordering of this and other Manning books, please visit www.manning.com. The publisher offers discounts on this book when ordered in quantity. For more information, please contact

Special Sales Department
Manning Publications Co.
20 Baldwin Road
PO Box 761
Shelter Island, NY 11964
Email: orders@manning.com

Manning Publications Co.
20 Baldwin Road
PO Box 761
Shelter Island, NY 11964

Development editor: Toni Arritola
Senior technical development editor: Al Scherer
Technical development editor: Mike Jensen
Review editor: Aleks Dragosavljević
Production editor: Andy Marinkovich
Copy editor: Michele Mitchell
Proofreader: Jason Everett
Technical proofreader: Chris Villanueva
Typesetter and cover designer: Marija Tudor

ISBN 9781617298936
Printed in the United States of America

contents

preface

I've been coding in one form or another since I was 11 years old, so by the time I landed my first job as a software engineer, I'd written quite a lot of code. Despite this, I quickly discovered that coding and software engineering are not the same thing. Coding as a software engineer meant that my code had to make sense to other people and not break when they changed things. It also meant that there were real people (sometimes lots of them) using and relying on my code, so the consequences of things going wrong were a lot more serious.

As a software engineer gets more experienced, they learn how the decisions they make in their everyday coding can have big consequences on whether software will work properly, keep working properly, and be maintainable by others. Learning how to write good code (from a software engineering point of view) can take many years. These skills are often picked up slowly and in an ad hoc way as engineers learn from their own mistakes or get piecemeal advice from more senior engineers that they work with.

This book aims to give new software engineers a jump-start in acquiring these skills. It teaches some of the most important lessons and theoretical underpinnings of writing code that will be reliable, maintainable, and adaptable to changing requirements. I hope that you find it useful.

acknowledgments

Writing a book is not a lone effort, and I'd like to thank everyone who had a hand in bringing this book into reality. In particular, I'd like to thank my development editor, Toni Arritola, for patiently guiding me through the process of authoring a book, and for her constant focus on the reader and high-quality teaching. I'd also like to thank my acquisition editor, Andrew Waldron, for believing in the idea for the book in the first place and for the many invaluable insights provided along the way. I'd also like to thank my technical development editor, Michael Jensen, for his deep technical insights and suggestions throughout the book. And thank you to my technical proofreader, Chris Villanueva, for carefully reviewing the code and technical content of the book, and for all the great suggestions.

I'd also like to thank all of the reviewers—Amrah Umudlu, Chris Villanueva, David Racey, George Thomas, Giri Swaminathan, Harrison Maseko, Hawley Waldman, Heather Ward, Henry Lin, Jason Taylor, Jeff Neumann, Joe Ivans, Joshua Sandeman, Koushik Vikram, Marcel van den Brink, Sebastian Larsson, Sebastián Palma, Sruti S, Charlie Reams, Eugenio Marchiori, Jing Tang, Andrei Molchanov, and Satyaki Upadhyay—who took the time to read the book at multiple stages throughout its development and provide precise and actionable feedback. It's hard to overstate just how important and useful this feedback has been.

Nearly all the concepts in this book are well-established ideas and techniques within the software engineering community, so as a final acknowledgement I'd like to say thank you to all those who have contributed to, and shared, this body of knowledge over the years.

about this book

Good Code, Bad Code introduces key concepts and techniques that professional software engineers regularly use to produce reliable and maintainable code. Rather than just enumerating do's and don'ts, the book aims to explain the core reasoning behind each concept and technique, as well as any trade-offs. This should help readers develop a fundamental understanding of how to think and code like a seasoned software engineer.

Who should read this book

This book is aimed at people who can already code but who want to improve their skills at coding as a software engineer in a professional environment. This book will be most useful to anyone with zero to three years' experience as a software engineer. More experienced engineers will probably find that they already know many of the things in the book, but I hope that they will still find it a useful resource for mentoring others.

How this book is organized: A roadmap

The book is organized into 11 chapters, spread across three parts. The first part introduces some more theoretical, high-level concepts that shape the way we think about code. The second part moves onto more practical lessons. Each chapter in part 2 is split into a series of topics that cover a particular consideration or technique. The third and final part of the book covers principles and practices that go into creating effective and maintainable unit tests.

The general pattern in individual sections of the book is to demonstrate a scenario (and some code) that can be problematic and to then show an alternative approach that eliminates some or all of the problems. In this sense, sections tend to progress from showing "bad" code to showing "good" code, with the caveat that the terms *bad* and *good* are subjective and context dependent. And as the book aims to emphasize, there are often nuances and trade-offs to consider, meaning this distinction is not always clear-cut.

Part 1, "In theory," sets the foundations for some overarching and slightly more theoretical considerations that shape our approach to writing code as software engineers.

- Chapter 1 introduces the concept of *code quality*, and in particular a practical set of goals for what we aim to achieve with high-quality code. It then expands these into six "pillars of code quality," which provide high-level strategies that can be employed in our everyday coding.
- Chapter 2 discusses *layers of abstraction*, a fundamental consideration that guides how we structure and split code into distinct parts.
- Chapter 3 highlights the importance of thinking about other engineers who will have to work with our code. It goes on to discuss *code contracts* and how thinking carefully about these can prevent bugs.
- Chapter 4 discusses errors and why thinking carefully about how to signal and handle them is a vital part of writing good code.

Part 2, "In practice," covers the first five pillars of code quality (established in chapter 1) in a more practical way with specific techniques and examples.

- Chapter 5 covers making code readable, which ensures that other engineers will be able to make sense of it.
- Chapter 6 covers avoiding surprises, which minimizes the chance of bugs by ensuring that other engineers will not misinterpret what a piece of code does.
- Chapter 7 covers making code hard to misuse, which minimizes the chance of bugs by making it difficult for engineers to accidentally produce code that is logically wrong or that violates assumptions.
- Chapter 8 covers making code modular, a key technique that helps ensure code exhibits clean layers of abstraction, and that it will be adaptable to changing requirements.
- Chapter 9 covers making code reusable and generalization. This makes adding new functionality or building new features easier and safer by preventing the need to reinvent the wheel.

Part 3, "Unit testing," introduces key principles and practices that go into writing effective unit tests.

- Chapter 10 introduces a number of principles and higher level considerations that influence how we unit test code.
- Chapter 11 builds on the principles in chapter 10 to provide a number of specific and practical suggestions for writing unit tests.

The ideal way to read this book is cover to cover, because the ideas in earlier parts of the book lay the foundations for subsequent parts. But despite this, the topics in part 2 (and chapter 11) are typically quite self-contained, and each span only a few pages, so most will be useful even if read in isolation. This is deliberate, with the aim of providing an effective way to quickly explain an established best practice to another engineer. This is intended to be useful for any engineers wishing to explain a specific concept in a code review or while mentoring another engineer.

About the code

The book is aimed at engineers who code in a statically typed, object-oriented programming language, such as one of the following: Java, C#, TypeScript, JavaScript (ECMAScript 2015 or later with a static type checker), C++, Swift, Kotlin, Dart 2, or similar. The concepts covered in this book are widely applicable whenever coding in a language like one of these.

Different programming languages have different syntaxes and paradigms for expressing logic and code structure. But in order to provide code examples in this book, it's necessary to standardize on some kind of syntax and set of paradigms. For this, the book uses a pseudocode that borrows ideas from a number of different languages. The aim with the pseudocode is to be explicit, clear, and easily recognizable to the greatest number of engineers. Please bear this utilitarian intent in mind; the book does not aim to suggest that any one language is better or worse than any other.

Similarly, where there is a trade-off between being unambiguous and being succinct, the pseudocode examples tend to err on the side of being unambiguous. One example of this is the use of explicit variable types, as opposed to inferred types with a keyword like *var*. Another example is the use of if-statements to handle nulls, rather than the more succinct (but perhaps less familiar) null coalescing and null conditional operators (see appendix B). In real codebases (and outside of the context of a book) engineers may wish to place a greater emphasis on succinctness.

liveBook discussion forum

Purchase of *Good Code, Bad Code: Think Like a Software Engineer* includes free access to a private web forum run by Manning Publications where you can make comments about the book, ask technical questions, and receive help from the author and from other users. To access the forum, go to https://livebook.manning.com/#!/book/good-code-bad-code/discussion. You can also learn more about Manning's forums and the rules of conduct at https://livebook.manning.com/#!/discussion.

Manning's commitment to our readers is to provide a venue where a meaningful dialogue between individual readers and between readers and the author can take place. It is not a commitment to any specific amount of participation on the part of the author, whose contribution to the forum remains voluntary (and unpaid). We suggest you try asking the author some challenging questions lest his interest stray! The forum and the archives of previous discussions will be accessible from the publisher's website as long as the book is in print.

How to use the advice in this book

While reading any book or article about software engineering, it's always worth remembering that it's a subjective topic and that the solutions to real-world problems are rarely clear-cut. In my experience, the best engineers approach everything they read with a healthy amount of skepticism and a desire to understand the fundamental thinking behind it. Opinions differ and evolve, and the tools and programming languages available are constantly improving. Understanding the reasons behind a particular piece of advice, its context, and its limits are essential for knowing when to apply it and when to ignore it.

This book aims to collect a number of useful topics and techniques to help guide engineers toward writing better code. Even though it's probably wise to consider these things, nothing in this book should be considered infallible or applied as a hard-and-fast rule that can never be broken. Good judgment is an essential ingredient of good engineering.

Further reading

This book aims to be a stepping stone into the world of coding as a software engineer. It should give the reader a broad idea of ways to think about code, things that can be problematic, and techniques for avoiding these problems. But the journey shouldn't end here; software engineering is a huge and ever evolving subject area, and it's highly advisable to read broadly and to keep up-to date with things. In addition to reading articles and blogs, some books on the subject that readers may find useful are as follows:

- *Refactoring: Improving the Design of Existing Code*, second edition, Martin Fowler (Addison-Wesley, 2019)
- *Clean Code: A Handbook of Agile Software Craftsmanship*, Robert C. Martin (Prentice Hall, 2008)
- *Code Complete: A Practical Handbook of Software Construction*, second edition, Steve McConnell (Microsoft Press, 2004)
- *The Pragmatic Programmer: Your Journey to Mastery*, 20th anniversary, second edition, David Thomas and Andrew Hunt (Addison-Wesley 2019)
- *Design Patterns: Elements of Reusable Object-Oriented Software*, Erich Gamma, Richard Helm, Ralph Johnson, and John Vlissides (Addison-Wesley, 1994)
- *Effective Java*, third edition, Joshua Bloch (Addison-Wesley, 2017)
- *Unit Testing: Principles, Practices and Patterns*, Vladimir Khorikov (Manning Publications, 2020)

about the author

TOM LONG is a software engineer at Google. He works as a tech lead, and among other tasks, regularly mentors new software engineers in professional coding best practices.

about the cover illustration

The figure on the cover of *Good Code, Bad Code* is captioned "Homme Zantiote," or a man from the island of Zakynthos in Greece. The illustration is taken from a collection of dress costumes from various countries by Jacques Grasset de Saint-Sauveur (1757–1810), titled *Costumes de Différents Pays,* published in France in 1797. Each illustration is finely drawn and colored by hand. The rich variety of Grasset de Saint-Sauveur's collection reminds us vividly of how culturally apart the world's towns and regions were just 200 years ago. Isolated from each other, people spoke different dialects and languages. In the streets or in the countryside, it was easy to identify where they lived and what their trade or station in life was just by their dress.

The way we dress has changed since then and the diversity by region, so rich at the time, has faded away. It is now hard to tell apart the inhabitants of different continents, let alone different towns, regions, or countries. Perhaps we have traded cultural diversity for a more varied personal life—certainly for a more varied and fast-paced technological life.

At a time when it is hard to tell one computer book from another, Manning celebrates the inventiveness and initiative of the computer business with book covers based on the rich diversity of regional life of two centuries ago, brought back to life by Grasset de Saint-Sauveur's pictures.

Part 1

In theory

The world of software engineering is full of advice and opinions on how best to write code. But life is rarely as simple as just absorbing as many of these as possible and then following them religiously. For a start, different pieces of advice from different sources can often contradict one another, so how do we know which one to follow? But more to the point: software engineering is not an exact science, and it can't be distilled down to a set of infallible rules (however hard we might try). Every project is different, and there are nearly always trade-offs to consider.

In order to write good code, we need to apply a sound sense of judgment to the scenario at hand and be able to think through the consequences (good and bad) of a particular way of doing something. For this, we need to understand the fundamentals: What are we actually trying to achieve when we write code? And what are the high-level considerations that help us get there? Part 1 aims to provide a solid grounding in these more theoretical aspects of writing good code.

1 Code quality

This chapter covers

- The reason code quality matters
- The four goals that high-quality code aims to achieve
- The six high-level strategies we can use to ensure code is of a high-quality
- How writing high-quality code actually saves time and effort in the medium to long term

You've probably used hundreds, maybe even thousands of different pieces of software in the past year. Every program installed on your computer, every app on your phone, and every self-service checkout you've had the pleasure of contending with—we interact with software a lot.

There are also many pieces of software that we depend on without even necessarily realizing it. We trust our bank, for example, to have a well-behaved backend system that isn't going to unexpectedly transfer the contents of our bank account to someone else, or suddenly decide that we're in millions of dollars of debt.

Sometimes we encounter pieces of software that are an absolute delight to use; they do exactly what we want, contain very few bugs, and are easy to use. But other times we encounter pieces of software that are absolutely horrible to use. They are full of bugs, crash all the time, and are unintuitive.

Some pieces of software are obviously less critical than others; an app on our phone containing a bug is probably annoying but not the end of the world. A bug in a bank's backend system, on the other hand, has the potential to ruin lives. Even issues in pieces of software that don't seem critical can ruin businesses. If users find a piece of software annoying or difficult to use, then there's a good chance that they will switch to an alternative.

Higher quality code tends to produce software that is more reliable, easier to maintain, and less buggy. Many of the principles around increasing code quality are concerned not just with ensuring that software is initially this way, but that it stays this way throughout its lifetime as requirements evolve and new scenarios emerge. Figure 1.1 illustrates some of the ways in which code quality can affect the quality of the software.

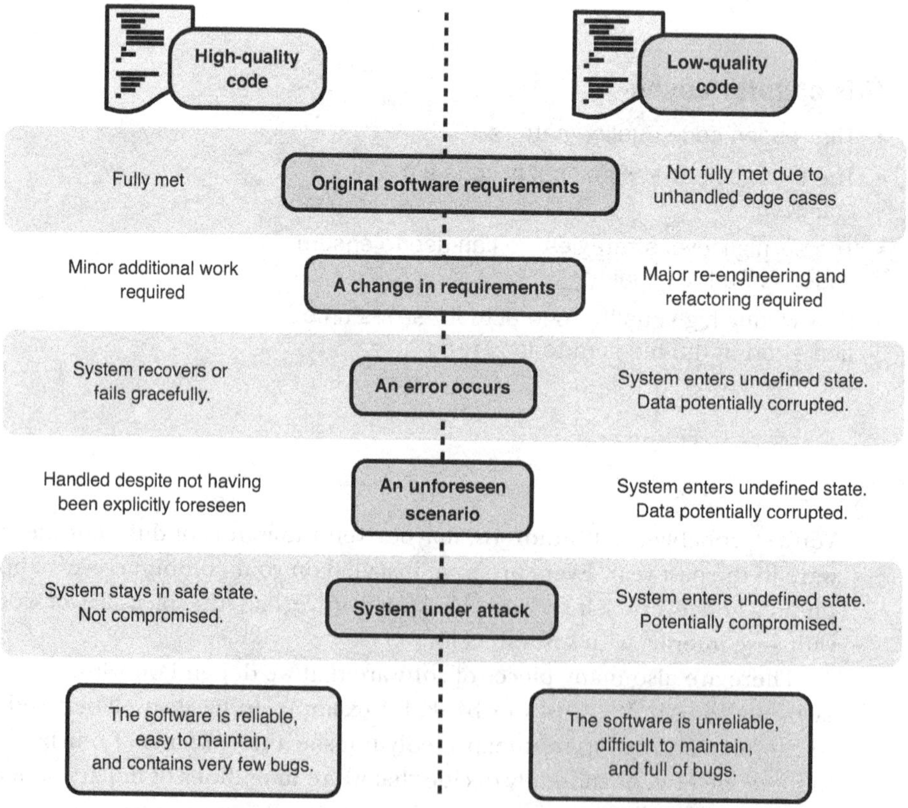

Figure 1.1 High-quality code maximizes the chance that the software will be reliable, maintainable, and meet its requirements. Low-quality code tends to do the opposite.

Good code is obviously not the only ingredient that goes into making good software, but it is one of the main ones. We can have the best product and marketing teams in the world, deploy on the best platforms, and build with the best frameworks, but at the end of the day everything a piece of software does happens because someone wrote a piece of code to make it happen.

The everyday decisions engineers make when writing code can seem small in isolation and sometimes insignificant, but they collectively determine whether a piece of software will be good or bad. If code contains bugs, is misconfigured, or doesn't handle error cases properly, then software built from it will likely be buggy and unstable and probably not do its job properly.

This chapter identifies four goals that high-quality code should aim to achieve. This is then expanded into six high-level strategies we can employ in our everyday work to ensure the code we write is of high quality. Later chapters in this book explore these strategies in increasing levels of detail, with many worked examples using pseudocode.

1.1 How code becomes software

Before we delve into talking about code quality, it's worth briefly discussing how code becomes software. If you already have familiarity with the software development and deployment process, then feel free to skip to section 1.2. If you're someone who knows how to code but you've never worked in a software engineering role before, then this section should give you a good high-level overview.

Software is made from code; that much is obvious and doesn't really need stating. What can be less obvious (unless you already have experience as a software engineer) is the process by which code becomes software running in the wild (in the hands of users, or performing business-related tasks).

Code generally doesn't become software running in the wild the moment an engineer writes it. There are usually various processes and checks in place to try and ensure that the code does what it's meant to and doesn't break anything. These are often referred to as the software development and deployment process.

We don't need detailed knowledge of this process for this book to make sense, but it'll help to at least know the high-level outline of it. To start, it's useful to introduce a few pieces of terminology:

- *Codebase*—The repository of code from which pieces of software can be built. This will typically be managed by a version control system such as git, subversion, perforce, etc.
- *Submitting code*—Sometimes called "committing code" or "merging a pull request," a programmer will typically make changes to the code in a local copy of the codebase. Once they are happy with the change they will submit it to the main codebase. Note: in some setups, a designated maintainer has to pull the changes into the codebase rather than the author submitting them.

- *Code review*—Many organizations require code to be reviewed by another engineer before it can be submitted to the codebase. This is a bit like having code proofread; a second pair of eyes will often spot issues the author of the code missed.
- *Pre-submit checks*—Sometimes called "pre-merge hooks," "pre-merge checks," or "pre-commit checks," these will block a change from being submitted to the codebase if tests fail or if the code does not compile.
- *A release*—A piece of software is built from a snapshot of the codebase. After various quality assurance checks, this is then released into the wild. You will often hear the phrase "cutting a release" to refer to the process of taking a certain revision of the codebase and making a release from it.
- *Production*—This is the proper term for *in the wild* when software is deployed to a server or a system (rather than shipped to customers). Once software is released and performing business-related tasks it is said to be running in production.

There are many variations on the process of how code becomes software running in the wild, but the key steps in the processes are usually the following:

1. An engineer will work on a local copy of the codebase to make changes.
2. Once they are happy, they will send these changes for a code review.
3. Another engineer will review the code and possibly suggest alterations.
4. Once both the author and the reviewer are happy, the code will be submitted to the codebase.
5. Releases will be periodically cut from the codebase. The frequency of this can vary between different organizations and teams (from the order of every few minutes to the order of every few months).
6. Any tests failing or the code not compiling will either block code from being submitted to the codebase or block the code from being released.

Figure 1.2 provides an outline of a typical software development and deployment process. Different companies and teams all have their own variations on this process, and the level to which parts of the process are automated can vary enormously.

It's worth noting that software development and deployment processes are enormous topics in their own right; many entire books have been written about them. There are also many different frameworks and ideologies around them, and it's well worth reading more about it if you're interested. This book is not primarily about these topics, so we won't cover them in any more detail than we just did. All you need to know for this book is the rough idea of how code becomes software.

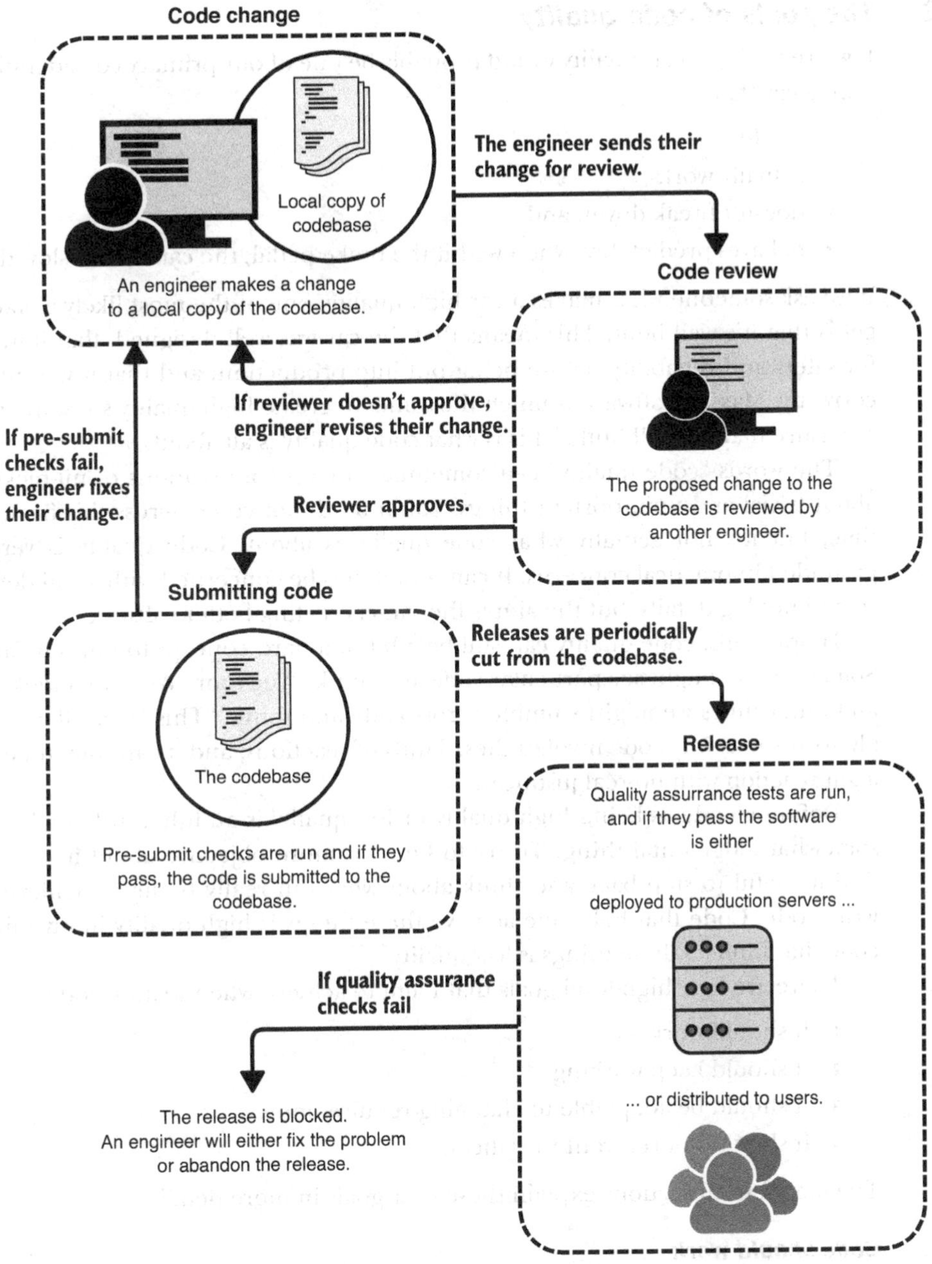

Figure 1.2 A simplified diagram of a typical software development and deployment process. The exact steps and the level of automation can vary greatly between different organizations and teams.

1.2 The goals of code quality

If we're buying a car, quality would probably be one of our primary considerations. We want a car that

- is safe,
- actually works,
- doesn't break down, and
- behaves predictably: when we hit the brake pedal, the car should slow down.

If we ask someone what makes a car high quality, one of the most likely answers we'll get is that it's well built. This means that the car was well designed, that it was tested for safety and reliability before being put into production, and that it was assembled correctly. Making software is much the same: to create high-quality software, we need to ensure that it's well built. This is what code quality is all about.

The words "code quality" can sometimes stir up connotations of nit-picky advice about trivial and unimportant things. You'll no doubt come across this from time to time, but it's not actually what code quality is about. Code quality is very much grounded in practical concerns. It can sometimes be concerned with small details and sometimes big details, but the aim is the same: creating better software.

Despite this, code quality can still be a bit of a hard concept to put our finger on. Sometimes we might see particular code and think, "Yuck" or "Wow, that looks hacky," and other times we might stumble across code and think, "This is excellent." It's not always obvious why code invokes these kinds of reactions, and it can sometimes just be a gut reaction with no real justification.

Defining code as being high quality or low quality is an inherently subjective and somewhat judgmental thing. To try to be a bit more objective about it; I personally find it useful to step back and think about what I'm really trying to achieve when I write code. Code that helps me achieve these things is high quality in my mind, and code that hinders these things is low quality.

There are four high-level goals that I aim to achieve when writing code:

1. It should work.
2. It should keep working.
3. It should be adaptable to changing requirements.
4. It should not reinvent the wheel.

The next few subsections explain these four goals in more detail.

1.2.1 Code should work

This one is so obvious it probably doesn't need stating, but I'll go ahead and say it anyway. When we write code, we are trying to solve a problem, such as implementing a feature, fixing a bug, or performing a task. The primary aim of our code is that it should work; it should solve the problem that we intend it to solve. This also implies that the code is bug free, because the presence of bugs will likely prevent it from working properly and fully solving the problem.

When defining what code "working" means, we need to capture all the requirements. For example, if the problem we are solving is particularly sensitive to performance (such as latency or CPU usage), then ensuring that our code is adequately performant comes under "code should work," because it's part of the requirements. The same applies to other important considerations such as user privacy and security.

1.2.2 Code should keep working

Code working can be a very transient thing; it might work today, but how do we make sure that it will still work tomorrow, or in a year's time? This might seem like an odd thing to worry about; why would code suddenly stop working? The point is that code does not live in isolation, and if we're not careful it can easily break as things around it change.

- Code likely depends on other code that will get modified, updated, and changed.
- Any new functionality required may mean that modifications are required to the code.
- The problem we're trying to solve might evolve over time: consumer preferences, business needs, and technology considerations can all change.

Code that works today but breaks tomorrow when one of these things changes is not very useful. It's often easy to create code that works but a lot harder to create code that keeps working. Ensuring that code keeps working is one of the biggest considerations that software engineers face and is something that needs to be considered at all stages of coding. Considering it as an afterthought or assuming that just adding some tests later on will achieve this are often not effective approaches.

1.2.3 Code should be adaptable to changing requirements

It's quite rare that a piece of code is written once and then never modified again. Continued development on a piece of software can span several months, usually several years, and sometimes even decades. Throughout this process requirements change:

- Business realities shift.
- Consumer preferences change.
- Assumptions get invalidated.
- New features are continually added.

Deciding how much effort to put into making code adaptable can be a tricky balancing act. On the one hand, we pretty much know that the requirements for a piece of software will evolve over time (it's extremely rare that they don't). But on the other hand, we often have no certainty about exactly how they will evolve. It's impossible to make perfectly accurate predictions about how a piece of code or software will change over time. But just because we don't know exactly *how* something will evolve doesn't mean that we should completely ignore the fact that it *will* evolve. To illustrate this, let's consider two extreme scenarios:

- *Scenario A*—We try to predict exactly how the requirements might evolve in the future and engineer our code to support all these potential changes. We will likely spend days or weeks mapping out all the ways that we think the code and software might evolve. We'll then have to carefully deliberate every minutiae of the code we write to ensure that it supports all these potential future requirements. This will slow us down enormously; a piece of software that might have taken three months to complete could now take a year or more. And at the end, it will probably have been a waste of time because a competitor will have beat us to market by several months, and our predictions about the future will probably turn out to be wrong anyway.
- *Scenario B*—We completely ignore the fact that the requirements might evolve. We write code to exactly meet the requirements as they are now and put no effort into making any of the code adaptable. Brittle assumptions get baked in all over the place, and solutions to subproblems are all bundled together into large inseparable chunks of code. We get the first version of the software launched within three months, but the feedback from the initial set of users makes it clear that we need to modify some of the features and add new ones if we want the software to be successful. The changes to the requirements are not massive, but because we didn't consider adaptability when writing the code, our only option is to throw everything away and start again. We then have to spend another three months rewriting the software, and if the requirements change again, we'll have to spend another three months rewriting it again after that. By the time we've created a piece of software that meets the users' needs, a competitor has once again beaten us to it.

Scenario A and scenario B represent two opposing extremes. The outcome in both scenarios is quite bad, and neither is an effective way to create software. Instead, we need to find an approach somewhere in the middle of these two extremes. There's no single answer for which point on the spectrum between scenario A and scenario B is optimal. It will depend on the kind of project we're working on and on the culture of the organization we work for.

Luckily, there are some generally applicable techniques we can adopt to ensure that code is adaptable without having to know exactly how it might be adapted in the future. We'll cover many of these techniques in this book.

1.2.4 Code should not reinvent the wheel

When we write code to solve a problem, we generally take a big problem and break it down into multiple smaller subproblems. For example, if we were writing code to load an image file, turn it into a grayscale image, and then save it again, the subproblems we need to solve are as follows:

- Load some bytes of data from a file.
- Parse the bytes of data into an image format.
- Transform the image to grayscale.

- Convert the image back into bytes.
- Save those bytes back to the file.

Many of these problems have already been solved by others; for example, loading some bytes from a file is likely something that the programming language has built-in support for. We wouldn't write our own code to do low-level communication with the file system. Similarly there is probably an existing library we can pull in to parse the bytes into an image.

If we do write our own code to do low-level communication with the file system or to parse some bytes into an image, then we are effectively reinventing the wheel. There are several reasons it's best to make use of an existing solution over reinventing it:

- *It saves time and effort*—If we made use of the built-in support for loading a file, it'd probably take only a few lines of code and a few minutes of our time. In contrast, writing our own code to do this would likely require reading numerous standards documents about file systems and writing many thousands of lines of code. It would probably take us many days if not weeks.
- *It decreases the chance of bugs*—If there is existing code somewhere to solve a given problem, then it should already have been thoroughly tested. It's also likely that it's already being used in the wild, so the chance of the code containing bugs is lowered, because if there were any, they've likely been discovered and fixed already.
- *It utilizes existing expertise*—The team maintaining the code that parses some bytes into an image are likely experts on image encoding. If a new version of JPEG-encoding comes out, then they'll likely know about it and update their code. By reusing their code we benefit from their expertise and future updates.
- *It makes code easier to understand*—If there is a standardized way of doing something, then there's a reasonable chance that another engineer will have seen it before. Most engineers have probably had to read a file at some point and will instantly recognize the built-in way of doing that and understand how it functions. If we write our own custom logic for doing this, then other engineers will not be familiar with it and won't instantly know how it functions.

The concept of not reinventing the wheel applies in both directions. If another engineer has already written code to solve a subproblem, then we should call their code rather than writing our own to solve it. But similarly, if we write code to solve a subproblem, then we should structure our code in a way that makes it easy for other engineers to reuse so that they don't need to reinvent the wheel.

The same classes of subproblems often crop up again and again, so the benefits of sharing code between different engineers and teams are often realized very quickly.

1.3 The pillars of code quality

The four goals we just looked at help us focus on what we're fundamentally trying to achieve, but they don't provide particularly specific advice about what to do in our everyday coding. It's useful to try to identify more specific strategies that will help us write code that meets these goals. This book will be centered around six such strategies, which I'll refer to (in an overly grand way) as "the six pillars of code quality." We'll start with a high-level description of each pillar, but later chapters will provide specific examples that show how to apply these in our everyday coding.

The six pillars of code quality:

1. Make code readable.
2. Avoid surprises.
3. Make code hard to misuse.
4. Make code modular.
5. Make code reusable and generalizable.
6. Make code testable and test it properly.

1.3.1 Make code readable

Consider the following passage of text. It's deliberately hard to read, so don't waste too much time deciphering it. Skim read and absorb what you can:

> *Take a bowl; we'll now refer to this as A. Take a saucepan; we'll now refer to this as B. Fill B with water and place on the hob. Take A and place butter and chocolate into it, 100 grams of the former, 185 grams of the latter. It should be 70% dark chocolate. Place A on top of B; leave it there until the contents of A have melted, then take A off of B. Take another bowl; we'll now refer to this as C. Take C and place eggs, sugar, and vanilla essence in it, 2 of the first, and 185 grams of the second, and half a teaspoon of the third. Mix the contents of C. Once the contents of A have cooled, add the contents of A to C and mix. Take a bowl; we'll refer to this as D. Take D and place flour, cocoa powder, and salt in it, 50 grams of the first, 35 grams of the second, and half a teaspoon of the third. Mix the contents of D thoroughly and then sieve into C. Mix contents of D just enough to fully combine them. We're making chocolate brownies by the way; did I forget to mention that? Take D and add 70 grams of chocolate chips, mix contents of D just enough to combine. Take a baking tin; we will refer to this as E. Grease and line E with baking paper. Place the contents of D into E. We will refer to your oven as F. You should have preheated F to 160°C by the way. Place E into F for 20 minutes, then remove E from F. Allow E to cool for several hours.*

Now some questions:

- What is the passage of text about?
- What will we end up with after following all the instructions?
- What ingredients, and how much of them, do we need?

We can find the answer to all these questions in the passage of text, but it's not easy; the text has poor *readability*. There are several issues that make the text less readable, including the following:

- There is no title, so we have to read the whole passage just to figure out what it is about.
- The passage is not nicely presented as a series of steps (or subproblems); it is instead presented as one big wall of text.

- Things are referred to with unhelpfully vague names, like "A" instead of "the bowl with melted butter and chocolate."
- Pieces of information are placed far away from where they're needed: ingredients and their quantities are separated, and the important instruction that the oven needs preheating is only mentioned at the end.

(In case you got fed up and stopped reading the passage of text, it's a recipe for chocolate brownies. There is a more readable version in appendix A in case you actually want to make them.)

Reading a piece of badly written code and trying to figure things out is not dissimilar from the experience we just had of reading the brownie recipe. In particular, we might struggle to understand the following things about the code:

- What it does
- How it does it
- What ingredients it needs (inputs or state)
- What we'll get after running that piece of code

At some point, another engineer will most likely need to read our code and understand it. If our code has to undergo a code review before being submitted, then this will happen almost immediately. But even ignoring the code review, at some point someone will find themselves looking at our code and trying to figure out what it does. This can happen when requirements change or the code needs debugging.

If our code has poor readability, other engineers will have to spend a lot of time trying to decipher it. There is also a high chance that they might misinterpret what it does or miss some important details. If this happens, then it's less likely that bugs will be spotted during code review, and it's more likely that new bugs will be introduced when someone else has to modify our code to add new functionality. Everything a piece of software does happens because of some code that makes it happen. If engineers can't understand what that code does, then it becomes almost impossible to make sure the software as a whole will do its job properly. Just like with a recipe, code needs to be readable.

In chapter 2, we'll see how defining the right layers of abstraction can help with this. And in chapter 5 we'll cover a number of specific techniques for making code more readable.

1.3.2 Avoid surprises

Being given a gift on your birthday or winning the lottery are both examples of nice surprises. When we're trying to get a specific task done, however, surprises are usually a bad thing.

Imagine you're hungry, so you decide to order some pizza. You get your phone out, find the number for the pizza restaurant, and hit dial. The line is silent for a weirdly long period of time but eventually connects and the voice on the other end asks you what you want.

"One large margherita for delivery please."

"Uh okay, what's your address?"

Half an hour later your order is delivered, you open the bag to find the following (figure 1.3).

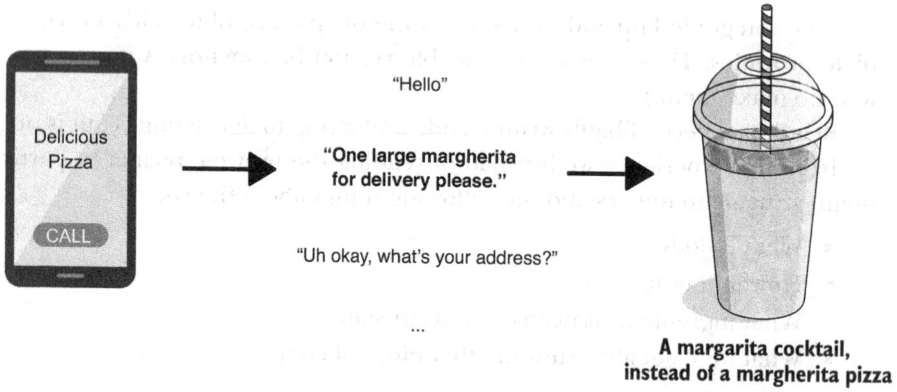

Figure 1.3 If you think you're talking to a pizza restaurant, when you're in fact talking to a Mexican restaurant, your order may still make sense, but you'll get a surprise when it's delivered.

Wow, that's surprising. Obviously someone has mistaken "margherita" (a type of pizza) for "margarita" (a type of cocktail), but that's kind of weird because the pizza restaurant doesn't serve cocktails.

It turns out that the custom dialer app you use on your phone has added a new "clever" feature. The developers of it observed that when users call a restaurant and find the line busy, 80% of them will immediately call a different restaurant, so they created a handy, time-saving feature: when you call a number that the dialer recognizes as a restaurant and the line is busy, it seamlessly dials the next restaurant number in your phone instead.

In this case that happened to be your favorite Mexican restaurant rather than the pizza restaurant you thought you were calling. The Mexican restaurant most definitely does serve margarita cocktails but not pizzas. The developers of the app had good intentions and thought they were making users' lives easier, but they created a system that does something surprising. We rely on our mental model of a phone call to determine what is happening based on what we hear. Importantly, if we hear a voice answer, then our mental model tells us we've been connected to the number we dialed.

The new feature in the dialer app modifies the behavior outside of what we would expect; it breaks our mental model's assumption that if a voice answers we have been connected to the number we dialed. It could well be a useful feature, but because its behavior is outside of a normal person's mental model, it needs to make explicit what is happening, like having an audio message that tells us that the number we called is busy and asking us if we'd like to be connected to another restaurant instead.

The dialer app is analogous to a piece of code. Another engineer using our code will use cues such as names, data types, and common conventions to build a mental model about what they expect our code to take as input, what it will do, and what it will return. If our code does something outside of this mental model, then it can very often lead to bugs creeping into a piece of software.

In the example of calling the pizza restaurant, it seemed like everything was working even after the unexpected happened: you ordered a margherita and the restaurant was happy to oblige. It was only much later, after it was too late to rectify, that you discovered you had inadvertently ordered a cocktail instead of food. This is analogous to what often happens in software systems when some code does something surprising: because the caller of the code doesn't know to expect it, they carry on unaware. It will often look like things are fine for a bit, but then later things will go horribly wrong when the program finds itself in an invalid state or a weird value is returned to a user.

Even with the best of intentions, writing code that does something helpful or clever can run the risk of causing surprises. If code does something surprising, then the engineer using that code will not know or think to handle that scenario. Often this will cause a system to limp on until some weird behavior manifests far away from the code in question. This might cause a mildly annoying bug, but it might also cause a catastrophic problem that corrupts some important data. We should be wary of causing surprises in our code and try to avoid them if we can.

In chapter 3, we'll see how thinking about code contracts is a fundamental technique that can help with this. Chapter 4 covers errors, which can be a cause of surprises if not signaled or handled appropriately. And chapter 6 looks at a number of more specific techniques for avoiding surprises.

1.3.3 Make code hard to misuse

If we look at the back of a TV, it will probably look something like figure 1.4. It will have a bunch of different sockets that we can plug cables into. Importantly, the sockets will have different shapes; the manufacturer of the TV has made it impossible to plug the power cord into the HDMI socket.

Imagine if the manufacturer had not done this and had instead made every socket the same shape. How many people do you think might accidentally end up plugging cables into the wrong sockets as they are fumbling around at the back of their TV? If someone plugged the HDMI cable into the power socket, then stuff would probably not

Figure 1.4 The sockets on the back of a TV are deliberately different shapes to make it hard to plug the wrong cables into the wrong holes.

work. That would be annoying but not too catastrophic. If someone plugged the power cable into the HDMI socket though, that might literally cause things to blow up.

Code we write is often called by other code and is a bit like the back of a TV. We expect that other code to "plug" certain things in, like input arguments or placing the system in a certain state before calling. If the wrong things get plugged into our code, then things might blow up; the system crashes, a database gets permanently corrupted, or some important data gets lost. Even if things don't blow up there's a good chance that the code is not going to work. There was a reason our code got called, and the incorrect stuff being plugged in might mean that an important task doesn't get performed or some weird behavior happens but goes unnoticed.

We can maximize the chance that code works and stays working by making things hard or impossible to misuse. There are numerous practical ways of doing this. Chapter 3 covers code contracts, which (similarly to avoiding surprises) is a fundamental technique that can help make code hard to misuse. Chapter 7 covers a number of more specific techniques for making code hard to misuse.

1.3.4 Make code modular

Modularity means that an object or system is composed of smaller components that can be independently exchanged or replaced. To demonstrate this, as well as the benefits of modularity, consider the two toys in figure 1.5.

The toy on the left is highly modular. The head, arms, hands, and legs can all be easily and independently exchanged or replaced without affecting other parts of the toy. The toy on the right, conversely, is highly non-modular. There is no easy way to exchange or replace the head, arms, hands, or legs.

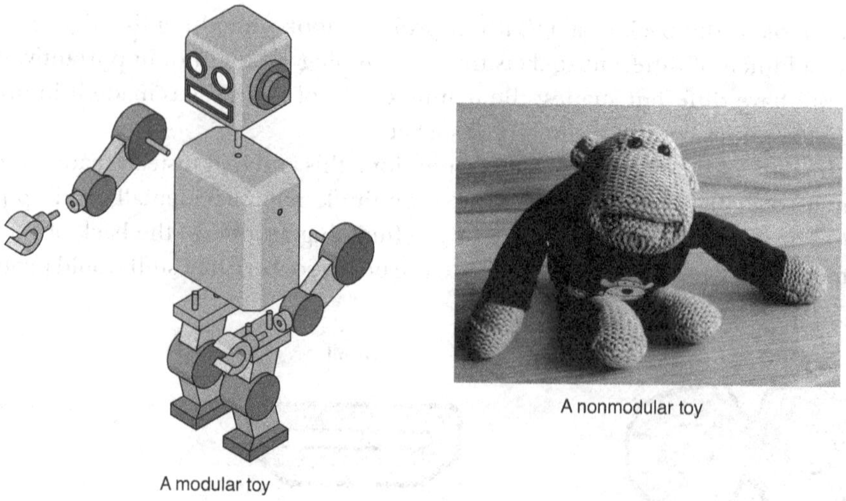

Figure 1.5 A modular toy can be easily reconfigured. A toy that has been stitched together is extremely hard to reconfigure.

One of the key features of a modular system (such as the toy on the left) is that the different components have well-defined interfaces, with as few points of interaction as possible. If we consider a hand as a component, then with the toy on the left there is a single point of interaction with a simple interface: a single peg and a single hole that it fits into. The toy on the right has an incredibly complex interface between a hand and the rest of the toy: 20-plus loops of thread on the hand and the arm interwoven into one another.

Now imagine that our job is maintaining these toys, and one day our manager tells us that there is a new requirement that the hands now need to have fingers. Which toy/system would we rather be working with?

With the toy on the left, we could manufacture a new design of the hand and then very easily exchange it with the existing ones. If our manager then changed their mind two weeks later, we'd have no trouble returning the toy to its previous configuration.

With the toy on the right, we'd probably have to get the scissors out, cut 20-plus strands of thread, and then stitch new hands directly onto the toy. We'd likely damage the toy in the process, and if our manager did change their mind two weeks later, we'd have a similarly laborious process to return the toy to the previous configuration.

Software systems and codebases are very much analogous to these toys. It's often beneficial to break a piece of code down into self-contained modules, where interactions between two adjacent modules happen in a single place and use a well-defined interface. This helps ensure that the code will be easier to adapt to changing requirements, because changes to one piece of functionality don't require lots of changes all over the place.

Modular systems are also generally easier to comprehend and reason about, because functionality is broken into manageable chunks and the interactions between the chunks of functionality are well defined and documented. This increases the chance that code will work in the first place and keep working in the future, because it's less likely that engineers will misunderstand what the code does.

In chapter 2, we'll see how creating clean layers of abstraction is a fundamental technique that can guide us toward more modular code. And in chapter 8, we'll look at a number of specific techniques for making code more modular.

1.3.5 Make code reusable and generalizable

Reusability and generalizability are two similar but slightly different concepts:

- *Reusability* means that something can be used to solve the same problem but in multiple scenarios. A hand drill is reusable because it can be used to drill holes in walls, in floor boards, and in ceilings. The problem is the same (a hole needs drilling), but the scenario is different (drilling into a wall versus into the floor versus into the ceiling).
- *Generalizability* means something can be used to solve multiple conceptually similar problems that are subtly different. A hand drill is also generalizable, because as well as being used to drill holes, it can also be used to drive screws

into things. The drill manufacturer recognized that rotating something is a general problem that applies to both drilling holes and driving screws, so they created a tool that generalizes to solve both problems.

In the case of the drill, we can immediately recognize the benefits of this. Imagine if we needed four different tools:

- A drill that only worked while being held level, meaning it was only useful for drilling into walls.
- A drill that only worked while being pointed down at a 90° angle, meaning it was only useful for drilling into the floor.
- A drill that only worked while being pointed up at a 90° angle, meaning it was only useful for drilling into the ceiling.
- An electric screwdriver for driving screws into things.

We'd have spent a lot more money acquiring this collection of four tools, we'd have to carry more stuff around with us, and we'd have to charge four times as many batteries—it's just wasteful. Thankfully someone created a drill that is both reusable and generalizable, and we only need one to do all these different jobs. There are no prizes for guessing that the hand drill here is yet another analogy for code.

Code takes time and effort to create, and once it's created it also takes ongoing time and effort to maintain. Creating code is also not without risks: however careful we are, some amount of the code we write will contain bugs, and the more of it we write, the more bugs we're likely to have. The point here is that the fewer lines of code we have in a codebase, the better. It might seem weird to say this when our job seems to involve being paid to write code, but really we're being paid to solve a problem, and code is just a means to that end. If we can solve that problem while exerting less effort and also reduce the chance that we're inadvertently creating other problems by introducing bugs, then great.

Making code reusable and generalizable allows us (and others) to use it in multiple places throughout a codebase, in more than one scenario, and to solve more than one problem. It saves time and effort and makes our code more reliable because we'll often be reusing logic that has already been tried and tested in the wild, meaning any bugs have likely already been discovered and fixed.

Code that is more modular also tends to be more reusable and generalizable. The chapters relating to modularity go hand-in-hand with the topic of reusability and generalizability. In addition, chapter 9 covers a number of techniques and considerations specific to making code more reusable and generalizable.

1.3.6 Make code testable and test it properly

As we saw earlier in the software development and deployment diagram (figure 1.2), tests are a vital part of the process of ensuring that bugs and broken functionality do not end up running in the wild. They're often the main defense at two of the key points in the process (figure 1.6):

- Preventing buggy or broken functionality from being submitted to the codebase
- Ensuring that a release with bugs or broken functionality is blocked and doesn't end up in the wild

Tests are therefore an essential part of ensuring that code works and that it keeps working.

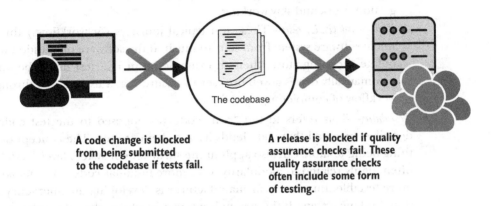

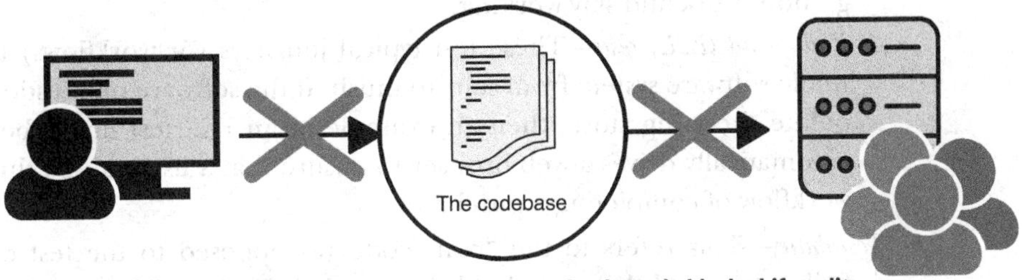
The codebase
A code change is blocked from being submitted to the codebase if tests fail.
A release is blocked if quality assurance checks fail. These quality assurance checks often include some form of testing.

Figure 1.6 Tests are vital for minimizing the chance that bugs and broken functionality enter the codebase and for ensuring they are not released into the wild if they do.

It's hard to overstate just how important testing is in software development. You've no doubt heard this multiple times before, and it becomes easy to start dismissing it as just another platitude, but it really is important. As we'll see at multiple points throughout the book,

- software systems and codebases tend to be too big and complicated for a single person to know every minute detail about them, and
- people (even exceptionally clever engineers) make mistakes.

These are more or less facts of life, and unless we lock the functionality of our code in with tests, then these have a habit of ganging up on us (and our code).

The title of this pillar of code quality contains two important concepts: "make code testable" and "test it properly." Testing and testability are related, but have different considerations:

- *Testing*—As the name suggests, this relates to testing our code or the software as a whole. Testing can be manual or automated. As engineers, we will usually strive to make our testing automated by writing test code that exercises the "real" code and checks that everything behaves as it should. There are different levels of testing. Three of the most common you will probably work with are as follows. *(Please note that this is not an exhaustive list; there are many ways of categorizing tests, and different organizations often use different nomenclatures.)*

- *Unit tests*—These usually test small units of code such as individual functions or classes. Unit testing is the level of testing engineers tend to work with most often in their everyday coding. This is the only level of testing this book will cover in any detail.
- *Integration tests*—A system is usually built up of multiple components, modules, or subsystems. The process of linking these components and subsystems together is known as *integration*. Integration tests try to ensure that these integrations work and stay working.
- *End-to-end (E2E) tests*—These test typical journeys (or workflows) through a whole software system from start to finish. If the software in question were an online shopping store, then an example of an E2E test might be one that automatically drives a web browser to ensure that a user can go through the workflow of completing a purchase.

- *Testability*—This refers to the "real" code (as opposed to the test code) and describes how well that code lends itself to being tested. The concept of something being testable can also apply at the subsystem or system level. Testability is often highly related to modularity, with more modular code (or systems) being more testable. Imagine a car manufacturer is developing an emergency pedestrian braking system. If the system is not very modular, then the only way to test it might be to install it in a real car, drive the car at a real pedestrian, and check that the car automatically comes to a stop. If this is the case, then the number of scenarios that the system can be tested in is limited, because the cost of each test is so high: building an entire car, renting a test track, and putting a real person at risk as they pretend to be a pedestrian in the road. The emergency braking system becomes a lot more testable if it's a distinct module that can be run outside of a real car. It can now be tested by feeding it a prerecorded video of a pedestrian stepping out and then checking that the system outputs the correct signal intended for the braking system. It's now very easy, cheap, and safe to test many thousands of different pedestrian scenarios.

If code is not testable, then it can become impossible to test it properly. To ensure that the code we write is testable, it's good to continually ask ourselves "How will we test this?" as we are writing the code. Therefore, testing should not be considered an afterthought: it's an integral and fundamental part of writing code at all stages. Chapters 10 and 11 are all about testing, but because testing is so integral to writing code, we will find that it crops up in numerous places throughout this book.

NOTE: TEST-DRIVEN DEVELOPMENT Because testing is so integral to writing code, some engineers advocate that the tests should be written before the code. This is one of the practices championed by the *test-driven development (TDD)* process. We'll discuss this more in chapter 10 (section 10.5).

Software testing is a huge topic, and to be upfront about it, this book will not come close to doing it justice. In this book, we'll cover some of the most important, and often overlooked, aspects of unit testing code because these are usually most useful in the course of everyday coding. But please be aware that by the end of this book we will only have scratched the surface of what there is to know about software testing.

1.4 Does writing high-quality code slow us down?

The answer to this question is that in the very short term it might seem like writing high-quality code slows us down. Writing code that is high quality usually requires a little more thought and effort than just coding the first thing that comes into our heads. But if we're writing anything more substantive than a small, run-once-then-throw-away utility, then writing high-quality code will usually speed up development times over the mid to long term.

Imagine we are putting a shelf up at home. There is the "proper" way of doing this, and then there is the quick, "hacky" way of doing this:

- *The proper way*—We attach brackets to the wall by drilling and screwing into something solid like the wall studs or masonry. We then mount the shelf on these brackets. Time taken: 30 minutes.
- *The hacky way*—We buy some glue and glue the shelf to the wall. Time taken: 10 minutes.

It seems like the hacky way of putting the shelf up can save us 20 minutes and also saves us the effort of getting the drill and screwdriver out. We chose the quick approach; now let's consider what happens next.

We glued the shelf to whatever the wall is surfaced with; this is most likely a layer of plaster. Plaster is not strong and can easily crack and come off in large chunks. As soon as we start using the shelf, the weight of items on it will likely cause the plaster to crack, and the shelf will fall and bring a large chunk of plaster with it. We now don't have a working shelf and also need to replaster and redecorate the wall (a job that will take several hours, if not days). Even if by some miracle the shelf doesn't fall down, we've created future problems for ourselves by putting it up the quick way. Imagine a couple of scenarios:

- We realize that we haven't put the shelf up quite level (a bug):
  - For the bracketed shelf, we can just add a smaller spacer between the bracket and the shelf. Time taken: 5 minutes.
  - For the glued shelf, we need to rip it off the wall; this will then take a big chunk of plaster with it. We now need to replaster the wall and then put the shelf back up. Time taken: several hours, if not days.
- We decide to redecorate the room (a new requirement):
  - We can take the bracketed shelf down by taking the screws out. We redecorate the room and then put the shelf back up afterward. Time taken for shelf-related work: 15 minutes.
  - For the glued shelf, we either leave the shelf up and then run the risk of dripping paint on it and having untidy edges where we have to paint or wallpaper

around it. Or we need to rip the shelf off the wall and deal with the fact that we'll need to replaster. Our choice is between doing a shoddy redecorating job or spending several hours or days replastering the wall.

You get the idea. It might have initially seemed like doing it properly and putting a bracketed shelf up was an unnecessary waste of 20 minutes, but in the long run, it's quite likely that it saves us a lot of time and hassle. In the case of the future redecoration project, we also saw how starting out with a quick, hacky solution then pushes us down a path of doing more things in a hacky way, like trying to paint or wallpaper around the shelf instead of taking it down while redecorating.

Writing code is very similar to this. Coding the first thing that comes into our heads, without considering the quality of the code, will likely save us some time initially. But we will quickly end up with a fragile, complicated codebase, which becomes increasingly hard to understand or reason about. Adding new features or fixing bugs will become increasingly difficult and slow as we have to deal with breakages and re-engineering things.

You may have heard the phrase "less haste, more speed" before; it's a reference to the observation that with many things in life, acting too hastily without thinking things through or doing them properly often leads to mistakes that reduce our overall speed. "Less haste, more speed" is an excellent summary of why writing high-quality code speeds us up; don't mistake haste for speed.

Summary

- To create good software, we need to write high-quality code.
- Before code becomes software running in the wild, it usually has to pass several stages of checks and tests (sometimes manual, sometimes automated).
- These checks help prevent buggy and broken functionality reaching users or business-critical systems.
- It's good to consider testing at every stage of writing code; it shouldn't be considered as an afterthought.
- It might seem like writing high-quality code slows us down initially, but it often speeds up development times in the mid to long term.

2 Layers of abstraction

This chapter covers

- How to break a problem down into subproblems with clean layers of abstraction
- How layers of abstraction can help us achieve a number of the pillars of code quality
- APIs and implementation details
- How to break code into distinct layers of abstraction using functions, classes, and interfaces

Writing code is about solving problems. These can be high-level problems, such as "We need a feature to allow users to share photos," all the way down to low-level problems such as "We need some code to add two numbers together." Even if we're not conscious of the fact we're doing it, when we solve a high-level problem, we usually do it by breaking it down into multiple, smaller subproblems. A problem statement such as "We need a system to allow users to share photos" might imply that we need to solve subproblems like storing photos, associating them with users, and displaying them.

How we solve problems and subproblems is important, but often just as important is how we structure the code that solves them. For example, should we just dump everything into one giant function or class, or should we try and break it out into multiple functions or classes? And if so, how should we do this?

How we structure code is one of the most fundamental aspects of code quality, and doing it well often comes down to creating clean *layers of abstraction.* This chapter will explain what this means and demonstrate how breaking problems down into distinct layers of abstraction, and structuring code to reflect this, can greatly improve its readability, modularity, reusability, generalizability, and testability.

This chapter and the following ones provide lots of pseudocode examples to demonstrate the topics being discussed. Before delving into these examples, it's important to spend a few moments explaining how the pseudocode convention in this book handles null values. Section 2.1 will go over this, while sections 2.2 onward will cover the main topics of this chapter.

2.1 Nulls and the pseudocode convention in this book

Before we get into looking at coding examples, it's important to explain how the pseudocode convention in this book handles null values.

Many programming languages have the concept of a value (or reference/pointer) being absent; the built-in way of doing this is often with a null. Historically nulls have straddled a dichotomy between being incredibly useful and incredibly problematic.

- They are useful because the concept of something being absent very often occurs: a value hasn't been provided, or a function is unable to provide the desired result.
- They are problematic because it's not always obvious when a value can/cannot be null, and engineers very often forget to check if a variable is null before accessing it. This very often leads to errors; you've likely seen a `NullPointerException`, `NullReferenceException`, or `Cannot read property of null` error before, probably more than you care to remember.

Due to how problematic nulls can be, you will sometimes see advice that advocates never using them, or at least never returning them from a function. This certainly helps avoid the problems of nulls, but it can require a lot of code gymnastics to follow this advice in practice.

Luckily, in more recent years the idea of *null safety* (also called *void safety*) has gained increased traction. This ensures that any variables or return values that can be null are marked as such and the compiler enforces that they are not used without first checking that they are not null.

Most of the significant new languages to come out in recent years support null safety. It can also be optionally enabled in more recent versions of languages like C#, and there are even ways to retrofit it into languages like Java. If the language we are using supports null safety, then it's probably a good idea to make use of it.

If the language we're using does not support null safety, then a good alternative to using nulls is to use an optional type. Many languages have support for this, including Java, Rust (called Option), and C++ (although there are nuances to consider in C++, which are covered in appendix B). Even in languages that don't support it as a standard feature, there are often third-party utilities that add support for it.

The pseudocode convention in this book assumes that there is null safety. By default, variables, function parameters, and return types are all non-nullable. But if the type is suffixed with a `'?'` then that means it can be null, and the compiler will enforce that it is not used without first checking that it's non-null. The following snippet demonstrates what some pseudocode using null safety looks like:

```
Element? getFifthElement(List<Element> elements) {    <-- The ? in Element? indicates that the return type can be null.
  if (elements.size() < 5) {
    return null;                                       <-- null is returned when the value can't be obtained.
  }
  return elements[4];
}
```

If the language we're using doesn't support null safety and we want to write this function using an optional type, then the following snippet demonstrates how the code we just saw could be rewritten:

```
Optional<Element> getFifthElement(List<Element> elements) {    <-- The return type is an Optional Element.
  if (elements.size() < 5) {
    return Optional.empty();                                   <-- Optional.empty() is returned instead of null.
  }
  return Optional.of(elements[4]);
}
```

If you want to know more about null safety and optional types, appendix B contains more information.

2.2 Why create layers of abstraction?

Writing code is often about taking a complicated problem and continually breaking it down into smaller subproblems. To demonstrate this, imagine we are writing a piece of code to run on a user's device and that we want to send a message to a server. We would probably hope to be able to write something like the code in listing 2.1. Notice how simple the code is; it's three lines and only requires dealing with four simple concepts:

- A URL for a server
- A connection
- Sending a message string
- Closing the connection

Listing 2.1 Sending a message to a server

```
HttpConnection connection =
    HttpConnection.connect("http://example.com/server");
connection.send("Hello server");
connection.close();
```

At a high level, this seems like quite a simple problem, and indeed the solution to it does look quite simple. But this is obviously not a simple problem: there is an immense amount of complexity involved in sending the string `"Hello server"` from the client device to the server, including the following:

- Serializing the string into a format that can be transmitted
- All the intricacies of the HTTP protocol
- TCP connections
- Whether the user is on WiFi or a cellular network
- Modulating data onto a radio signal
- Data transmission errors and correction

In this example, there is a high-level problem we care about: sending a message to a server. But to do this there are many subproblems that need to be solved (such as all the ones just listed). Luckily for us, other engineers have already solved all these subproblems, but not only have they solved them, they've solved them in a way that means we don't even need to be aware of them.

We can think of the solutions to problems and subproblems as forming a series of layers. At the top-most layer, we care about sending a message to a server, and we can write code to do this without having to know anything about how the HTTP protocol is implemented. Similarly, the engineer who wrote the code to implement the HTTP protocol probably didn't have to know anything about how data is modulated onto a radio signal. The engineer who implemented the `HttpConnection` code was able to think of physical data transmission as an abstract concept, and, in turn, we are able to think of an HTTP connection as an abstract concept. This is known as *layers of abstraction.* Figure 2.1 shows some of the layers of abstraction involved in sending a message to a server.

It's worth taking another moment to appreciate just how simple the code for sending a message to a server is when compared to the vast complexity involved in actually doing it:

- It took three lines of simple code.
- It only involved dealing with four simple concepts:
  - A URL for a server
  - A connection
  - Sending a message string
  - Closing the connection

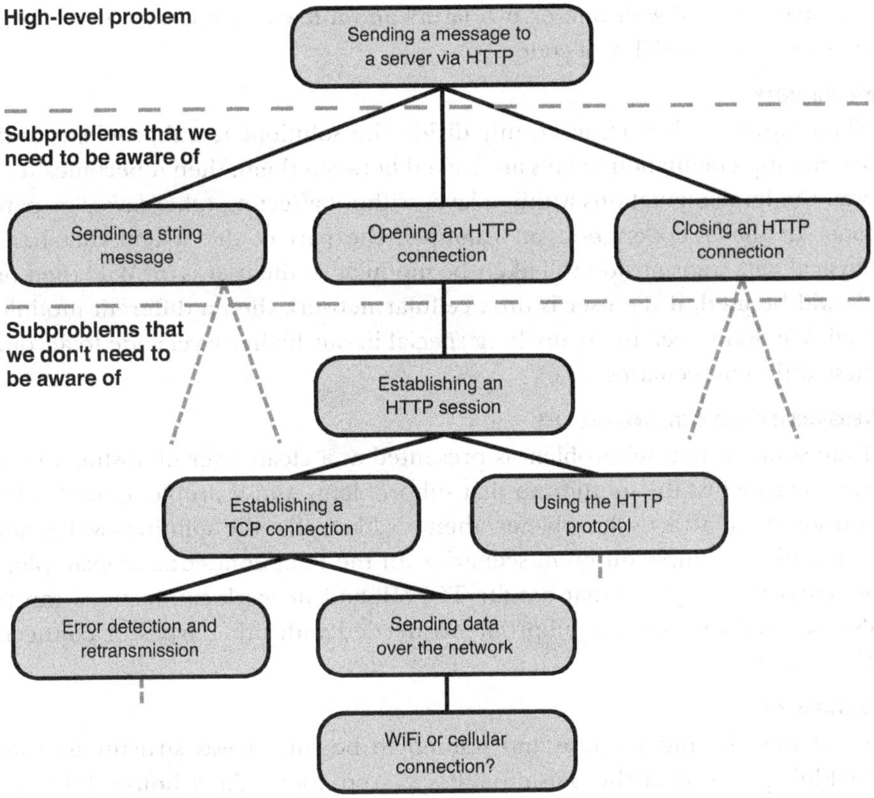

Figure 2.1 When sending a message to a server, we can reuse the solutions to subproblems that others have already created. The clean layers of abstraction also mean that we only have to be aware of a few concepts in order to solve the high-level problem we care about.

More generally, if we do a good job of recursively breaking a problem down into subproblems and creating layers of abstraction, then no individual piece of code will ever seem particularly complicated, because it will be dealing with just a few easily comprehended concepts at a time. This should be our aim when solving a problem as a software engineer: even if the problem is incredibly complicated we can tame it by identifying the subproblems and creating the correct layers of abstraction.

2.2.1 *Layers of abstraction and the pillars of code quality*

Building clean and distinct layers of abstraction goes a long way to achieving four of the pillars of code quality that we saw in chapter 1. The following subsections explain why.

READABILITY

It's impossible for engineers to understand every minutiae of every piece of code in a codebase, but it's quite easy for them to understand and use a few high-level abstractions at a time. Creating clean and distinct layers of abstraction means that engineers only need to deal with one or two layers and a few concepts at a time. This greatly increases the readability of code.

MODULARITY

When layers of abstraction cleanly divide the solutions to subproblems and ensure that no implementation details are leaked between them, then it becomes very easy to swap the implementations within a layer without affecting other layers or parts of the code. In the `HttpConnection` example, the part of the system that handles the physical data transmission will likely be modular. If the user is on WiFi then one module will be used; if the user is on a cellular network then a different module will be used. We don't need to do anything special in our higher level code to accommodate these different scenarios.

REUSABILITY AND GENERALIZABILITY

If the solution to a subproblem is presented as a clean layer of abstraction, then it's easy to reuse just the solution to that subproblem. And if problems are broken down into suitably abstract subproblems, then it's likely that the solutions will generalize to be useful in multiple different scenarios. In the `HttpConnection` example, most of the parts of the system that handle TCP/IP and network connections can probably also be used to solve the subproblems needed with other types of connection like WebSockets.

TESTABILITY

If you were buying a house and wanted to be sure it was structurally sound, you wouldn't just look at the outside and say "Yep, looks like a house. I'll buy it." You would want a surveyor to check that the foundations aren't subsiding, that the walls aren't cracked, and that any timber structures aren't rotten. Similarly, if we want reliable code, then we also need to ensure that the solution to each subproblem is sound and working. If the code is split cleanly into layers of abstraction, then it becomes a lot easier to fully test the solution to each subproblem.

2.3 Layers of code

In practice, the way we create layers of abstraction is by dividing code into different units, where one unit depends on another, creating a dependency graph (figure 2.2). In most programming languages we have several constructs at our disposal for breaking code into different units. More often than not we will have the following:

- Functions
- Classes (and potentially other class-like things such as structs and mixins)
- Interfaces (or an equivalent construct)
- Packages, namespaces, or modules
  - I mention these for completeness, but we won't actually cover them in this book, as these higher levels of code structuring are often dictated largely by organizational and system design considerations, neither of which are in the scope of this book.

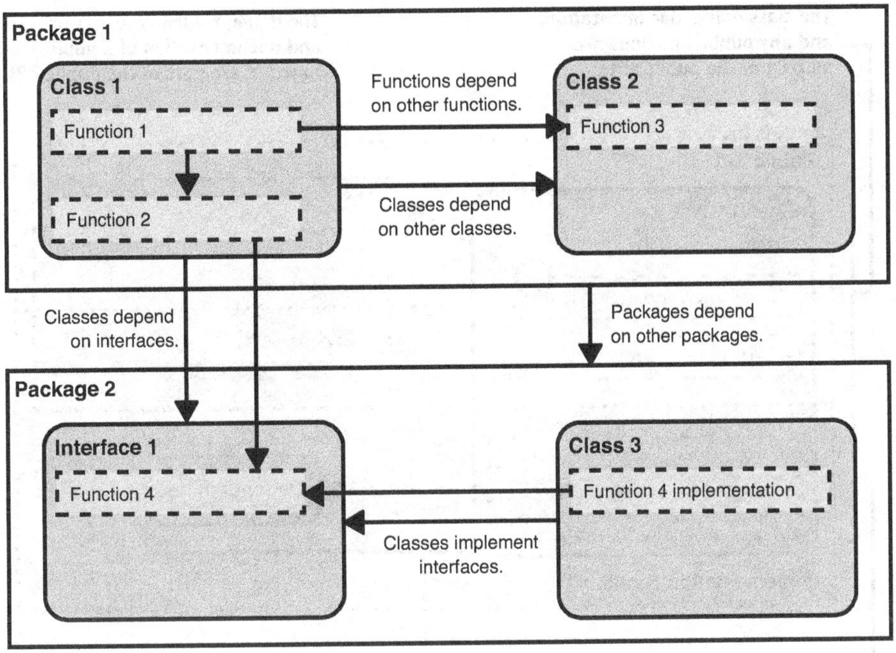

Figure 2.2 Units of code depend on other units of code, forming a dependency graph.

The next few sections will explore how best to break code into clean layers of abstraction by using functions, classes, and interfaces.

2.3.1 APIs and implementation details

When writing some code, there are often two aspects we need to think about:

- Things that callers of our code will see:
  - Which classes, interfaces, and functions we make public
  - What concepts things expose in their names, input parameters, and return types
  - Any extra information that callers need to know to use the code correctly (such as the order in which to call things)
- Things that callers of our code will not see: implementation details.

If you've ever worked with *services* (building them or calling them), then you will likely be familiar with the term *application programming interface (API)*. This formalizes the concept of things that callers of a service need to know, and all the implementation details of the service remain hidden behind the API.

It's often useful to think of the code we write as exposing a mini API that other pieces of code can use. Engineers often do this, and you will likely hear them talking

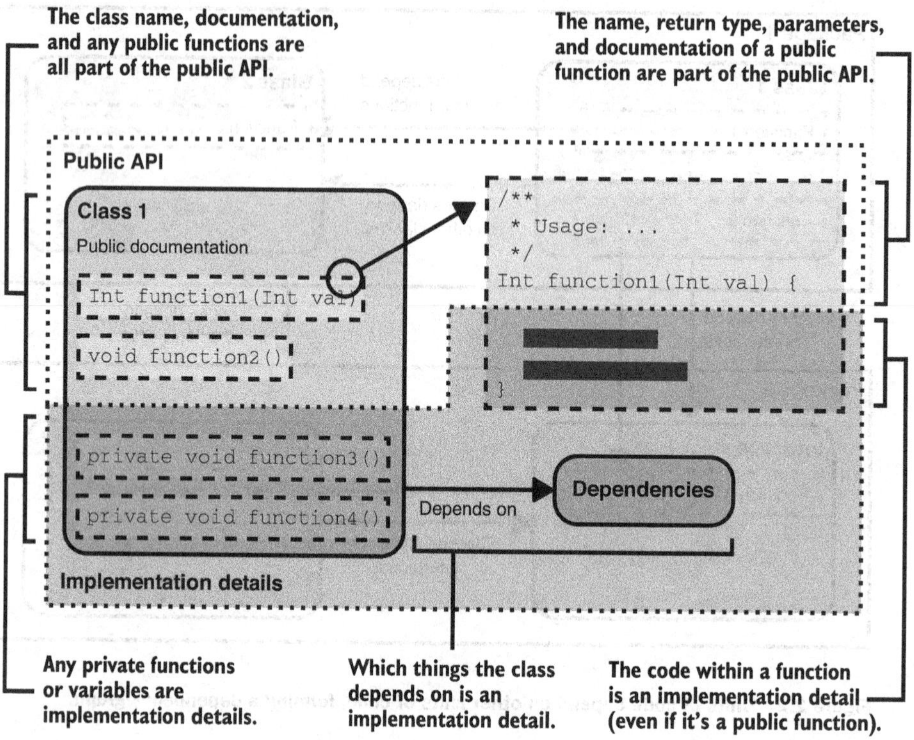

Figure 2.3 We can think of the parts of our code that callers should be aware of as exposing a public API. Anything not exposed in the public API is an implementation detail.

of classes, interfaces, and functions as "exposing an API." Figure 2.3 provides an example of how the different aspects of a class can be divided between being part of a public API and implementation details.

Thinking about code in terms of APIs can help create clean layers of abstraction because the API defines what concepts are exposed to callers, and everything else is an implementation detail. If we're writing or modifying some code, and something that should be an implementation detail leaks into the API (via an input parameter, return type, or public function), then it's obvious that the layers of abstraction are not as clean and distinct as they probably should be.

We'll use this concept of code exposing an API at multiple places throughout this book, as it's a useful and succinct way to refer to the layer of abstraction a piece of code provides.

2.3.2 Functions

The threshold at which it's beneficial to break out some logic into a new function is often quite low. The code inside each function should ideally read like a single, short, well-written sentence. To demonstrate this, consider the following example of a function that tries to do too much (listing 2.2). The function finds the address of a vehicle owner and then sends them a letter if one is found. The function contains all the nuts-and-bolts logic for finding the owner's address, as well as the function call to send the letter. This makes it hard to understand, as it deals with too many concepts at once. In listing 2.2, we can also see how doing too much inside a single function can lead to other issues that make the code hard to understand, such as deeply nested if-statements (chapter 5 will cover this in more detail).

Listing 2.2 A function that does too much

```
SentConfirmation? sendOwnerALetter(
    Vehicle vehicle, Letter letter) {
  Address? ownersAddress = null;
  if (vehicle.hasBeenScraped()) {
    ownersAddress = SCRAPYARD_ADDRESS;
  } else {
    Purchase? mostRecentPurchase =
        vehicle.getMostRecentPurchase();
    if (mostRecentPurchase == null) {
      ownersAddress = SHOWROOM_ADDRESS;
    } else {
      ownersAddress = mostRecentPurchase.getBuyersAddress();
    }
  }
  if (ownersAddress == null) {
    return null;
  }
  return sendLetter(ownersAddress, letter);
}
```

The nuts-and-bolts logic for finding the owner's address

Logic for conditionally sending the letter

If the `sendOwnerALetter()` function were translated into a sentence it would read, "Find the owner's address (which will be the scrapyard address if the vehicle has been scrapped, or the showroom address if the vehicle has not been sold yet, or the registered buyer's address if there is one) and if found, send them a letter." That is not a nice sentence: it requires dealing with several different concepts all in one go, and the sheer volume of words means we'd probably have to take several attempts at reading it to be sure we'd properly understood it.

It would be much nicer if we could have a function that translated into something like, "Find the owner's address (more details below), and if found, send them a letter." A good strategy to try and ensure that functions can be translated into nice sentences like this is to limit a single function to either of the following:

- Performing one single task
- Composing more complex behavior by just calling other well-named functions

This is not an exact science, because "one single task" is open to interpretation, and even when composing more complex behavior by just calling other functions, we will likely still need some control flow (like an if-statement, or a for-loop). So once we've written a function, it's worth trying to read it as a sentence. If it's difficult to do this, or the sentence gets very clunky, then it's likely that the function is too long, and it would be beneficial to break it into smaller functions.

In the case of `sendOwnerALetter()` we've already established that it doesn't translate into a nice sentence, and it also clearly doesn't follow the strategy just mentioned. The function performs two tasks: finding the owner's address and triggering the sending of a letter. But instead of doing this by just composing functionality out of other functions, it contains the nuts-and-bolts logic for finding the owner's address.

A better approach would be to split the logic to find the owner's address into a separate function, so the `sendOwnerALetter()` function now translates into the more ideal sentence. Listing 2.3 shows what this looks like. Anyone reading it after this change can easily understand how it solves the given subproblem:

1. Get the owner's address.
2. Send a letter to the owner if an address was found.

Another benefit of the new code in listing 2.3 is that the logic to find the owner's address is now more easily reusable. In the future, there might be a request to build a feature that displays just the owner's address without sending a letter. The engineer building this could reuse the `getOwnersAddress()` function within the same class, or move it to an appropriate helper class and make it public relatively easily.

Listing 2.3 Smaller functions

```
SentConfirmation? sendOwnerALetter(Vehicle vehicle, Letter letter) {
  Address? ownersAddress = getOwnersAddress(vehicle);    // Get the owner's address.
  if (ownersAddress == null) {
    return null;
  }
  return sendLetter(ownersAddress, letter);    // Send a letter to the owner if an address was found.
}

private Address? getOwnersAddress(Vehicle vehicle) {    // Function to find owner's address. Can be easily reused.
  if (vehicle.hasBeenScraped()) {
    return SCRAPYARD_ADDRESS;
  }
  Purchase? mostRecentPurchase = vehicle.getMostRecentPurchase();
  if (mostRecentPurchase == null) {
    return SHOWROOM_ADDRESS;
  }
  return mostRecentPurchase.getBuyersAddress();
}
```

Making functions small and focused is one of the best ways to ensure that code is readable and reusable. When churning out code, it's quite easy to end up writing a function that's too long and not very readable. So after writing the first cut of our code, and before sending it for review, it's often worth taking a critical look at it. Whenever we see a function that's hard to translate into a sentence, we should consider breaking out parts of the logic into well-named helper functions.

2.3.3 Classes

Engineers often debate what the ideal size for a single class is, and many theories and rules of thumb have been put forward such as the following:

- *Number of lines*—You will sometimes hear guidance such as "a class shouldn't be longer than 300 lines of code."
  - It's very often (but not always) true that a class that is longer than 300 lines is handling too many concepts and should be broken up. This rule of thumb does not imply that a class that is 300 lines or fewer is an appropriate size. It serves only as a warning that something might be wrong but is not an assurance that anything is right. Rules like this are, therefore, often of quite limited practical use.
- *Cohesion*[1]—This is a gauge of how well the things inside a class "belong" together, with the idea being that a good class is one that is highly cohesive. There are many ways in which things might be classified as being cohesive to one another. Here are a couple of examples:
  - *Sequential cohesion*—This occurs when the output of one thing is needed as an input to another thing. A real-world example of this might be making a cup of fresh coffee. We can't brew the coffee until we grind the beans; the output of the bean-grinding process is an input to the coffee-brewing process. We might therefore conclude that grinding and brewing are cohesive to one another.
  - *Functional cohesion*—This occurs when a group of things all contribute to achieving a single task. The definition of a *single task* can be highly subjective, but a real-world example might be if you were to keep all your cake-making equipment in a single dedicated drawer in your kitchen. You've decided that mixing bowls, wooden spoons, and cake tins are all cohesive and belong together because they all contribute to the same functional task: making cakes.
- *Separation of concerns*[2]—This is a design principle that advocates that systems should be separated into individual components that each deal with a distinct problem (or concern). A real-world example of this is how a games console is usually separate from a TV, rather than being bundled together into a single inseparable appliance. The games console is concerned with running a game, and the TV is concerned with displaying a moving picture. This allows for more configurability: one person buying a games console might live in a small apartment and only have room for a small TV, while someone else with more space might want to plug it into a 292-inch wall TV. The separation of these items also allows us to upgrade one without having to upgrade the other. When a newer, faster games console comes out, we don't have to also incur the cost of a new TV.

---

1 The idea of using cohesion as a metric for assessing software structure was first introduced by Larry L. Constantine in the 1960s and later expanded on by Wayne P. Stevens, Glenford J. Myers, and Larry L. Constantine in the 1970s.

2 The term *separation of concerns* is widely believed to have been coined by Edsger W. Dijkstra in the 1970s.

The ideas of cohesion and separation of concerns generally require us to make a decision about the level at which it's useful to consider a group of related things *one thing*. This can often be trickier than it might seem because it can be highly subjective. To one person, grouping grinding and coffee brewing together might make perfect sense, but to another person who just wants to grind spices for cooking, this might seem like a very unhelpful way of grouping things, because they obviously don't want to brew their spices.

I've not met many engineers who are completely unaware of these rules of thumb, or who would disagree with a statement like "A class should be cohesive and ideally concerned with one single thing." But despite knowing this advice, many engineers still write classes that are way too big. Classes often end up being too big when engineers don't think carefully enough about how many different concepts they are introducing within a single class and which pieces of logic might be appropriate for being reused or reconfigured. This can sometimes happen when a class is first authored, and it can sometimes happen as a class grows organically over time, so it's important to think about whether a class is getting too big, both when modifying existing code as well as when writing completely new code.

Rules of thumb like "a class should only be concerned with one thing" or "a class should be cohesive" exist to try and guide engineers to create higher quality code. But we still need to think carefully about what we're fundamentally trying to achieve. With regard to layers of code and creating classes, four of the pillars that were defined in chapter 1 capture what we should be trying to achieve:

- *Make code readable*—The greater the number of different concepts that we bundle together in a single class, the less readable that class is going to be. Human brains are not good at consciously thinking about a lot of things simultaneously. The more cognitive load we put on other engineers trying to read the code, the longer it will take them, and the more likely they are to misinterpret it.
- *Make code modular*—Using classes and interfaces is one of the best ways to make code modular. If the solution to a subproblem is self-contained inside its own class, and other classes only interact with it via a few well thought–out public functions, then it will be easy to swap out that implementation with another one should we need to.
- *Make code reusable and generalizable*—If solving a problem requires solving two subproblems, then there's a reasonable chance that someone else might also need to solve one of those subproblems in the future. If we bundle the solution to both subproblems together in one class, then it reduces the chance someone else will be able to reuse one of them.
- *Make code testable and test it properly*—The previous section used the house analogy, where we'd want to check the soundness of all parts of a house before buying it, not just its external appearance. Likewise, if logic is broken into classes, then it becomes a lot easier to properly test each piece of it.

Figure 2.4 illustrates how a class that's too big can end up achieving the opposite of these four pillars.

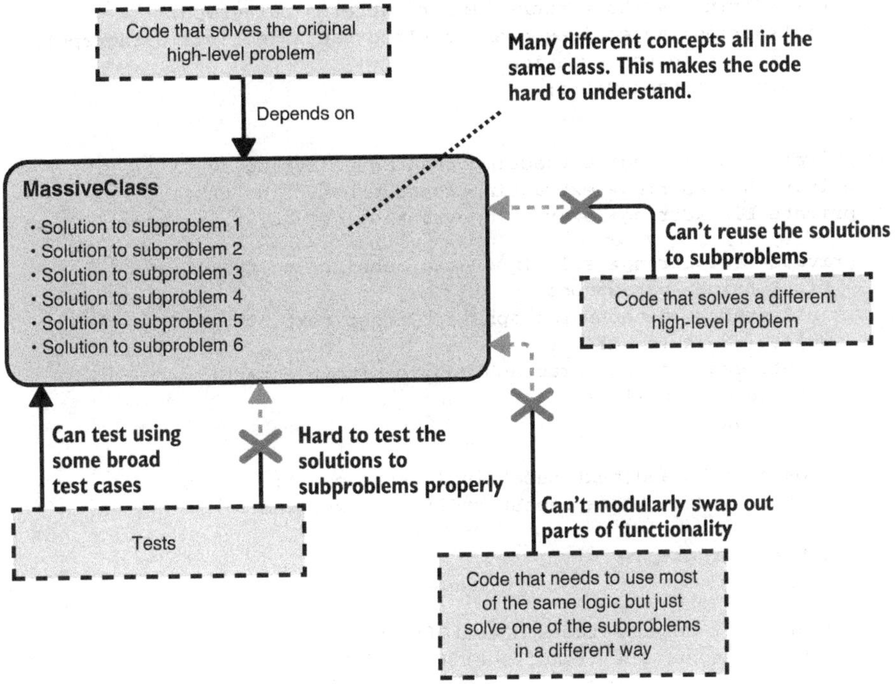

Figure 2.4 Not breaking code into appropriately sized classes often results in code that deals with too many concepts at once, and that is less readable, modular, reusable, generalizable, and testable.

To demonstrate how these pillars can help us structure our classes, let's look at some code. Listing 2.4 contains a class that can be used to summarize a passage of text. It does this by splitting the text into paragraphs and filtering out any paragraphs it determines to have a low importance score. In solving the problem of summarizing text, the author of this class has to solve subproblems. They've kind of created some layers of abstraction by dividing things into separate functions, but they've still just dumped everything into a single class, meaning the separation between the layers of abstraction is not very distinct.

Listing 2.4 A class that's too big

```
class TextSummarizer {
  ...

  String summarizeText(String text) {
    return splitIntoParagraphs(text)
        .filter(paragraph -> calculateImportance(paragraph) >=
            IMPORTANCE_THRESHOLD)
        .join("\n\n");
  }

  private Double calculateImportance(String paragraph) {
    List<String> nouns = extractImportantNouns(paragraph);
```

```
    List<String> verbs = extractImportantVerbs(paragraph);
    List<String> adjectives = extractImportantAdjectives(paragraph);
    ... a complicated equation ...
    return importanceScore;
  }

  private List<String> extractImportantNouns(String text) { ... }
  private List<String> extractImportantVerbs(String text) { ... }
  private List<String> extractImportantAdjectives(String text) { ... }

  private List<String> splitIntoParagraphs(String text) {
    List<String> paragraphs = [];
    Int? start = detectParagraphStartOffset(text, 0);
    while (start != null) {
      Int? end = detectParagraphEndOffset(text, start);
      if (end == null) {
        break;
      }
      paragraphs.add(text.subString(start, end));
      start = detectParagraphStartOffset(text, end);
    }
    return paragraphs;
  }

  private Int? detectParagraphStartOffset(
      String text, Int fromOffset) { ... }

  private Int? detectParagraphEndOffset(
      String text, Int fromOffset) { ... }
}
```

If we spoke to the author of this class, they might well claim that it's only concerned with one thing: summarizing a passage of text. And at a high level, they'd be kind of right. But the class clearly contains code that solves a bunch of subproblems:

- Splitting the text into paragraphs
- Calculating an importance score for a string of text
  - This further divides into the subproblems of finding the important nouns, verbs, and adjectives

Based on this observation, another engineer might argue back and say, "No, this class is concerned with multiple different things. It should be broken up." In this scenario both the engineers agree with the notion that the class should be cohesive and concerned with one thing, but they disagree about whether solving the associated subproblems count as different concerns or intrinsic parts of the main problem. To better judge whether this class should be broken up, it might be better to look at how it stacks up against the pillars we just mentioned. If we do this, we will likely conclude that the class in its current form is low-quality code, based on the following (also illustrated in figure 2.5):

- *The code is not as readable as it could be.* When we initially read the code, it's a wall of several different concepts such as splitting text into paragraphs, extracting things like important nouns, and calculating importance scores. It takes some time to figure out which of these concepts is needed for solving which of the subproblems.

- *The code is not particularly modular.* This makes it hard to reconfigure or modify the code. This algorithm is no doubt quite a naive way of summarizing a passage of text and is likely something that engineers will want to iterate on over time. It's hard to reconfigure the code to try out new things without modifying it for every caller. It'd be better if the code were modular, so we could swap in a new way of calculating the importance score for example.
- *The code is not reusable.* When working on solving a different problem, we might end up needing to solve some of the same subproblems that were solved here. If we had to build a feature to count how many paragraphs a passage of text contained, then it'd be great if we could just reuse the `splitIntoParagraphs()` function. Currently we can't do this, and we'd have to re-solve this subproblem ourselves, or else refactor the `TextSummarizer` class. Making the `splitIntoParagraphs()` function public to allow reuse might seem tempting, but would not be a good idea: it would pollute the public API of the `TextSummarizer` class with a seemingly unrelated concept, and it would make it awkward to modify this functionality within the `TextSummarizer` class in the future, since other external code would start depending on the `splitIntoParagraphs()` function.

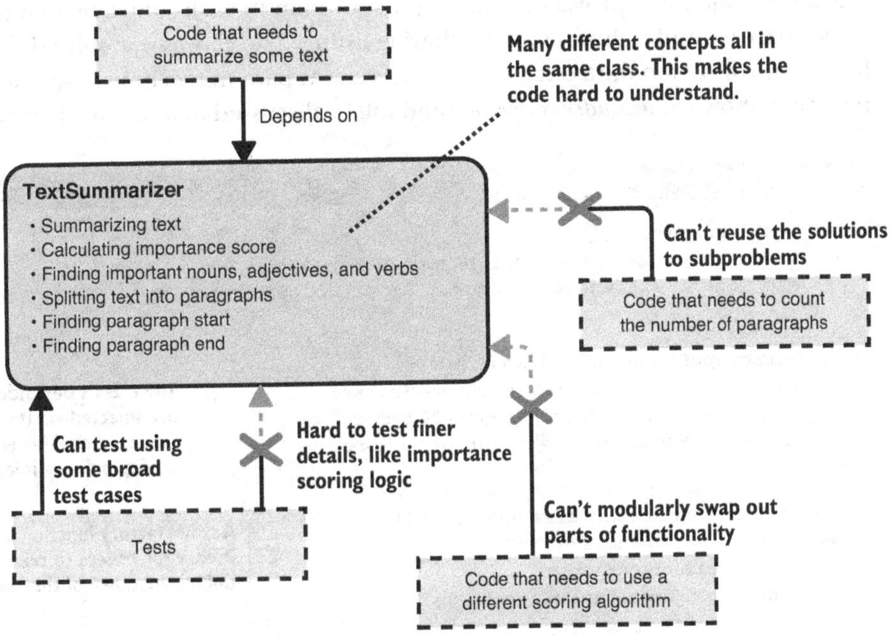

Figure 2.5 The `TextSummarizer` class contains with too many different concepts and results in code that is less readable, modular, reusable, generalizable, and testable.

- *The code is not generalizable.* The whole solution assumes that the text being input is plain text. But we might want to start summarizing web pages at some point in the near future. In that case we might want to input a passage of HTML rather than plain text. If the code were more modular, then we could perhaps swap out the logic that splits the text into paragraphs with something that could split HTML into paragraphs.
- *The code is hard to test properly.* Many of the subproblems being solved actually have quite complicated solutions. Splitting the text into paragraphs looks like a nontrivial problem, and calculating the importance score is a particularly involved algorithm. Currently all that can be tested is the overall behavior via the `summarizeText()` function, but it'll be hard to properly test all the intricacies of whether the importance score code is working by just calling `summarizeText()`. We could start making other functions public (such as `calculateImportance()`) so that we can test them properly, but this would then clutter the public API of `TextSummarizer`. We could add a comment saying, "Only publicly visible for testing," but this just increases the cognitive load on other engineers even further.

The `TextSummarizer` class is clearly too big and handles too many different concepts, and this is reducing the code quality. The next section shows how this code could be improved.

How to improve the code

The code could be improved by splitting the solution to each subproblem into its own respective class and is shown in the following listing. The classes that solve the subproblems are provided to the `TextSummarizer` class as parameters in its constructor. This pattern is known as *dependency injection* and will be discussed in more detail in chapter 8.

Listing 2.5 One class per concept

```
class TextSummarizer {
  private final ParagraphFinder paragraphFinder;
  private final TextImportanceScorer importanceScorer;

  TextSummarizer(
      ParagraphFinder paragraphFinder,
      TextImportanceScorer importanceScorer) {
    this.paragraphFinder = paragraphFinder;
    this.importanceScorer = importanceScorer;
  }

  static TextSummarizer createDefault() {
    return new TextSummarizer(
        new ParagraphFinder(),
        new TextImportanceScorer());
  }

  String summarizeText(String text) {
    return paragraphFinder.find(text)
```

The class's dependencies are injected via its constructor. This is known as dependency injection.

A static factory function to make it easy for callers to create a default instance of the class

```
        .filter(paragraph ->
            importanceScorer.isImportant(paragraph))
        .join("\n\n");
  }
}

class ParagraphFinder {
  List<String> find(String text) {
    List<String> paragraphs = [];
    Int? start = detectParagraphStartOffset(text, 0);
    while (start != null) {
      Int? end = detectParagraphEndOffset(text, start);
      if (end == null) {
        break;
      }
      paragraphs.add(text.subString(start, end));
      start = detectParagraphStartOffset(text, end);
    }
    return paragraphs;
  }

  private Int? detectParagraphStartOffset(
      String text, Int fromOffset) { ... }

  private Int? detectParagraphEndOffset(
      String text, Int fromOffset) { ... }
}

class TextImportanceScorer {
  ...
  Boolean isImportant(String text) {
    return calculateImportance(text) >=
        IMPORTANCE_THRESHOLD;
  }

  private Double calculateImportance(String text) {
    List<String> nouns = extractImportantNouns(text);
    List<String> verbs = extractImportantVerbs(text);
    List<String> adjectives = extractImportantAdjectives(text);
    ... a complicated equation ...
    return importanceScore;
  }

  private List<String> extractImportantNouns(String text) { ... }
  private List<String> extractImportantVerbs(String text) { ... }
  private List<String> extractImportantAdjectives(String text) { ... }
}
```

The solutions to subproblems are split into their own classes.

The code is now a lot more readable, because each class requires someone reading it to deal with only a few concepts at a time. We can look at the `TextSummarizer` class and within a few seconds know all the concepts and steps that form the high-level algorithm:

- Find the paragraphs.
- Filter out the ones that aren't important.
- Join the paragraphs that are left.

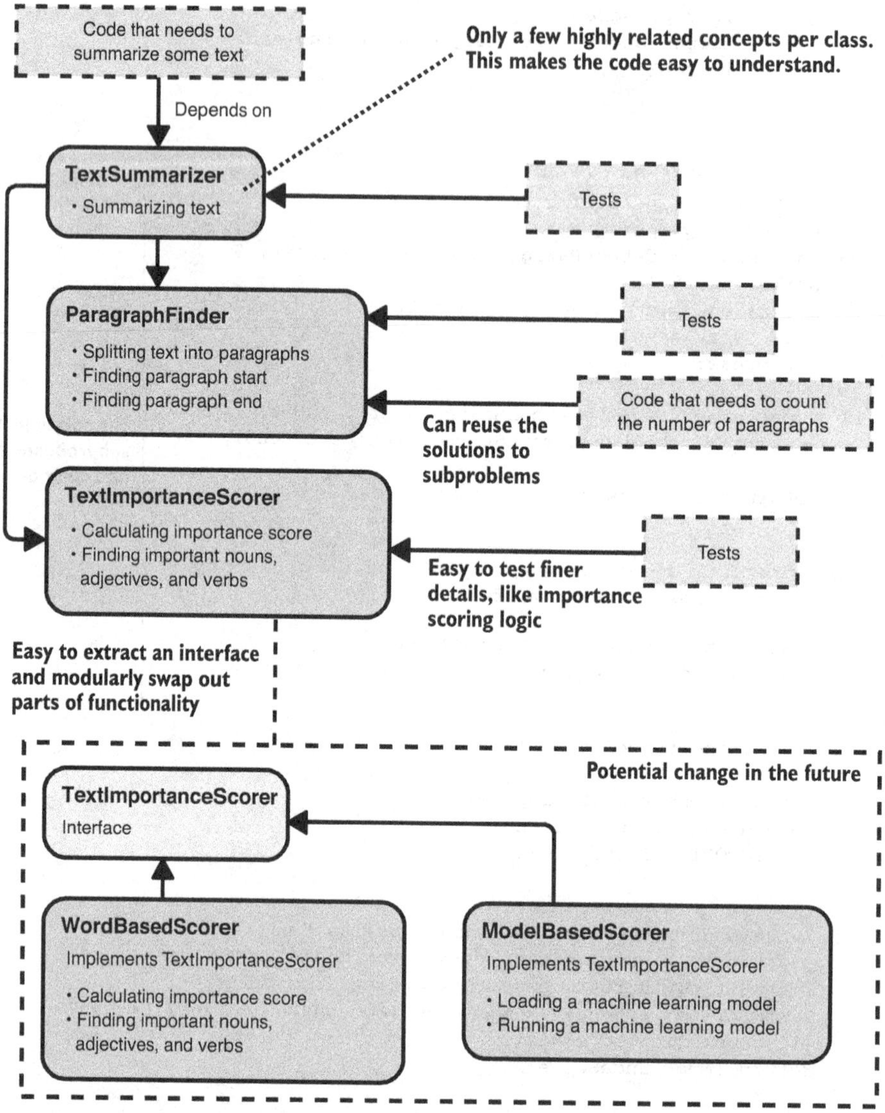

Figure 2.6 Breaking code into appropriately sized layers of abstraction results in code that deals with only a few concepts at once. This makes the code more readable, modular, reusable, generalizable, and testable.

If that's all we wanted to know, then great; job done. If we didn't really care how scores were calculated but wanted to know how paragraphs were found, then we can move to the `ParagraphFinder` class and quickly understand how that subproblem is solved.

As shown in figure 2.6, there are numerous other benefits:

- *The code is now more modular and reconfigurable.* If we wanted to try out a different way of scoring text, then it would be trivial to extract `TextImportanceScorer` into an interface and create an alternative implementation of it. We'll discuss this in the next section.

- *The code is more reusable.* We can quite easily use the `ParagraphFinder` class in other scenarios now if we wanted to.
- *The code is more testable.* It's easy to write comprehensive and focused tests for each of the subproblem classes.

Large classes that do too many things are all too common in a lot of codebases, and as this section demonstrates, this often leads to a reduction in code quality. It's good to think carefully when designing a class hierarchy about whether it meets the pillars of code quality that were just discussed. Classes can often grow organically over time to become too big, so it helps to think about these pillars when modifying existing classes, as well as when authoring new ones. Breaking code down into appropriately sized classes is one of the most effective tools for ensuring we have good layers of abstraction, so it's worth spending time and thought on getting it right.

2.3.4 Interfaces

One approach sometimes used to force layers to be distinct and to ensure that implementation details are not leaked between layers is to define an interface that determines which public functions will be exposed by that layer. The actual class containing the code for the layer will then implement this interface. The layers of code above this would only depend on the interface and never the concrete class that implements the logic.

If we have more than one implementation for a given abstract layer, or if we think that we will be adding more in the future, then it's usually a good idea to define an interface. To demonstrate this, consider the example we saw in the previous section for summarizing text. An important subproblem is scoring pieces of text (in this case, paragraphs) to determine whether they could be omitted from the summary. The original code uses quite a naive solution based on finding important words.

A more robust approach might be to use machine learning to train a model to determine whether a piece of text is important. This is likely something we'd want to experiment with, try out in development mode first, and maybe release as an optional beta. We don't want to simply replace the old logic with the model-based approach in one go; we need a way to configure the code with either of the approaches.

One of the best ways to do this is to extract the `TextImportanceScorer` class into an interface and then have an implementation class for each of the approaches to solving this subproblem. The `TextSummarizer` class would only ever depend on the `TextImportanceScorer` interface and never on any of the concrete implementations. Figure 2.7 shows how this might look in terms of the dependencies between the different classes and the interface.

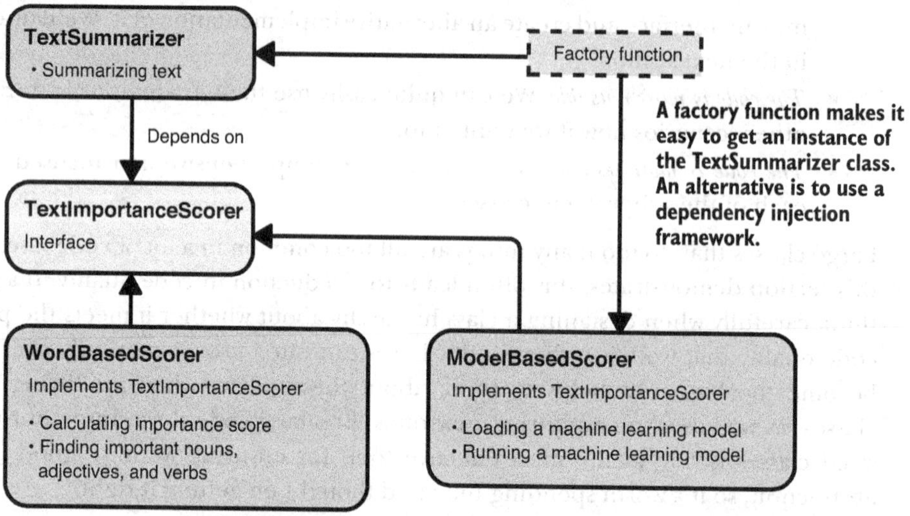

Figure 2.7 By defining an interface to represent a layer of abstraction, we can easily swap implementations for solving the given subproblem. This makes code more modular and configurable.

The code in the following listing shows how the new interface and implementation classes might look.

Listing 2.6 An interface and implementations

```
interface TextImportanceScorer {
  Boolean isImportant(String text);
}


class WordBasedScorer implements TextImportanceScorer {
  ...
  override Boolean isImportant(String text) {
    return calculateImportance(text) >=
        IMPORTANCE_THRESHOLD;
  }

  private Double calculateImportance(String text) {
    List<String> nouns = extractImportantNouns(text);
    List<String> verbs = extractImportantVerbs(text);
    List<String> adjectives = extractImportantAdjectives(text);
    ... a complicated equation ...
    return importanceScore;
  }

  private List<String> extractImportantNouns(String text) { ... }
  private List<String> extractImportantVerbs(String text) { ... }
  private List<String> extractImportantAdjectives(String text) { ... }
}
```

- TextImportanceScorer is now an interface rather than a class.
- The original TextImportanceScorer class is renamed and implements the new interface.
- Function marked with "override" to indicate that it overrides the function from the interface

```
class ModelBasedScorer implements TextImportanceScorer {
  private final TextPredictionModel model;
  ...

  static ModelBasedScorer create() {
    return new ModelBasedScorer(
        TextPredictionModel.load(MODEL_FILE));
  }

  override Boolean isImportant(String text) {
    return model.predict(text) >=
        MODEL_THRESHOLD;
  }
}
```

The new model-based scorer also implements the interface.

It's now straightforward to configure the `TextSummarizer` to use either the `WordBasedScorer` or the `ModelBasedScorer` using one of two factory functions. The following listing shows what the code for two factory functions to create an instance of the `TextSummarizer` class might look like.

Listing 2.7 Factory functions

```
TextSummarizer createWordBasedSummarizer() {
  return new TextSummarizer(
      new ParagraphFinder(), new WordBasedScorer());
}

TextSummarizer createModelBasedSummarizer() {
  return new TextSummarizer(
      new ParagraphFinder(), ModelBasedScorer.create());
}
```

Interfaces are an extremely useful tool for creating code that provides clean layers of abstraction. Whenever we need to switch between two or more different concrete implementations for a given subproblem, it's usually best to define an interface to represent the layer of abstraction. This will make our code more modular and much easier to reconfigure.

INTERFACES FOR EVERYTHING?

If you have only one implementation of a given layer of abstraction, and you don't envision adding more in the future, then it's really up to you (and your team) to decide whether you think hiding layers behind an interface is worth it. Some software engineering philosophies make a point of encouraging this. If we were to follow this and hide the `TextSummarizer` class we just saw behind an interface, then it would look something like the following in listing 2.8. Under this regime, `TextSummarizer` is the interface that layers of code above this one would depend on; they would never depend directly on the `TextSummarizerImpl` implementation class.

Listing 2.8 An interface and a single implementation

```
interface TextSummarizer {
  String summarizeText(String text);
}

class TextSummarizerImpl implements TextSummarizer {
  . . .

  override String summarizeText(String text) {
    return paragraphFinder.find(text)
        .filter(paragraph ->
            importanceScorer.isImportant(paragraph))
        .join("\n\n");
  }
}
```

Only functions defined in the interface will be visible to users of this layer of abstraction.

TextSummarizerImpl is the only class that implements the TextSummarizer interface.

Even though there is only one implementation of `TextSummarizer`, and even if we can't envision ever adding another implementation of it in the future, there are some benefits to this approach:

- *It makes the public API very clear*—There's no confusion about which functions engineers using this layer should/shouldn't use. If an engineer adds a new public function to the `TextSummarizerImpl` class, then it won't be exposed to layers of code above this since they only depend on the `TextSummarizer` interface.
- *We may have guessed wrong about only needing one implementation*—When originally writing the code, we may have been absolutely sure that we would not need a second implementation, but after a month or two, this assumption may prove wrong. Maybe we realize that summarizing text by just omitting a few paragraphs is not very effective and decide to experiment with another algorithm that summarizes text in a completely different way.
- *It can make testing easier*—If our implementation class did something particularly complicated or depended on network I/O, for example, then we might want to substitute it with a mock or a fake implementation during testing. Depending on the programming language we are using, we may need to define an interface to do this.
- *The same class can solve two subproblems*—It's sometimes possible for a single class to provide the implementation to two or more different layers of abstraction. An example of this is how a `LinkedList` implementation class might implement both a `List` and a `Queue` interface. This means it can be used as a queue in one scenario without allowing code in that scenario to also use it as a list. This can greatly increase the generalizability of code.

On the other hand, the downsides of defining an interface are as follows:

- *It's a bit more effort*—We have to write a few more lines of code (and maybe a new file) to define the interface.

- *It can make code more complicated*—When another engineer wants to understand the code, it can be harder for them to navigate the logic. If they want to understand how a certain subproblem is being solved, then instead of just directly navigating to the class that implements the layer below, they have to navigate to the interface and then find the concrete class that implements that interface.

In my personal experience, taking an extreme stance and hiding every single class behind an interface often gets out of hand and can create code that becomes unnecessarily complex to understand and modify. My advice is to use an interface where it provides an appreciable benefit, but not to do it just for the sake of doing it. Despite this, it's still important to concentrate on creating clean and distinct layers of abstraction. Even if we don't define an interface, we should still think very carefully about which public functions our classes expose and make sure no implementation details are leaked. In general, whenever we write or modify a class we should ensure that it would be a trivial job to hide it behind an interface at some later time if we needed to.

2.3.5 When layers get too thin

Despite the benefits, there are some overheads associated with breaking code into distinct layers, such as the following:

- More lines of code, due to all the boilerplate required to define a class or import dependencies into a new file.
- The effort required to switch between files or classes when following a chain of logic.
- If we end up hiding a layer behind an interface, then it requires more effort to figure out which implementation is used in which scenarios. This can make understanding logic or debugging more difficult.

These costs are generally quite low compared with all the benefits of having code that is split into distinct layers, but it's worth remembering that there's no point in splitting code just for the sake of it. There can come a point where the costs outweigh the benefits, so it's good to apply common sense.

Listing 2.9 shows what the code might look like if the `ParagraphFinder` class seen previously were split into more layers by breaking the start and end offset finders into their own classes behind a common interface. The layers of code are probably now too thin, because it's hard to envisage the `ParagraphStartOffsetDetector` and `ParagraphEndOffsetDetector` classes being used by anything other than the `ParagraphFinder` class.

Listing 2.9 Layers of code that are too thin

```
class ParagraphFinder {
  private final OffsetDetector startDetector;
  private final OffsetDetector endDetector;
  ...
```

```
    List<String> find(String text) {
      List<String> paragraphs = [];
      Int? start = startDetector.detectOffset(text, 0);
      while (start != null) {
        Int? end = endDetector.detectOffset(text, start);
        if (end == null) {
          break;
        }
        paragraphs.add(text.subString(start, end));
        start = startDetector.detectOffset(text, end);
      }
      return paragraphs;
    }
  }

  interface OffsetDetector {
    Int? detectOffset(String text, Int fromOffset);
  }

  class ParagraphStartOffsetDetector implements OffsetDetector {
    override Int? detectOffset(String text, Int fromOffset) { ... }
  }

  class ParagraphEndOffsetDetector implements OffsetDetector {
    override Int? detectOffset(String text, Int fromOffset) { ... }
  }
```

Even if we could imagine the class `ParagraphFinder` being useful elsewhere, it's certainly hard to imagine that anyone would use `ParagraphStartOffsetDetector` and not the equivalent `ParagraphEndOffsetDetector`, because their implementations need to have a mutually coherent idea of how to detect the start and end of a paragraph.

Deciding on the correct thickness of layers of code is important; codebases become completely unmanageable without having meaningful layers of abstraction. If we make the layers too thick, then multiple abstractions will end up being merged, making code that is not modular, reusable, or readable. If we make the layers too thin, then we can end up dissecting what should be a single layer of abstraction into two, which can lead to unnecessary complexity and might also mean that adjacent layers are not as well decoupled as they should be. In general, having layers that are too thick often causes a worse set of problems than having layers that are too thin, so if we're unsure, then it's often better to err on the side of making the layers too thin.

As we saw earlier with classes, it's hard to come up with a single rule or piece of advice that will tell us definitively whether a layer is too thick, as it will often depend on the nature of the real-world problem that we're solving. The best advice is to use our judgment and to think carefully about whether the layers we have created will ensure that the code is readable, reusable, generalizable, modular, and testable. And remember: even for engineers with decades of experience, it can often take a few iterations of designing or reworking the code, before submitting it to the codebase, to get the layers of abstraction right.

2.4 What about microservices?

In a microservices architecture, the solutions to individual problems are deployed as standalone services rather than just being libraries that are compiled into a single program. This means that the system is broken up into a number of smaller programs that are each dedicated to a set task. These smaller programs are deployed as dedicated services that can be remotely called through APIs. Microservices have a number of benefits and have become increasingly popular in recent years. They are the go-to architecture for many organizations and teams now.

One argument you will sometimes hear is that when using microservices, code structure and creating layers of abstraction in code are not important. The reason is that the microservices themselves provide the clean layer of abstraction, and it therefore doesn't really matter how the code inside is structured or broken up. Although it's true that microservices typically provide quite clean layers of abstraction, they're usually of a size and scope that mean it's still useful to think properly about the layers of abstraction within them.

To demonstrate this, imagine that we work for an online retailer on a team that develops and maintains a microservice for checking and modifying stock levels. Our microservice is called whenever any of the following occur:

- A new delivery of stock arrives at a warehouse
- The store frontend needs to know if an item is in stock, so it can display that to the user
- A customer purchases something

Nominally, this microservice only does one thing: manage stock levels. But it's probably immediately obvious that there are multiple subproblems that need solving to do this "one thing":

- Dealing with the concept of items (what it's actually keeping track of)
- Handling the fact that there are different warehouses and locations that the stock might be in
- The notion that an item might be in stock for customers in one country but not another, depending on which warehouses they are within delivery range of
- Interfacing with the database that the actual stock levels are stored in
- Interpreting the data returned by the database

All the things that were previously said about solving a problem by breaking it down into subproblems still applies, even within this microservice. For example, determining if an item is in stock for a customer involves the following:

- Determining which warehouses are within range of that customer
- Querying the datastore to find the stock of the item in any of those warehouses
- Interpreting the data format returned by the database
- Returning an answer back to the caller of the service

What's more, it's very likely that other engineers might want to reuse some of this logic. There are probably other teams within the company that track analytics and trends to figure out which items the company should discontinue, stock more of, or run special offers on. For efficiency and latency reasons, they'll most likely be using a pipeline to scan directly over the stock database, rather than calling our service, but they might still need some logic to help them interpret the data returned by the database, so it'd be good if they could just reuse our code that does that.

Microservices can be an extremely good way to break up a system and make it more modular, but it usually doesn't change the fact that we'll still need to solve multiple subproblems to implement the service. Creating the right abstractions and layers of code is still important.

Summary

- Breaking code into clean and distinct layers of abstraction makes it more readable, modular, reusable, generalizable, and testable.
- We can use functions, classes, and interfaces (as well as other language-specific features) to break our code into layers of abstraction.
- Deciding how to break code into layers of abstraction requires using our judgment and knowledge about the problem we're solving.
- The problems that come from having layers that are too thick are usually worse than the problems that come from having layers that are too thin. If we're unsure, it can often be best to err on the side of making layers too thin.

3 Other engineers and code contracts

> ***This chapter covers***
> - How other engineers will interact with our code
> - Code contracts and small print in code contracts
> - How minimizing small print can help prevent misuse and surprises
> - If we can't avoid small print, how checks and assertions can be used to enforce it

Writing and maintaining software is usually a team effort. Companies that create software will typically employ multiple engineers: it could be a team of two working on a single product or thousands of engineers working across hundreds of different products. The exact number doesn't really matter; the point is that other engineers will end up having to interact with the code we write, and in turn, we will have to interact with the code they write.

Two of the pillars of code quality introduced in chapter 1 were "avoid surprises" and "make code hard to misuse." These relate to what might happen (and what might go wrong) when other engineers interact with our code. This chapter will discuss different techniques for conveying important details of the code to other engineers (with some techniques being more reliable than others). This will then be formalized with the concept of code contracts and small print. The final two sections of this chapter will go through a worked example of some code that is too open to misuse and misinterpretation and show how to improve the code. Chapters 6 and 7 will provide many more specific examples that build on this chapter.

3.1 Your code and other engineers' code

If you're writing code as part of a team, then the code you write will likely be built on top of layers of code that other engineers have written, and others will likely build layers on top of your code. If you've solved various subproblems along the way and broken them into clean layers of abstraction, then other engineers will likely also want to reuse some of these for completely different problems that you may not even have considered.

To demonstrate this, imagine that you work for a company that runs an online magazine where users can find and read articles. You are tasked to write a text-summarization feature to summarize articles for users as they are trying to find something to read. You end up writing the code we saw in the previous chapter, with the `TextSummarizer` and associated classes. (If you can't remember the exact code or skipped that chapter, then no worries.) Figure 3.1 shows how the text-summarization code you wrote might end up being used in the software. You can see that your code depends on lower layers of code written by other engineers, and in turn other engineers are depending on your code to solve higher level problems. You can also see that your code is being reused for multiple pieces of functionality. You may have initially anticipated its use only for article summarization, but other engineers have gone on to reuse it (or parts of it) for summarizing comments and for estimating the reading times of articles.

Another important thing to keep in mind is that requirements change and evolve all the time: priorities change, new features are added, and systems sometimes need to be migrated to new technologies. This means that code and software also change all the time. Figure 3.1 is very much a snapshot in time; it's unlikely that the piece of software will look exactly like this in a year, or even a few months' time.

A group of engineers all continually making modifications to a codebase make it a busy place. And as with any busy place, if things are fragile, they'll get broken. There's a reason you don't get your fine glassware out when you're having a massive party, and why barriers at stadiums tend to be made out of metal and be bolted to the ground: fragile things and busy places don't mix well.

To withstand this kind of "footfall" from other engineers, code needs to be robust and easy to use. One of the main considerations when writing high-quality code is understanding and preempting what bad things might happen when other engineers make changes, or need to interact with your code, and how you can mitigate against these. Unless you literally work in a one-engineer company and you never forget anything, you can't write high-quality code without considering other engineers.

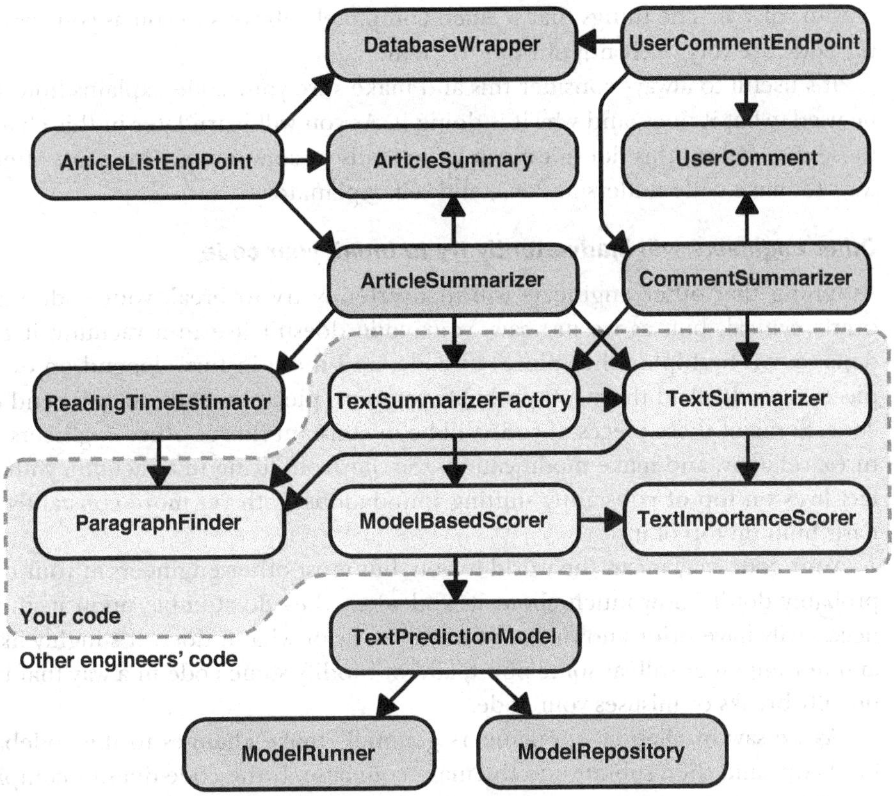

Figure 3.1 The code you write rarely lives in isolation. It will depend on code written by other engineers, and other engineers will in turn write code that depends on your code.

When writing code, it's useful to consider the following three things (the next three subsections will explore them in more detail):

- Things that are obvious to you are not obvious to others.
- Other engineers will inadvertently try to break your code.
- In time, you will forget about your own code.

3.1.1 Things that are obvious to you are not obvious to others

When you get down to writing some code, you have probably already spent hours or days thinking about the problem you are solving. You may have been through several stages of design, user experience testing, product feedback, or bug reports. You might be so familiar with your logic that things seem obvious, and you barely need to think about why something is the way it is or why you are solving the problem the way you are.

But remember, at some point another engineer will probably need to interact with your code, make changes to it, or make changes to something it depends on. They will not have had the benefit of all your time to understand the problem and think about how to solve it. The things that seemed completely obvious to you as you were writing the code are very likely not obvious to them.

It's useful to always consider this and make sure your code explains how it should be used, what it does, and why it is doing it. As you will learn later in this chapter and those that follow, this doesn't mean write loads of comments. There are often better ways to make code understandable and self-explanatory.

3.1.2 Other engineers will inadvertently try to break your code

Assuming that other engineers will inadvertently try to break your code may seem overly cynical, but, as we just saw, your code doesn't live in a vacuum; it probably depends on multiple other pieces of code, and these in turn depend on even more pieces of code. And there are probably yet more pieces of code that depend on your code. Some of these pieces of code will be in constant flux as other engineers add features, refactor, and make modifications. So, far from living in a vacuum, your code in fact lives on top of constantly shifting foundations, with yet more constantly moving parts built on top of it.

Your code may mean the world to you, but most other engineers at your company probably don't know much about it, and when they do stumble upon it, they won't necessarily have prior knowledge of why it exists or what it does. It's highly likely that another engineer will, at some point, add or modify some code in a way that unintentionally breaks or misuses your code.

As we saw in chapter 1, engineers generally make changes to the codebase in a local copy and then submit it to the main codebase. If the code doesn't compile, or if tests fail, then they won't be able to submit their change. If another engineer makes a change that breaks or misuses your code, then you want to ensure that their change does not get submitted into the main codebase until they've fixed the issue they've caused. The only two reliable ways to do this are to ensure that, when something is broken, either the code stops compiling or some tests start failing. A lot of the considerations around writing high-quality code are ultimately about ensuring that one of these two things happens when something is broken.

3.1.3 In time, you will forget about your own code

The details of your code may seem so fresh and foremost in your mind right now that you can't imagine ever forgetting them, but after time they will no longer be fresh in your mind, and you will start to forget things. When a new feature comes along, or a bug gets assigned to you in a year's time from now, you might have to modify that code you wrote and may no longer remember all the ins and outs of it.

All the words that were just said about things not being obvious to others, or about others breaking your code, will likely apply to you at some point. Looking at code that you wrote a year or two ago is not much different from looking at code written by someone else. Make sure your code is understandable even to someone with little or no context, and make it hard to break. You'll not only be doing everyone else a favor, but you'll be doing your future self one too.

3.2 How will others figure out how to use your code?

When another engineer needs to make use of your code or modify some code that is depending on your code, they will need to figure out how to use your code and what it does. Specifically, they will need to understand the following:

- In what scenarios they should call the various functions you provide
- What the classes you have created represent and when they should be used
- What values they should call things with
- What actions your code will perform
- What values your code can return

As you just read in the previous section, after a year there is a good chance that you yourself will forget all these details about your code, so you can consider your future self as essentially being another engineer for the sake of everything written in this book.

In order to figure out how to use your code, there are a few things that another engineer could do:

- Look at the names of things (functions, classes, enums etc.).
- Look at the data types of things (function and constructor parameter types and return value types).
- Read any documentation or function-/class-level comments.
- Come and ask you in person, or over chat/email.
- Look at your code (the nuts-and-bolts implementation details of the functions and classes you have written).

As we'll see in the following subsections, only the first three of these are actually practical, and within those three the naming of things and data types tend to be more reliable than documentation.

3.2.1 Looking at the names of things

In practice, looking at the names of things is one of the main ways in which engineers figure out how to use a new piece of code. The names of packages, classes, and functions read a bit like the table of contents of a book: they're a convenient and quick way to find code that will solve a subproblem. When using the code, it's very hard to ignore the names of things: if a function is called `removeEntry()` then it's hard to confuse it with a function called `addEntry()`.

Naming things well is therefore one of the best ways to convey to another engineer how your code should be used.

3.2.2 Looking at the data types of things

If done properly, looking at the data types of things can be a very reliable way of ensuring your code is used correctly. In any compiled, statically typed language, engineers have to be aware of the data types of things and get them correct or the code will not even compile. Therefore, enforcing how your code can be used using the type system is one of the best ways to ensure that other engineers can't misuse or misconfigure your code.

3.2.3 Reading documentation

Documentation about how to use your code can exist in more than one form and includes the following:

- Informal function and class-level comments
- More formal in-code documentation (such as JavaDoc)
- External documentation (such as a README.md, a web page, or a document with instructions)

These can all be extremely useful but are only somewhat reliable as a way of ensuring that others will know how to use your code correctly:

- There's no guarantee that other engineers will read these, and in fact they often don't, or they don't read them fully.
- Even if they do read them, they might misinterpret them. You may have used terms that they are unfamiliar with or wrongly assumed the other engineers' level of familiarity with the problem your code solves.
- Your documentation may be out of date. Engineers regularly forget to update documentation when they make changes to code, so it is inevitable that some amount of documentation for code will be out of date and incorrect.

3.2.4 Asking you in person

If you work in a team, then you will probably find that other engineers often ask you questions about how to use your code, and if the code is fresh in your mind then this approach can be quite effective. It can't be relied on as a way of explaining how to use a piece of code though:

- The more code you write, the more time you'll spend answering questions about it. Eventually you will run out of hours in the day to answer all these questions.
- You might be on vacation for two weeks, meaning people obviously can't ask you anything.
- After a year, you yourself will probably forget about the code, so there is only actually a limited timeframe in which this approach would even work.
- You might leave the company, and then the knowledge about how to use the code would be forever lost.

3.2.5 Looking at your code

If another engineer were to look at the nuts-and-bolts implementation details of your code, then they would probably get the most definitive answer about how to use it, but this approach doesn't scale and quickly becomes impractical. When another engineer decides to use your code as a dependency, it is probably just one of many pieces of code they are depending on. If they always have to look at the implementation details of every dependency to figure out how to use them all, then they will end up having to read through thousands of lines of existing code every time they implement a feature.

It gets worse though. These dependencies will have dependencies of their own, so if every engineer working on the codebase had taken the attitude, "You'll have to read my code to understand how to use it," then it would likely be necessary to read the implementations of some or all of the sub-dependencies too, and there might be hundreds of these. Before you know it, every engineer would need to read hundreds of thousands of lines of code just to implement a moderately sized feature.

The whole point in creating layers of abstraction is to ensure that engineers have to deal with only a few concepts at a time and that they can use a solution to a subproblem without having to know exactly how that problem was solved. Requiring engineers to read implementation details to know how to use a piece of code obviously negates a lot of the benefits of layers of abstraction.

3.3 Code contracts

You may have previously come across the term *programming by contract* (or *design by contract*[1]). It's a principle that formalizes some of the concepts that were discussed in the previous section about how others can know how to use your code and what they can expect your code to do. Under this philosophy, engineers think about the interactions between different pieces of code as though they were a contract: callers are required to meet certain obligations, and in return, the code being called will return a desired value or modify some state. Nothing should be unclear or a surprise because everything should be defined in this contract.

Engineers sometimes find it useful to formally divide the terms on their code's contract into different categories:

- *Preconditions*—Things that should be true before calling the code, such as what state the system should be in and what inputs should be supplied to the code
- *Postconditions*—Things that should be true after the piece of code has been called, such as the system being placed into a new state or certain values being returned
- *Invariants*—Things that should remain unchanged when comparing the state of the system before and after the code was called

Even if you're not deliberately programming by contract or you've never even heard of the term before, the code you write will almost certainly have some kind of contract. If you write a function that has any input parameters, returns a value, or modifies some state, then you have created a contract because you are placing an obligation onto the caller of the code to set something up or provide an input (a precondition) and giving them an expectation about what will happen or be returned (a postcondition).

1 The term *design by contract* was first introduced by Bertrand Meyer in the 1980s and is a central feature of the Eiffel programming language and methodology.

Problems arise with code contracts when engineers are unaware of some or all of the terms of them. When you are writing code, it's important to think about what the contract is and how you will ensure that anyone using your code will be aware of it and follow it.

3.3.1 *Small print in contracts*

In real life, contracts tend to have a mixture of things that are unmistakably obvious and things that are in the small print and therefore less obvious. Everyone knows that they really should read the small print of every contract they enter, but most people don't. Do you carefully read every sentence of every terms and conditions text thrown at you?

To demonstrate this distinction between things that are obvious and things that are in the small print, let's consider a real-world example of a contract: using an electric scooter rental app. After having signed up and entered your credit card number, the app allows you to find a scooter near you, reserve it, ride it, and then end the rental when you're done. The screen where you book the rental looks like figure 3.2. When you click RESERVE you are entering a contract.

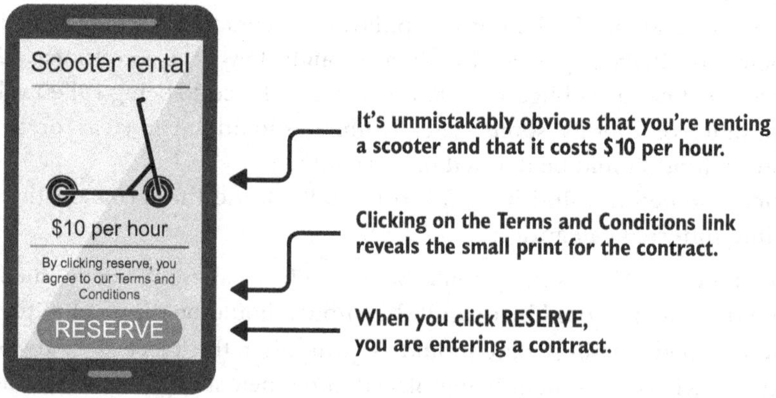

Figure 3.2 Renting an electric scooter using an app is a real-world example of entering a contract. What you are renting and the cost are unmistakable parts of the contract.

We can dissect this contract into the parts that are unmistakable and the parts that are small print:

- The unmistakable parts of the contract:
  - You are renting an electric scooter.
  - The rental will cost $10/hour.
- The small print of the contract. If you were to click the Terms and Conditions link and read the small print (figure 3.3), you would find that it says the following:
  - If you crash the scooter, you'll have to pay for it.

  - You'll be fined $100 if you take the scooter beyond the city limits.
  - If you go faster than 30 mph on the scooter, you will be fined $300, as this damages the scooter's motor. There is no speed restrictor on the scooter, and it can easily exceed this speed, so users are solely responsible for monitoring their speed and not going faster than this.

The first two of the terms in the small print are not really that surprising; we could probably have guessed that there'd be something like that in there. The third one about not going faster than 30 mph, on the other hand, is potentially a gotcha, and unless you'd read the small print carefully and knew this, it could result in a surprising and hefty fine.

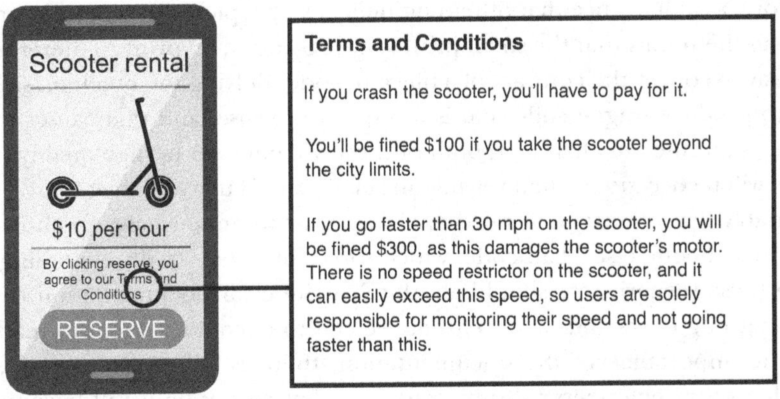

Figure 3.3 Contracts usually contain small print, such as things in the terms and conditions.

When defining the contract for a piece of code there are similarly parts that are unmistakable and parts that are more like small print:

- The unmistakable parts of the contract:
  - *Function and class names*—A caller can't use the code without knowing these.
  - *Parameter types*—The code won't even compile if the caller gets these wrong.
  - *Return types*—A caller has to know the return type of a function to be able to use it, and the code will likely not compile if they get it wrong.
  - *Any checked exceptions* (if the language supports them)—The code won't compile if the caller doesn't acknowledge or handle these.
- The small print:
  - *Comments and documentation*—Much like small print in real contracts, people really should read these (and read them fully), but in reality, they often don't. Engineers need to be pragmatic to this fact.

- *Any unchecked exceptions*—If these are listed in comments then they are small print. Sometimes they won't even be in the small print, if for example a function a few layers down throws one of these and the author of a function farther up forgot to mention it in their documentation.

Making the terms of a code contract unmistakable is much better than relying on the small print. People very often don't read small print, and even if they do they might only skim read it and get the wrong idea. And, as discussed in the previous section, documentation has a habit of becoming out-of-date, so the small print isn't even always correct.

3.3.2 Don't rely too much on small print

Small print in the form of comments and documentation is often overlooked. There is, therefore, a high chance that other engineers using a piece of code will not be fully aware of all the things that the small print states. Using small print is, therefore, not a reliable way to convey the contract of a piece of code. Relying too much on small print is likely to produce fragile code that is too easy to misuse, and that causes surprises, and as we established in chapter 1, both of these are enemies of high-quality code.

There will be occasions when relying on small print is unavoidable; some problems will invariably have caveats that need explaining, or we might have no choice but to depend on someone else's bad code, which forces our code to do something slightly weird. In these scenarios we should absolutely write clear documentation to explain this to other engineers and do everything we can to encourage them to read it. But, despite the importance of the documentation, there is still, unfortunately, a high chance that other engineers will not read it or that over time it will become out-of-date, so it's really not ideal. Chapter 5 will discuss comments and documentation in more detail. In general, it's a good idea to document things that might otherwise not be clear, but it's usually best not to rely too much on other engineers actually reading it. If it's possible to make things clear using the unmistakably obvious parts of the code contract instead, then this is often preferable.

To demonstrate this, the following example (listing 3.1) shows code for a class to load and access some user settings. It defines a contract for how the class should be used, but it relies heavily on callers of the class having read all the small print to be able to use it: after constructing the class, callers are required to call a function to load some settings and then an initializer function. If they fail to do all these things in the right order, then the class is in an invalid state.

Listing 3.1 Code with lots of small print

```
class UserSettings {

  UserSettings() { ... }
```

```
  // Do not call any other functions until the settings have
  // been successfully loaded using this function.
  // Returns true if the settings were successfully loaded.
  Boolean loadSettings(File location) { ... }

  // init() must be called before calling any other functions, but
  // only after the settings have been loaded using loadSettings().
  void init() { ... }

  // Returns the user's chosen UI color, or null if they haven't
  // chosen one, or if the settings have not been loaded or
  // initialized.
  Color? getUiColor() { ... }
}
```

Pieces of documentation like these are small print in the code's contract.

A null return value can mean one of two things here: the user didn't choose a color or the class has not been fully initialized.

Let's spell the contract here out:

- The unmistakable parts of the contract:
  - The class is called `UserSettings`, so it obviously contains user settings.
  - `getUiColor()` almost certainly returns the UI color chosen by the user. It can return either a color or null. Without reading the comments, there is some ambiguity about what null means, but the most likely guess might be that it means the user didn't choose a color.
  - `loadSettings()` accepts a file and returns a Boolean. Even without reading the comment, a likely guess is that this returning true indicates success and false indicates failure.
- The small print:
  - The class needs to be set up with a very specific series of function calls: first `loadSettings()` needs to be called. If it returns true, then `init()` needs to be called, and only then can the class be used.
  - If `loadSettings()` returns false, then no other functions in the class should be called.
  - `getUiColor()` returning null can in fact indicate one of two things: that the user didn't choose a color or that the class hasn't been set up yet.

This is a horrible contract. If an engineer using this class doesn't very carefully read all the small print, then there is a high chance that they will not set this class up correctly. If they don't set the class up correctly, then this might not even be obvious, because the function `getUiColor()` has overloaded the meaning of null (and they wouldn't know this unless they read the small print).

To demonstrate how this can be problematic, consider the code in listing 3.2. If `userSettings` has not been correctly set up before calling the `setUiColor()` function, then the program won't crash, and it'll do something vaguely sensible, but there is clearly a bug here: we're ignoring the user's chosen UI color.

Listing 3.2 Code with a potential bug in it

```
void setUiColor(UserSettings userSettings) {
  Color? chosenColor = userSettings.getUiColor();
  if (chosenColor == null) {
    ui.setColor(DEFAULT_UI_COLOR);        <-- Uses a default color if getUiColor()
    return;                                   returns null. This can happen if either
  }                                           the user didn't choose a color or if the
  ui.setColor(chosenColor);                   UserSettings class is in an invalid state.
}
```

Figure 3.4 enumerates all the ways in which this code can be misconfigured and potentially cause bugs. Currently, the only mitigation against this misuse is the small print, and as we established, small print is generally not a reliable way to convey a code contract. The code as is creates a high chance that bugs will creep into the software.

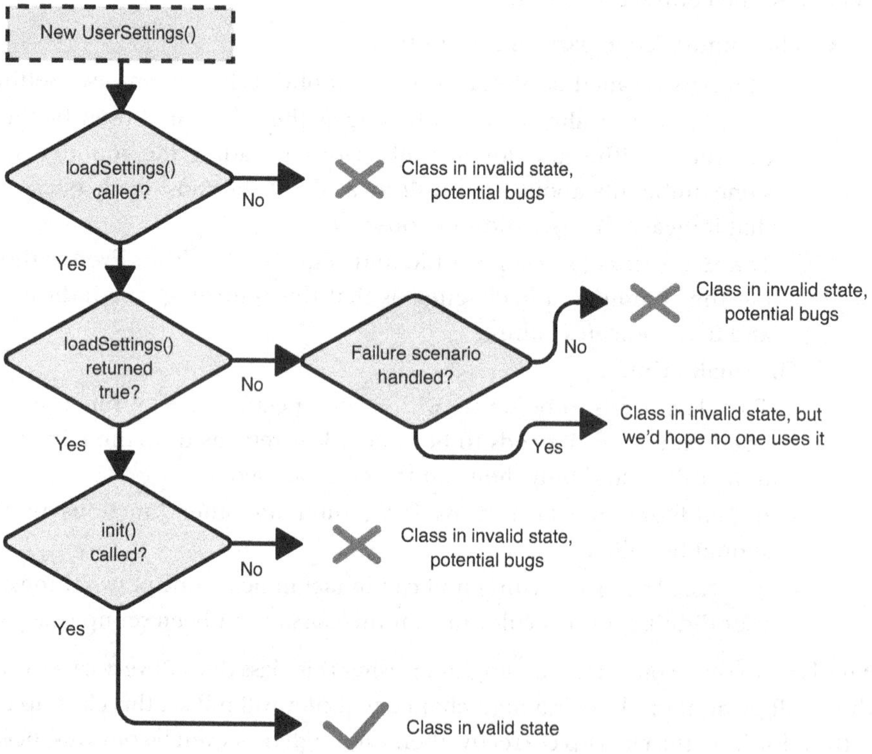

Figure 3.4 The more ways there are to misuse a piece of code, the more likely it is to be misused, and the more likely there are to be bugs in the software.

How to eliminate the small print

We saw previously how relying on small print is unreliable because it's too easily overlooked. In the real-world contract example with the scooter that we saw earlier, it would be better if going faster than 30 mph were just impossible. The scooter company could fit a speed restrictor to the scooter so that the motor stopped supplying power whenever the speed approached 30 mph and started supplying power again only once the speed dropped. If they did this, then there'd be no need for a clause in the small print, and it would probably completely eradicate the problem of the scooter motors getting damaged in this way.

We can apply the same principle to code: it's better to just make it impossible to do the wrong thing rather than relying on small print to try to ensure that other engineers use a piece of code correctly. It's often possible to shift parts of the code contract from small print to being impossible (or at least unmistakable) by thinking carefully about what states the code can get into or what data types it takes as input or returns. The aim is to ensure that if the code is misused or misconfigured, then it won't even compile.

The `UserSettings` class could be modified to use a static factory function that ensures that it's only possible to get a fully initialized instance of the class. This means that any piece of code anywhere else that uses an instance of `UserSettings` is guaranteed to have a fully initialized version of it. In the following example (listing 3.3), the `UserSettings` class has been modified in the following ways:

- A static factory function called `create()` has been added. This handles the loading of settings and initialization and only ever returns an instance of the class that's in a valid state.
- The constructor has been made private to force code external to the class to use the `create()` function.
- The `loadSettings()` and `init()` functions have been made private to prevent code external to the class from calling them, which could otherwise place an instance of the class into an invalid state.
- Because an instance of the class is now guaranteed to be in a valid state, the `getUiColor()` function no longer needs to overload the meaning of null. A null return value now only means that the user didn't provide a color.

Listing 3.3 Code with almost no small print

```
class UserSettings {

  private UserSettings() { ... }

  static UserSettings? create(File location) {
    UserSettings settings = new UserSettings();
    if (!settings.loadSettings(location)) {
      return null;
    }
    settings.init();
    return settings;
  }
```

The constructor is private. This forces engineers to use the create() function instead.

Calling this function is the only way to create an instance of UserSettings.

If loading the settings failed, then return null. This prevents anyone ever getting an instance of this class that's in an invalid state.

```
  private Boolean loadSettings(File location) { ... }

  private void init() { ... }

  // Returns the user's chosen UI color, or null if they haven't
  // chosen one.
  Color? getUiColor() { ... }
}
```

Any functions that change the class's state are private.

A null return value can now only mean one thing: the user didn't choose a color.

These changes have successfully eliminated nearly all the small print from the `UserSettings` class's contract, and instead made it impossible to create an instance of the class in an invalid state. The only bit of small print that remains is to explain what a null return value from `getUiColor()` signifies, but even this is probably not needed, as most users of the class would probably guess this is what null means, and it's no longer overloaded with also indicating that the class is in an invalid state.

Figure 3.5 shows how the class can now be used, in particular, how it's now impossible to acquire an instance of the class in an invalid state. If you have some familiarity with this already, then you may have spotted that the technique employed here was to eliminate any *state* or *mutability* from being exposed outside of the class.

NOTE: STATE AND MUTABILITY? If you're not familiar with the terms *state* or *mutability*, then you will be by the end of this book. Many ways of improving code quality revolve around minimizing them. An object's state refers to any values or data held within it. An object is mutable if it's possible to modify any of these values after having created the object. Conversely if it's not possible to modify any of these values after creation, then an object is immutable. We'll discuss this in detail in chapter 7.

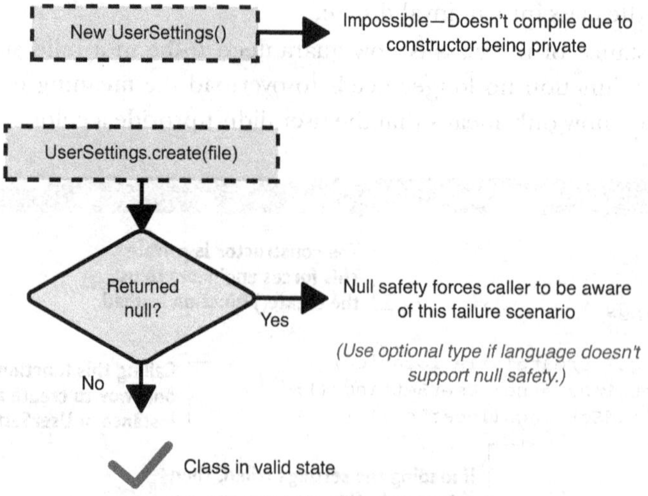

Figure 3.5 If code is impossible to misuse, then it's a lot less likely that bugs will creep into the software when other engineers need to use it.

It's worth mentioning that the `UserSettings` class is still not perfect. For example, indicating that loading the settings failed by returning null doesn't make the code very debuggable; it would probably be useful to have error information about why it failed. The next chapter will explore ways of handling errors, and we'll see various alternatives that could be used here instead.

The code in this section is just one example of how too much small print can lead to poor quality code that is easy to misuse and that causes surprises. There are numerous other ways in which too much small print can make code fragile and error prone, and we'll explore a bunch of them in later chapters.

3.4 Checks and assertions

An alternative to using the compiler to enforce a code contract is to use runtime enforcement instead. This is generally not as robust as compile-time enforcement, because discovering a breach of the code contract will rely on a test (or a user) encountering the issue while running the code. This is in contrast to compile-time enforcement, which makes breaching the contract logically impossible in the first place.

Nonetheless there are sometimes scenarios where there is no practical way to enforce a contract using the compiler. And when this happens, enforcing the contract with a runtime check is better than not enforcing the contract.

3.4.1 Checks

A common way to enforce the conditions of a code contract is to use *checks*. These are additional logic that check that a code's contract has been adhered to (such as constraints on input parameters, or setup that should have been done), and if it hasn't, then the check throws an error (or similar) that will cause an obvious and unmissable failure. (Checks are closely related to *failing fast*, which is discussed in the next chapter.)

To continue the electric scooter analogy, adding a check would be a bit like adding a failsafe to the scooter's firmware that means that the scooter will completely shut down if the rider hits 30 mph. The rider would then have to pull over and find the hard reset button and wait for the scooter to reboot before they could continue. This prevents the motor getting damaged, but it causes the scooter to abruptly shut down, which is at best kind of annoying and at worst kind of dangerous, if, for example, the rider were in a column of traffic on a busy road. It's still probably better than damaging the motor and getting fined $300, but the solution using a speed restrictor was nicer, because it made it impossible for the bad situation to happen in the first place.

The naming of checks is often divided into subcategories based on what kind of contract condition they are enforcing:

- *Precondition checks*—For example, checking an input argument is correct, that some initialization has been performed, or more generally that the system is in a valid state before running some code
- *Postcondition checks*—For example, checking a return value is correct or that the system is in a valid state after running some code

We saw that the `UserSettings` class could be made less error prone by making it impossible to misconfigure. An alternative might be to use precondition checks. If the author of the class had done this, then code would look something like the example in the following listing.

Listing 3.4 Using checks to enforce a contract

```
class UserSettings {

  UserSettings() { ... }

  // Do not call any other functions until the settings have
  // been successfully loaded using this function.
  // Returns true if the settings were successfully loaded.
  bool loadSettings(File location) { ... }

  // init() must be called before calling any other functions, but
  // only after the settings have been loaded using loadSettings().
  void init() {
    if (!haveSettingsBeenLoaded()) {
      throw new StateException("Settings not loaded");
    }
    ...
  }

  // Returns the user's chosen UI color, or null if they haven't
  // chosen one.
  Color? getUiColor() {
    if (!hasBeenInitialized()) {
      throw new StateException("Settings not initialized");
    }
    ...
  }
}
```

Exceptions are thrown if the class is used in an invalid way.

This is an improvement over the original code with loads of small print because it's less likely that bugs will go unnoticed; if the class is used before being set up, then a loud failure will happen. But this is less ideal than the solution we saw that made misuse impossible.

> **NOTE: CHECKS IN DIFFERENT LANGUAGES** Listing 3.4 implemented a precondition check in a custom way by throwing a `StateException`. Some languages have built-in support and therefore a nicer syntax for checks, while others require a more manual approach or use of a third-party library. If you decide to use checks, then make sure you look up the best way of implementing them in whatever language you're using.

The hope with a check is that if someone is misusing the code it will be revealed during development, or during testing, and it will be noticed and fixed before the code is shipped to customers or used in the wild. This is much better than the program silently getting into a bad state that might only manifest as weird bugs that aren't immediately obvious. But the effectiveness of checks is not guaranteed:

- If the condition being checked is broken only in some obscure scenario that no one thought to test (or that fuzz testing doesn't simulate), then the bug may still not be revealed until the code is released and in the hands of real users.
- Despite the check causing a loud failure, there is still a risk that no one notices. Exceptions might be caught at some higher level in the program and just logged to prevent full on crashes. If an engineer working on the code didn't bother to check these logs, then they might not notice. If this happens, then it is a sign of a pretty serious problem with a team's development practices (or exception handling), but stuff like this does unfortunately happen more often than it should.

Sometimes having small print in a piece of code's contract is unavoidable, and in these instances it can be a good idea to add checks to ensure that the contract is adhered to. But it's better to just avoid small print in the first place if possible. If we find ourselves adding lots of checks to a piece of code, then it might be a sign that we should instead think about how to eliminate the small print.

Fuzz testing

Fuzz testing is a type of testing that tries to generate inputs that might reveal bugs or misconfiguration in a piece of code or software. For example, if we have a piece of software that takes a user-provided input in the form of a string, then a fuzz test might generate lots of different random strings and provide them as input, one after another, to see if a failure happens or an exception is thrown. If, for example, a string containing a certain character causes the program to crash, then we'd hope that fuzz testing would reveal this.

If we use fuzz testing, then including checks (or assertions, see next section) in our code, can help increase the chance that the fuzz testing will reveal any misconfiguration or bugs, because fuzz testing usually relies on an error or exception being thrown and won't catch more subtle bugs that simply results in weird behavior.

3.4.2 Assertions

Many languages have built-in support for *assertions*. Assertions are conceptually very similar to checks in that they are a way to try to enforce that the code contract is adhered to. When the code is compiled in a development mode, or when tests are run, assertions behave in much the same way as checks: a loud error or exception will be thrown if a condition is broken. The key difference between assertions and checks is that assertions are normally compiled out once the code is built for release, meaning no loud failure will happen when the code is being used in the wild. The reason for compiling them out when the code is released can be twofold:

- *To improve performance*—Calculating whether a condition has been broken obviously requires some CPU cycles. If we have an assertion in a piece of code that is run a lot, then it can noticeably degrade overall performance of a piece of software.

- *To make code less likely to fail*—Whether this is a valid motivation will really depend on our particular application. This increases the chance that bugs will go unnoticed, but if we are working on a system where availability is more important than avoiding some potentially buggy behavior, then it might be the right trade-off.

There is usually a way to leave assertions enabled even in release builds of the code, and many development teams do this. In this case, assertions are not really any different from checks, except for some details about what kind of errors or exceptions they might throw.

If the author of the `UserSettings` class has used assertions instead of checks, then the `getUiColor()` function would look something like the following listing.

Listing 3.5 Using an assertion to enforce a contract

```
class UserSettings {
  ...

  // Returns the user's chosen UI color, or null if they haven't
  // chosen one.
  Color? getUiColor() {
    assert(hasBeenInitialized(), "Settings not initialized");
    ...
  }
}
```

The assertion will cause an error or exception to be thrown if the class is used in an invalid way.

What was said about checks is also true of assertions: when we have small print in our code's contract it's good to enforce it. But it's even better to just avoid small print in the first place.

Summary

- Codebases are in a constant state of flux, with multiple engineers typically making changes.
- It's useful to think about how other engineers might break or misuse code and engineer it in a way that minimizes the chances of this or makes it impossible.
- When we write code, we are invariably creating some kind of code contract. This can contain things that are unmistakably obvious and things that are more like small print.
- Small print in code contracts is not a reliable way to ensure other engineers adhere to the contract. Making things unmistakably obvious is usually a better approach.
- Enforcing a contract using the compiler is usually the most reliable approach. When this is not feasible, an alternative is to enforce a contract at runtime using checks or assertions.

4 Errors

This chapter covers

- The distinction between errors a system can recover from and those it cannot recover from
- Failing fast and failing loudly
- Different techniques for signaling errors and considerations for choosing which to use

The environment in which our code runs tends to be imperfect: users will provide invalid inputs, external systems will go down, and our code and other code around it will often contain some number of bugs. Given this, errors are inevitable; things can and will go wrong, and as a result we can't write robust and reliable code without thinking carefully about error cases. When thinking about errors, it's often useful to distinguish between errors from which a piece of software might want to recover and those from which there is no sensible way to recover. This chapter starts by exploring this distinction before exploring techniques we can use to ensure that errors don't go unnoticed and that they're handled appropriately.

Talking about errors, and in particular how to signal and handle them, is a bit of a can of worms, and we're about to open it. Many software engineers and even programming language designers have different (and sometimes strongly held) opinions about how code should signal and handle errors. The second half of this chapter attempts to give a reasonably broad overview of the main techniques you're likely to encounter and the arguments around using them. But just to warn you, this is a big and somewhat divisive topic, and as a result this chapter is relatively long.

4.1 Recoverability

When thinking about a piece of software, it's often necessary to think about whether there is a realistic way to recover from a particular error scenario. This section will describe what is meant by an error being one that can or cannot be recovered from. It will then go on to explain how this distinction is often context dependent, meaning engineers have to think carefully about how their code might be used when deciding what to do when an error occurs.

4.1.1 Errors that can be recovered from

Many errors are not fatal to a piece of software, and there are sensible ways to handle them gracefully and recover. An obvious example of this is if a user provides an invalid input (such as an incorrect phone number); it would not be a great user experience if, upon entering an invalid phone number, the whole application crashed (potentially losing unsaved work). Instead, it's better to just provide the user with a nice error message stating that the phone number is invalid and ask them to enter a correct one.

In addition to things like invalid user inputs, other examples of errors that we likely want a piece of software to recover from are the following:

- *Network errors*—If a service that we depend on is unreachable, then it might be best to just wait a few seconds and retry, or else ask the user to check their network connection if our code runs on the user's device.
- *A noncritical task error*—For example, if an error occurs in a part of the software that just logs some usage statistics, then it's probably fine to continue execution.

Generally, most errors caused by something external to a system are things that the system as a whole should probably try to recover from gracefully. This is because they are often things that we should actively expect to happen: external systems and networks go down, files get corrupted, and users (or hackers) will provide invalid inputs.

Note that this is referring to the system as a whole. As we'll see in a bit, low-level code is often not well placed to try and recover from errors, and it's often necessary to signal an error to higher level code that knows how the error should be handled.

4.1.2 Errors that cannot be recovered from

Sometimes errors occur and there is no sensible way for a system to recover from them. Very often these occur due to a programming error where an engineer somewhere has "screwed something up." Examples of these include the following:

- A resource that should be bundled with the code is missing.
- Some code misuses another a piece of code, such as the following examples:
  - Calling it with an invalid input argument
  - Not pre-initializing some state that is required

If there is no conceivable way that an error can be recovered from, then the only sensible thing a piece of code can do is try to limit the damage and maximize the likelihood that an engineer notices and fixes the problem. Section 4.2 discusses the concepts of *failing fast* and *failing loudly*, which are central to this.

4.1.3 Often only the caller knows if an error can be recovered from

Most types of errors manifest when one piece of code calls another piece of code. Therefore, when dealing with an error scenario, it's important to think carefully about what other code might be calling our code, in particular the following:

- Would the caller potentially want to recover from the error?
- If so, how will the caller know that they need to handle the error?

Code is often reused and called from multiple places, and if we're aiming to create clean layers of abstraction, then it's generally best to make as few assumptions as possible about potential callers of our code. This means that when we're writing or modifying a function, we are not always in a position to know whether an error state is one that can or should be recovered from.

To demonstrate this, consider listing 4.1. It contains a function that parses a phone number from a string. If the string is an invalid phone number, then that constitutes an error, but can a piece of code calling this function (and the program as whole) realistically recover from this error?

Listing 4.1 Parsing a phone number

```
class PhoneNumber {
  ...
  static PhoneNumber parse(String number) {
    if (!isValidPhoneNumber(number)) {
      ... some code to handle the error ...     <-- Can the program recover from this?
    }
    ...
  }
  ...
}
```

The answer to the question of whether the program can recover from this error is that we don't know unless we know how this function is being used and where it's being called from.

If the function is being called with a hard-coded value that is not a valid phone number, then it's a programming error. This is likely not something that the program can recover from. Imagine this is being used in some call-forwarding software for a company that redirects every call to the head office; there is absolutely no way the program can recover from this:

```
PhoneNumber getHeadOfficeNumber() {
  return PhoneNumber.parse("01234typo56789");
}
```

Conversely, if the function is being called with a user-provided value (as in the following snippet) and that input is an invalid phone number, then it is probably something that the program can and should recover from. It would be best to show a nicely formatted error message in the UI informing the user that the phone number is invalid.

```
PhoneNumber getUserPhoneNumber(UserInput input) {
  return PhoneNumber.parse(input.getPhoneNumber());
}
```

Only the caller of the `PhoneNumber.parse()` function is in a position to know whether the phone number being invalid is something that the program can recover from. In scenarios like this, the author of a function like `PhoneNumber.parse()` should assume that the phone number being invalid is something that callers may want to recover from.

More generally, if any of the following are true, then an error caused by anything supplied to a function should probably be considered as something that a caller might want to recover from:

- We don't have exact (and complete) knowledge about everywhere our function might be called from and where values supplied in those calls originate from.
- There's even the slimmest chance that our code might be reused in the future, meaning our assumptions about where it's called from and the origins of any values may become invalid.

The only real exception to this is where the code's contract makes it clear that a certain input is invalid and a caller has an easy and obvious way to validate the input before calling the function. An example of this might be an engineer calling a list getter with a negative index (in a language that doesn't support this); it should be obvious that a negative index would be invalid, and the caller has an easy and obvious way to check this before calling the function if there's a risk that the index could be negative. For scenarios like this, we can probably safely assume it's a programming error and treat it as something that cannot be recovered from. But it's still good to appreciate that what might seem obvious to us about how our code should be used might not be obvious to others. If the fact that a certain input is invalid is buried deep in the small print of the code contract, then other engineers are likely to miss it.

Determining that callers might want to recover from an error is all well and good, but if callers are not even aware that the error can happen, then they're unlikely to handle it properly. The next section explains this in more detail.

4.1.4 Make callers aware of errors they might want to recover from

When some other code calls our code, it will often have no practical way of knowing beforehand that its call will result in an error. For example, what is or isn't a valid phone number might be quite a complicated thing to determine. "01234typo56789" might be an invalid phone number, but "1-800-I-LOVE-CODE" might be perfectly valid, meaning the rules determining this are, clearly, somewhat complicated.

In the previous phone number example (repeated in listing 4.2), the `PhoneNumber` class provides a layer of abstraction for dealing with the ins and outs of phone numbers; callers are shielded from the implementation details, and thus complexity, of the rules that determine what is/isn't a valid phone number. It would therefore be unreasonable to expect callers to call `PhoneNumber.parse()` with only valid inputs, because the whole point in the `PhoneNumber` class is to prevent callers from having to worry about the rules that determine this.

Listing 4.2 Parsing a phone number

```
class PhoneNumber {                          <-- The layer of abstraction for phone numbers
  ...
  static PhoneNumber parse(String number) {
    if (!isValidPhoneNumber(number)) {
      ... some code to handle the error ...
    }
    ...
  }
  ...
}
```

Further to this, because callers to `PhoneNumber.parse()` are not experts on phone numbers, they might not even realize that the concept of a phone number being invalid exists, or even if they do, they might not expect validation to happen at this point. They might expect it to happen only when the number is dialed, for example.

The author of the `PhoneNumber.parse()` function should therefore make sure that callers are aware of the possibility that an error might occur. Failure to do this could result in surprises when the error does occur and no one has written any code to actually handle it. This might lead to user-visible bugs or failures in business-critical logic. Sections 4.3 and 4.5 cover how we can ensure that a caller is aware that an error can happen in detail.

4.2 Robustness vs. failure

When an error occurs, there is often a choice to be made between

- failing, which could entail either making a higher layer of code handle the error or else making the entire program crash, or
- trying to deal with the error and carrying on.

Carrying on can sometimes make code more robust, but it can also mean that errors go unnoticed and that weird things start happening. This section explains why failure can often be the best option but how robustness can be built in at appropriate levels in the logic.

4.2.1 Fail fast

Imagine we are in the business of foraging for rare wild truffles and selling them to high-end restaurants. We want to buy a dog that can help us find truffles by sniffing them out. We have two options:

1 A dog that is trained to stop and bark as soon as it discovers a truffle. Whenever it does this, we look where its nose is pointing, dig, and presto: we've found the truffle.
2 A dog that, after finding a truffle, stays silent, walks for 10 meters or more in random directions, and only then starts barking.

Which of these dogs should we choose? Hunting for bugs in code is a bit like hunting for truffles with a dog; at some point the code will bark at us by exhibiting some bad behavior or throwing an error. We'll know where the code started barking: either where we saw the bad behavior or a line number in a stack trace. But if the barking doesn't start anywhere near the actual source of the bug, then it's not very useful.

Failing fast is about ensuring that an error is signaled as near to the real location of a problem as possible. For an error that can be recovered from, this gives the caller the maximum chance of being able to recover gracefully and safely from it; for an error that cannot be recovered from, it gives engineers the maximum chance of being able to quickly identify and fix the problem. In both cases, it also prevents a piece of software from ending up in an unintended and potentially dangerous state.

A common example of this is when a function is called with an invalid argument. Failing fast would mean throwing an error as soon as that function is called with the invalid input, as opposed to carrying on running only to find that the invalid input causes an issue somewhere else in the code sometime later.

Figure 4.1 illustrates what can happen if code doesn't fail fast: the error may only manifest far away from the actual location of the error, and it can require significant engineering effort to work backward through the code to find and fix the error.

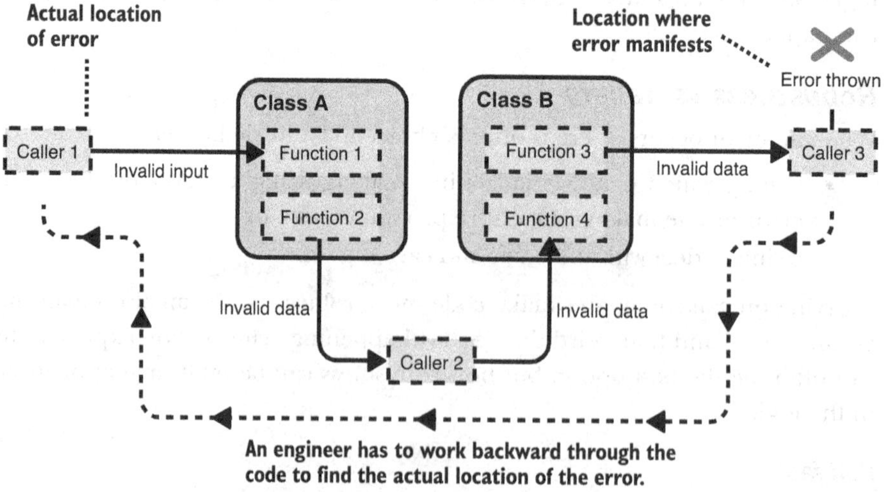

Figure 4.1 If code doesn't fail fast when an error occurs, then the error may only manifest much later in some code far away from the actual location of the error. It can require considerable engineering effort to track down and fix the problem.

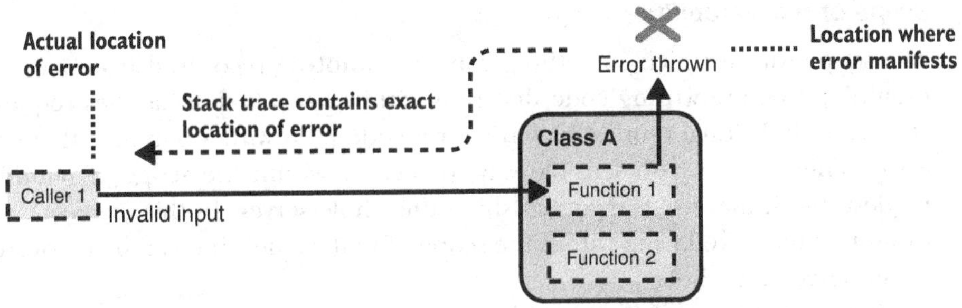

Figure 4.2 If code fails fast when an error occurs, then the exact location of the error will usually be immediately obvious.

In contrast, figure 4.2 shows how failing fast can improve the situation considerably. When failing fast, the error will manifest near to its actual location, and a stack trace will often provide the exact line number in the code where it can be found.

In addition to making things hard to debug, not failing fast can cause code to limp on and potentially cause damage. An example of this might be saving some corrupted data to a database: a bug that may only be noticed several months later, by which time a lot of important data may have been destroyed for good.

As with the dog and the truffle, it's a lot more useful if code barks as near to the real source of the problem as possible. If the error can't be recovered from, then it's also important to make sure that code does indeed bark (and bark loudly) when there's a bug, as the next section discusses; this is known as *failing loudly*.

4.2.2 Fail loudly

If an error occurs that the program can't recover from, then it's very likely a bug caused by a programming error or some mistake made by an engineer. We obviously don't want a bug like this in the software and most likely want to fix it, but we can't fix it unless we first know about it.

Failing loudly is simply ensuring that errors don't go unnoticed. The most obvious (and violent) way to do this is to crash the program by throwing an exception (or similar). An alternative is to log an error message, although these can sometimes get ignored depending on how diligent engineers are at checking them and how much other noise there is in the logs. If the code is running on a user's device, then we might want to send an error message back to the server to log what has happened (as long as we have the user's permission to do this, of course).

If code fails fast and fails loudly, then there is a good chance that a bug will be discovered during development or during testing (before the code is even released). Even if it's not, we'll likely start seeing the error reports quite soon after release and will have the benefit of knowing exactly where the bug occurred in the code from looking at the report.

4.2.3 Scope of recoverability

The scope within which something can or cannot be recovered from can vary. For example, if we are writing code that runs within a server that handles requests from clients, an individual request may trigger a code path with a bug in it that causes an error. There may be no sensible way to recover within the scope of handling that request, but it may not warrant crashing the whole server. In this scenario, the error cannot be recovered from within the scope of that request but can be recovered from by the server as a whole.

It's generally good to try and make software robust; crashing a whole server because of one bad request would probably not be a good idea. But it's also important to make sure that errors don't go unnoticed, so the code needs to fail loudly. There is often a dichotomy between these two aims. The loudest way to fail is to crash the program, but this obviously makes the software less robust.

The solution to this dichotomy is to ensure that if programming errors are caught, they are logged and monitored in a way that ensures that engineers will notice them. This usually involves logging detailed error information so that an engineer can debug what happened and ensuring that error rates are monitored and engineers are alerted if the error rate gets too high (figure 4.3 illustrates this).

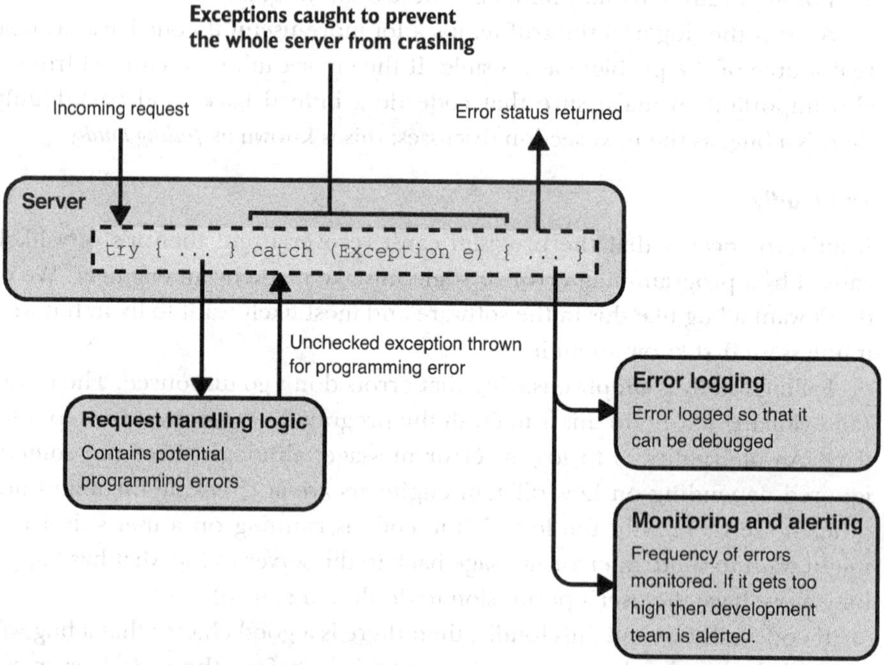

Figure 4.3 In a server a programming error may occur when processing a single request. Because requests are independent events, it might be best not to crash the whole server when this happens. The error cannot be recovered from within the scope of a single request but can be recovered from by server as a whole.

NOTE: SERVER FRAMEWORKS Most server frameworks contain built-in functionality to isolate errors for individual requests and map certain types of errors to different error responses and handling. It's therefore unlikely that we'd have to write our own try–catch statement, but something conceptually similar to this will be happening inside the server framework.

As a word of caution, this technique of catching all types of errors and then logging them instead of signaling them to a higher level in the program should be applied with extreme care. There are often only a handful of places (if any) in a program where it's appropriate to do this, such as very high-level entry points into the code or branches of logic that are genuinely independent of, or noncritical to, the correct functioning of the rest of the program. As we'll see in the next section, catching and logging errors (instead of signaling them) can result in them being hidden, which can cause problems.

4.2.4 Don't hide errors

As we just saw, robustness can be built in by isolating independent or noncritical parts of code to ensure they don't crash the entire piece of software. This usually needs to be done carefully, sparingly, and in reasonably high-level code. Catching errors from non-independent, critical, or low-level parts of code and then carrying on regardless can often lead to software that doesn't properly do what it's meant to. And if errors are not appropriately logged or reported, then problems might go unnoticed by the engineering team.

Sometimes it can seem tempting to just hide an error and pretend it never happened. This can make the code look a lot simpler and avoid a load of clunky error handling, but it's almost never a good idea. Hiding errors is problematic for both errors that can be recovered from and errors that cannot be recovered from:

- Hiding an error that a caller might want to recover from denies that caller the opportunity to gracefully recover from it. Instead of being able to display a precise and meaningful error message, or fall back to some other behavior, they are instead completely unaware that anything has gone wrong, meaning the software will likely not do what it is meant to.
- Hiding an error that can't be recovered from likely conceals a programming error. As was established in the earlier subsections about failing fast and failing loudly, these are errors that the development team really needs to know about so they can be fixed. Hiding them means that the development team may never know about them, and the software will contain bugs that may go unnoticed for quite some time.
- In both scenarios, if an error occurs it generally means that the code is not able to do the thing that a caller was expecting it to do. If the code tries to hide the error, then the caller will assume that everything worked fine, when in fact it didn't. The code will likely limp on but then output incorrect information, corrupt some data, or eventually crash.

The next few subsections cover some of the ways in which code can hide the fact that an error has occurred. Some of these techniques are useful in other scenarios, but when it comes to handling errors, they are all generally a bad idea.

RETURNING A DEFAULT VALUE

When an error occurs and a function is unable to return a desired value it can sometimes seem simpler and easier to just return a default value. The alternative of adding code to do proper error signaling and handling can seem like a lot of effort in comparison. The problem with default values is they hide the fact that an error has occurred, meaning callers of the code will likely carry on as though everything is fine.

Listing 4.3 contains some code to look up the balance of a customer's account. If an error occurs while accessing the account store, then the function returns a default value of zero. Returning a default value of zero hides the fact that an error has occurred and makes it indistinguishable from the scenario of the customer genuinely having a balance of zero. If a customer with a credit balance of $10,000 logged in one day to find their balance displayed as zero, they would probably freak out. It would be better to signal the error to the caller, so they can instead display an error message to the user saying, "Sorry we can't access this information right now."

Listing 4.3 Returning a default value

```
class AccountManager {
  private final AccountStore accountStore;
  ...

  Double getAccountBalanceUsd(Int customerId) {
    AccountResult result = accountStore.lookup(customerId);
    if (!result.success()) {
      return 0.0;
    }
    return result.getAccount().getBalanceUsd();
  }
}
```

A default value of zero is returned if an error occurs.

There can be scenarios where having default values in code can be useful, but they're almost never appropriate when it comes to dealing with errors. They break the principles of failing fast and failing loudly because they cause the system to limp on with incorrect data, and mean that the error will manifest in some weird way later on.

THE NULL OBJECT PATTERN

A null object is conceptually similar to a default value but expands the idea to cover more complicated objects (like classes). A null object will look like a genuine return value, but all its member functions will either do nothing or return a default value that's intended to be innocuous.

Examples of the null object pattern can vary from something as simple as returning an empty list to something as complicated as implementing a whole class. Here we will just concentrate on the example of an empty list.

Listing 4.4 contains a function to look up all the unpaid invoices for a customer. If the query to the `InvoiceStore` fails, then the function returns an empty list. This could easily lead to bugs in the software. A customer may owe thousands of dollars in unpaid invoices, but if the `InvoiceStore` happens to be down on the day an audit is run, then the error will lead the caller to believe that the customer has no unpaid invoices.

Listing 4.4 Returning an empty list

```
class InvoiceManager {
  private final InvoiceStore invoiceStore;
  ...

  List<Invoice> getUnpaidInvoices(Int customerId) {
    InvoiceResult result = invoiceStore.query(customerId);
    if (!result.success()) {
      return [];                    <-- An empty list is returned
    }                                   if an error occurs.
    return result
        .getInvoices()
        .filter(invoice -> !invoice.isPaid());
  }
}
```

The null object pattern is covered in more detail in chapter 6. As far as design patterns go, it's a bit of a double-edged sword; there are a few scenarios where it can be quite useful, but as the preceding example shows, when it comes to error handling, it's often not a good idea to use it.

DOING NOTHING

If the code in question does something (rather than returning something), then one option is to just not signal that an error has happened. This is generally bad, as callers will assume that the task the code was meant to perform has been completed. This is very likely to create a mismatch between an engineer's mental model of what the code does and what it does in reality. This can cause surprises and create bugs in the software.

Listing 4.5 contains some code to add an item to a `MutableInvoice`. If the item being added has a price in a different currency to that of the `MutableInvoice`, then that is an error, and the item will not be added to the invoice. The code does nothing to signal that this error has occurred and that the item has not been added. This is very likely to cause bugs in the software, as anyone calling the `addItem()` function would expect that the item has been added to the invoice.

Listing 4.5 Do nothing when an error occurs

```
class MutableInvoice {
  ...
  void addItem(InvoiceItem item) {
    if (item.getPrice().getCurrency() !=
```

```
            this.getCurrency()) {
          return;                          <--  If there is a mismatch in
        }                                       currencies, the function returns.
        this.items.add(item);
      }
      ...
    }
```

The previous scenario is an example of not signaling an error. Another scenario that we may come across is code that actively suppresses an error that another piece of code signals. Listing 4.6 shows what this might look like. A call to `emailService.sendPlainText()` can result in an `EmailException` if an error occurs in sending an email. If this exception occurs then the code suppresses it and doesn't signal anything to the caller to indicate that the action failed. This is very likely to cause bugs in the software, as a caller to this function will assume that the email has been sent, when in fact it may not have been.

Listing 4.6 Suppressing an exception

```
class InvoiceSender {
  private final EmailService emailService;
  ...

  void emailInvoice(String emailAddress, Invoice invoice) {
    try {
      emailService.sendPlainText(
          emailAddress,
          InvoiceFormat.plainText(invoice));     The EmailException is caught
    } catch (EmailException e) { }          <--  and then completely ignored.
  }
}
```

A slight improvement on this would be if an error were logged when the failure happens (listing 4.7), but this is still almost as bad as the original code in listing 4.6. It's a slight improvement because at least an engineer might notice these errors if they looked in the logs. But it's still hiding the error from the caller, meaning they will assume that the email has been sent, when in fact it has not.

Listing 4.7 Catching an exception and logging an error

```
class InvoiceSender {
  private final EmailService emailService;
  ...

  void emailInvoice(String emailAddress, Invoice invoice) {
    try {
      emailService.sendPlainText(
          emailAddress,
          InvoiceFormat.plainText(invoice));
    } catch (EmailException e) {
```

```
      logger.logError(e);     <-- The EmailException
    }                             is logged.
  }
}
```

NOTE: BE CAREFUL ABOUT WHAT IS LOGGED Another thing that should make us nervous about the code in listing 4.7 is that the `EmailException` might contain an email address that could contain a user's personal information and be subject to specific data handling policies. Logging that email address to an error log might break those data handling policies.

As the examples demonstrate, hiding errors is almost never a good idea. If a company had the code from the previous few listings in their codebase they'd likely have a lot of unpaid invoices and an unhealthy looking balance sheet. Hiding errors can have real-world (and sometimes severe) consequences. It's better to signal when an error has occurred, and the next section covers how to do this.

4.3 Ways of signaling errors

When an error does occur, it's generally necessary to signal this to some higher level in the program. If it's not possible to recover from the error, then this generally means causing some much higher level in the program to abort and log the error, or maybe even terminate execution of the whole program. If it is potentially possible to recover from the error, this generally means signaling it to the immediate caller (or maybe a caller one or two levels up the call chain) so that they can handle it gracefully.

There are a number of ways of doing this, and the options we have for doing it will depend on what error handling features the language we are using supports. Broadly speaking, the ways of signaling an error fall into two categories:

- *Explicit*—The immediate caller of our code is forced to be aware that the error might happen. Whether they then handle it, pass it on to the next caller, or just ignore it is up to them. But whatever they do, it will be an active choice, and there's almost no way they could be oblivious to it: the possibility of the error occurring is in the unmistakable part of our code's contract.
- *Implicit*—The error gets signaled, but callers of our code are free to be oblivious to it. For a caller to know that the error might happen often requires active effort, like reading the documentation or the code. If the error is mentioned in documentation, then it's part of the small print of the code contract. Sometimes the error will not even be mentioned here, in which case it's not part of the written contract at all.

To emphasize, in this categorization we are referring to whether the possibility of an error occurring is explicit or implicit from the perspective of an engineer using a piece of code. This is not about whether the error causes stuff to ultimately fail loudly or fail quietly, it's about ensuring that callers are aware of scenarios they need to be aware of (by using explicit techniques) and that they are not burdened with having to handle scenarios that they can't do anything sensible for (by using implicit techniques). Table 4.1 lists some examples of explicit and implicit error-signaling techniques.

Table 4.1 Explicit and implicit error-signaling techniques

	Explicit error-signaling techniques	Implicit error-signaling techniques
Location in code's contract	Unmistakable part	Small print if documented, otherwise not even in the small print
Caller aware that error can happen?	Yes	Maybe
Example techniques	Checked exception Nullable return type (*if null safety*) Optional return type Result return type Outcome return type (*if return value checking enforced*) Swift errors	Unchecked exception Returning a magic value (*should be avoided*) Promise or future Assertion Check (*depending on implementation*) Panic

The following subsections will explore some of the techniques listed in table 4.1, with examples of how to use them and explanations of why they are explicit or implicit techniques.

4.3.1 Recap: Exceptions

Many programming languages have the concept of *exceptions*. These are designed as a way for a piece of code to signal an error or exceptional circumstance. When an exception is thrown, it unwinds the call stack, either until a caller that handles the exception is encountered or else until the call stack is fully unwound, at which point the program will terminate and output an error message.

An implementation of an exception is generally a fully fledged class. Languages usually have some off-the-shelf ones that we can use, but we are also free to define our own and encapsulate information about an error inside them.

Java has the concept of both *checked exceptions* and *unchecked exceptions*. Most mainstream languages that support exceptions only have the concept of unchecked exceptions, so when talking about almost any language other than Java, the word *exception* usually implies *unchecked exception*.

4.3.2 Explicit: Checked exceptions

With a checked exception, the compiler forces the caller to acknowledge that it can happen by either writing code to handle it or else declaring that the exception can be thrown in their own function signature. Using checked exceptions is therefore an explicit way of signaling an error.

SIGNALING USING A CHECKED EXCEPTION

To demonstrate and contrast different error-signaling techniques, we'll use the example of a function that calculates the square root of a number. Whenever the function is provided with a negative number as an input, this constitutes an error that needs to be signaled somehow. Obviously most languages already have an inbuilt way of calculating a square root, so we probably wouldn't write our own function to do this in real life, but it's a nice, simple example for our purposes here.

Listing 4.8 shows what this function might look like if it throws a checked exception called `NegativeNumberException` when it's supplied with a negative number. In Java, extending the class `Exception` makes an exception be a checked one (this Java paradigm is shown in listing 4.8). As well as signaling the error, `NegativeNumberException` also encapsulates the erroneous value that caused the error to help with debugging. The `getSquareRoot()` function signature contains `throws NegativeNumberException` to indicate that it can throw this checked exception; the code wouldn't compile if this were omitted.

Listing 4.8 Throwing a checked exception

```
class NegativeNumberException extends Exception {
  private final Double erroneousNumber;

  NegativeNumberException(Double erroneousNumber) {
    this.erroneousNumber = erroneousNumber;
  }

  Double getErroneousNumber() {
    return erroneousNumber;
  }
}

Double getSquareRoot(Double value)
    throws NegativeNumberException {
  if (value < 0.0) {
    throw new NegativeNumberException(value);
  }
  return Math.sqrt(value);
}
```

- A class to represent a specific type of checked exception
- Encapsulates extra information: the number that caused the error
- Functions must declare which checked exceptions they can throw.
- A checked exception is thrown if there's an error.

HANDLING A CHECKED EXCEPTION

Any other function calling the `getSquareRoot()` function must either catch the `NegativeNumberException` or else mark that it can be thrown in its own function signature.

Listing 4.9 shows a function that calls `getSquareRoot()` with a value and displays the result in the UI. The function catches the `NegativeNumberException` if it is thrown and displays an error message that explains what number caused the error.

Listing 4.9 Catching a checked exception

```
void displaySquareRoot() {
  Double value = ui.getInputNumber();
  try {
    ui.setOutput("Square root is: " + getSquareRoot(value));
  } catch (NegativeNumberException e) {
    ui.setError("Can't get square root of negative number: " +
        e.getErroneousNumber());
  }
}
```

NegativeNumberException is caught if it's thrown by getSquareRoot().

Error information from the exception is displayed

If the `displaySquareRoot()` function doesn't catch the `NegativeNumberException`, then it has to declare that the exception can be thrown in its own function signature (the following listing shows this). This then moves the decision about how to handle the error to whatever code called the `displaySquareRoot()` function.

Listing 4.10 Not catching a checked exception

```
void displaySquareRoot() throws NegativeNumberException {
  Double value = ui.getInputNumber();
  ui.setOutput("Square root is: " + getSquareRoot(value));
}
```

The NegativeNumberException is declared in the displaySquareRoot() function signature.

If the `displaySquareRoot()` function neither caught the `NegativeNumberException` nor declared it in its own function signature, then the code would not compile. This is what makes a checked exception an explicit way of signaling an error because the caller is forced to acknowledge it in some form.

4.3.3 *Implicit: Unchecked exceptions*

With unchecked exceptions, other engineers are free to be completely oblivious to the fact a piece of code might throw one. It's often advisable to document what unchecked exceptions a function might throw, but engineers very often forget to do this. Even if they do, this only makes the exception part of the small print in the code contract. As we saw earlier, small print is often not a reliable way to convey a piece of code's contract. Unchecked exceptions are therefore an implicit way of signaling an error because there's no guarantee that the caller will be aware that the error can happen.

SIGNALING USING AN UNCHECKED EXCEPTION

Listing 4.11 shows the `getSquareRoot()` function and `NegativeNumberException` from the previous subsection, but with it modified so that `NegativeNumberException` is now an unchecked exception. As previously mentioned, in most languages all exceptions are unchecked exceptions, but in Java extending the class `RuntimeException` makes an exception unchecked (this Java paradigm is shown in listing 4.11). The `getSquareRoot()` function now does not need to declare that it can throw an exception. The `NegativeNumberException` is mentioned in the functions documentation as this is advisable but not enforced.

Listing 4.11 Throwing an unchecked exception

```
class NegativeNumberException extends RuntimeException {
  private final Double erroneousNumber;

  NegativeNumberException(Double erroneousNumber) {
    this.erroneousNumber = erroneousNumber;
  }

  Double getErroneousNumber() {
    return erroneousNumber;
  }
}

/**
 * @throws NegativeNumberException if the value is negative
 */
Double getSquareRoot(Double value) {
  if (value < 0.0) {
    throw new NegativeNumberException(value);
  }
  return Math.sqrt(value);
}
```

- A class to represent a specific type of unchecked exception
- It's advisable (but not enforced) that functions document what unchecked exceptions they can throw.
- An unchecked exception is thrown if there's an error.

HANDLING AN UNCHECKED EXCEPTION

Another function calling the `getSquareRoot()` function can choose to catch the `NegativeNumberException` in exactly the same way as the previous example when it was a checked exception (repeated in the following listing).

Listing 4.12 Catching an unchecked exception

```
void displaySquareRoot() {
  Double value = ui.getInputNumber();
  try {
    ui.setOutput("Square root is: " + getSquareRoot(value));
  } catch (NegativeNumberException e) {
    ui.setError("Can't get square root of negative number: " +
        e.getErroneousNumber());
  }
}
```

- NegativeNumberException is caught if it's thrown by getSquareRoot().

Importantly, a function calling `getSquareRoot()` is not required to acknowledge the exception. If it didn't catch the exception, then there is no requirement that it declares it in its own function signature, or even in its own documentation. Listing 4.13 shows a version of the `displaySquareRoot()` function that neither handles nor declares the `NegativeNumberException`. Because `NegativeNumberException` is an unchecked exception this would compile absolutely fine. If a `NegativeNumber-Exception` were thrown by `getSquareRoot()`, it would either bubble up to a caller that does catch it, or else the program would terminate.

Listing 4.13 Not catching an unchecked exception

```
void displaySquareRoot() {
  Double value = ui.getInputNumber();
  ui.setOutput("Square root is: " + getSquareRoot(value));
}
```

As we can see, a caller of a function that throws an unchecked exception is free to be completely oblivious to the fact that the exception might be thrown. This makes unchecked exceptions an implicit way of signaling an error.

4.3.4 Explicit: Nullable return type

Returning a null from a function can be an effective, simple way to indicate that a certain value could not be calculated (or acquired). If the language we are using supports null safety, then the caller will be forced to be aware that the value might be null and handle it accordingly. Using a nullable return type (when we have null safety) is therefore an explicit way of signaling an error.

If we're using a language that doesn't support null safety, then using an optional return type can be a good alternative. This was discussed in chapter 2, and more information about optionals is also available in appendix B at the end of the book.

SIGNALING USING A NULL

Listing 4.14 shows the `getSquareRoot()` function, but this time modified so that it returns null if the input value is negative. One issue with returning null is that it gives no information about why the error occurred, so it can often be necessary to add a comment or documentation to explain what null signifies.

Listing 4.14 Returning a null

```
// Returns null if the supplied value is negative
Double? getSquareRoot(Double value) {
  if (value < 0.0) {
    return null;
  }
  return Math.sqrt(value);
}
```

- A comment is required to explain when a null might be returned. (annotates the comment line)
- The ? in Double? indicates that the return value can be null. (annotates the signature)
- null is returned if an error occurs. (annotates `return null;`)

HANDLING A NULL

Because the language supports null safety, a caller is forced to check whether the value returned by `getSquareRoot()` is null before they can use it. The following listing shows the `displaySquareRoot()` function but this time handling a nullable return type.

Listing 4.15 Handling a null

```
void displaySquareRoot() {
  Double? squareRoot = getSquareRoot(ui.getInputNumber());
```

```
  if (squareRoot == null) {
    ui.setError("Can't get square root of a negative number");
  } else {
    ui.setOutput("Square root is: " + squareRoot);
  }
}
```

The return value of getSquareRoot() needs to be checked for null.

It's not entirely true to say that a caller is forced to check whether the value is null. They could always just cast the value to non-null, but this is still an active decision and in doing so they've had to acknowledge that the value could be null.

4.3.5 Explicit: Result return type

One of the problems with returning a null or an optional return type is that we can't convey any error information. In addition to informing a caller that a value couldn't be acquired, it may also be useful to tell them why it couldn't be acquired. If this is the case, then using a result type might be appropriate.

Languages like Swift, Rust, and F# have built-in support for this and provide some nice syntax to make them easy to use. We can make our own result type in any language, but without the built-in syntax, using them can be a little clunkier.

Listing 4.16 provides a basic example of how we might define our own result type in a language that doesn't have built-in support for it.

Listing 4.16 A simple result type

```
class Result<V, E> {
  private final Optional<V> value;
  private final Optional<E> error;

  private Result(Optional<V> value, Optional<E> error) {
    this.value = value;
    this.error = error;
  }

  static Result<V, E> ofValue(V value) {
    return new Result(Optional.of(value), Optional.empty());
  }

  static Result<V, E> ofError(E error) {
    return new Result(Optional.empty(), Optional.of(error));
  }

  Boolean hasError() {
    return error.isPresent();
  }

  V getValue() {
    return value.get();
  }

  E getError() {
    return error.get();
  }
}
```

Generic/template types used so that the class can be used with any types of value and error

Private constructor to force callers to use one of the static factory functions

Static factory functions, meaning that the class can only be instantiated with either a value or an error but not both

> **Result type implementations**
>
> Real implementations of result types will often be more sophisticated than the example in listing 4.16. They'll often make better use of language constructs such as enums and provide helper functions for transforming results.
>
> The Rust and Swift implementations of Result can be a good source of inspiration:
>
> https://doc.rust-lang.org/beta/core/result/enum.Result.html
> https://developer.apple.com/documentation/swift/result

If we define our own result type (because the language doesn't have it built in), then it relies on other engineers being familiar with how to use it. If another engineer doesn't know to check the `hasError()` function before calling `getValue()`, then it defeats the point, although a diligent engineer would likely be able to figure this out quite quickly, even if they'd never encountered a result type before.

Assuming that the language supports the result type, or that other engineers are familiar with it (if we define our own), then using it as a return type makes it clear that an error might occur. Using a result return type is therefore an explicit way of signaling an error.

SIGNALING USING A RESULT

Listing 4.17 shows the `getSquareRoot()` function, but this time with it modified to return a result type. `NegativeNumberError` is a custom error, and the return type of `getSquareRoot()` signifies that this error can potentially occur. `NegativeNumberError` encapsulates extra information about the error: the erroneous number that caused it.

Listing 4.17 Returning a result type

```
class NegativeNumberError extends Error {            // A class to represent a
  private final Double erroneousNumber;              // specific type of error

  NegativeNumberError(Double erroneousNumber) {      // Encapsulates extra information:
    this.erroneousNumber = erroneousNumber;          // the number that caused the error
  }

  Double getErroneousNumber() {
    return erroneousNumber;
  }
}

Result<Double, NegativeNumberError> getSquareRoot(Double value) {   // Return type signifies that a NegativeNumberError can happen.
  if (value < 0.0) {
    return Result.ofError(new NegativeNumberError(value));          // An error result is returned if an error occurs.
  }
  return Result.ofValue(Math.sqrt(value));                          // The answer is wrapped in a result.
}
```

HANDLING A RESULT

It will be obvious to an engineer calling `getSquareRoot()` that the return type is Result. Assuming that they are familiar with the usage of Result, they will know that `hasError()` must first be called to check if an error occurred, and if one didn't occur, then `getValue()` can be called to access the value. If an error has occurred, then the details can be accessed by calling `getError()` on the result. The following listing shows this.

Listing 4.18 Returning a result type

```
void displaySquareRoot() {
  Result<Double, NegativeNumberError> squareRoot =
      getSquareRoot(ui.getInputNumber());
  if (squareRoot.hasError()) {
    ui.setError("Can't get square root of a negative number: " +
        squareRoot.getError().getErroneousNumber());
  } else {
    ui.setOutput("Square root is: " + squareRoot.getValue());
  }
}
```

The squareRoot result has to be checked for an error.

Detailed error information displayed to user

> **Nicer syntax**
>
> Languages with built-in support for result types will sometimes have more succinct syntaxes for handling them than that shown in listing 4.18. There are also numerous helper functions we could add to a custom implementation of a result type to create nicer control flow, such as things like the `and_then()` function in the Rust implementation: http://mng.bz/Jv5P

4.3.6 *Explicit: Outcome return type*

Some functions just do something rather than acquiring a value and returning it. If an error can occur while doing that thing and it would be useful to signal that to the caller, then one approach is to modify the function to return a value indicating the outcome of the operation. As we'll see in a moment, returning an outcome return type is an explicit way of signaling an error as long as we can enforce that callers check the return value.

SIGNALING USING AN OUTCOME

Listing 4.19 shows some code to send a message on a channel. The message can be sent only if the channel is open. If the channel is not open then that is an error. The `sendMessage()` function signals if an error has occurred by returning a Boolean. If the message is sent, then the function returns true. If an error occurs, it returns false.

Listing 4.19 Returning an outcome

```
Boolean sendMessage(Channel channel, String message) {
  if (channel.isOpen()) {
    channel.send(message);
```

The function returns a Boolean.

```
    return true;
  }
  return false;
}
```

true is returned if the message was sent.

false is returned if an error occurred.

If we have a more complicated scenario, then we might find it more appropriate to use a more sophisticated outcome type than a simple Boolean. An enum is useful if there are more than two possible outcome states or if it's not obvious from the context what true and false mean. If we require more detailed information, then defining an entire class to encapsulate this can be another good option.

HANDLING AN OUTCOME

In the example of using a Boolean as a return type, handling the outcome is quite straightforward. The function call can just be placed in an if-else statement and the appropriate handling logic placed in each branch. The following listing shows code to send the message "hello" on a channel and display a message in the UI to indicate if the message was sent.

Listing 4.20 Handling an outcome

```
void sayHello(Channel channel) {
  if (sendMessage(channel, "hello")) {
    ui.setOutput("Hello sent");
  } else {
    ui.setError("Unable to send hello");
  }
}
```

Success scenario handled

Failure scenario handled

ENSURING AN OUTCOME IS NOT IGNORED

One of the problems with an outcome return type is that it's quite easy for a caller to ignore the return value or not even be aware that the function returns a value. This can limit how explicit an outcome return type is as a way of signaling an error. To demonstrate this, a caller could write the code in the following listing. The code completely ignores the outcome return value from `sendMessage()` and in doing so tells the user that the message has been sent when, in fact, it might not have been.

Listing 4.21 Ignoring an outcome

```
void sayHello(Channel channel) {
  sendMessage(channel, "hello");
  ui.setOutput("Hello sent");
}
```

The outcome return value is ignored.

In some languages there is a way to mark a function such that a compiler warning is generated if a caller ignores the return value of the function. The name and usage of these vary from language to language, but some examples are as follows:

- `CheckReturnValue` annotation in Java (from the javax.annotation package)

- `MustUseReturnValue` annotation that can be used in C# (from https://www.jetbrains.com/help/resharper)
- `[[nodiscard]]` attribute in C++

If the `sendMessage()` function had been marked with one of these, then the code in listing 4.21 would produce a compiler warning that would likely be noticed by the engineer writing the code. The following listing shows what the `sendMessage()` function would look like if it were marked with an `@CheckReturnValue` annotation.

Listing 4.22 Using a CheckReturnValue annotation

```
@CheckReturnValue
Boolean sendMessage(Channel channel, String message) {
  ...
}
```

Indicates that the return value of the function should not be ignored by callers

The author of the code in listing 4.21 would likely notice the compiler warning and modify their code to the version we saw earlier that handled it (repeated in the following listing).

Listing 4.23 Forced to check a return value

```
void sayHello(Channel channel) {
  if (sendMessage(channel, "hello")) {
    ui.setOutput("Hello sent");
  } else {
    ui.setError("Unable to send hello");
  }
}
```

Success scenario handled

Failure scenario handled

4.3.7 *Implicit: Promise or future*

When writing code that executes asynchronously, it's common to create a function that returns a *promise* or a *future* (or an equivalent concept). In many languages (but not all), a promise or a future can also convey an error state.

A consumer of the promise or future is typically not forced to handle an error that may have occurred, and they would not know that they need to add error handling unless they were familiar with the small print in the code contract for the function in question. This therefore makes error signaling using a promise or a future an implicit technique.

> **Asynchronous?**
>
> If a process is *synchronous*, then it means that tasks are performed one at a time: a task can't begin until the previous task has completely finished. If we are making a cake, then we can't bake the cake in the oven until we've first mixed the cake batter.

> ***(continued)***
>
> This is an example of a synchronous process: the act of baking the cake is blocked by the need to first mix the cake.
>
> If a process is *asynchronous*, then it means we can perform different tasks while waiting for other tasks to finish. While our cake is baking in the oven, we might use the otherwise wasted time to make the frosting for the cake. This is an example of an asynchronous process: we can make the frosting without having to wait for the cake to be baked.
>
> When code has to wait for something to happen (like a server returning a response), it's common to write it in an asynchronous way. This means the code can do other things while waiting for the server.
>
> Most programming languages provide ways of executing code asynchronously. Exactly how to do this can vary a lot between different languages, so it's worth looking it up for whatever language you use. The use of an asynchronous function and promise in the following code examples most closely resembles the JavaScript paradigm. If you're not familiar with this and would like to find out more, the following reference page provides a good overview with examples: http://mng.bz/wOwW

SIGNALING USING A PROMISE

Listing 4.24 shows the `getSquareRoot()` function, but this time modified to be an asynchronous function that returns a promise and waits for one second before running. (You'll have to use your imagination as to why someone would actually write this particular code.) If an error is thrown inside the function, then the promise will become *rejected*; otherwise the promise will be *fulfilled* with the returned value.

Listing 4.24 An asynchronous function

```
class NegativeNumberError extends Error {      <-- A class to represent a
  ...                                              specific type of error
}
                                                   async marks the function
Promise<Double> getSquareRoot(Double value) async {   <-- as being asynchronous.
  await Timer.wait(Duration.ofSeconds(1));     <-- Waits one second
  if (value < 0.0) {                               before actually running
    throw new NegativeNumberError(value);     <-- An error thrown inside the
  }                                               function will cause the
  return Math.sqrt(value);   <-- A returned value promise to be rejected.
}                                causes the promise
                                 to be fulfilled.
```

HANDLING A PROMISE

Listing 4.25 shows the `displaySquareRoot()` function modified to call the asynchronous version of `getSquareRoot()`. The promise returned by `getSquareRoot()` has two member functions that can be used to set callbacks. The `then()` function can be used to set a callback function that is called if and when the promise is fulfilled, and the `catch()` function can be used to set a callback that is called if and when the promise is rejected.

Listing 4.25 Consuming a promise

```
void displaySquareRoot() {
  getSquareRoot(ui.getInputNumber())
      .then(squareRoot ->
          ui.setOutput("Square root is: " + squareRoot))
      .catch(error ->
          ui.setError("An error occurred: " + error.toString()));
}
```

then() callback called if and when the promise is fulfilled

catch() callback called if and when the promise is rejected

WHY PROMISES ARE AN IMPLICIT SIGNALING TECHNIQUE

To know that an error can occur and that the promise may be rejected, we need to know either the small print or implementation details of whatever function generated the promise. Without knowing these, a consumer of a promise can easily be unaware of a potential error state and may only provide a callback via the `then()` function. When no callback has been provided via the `catch()` function, the error might be caught by some higher level error handler, or it might just go completely unnoticed (depending on the language and set up).

Promises and futures can be an excellent way to return values from asynchronous functions. But because the caller is free to be completely unaware of the potential error scenario, using a promise or future is an implicit way of signaling an error.

MAKING A PROMISE EXPLICIT

If we're returning a promise or a future and want to use an explicit error-signaling technique, then one option is to return a promise of a result type. If we do this, then the `getSquareRoot()` function would look like the following listing. This can be a useful technique, but the code starts to get quite clunky, so it doesn't appeal to everyone.

Listing 4.26 A promise of a result

```
Promise<Result<Double, NegativeNumberError>> getSquareRoot(
    Double value) async {
  await Timer.wait(Duration.ofSeconds(1));
  if (value < 0.0) {
    return Result.ofError(new NegativeNumberError(value));
  }
  return Result.ofValue(Math.sqrt(value));
}
```

The return type is quite clunky.

4.3.8 Implicit: Returning a magic value

A *magic value* (or an error code) is a value that fits into the normal return type of a function, but which has a special meaning. An engineer has to either read the documentation or the code itself to be aware that a magic value might be returned. This makes them an implicit error-signaling technique.

A common way of signaling an error using a magic value is to return minus one. The following listing shows what this looks like for the `getSquareRoot()` function.

Listing 4.27 Returning a magic value

```
// Returns -1 if a negative value is supplied
Double getSquareRoot(Double value) {
  if (value < 0.0) {
    return -1.0;
  }
  return Math.sqrt(value);
}
```

Comment warning that the function can return minus one

Minus one returned if an error occurs

Magic values can easily cause surprises and lead to bugs because they need to be handled, but nothing in the unmistakably obvious part of the code contract informs callers of this. The problems that magic values can cause are discussed in detail in chapter 6, so we won't discuss them in detail here. But the important point to remember for this chapter is that magic values are often not a good way to signal an error.

4.4 Signaling errors that can't be recovered from

When an error occurs that there is no realistic prospect of a program recovering from, then it is best to fail fast and to fail loudly. Some common ways of achieving this are the following:

- Throwing an unchecked exception
- Causing the program to *panic* (if using a language that supports panics)
- Using a check or an assertion (as covered in chapter 3)

These will cause the program (or scope of irrecoverability) to exit, which should mean that engineers notice something is wrong, and the error message produced will usually provide a stack trace or line number to give a clear indication of where the error has occurred.

Using an implicit technique (like those just mentioned) prevents the need for every caller higher up the call chain to write code to acknowledge or handle the error scenario. When there's no conceivable way that an error could be recovered from, this makes sense, because there is nothing sensible that a caller could do other than just pass the error onto the next caller.

4.5 Signaling errors that a caller might want to recover from

This is where things get interesting because software engineers (and programming language designers) don't all agree on what the best practices are regarding signaling errors that a caller might want to recover from. The debate here is generally between using unchecked exceptions versus explicit error-signaling techniques (such as checked exceptions, safe nulls, optional types, or result types). There are valid arguments and counterarguments to both sides of this, and I will try to summarize them in this section.

Before I do, it's worth remembering that what is likely more important than any of the following arguments is that you and your team agree on what your philosophy is.

The worst possible situation is that half your team writes code that follows one practice regarding error signaling and handling, and the other half follows a completely different practice. You will have a nightmare of a time whenever the pieces of code have to interact with each other.

The following arguments, as presented, will likely sound a bit all or nothing, but bear in mind that if you speak to another engineer, then you will probably find that their opinions on error signaling and handling are more nuanced.

NOTE: LEAKING IMPLEMENTATION DETAILS Another thing to consider for errors that a caller might want to recover from is that callers should ideally not have to know implementation details of the code they're calling in order to handle errors it might signal. This is discussed in the context of modularity in chapter 8 (sections 8.6 and 8.7).

4.5.1 Arguments for using unchecked exceptions

Some common arguments for why it's better to use unchecked exceptions even for errors that can potentially be recovered from are as follows.

Improving code structure

Some engineers argue that throwing an unchecked exception (instead of using an explicit technique) can improve the code structure because most error handling can be performed in a distinct place in a higher layer of the code. The errors bubble up to this layer, and the code in between doesn't have to be cluttered with loads of error handling logic. Figure 4.4 demonstrates what this might look like.

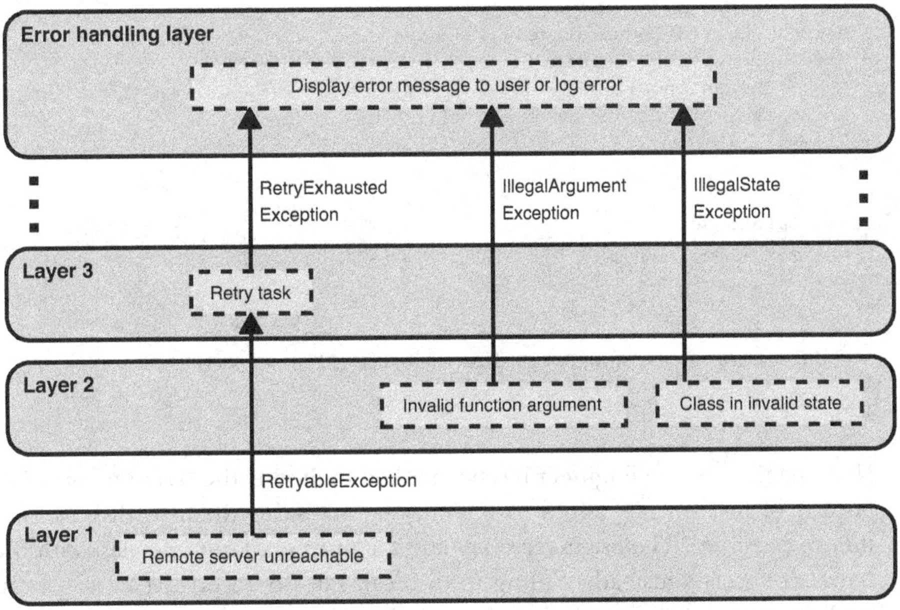

Figure 4.4 Some engineers argue that using unchecked exceptions can improve code structure because the majority of error handling can be performed in a few distinct layers.

Layers in the middle can handle some of the exceptions if they want to (such as retrying certain tasks), but otherwise errors will just bubble up to the topmost error handling layer. If this were a user application the error handling layer might show an overlay on the UI to display the error message; or if this were a server or backend process, then the error message might be logged somewhere. The key advantage of this approach is that the logic for handling errors can be kept contained in a few distinct layers rather than being spread throughout the code.

BEING PRAGMATIC ABOUT WHAT ENGINEERS WILL DO

Some argue that with more explicit error-signaling techniques (return types and checked exceptions) engineers eventually get fed up and do the wrong thing, for example catching an exception and ignoring it, or casting a nullable type to non-null without checking it.

To demonstrate this, imagine that the code in listing 4.28 existed somewhere in the codebase. The listing contains code to log the temperature to a data logger, which in turn uses an `InMemoryDataStore` to store the logged data. Nothing in this initial version of the code can cause an error, so no error-signaling or handling techniques are required.

Listing 4.28 Initial code with no error scenarios

```
class TemperatureLogger {
  private final Thermometer thermometer;
  private final DataLogger dataLogger;
  ...

  void logCurrentTemperature() {
    dataLogger.logDataPoint(
        Instant.now(),
        thermometer.getTemperature());
  }
}

class DataLogger {
  private final InMemoryDataStore dataStore;
  ...

  void logDataPoint(Instant time, Double value) {
    dataStore.store(new DataPoint(time.toMillis(), value));
  }
}
```

Now imagine that an engineer has been asked to modify the `DataLogger` class so that instead of just storing values to memory it now saves them to disk to ensure that they're persisted. The engineer swaps the `InMemoryDataStore` class with the `DiskDataStore` class instead. Writing to disk can fail, so an error can now occur. If an explicit error-signaling technique is used, then the error would either need to be handled or else explicitly passed on to the next caller up the chain.

In this scenario, we'll demonstrate this by `DiskDataStore.store()` throwing a checked exception (`IOException`), but the principle is the same with any other explicit error-signaling technique. Because `IOException` is a checked exception it either needs to be handled or else put in the `DataLogger.logDataPoint()` function's signature. There's no sensible way to handle this error within the `DataLogger.logDataPoint()` function, but adding it to the function signature will require modifying every call site, and potentially multiple call sites in the layers above those. Daunted by this amount of work, the engineer decides to just hide the error instead and writes the code in the following listing.

Listing 4.29 Hiding a checked exception

```
class DataLogger {
  private final DiskDataStore dataStore;
  ...

  void logDataPoint(Instant time, Double value) {
    try {
      dataStore.store(new DataPoint(time.toMillis(), value));
    } catch (IOException e) {}        <-- The IOException error
  }                                       is hidden from callers.
}
```

As was discussed earlier in this chapter, hiding errors is almost never a good idea. The `DataLogger.logDataPoint()` function now doesn't always do what it claims to do; sometimes data points will not be saved, but the caller will not be aware of this. Using explicit error-signaling techniques can sometimes cause a cascade of work that needs to be done to repeatedly signal an error up through the layers of code, and this can encourage engineers to cut corners and do the wrong things. The need to be pragmatic about this is one of the most frequently expressed arguments in favor of using unchecked exceptions.

4.5.2 Arguments for using explicit techniques

Some common arguments for why it's better to use explicit error-signaling techniques for errors that can potentially be recovered from are as follows.

Graceful error handling

If using unchecked exceptions, then it's difficult to have a single layer that can gracefully handle all errors. For example, if a user input is invalid, it probably makes sense to have a nice error message right next to that input field. If the engineer writing the code that processes the inputs wasn't aware of the error scenario and left it to bubble up to a higher level, then this might result in a less user-friendly error message such as a generic message overlaid on the UI.

Forcing callers to be aware of potential errors (by using a return type or a checked exception) means that there is a greater chance that these errors will be handled gracefully. With an implicit technique, a caller might not be aware that an error scenario can happen, so how would they know to handle it?

ERRORS CAN'T BE ACCIDENTALLY IGNORED

There may be some errors that really do need to be handled by certain callers. If an unchecked exception is used, then doing the wrong thing (not handling the error) happens by default rather than being an active decision. This is because it's easy for an engineer (and code reviewer) to be completely unaware that a certain error might happen.

If using a more explicit error-signaling technique like a return type or a checked exception, then yes, engineers can still do the wrong thing (like catching an excep-

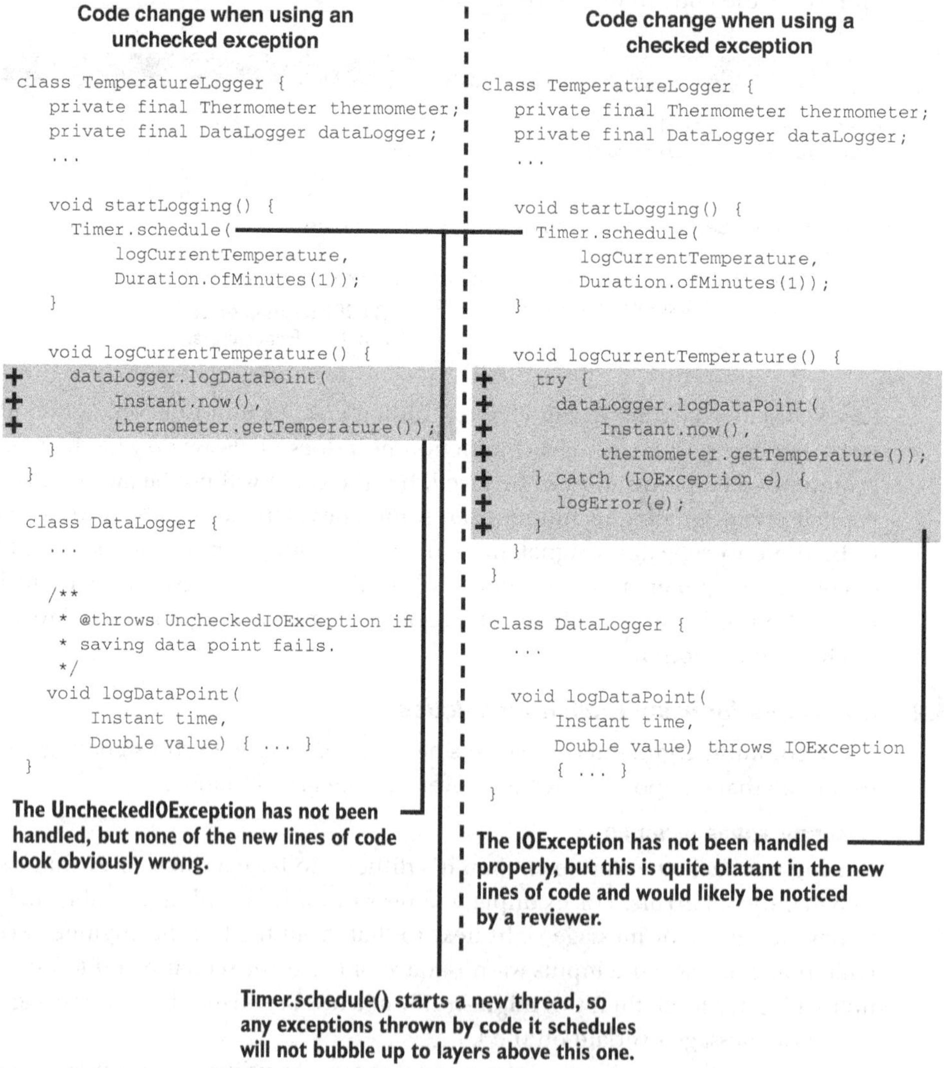

Figure 4.5 When using explicit error-signaling techniques, not handling an error properly will often result in a deliberate and blatant transgression in the code. By contrast, when using an unchecked exception, it may not be obvious from the code that an error has not been handled properly.

tion and ignoring it), but this usually requires active effort and results in quite a blatant transgression in the code. This makes it more likely that issues like this can be weeded out in code reviews, because it will be obvious to the reviewer. With more explicit error-signaling techniques, the wrong thing doesn't happen by default or by accident.

Figure 4.5 contrasts how a code change might look to a reviewer if using an unchecked exception versus a checked exception. The fact that something bad is happening in the code is not at all obvious when using an unchecked exception, whereas it's extremely obvious in the case where a checked exception is used. Other explicit error-signaling techniques (such as an outcome return type enforced with an `@CheckReturnValue` annotation) would force the engineer's transgression to be similarly obvious in the code change.

BEING PRAGMATIC ABOUT WHAT ENGINEERS WILL DO

Arguments around engineers doing the wrong thing because they get fed up with error handling also apply against using unchecked exceptions. There's no guarantee that unchecked exceptions get properly documented throughout a codebase, and from my personal experience, they often don't. This means there is often no certainty about exactly which unchecked exceptions some code might throw, and this can turn catching them into a frustrating game of whack-a-mole.

Listing 4.30 contains a function to check if a data file is valid. It does this by checking whether any exceptions are thrown that would indicate that the file is invalid. `DataFile.parse()` throws a number of different unchecked exceptions, which have not all been documented. The author of the `isDataFileValid()` function has added code to catch three of these unchecked exceptions.

Listing 4.30 Catching multiple types of unchecked exceptions

```
Boolean isDataFileValid(byte[] fileContents) {
  try {
    DataFile.parse(fileContents);
    return true;
  } catch (InvalidEncodingException |
           ParseException |
           UnrecognizedDataKeyException e) {
    return false;
  }
}
```

- `DataFile.parse(fileContents)`: Can throw a number of undocumented, unchecked exceptions
- `catch (...)`: Catches three different types of unchecked exception

After releasing their code, the author of the `isDataFileValid()` function notices that they're seeing a lot of crash reports. They investigate and find that the failures are due to yet another undocumented, unchecked exception: `InvalidDataRange-Exception`. At this point the author of the code might be so fed up with playing whack-a-mole with all these unchecked exceptions that they decide to instead catch all types of exceptions and be done with it. They write the code in the following listing.

Listing 4.31 Catching all types of exceptions

```
Boolean isDataFileValid(byte[] fileContents) {
  try {
    DataFile.parse(fileContents);
    return true;
  } catch (Exception e) {      <-- Catches every type of exception
    return false;
  }
}
```

Catching every type of exception in code like this is often a bad idea. This will hide almost every type of error, including a lot that the program cannot realistically recover from. There might be some severe programming error that is now hidden. This could be a bug in the `DataFile.parse()` function, or it could be some severe misconfiguration in the software that results in something like a `ClassNotFoundException`. Either way, these programming errors will now go completely unnoticed, and the software will fail in a silent and weird way.

A transgression like the code in listing 4.31 is quite blatant, so we'd hope that it gets weeded out during a code review. But if we're worried that our code-review process is not robust enough to catch transgressions like this, then it's worth realizing that we likely have a problem whether we decide to use unchecked exceptions or explicit error-signaling techniques. The real problem is that we have engineers doing sloppy things and no robust process to weed these out.

> **Sticking to standard exception types**
>
> In order to avoid this exception whack-a-mole, an approach sometimes favored by engineers using unchecked exceptions is to prefer using (or subclassing) standard exception types (like `ArgumentException` or `StateException`). It's more likely that other engineers will predict that these might be thrown and handle them appropriately, and it limits the number of exception types that engineers usually need to worry about.
>
> A downside of this is that it can limit the ability to distinguish between different error scenarios: one cause of a `StateException` might be something a caller wants to recover from, while another cause might not be. As you've probably gathered by now, the topic of error signaling and handling is an imperfect science, and there are pros and cons to consider with any technique.

4.5.3 My opinion: Use an explicit technique

My opinion is that it's best to avoid using an unchecked exception for an error that a caller might want to recover from. In my experience, the usage of unchecked exceptions very rarely gets documented fully throughout a codebase, meaning it can become near impossible for an engineer using a function to have any certainty about what error scenarios may happen and which they need to handle.

I have seen too many bugs and outages caused by the use of undocumented, unchecked exceptions for errors that the caller would have liked to recover from if only the engineer writing that code were aware of the exception, so my personal preference is to use explicit error-signaling techniques when there is a chance that a caller might want to recover.

As this section already discussed, this approach is not without some downsides, but in my experience the downsides of using unchecked exceptions for these kinds of errors are worse. As I said earlier, though, what's potentially even worse is if you work on a team where some engineers follow one approach and some follow another, so it's best that you and your team agree on a philosophy around error signaling and stick to it.

4.6 Don't ignore compiler warnings

Chapter 3 covered some techniques for ensuring that a compiler error occurs if code is broken or misused. In addition to compiler errors, most compilers also emit warnings. A compiler warning often flags code that is suspicious in some way, and this can be an early warning that there might be a bug. Paying attention to these warnings can be a great way to identify and weed out programming errors long before the code gets anywhere near the codebase.

To demonstrate this, consider the code in listing 4.32. It's for a class to store some information about a user. It contains a bug because the `getDisplayName()` function incorrectly returns the user's real name, rather than their display name.

Listing 4.32 Code that causes a compiler warning

```
class UserInfo {
  private final String realName;
  private final String displayName;

  UserInfo(String realName, String displayName) {
    this.realName = realName;
    this.displayName = displayName;
  }

  String getRealName() {
    return realName;
  }

  String getDisplayName() {
    return realName;          <-- The user's real name is
  }                               erroneously returned.
}
```

This code would compile, but the compiler would likely spit out a warning along the lines of "WARNING: private member 'UserInfo.displayName' can be removed as the value assigned to it is never read." If we ignored this warning then we might not realize that this bug exists. We could hope that testing would catch it, but if it didn't, this could actually be quite a serious bug that violates users' privacy in a bad way.

Most compilers can be configured so that any warnings become errors and prevent the code from compiling. This may seem a bit over the top and draconian, but it's actually incredibly useful, as it forces engineers to notice warnings and act accordingly.

If the warning is not actually anything to be concerned about, then there will usually be a mechanism in the language to suppress a specific warning (without having to turn off all warnings). For example, if there were a valid reason for having an unused variable in the `UserInfo` class, then the warning could be suppressed. The following listing shows what this might look like.

Listing 4.33 Suppressing a compiler warning

```
class UserInfo {
  private final String realName;

  // displayName is unused for now, as we migrate away from
  // using real names. This is a placeholder that will be used
  // soon. See issue #7462 for details of the migration.
  @Suppress("unused")                                  <-- The warning is
  private final String displayName;                        suppressed.

  UserInfo(String realName, String displayName) {
    this.realName = realName;
    this.displayName = displayName;
  }

  String getRealName() {
    return realName;
  }

  String getDisplayName() {
    return realName;
  }
}
```

It can be tempting to dismiss compiler warnings as not being that important; after all, the code still compiles so it's easy to assume that nothing is catastrophically wrong. Although warnings are just that—warnings—they can often be a sign that there is something wrong with the code, and in some scenarios this could be quite a serious bug. As the previous examples show, it's good to make sure that compiler warnings are noticed and acted on. Ideally, there should be no warnings when our code is built because every issue has either been fixed or explicitly suppressed with a valid explanation of why.

Summary

- There are broadly two types of error:
  - Those that a system can recover from
  - Those that a system cannot recover from
- Often only the caller of a piece of code knows if an error generated by that code can be recovered from.

- When an error does occur it's good to fail fast, and if the error can't be recovered from to also fail loudly.
- Hiding an error is often not a good idea, and it's better to signal that the error has occurred.
- Error-signaling techniques can be divided into two categories:
  - *Explicit*—In the unmistakable part of the code's contract. Callers are aware that the error can happen.
  - *Implicit*—In the small print of the code's contract, or potentially not in the written contract at all. Callers are not necessarily aware that the error can happen.
- Errors that cannot be recovered from should use implicit error-signaling techniques.
- For errors that can potentially be recovered from:
  - Engineers don't all agree on whether explicit or implicit techniques should be used.
  - My opinion is that explicit techniques should be used.
- Compiler warnings can often flag that something is wrong with the code. It's good to pay attention to them.

Part 2

In practice

Chapter 1 established the grandly named "six pillars of code quality." These provide some high-level strategies that can help ensure our code is of high quality. In part 2, we delve deeper into the first five of these in a more practical way.

Each chapter in part 2 concentrates on one of the pillars of code quality, with each section within the chapters demonstrating a particular consideration or technique. The general pattern is to first show a common way in which code can be problematic and to then show how a particular technique can be used to improve the situation. Each section within the chapters is designed to be relatively self-contained, and my hope is that they can provide a useful reference for anyone wishing to explain a particular concept or consideration to another engineer (for example, during a code review).

Please note that the list of topics within each chapter is not exhaustive. For example, chapter 7 discusses six specific topics for making code hard to misuse. This is not to suggest that these are the only six things we ever need to consider in order to make our code hard to misuse. But the aim is that by understanding the reasoning behind these six things, in combination with the more theoretical things we learned in part 1, we'll be able to develop a broader sense of judgment that can guide us in whatever scenario we might find ourselves.

5 Make code readable

This chapter covers

- Techniques for making code self-explanatory
- Ensuring that details within the code are clear to others
- Using language features for the right reasons

Readability is inherently a subjective thing, and it's therefore hard to put a solid definition on exactly what it means. The essence of readability is ensuring that engineers can quickly and accurately understand what some code does. Actually achieving this often requires being empathetic and trying to imagine how things might be confusing or open to misinterpretation when seen from someone else's point of view.

This chapter should provide a solid grounding in some of the most common and effective techniques for making code more readable. It's worth remembering, though, that each real-life scenario is different and has its own set of considerations, so using common sense and applying good judgment are both essential.

5.1 Use descriptive names

Names are needed to uniquely identify things, but they often also provide a brief summary of what the thing is. The word *toaster* uniquely identifies an appliance in your kitchen, but it also gives a massive hint as to what it does: it toasts things. If we, instead, insisted on referring to a toaster as "object A," then it would be quite easy to forget what exactly "object A" is and what it does.

The same principle applies when naming things in code. Names are needed to uniquely identify things like classes, functions, and variables. But how we name things is also a great opportunity to make the code more readable by ensuring that things are referred to in a self-explanatory way.

5.1.1 Nondescriptive names make code hard to read

Listing 5.1 is a somewhat extreme example of what some code might look like if no effort whatsoever was put into using descriptive names. Spend 20–30 seconds looking at it and see how hard it is to have any idea what it does.

Listing 5.1 Nondescriptive names

```
class T {
  Set<String> pns = new Set();
  Int s = 0;
  ...
  Boolean f(String n) {
    return pns.contains(n);
  }

  Int getS() {
    return s;
  }
}

Int? s(List<T> ts, String n) {
  for (T t in ts) {
    if (t.f(n)) {
      return t.getS();
    }
  }
  return null;
}
```

If you were asked to describe what this code does, what would you say? Unless you've already glanced ahead, you probably have no idea what this code does, or what concepts the strings, integers, and class even represent.

5.1.2 Comments are a poor substitute for descriptive names

One way to improve this might be to add some comments and documentation. If the author had done this, then the code might look something like listing 5.2. This makes things a little better, but there are still a bunch of problems:

- The code is now a lot more cluttered, and the author and other engineers now have to maintain all these comments and documentation as well as the code itself.
- Engineers need to continually scroll up and down the file to make sense of things. If an engineer is all the way at the bottom of the file looking at the `getS()` function and forgets what the variable `s` is for, then they have to scroll all the way to the top of the file to find the comment explaining what `s` is. If the class `T` is several hundred lines long, then this gets annoying quite quickly.
- If an engineer is looking at the body of the function `s()`, it's still a complete mystery as to what a call like `t.f(n)` is doing or returning, unless they go and look at the code for the class `T`.

Listing 5.2 Comments instead of descriptive names

```
/** Represents a team. */
class T {
  Set<String> pns = new Set();  // Names of players in the team.
  Int s = 0;  // The team's score.
  ...
  /**
   * @param n the players name
   * @return true if the player is in the team
   */
  Boolean f(String n) {
    return pns.contains(n);
  }

  /**
   * @return the team's score
   */
  Int getS() {
    return s;
  }
}

/**
 * @param ts a list of all teams
 * @param n the name of the player
 * @return the score of the team that the player is on
 */
Int? s(List<T> ts, String n) {
  for (T t in ts) {
    if (t.f(n)) {
      return t.getS();
    }
  }
  return null;
}
```

Some of the documentation in listing 5.2 might well be useful: documenting what parameters and return types represent can help other engineers understand how to use the code. But comments should not be used as a substitute for giving things descriptive names. Section 5.2 discusses the use of comments and documentation in more detail.

5.1.3 Solution: Make names descriptive

Using descriptive names can transform the impenetrable code we just saw into something that is suddenly very easy to understand. The following listing shows what the code looks like with descriptive names.

Listing 5.3 Descriptive names

```
class Team {
  Set<String> playerNames = new Set();
  Int score = 0;
  ...
  Boolean containsPlayer(String playerName) {
    return playerNames.contains(playerName);
  }

  Int getScore() {
    return score;
  }
}

Int? getTeamScoreForPlayer(List<Team> teams, String playerName) {
  for (Team team in teams) {
    if (team.containsPlayer(playerName)) {
      return team.getScore();
    }
  }
  return null;
}
```

The code is now much easier to understand:

- Variables, functions, and classes are now self-explanatory.
- Pieces of code now make more sense even when seen in isolation; it's very obvious what a call like `team.containsPlayer(playerName)` is doing and returning without even having to look at the code for the `Team` class. Previously this function call looked like `t.f(n)`, so this is clearly a big improvement in readability.

The code is also less cluttered than if comments had been used, and engineers can concentrate on maintaining the code without also having to keep a collection of comments maintained alongside it.

5.2 Use comments appropriately

Comments or documentation in code can serve various purposes, such as the following:

- Explaining *what* some code does
- Explaining *why* some code does what it does
- Providing other information such as usage instructions

This section will concentrate on the first two of these: using comments to explain *what* and to explain *why*. Other information like usage instructions generally form part of the code's contract and were discussed in chapter 3.

High-level comments summarizing what a large chunk of code (like a class) does can often be useful. When it comes to the lower level, line-by-line details of code, however, comments explaining what code does are often not the most effective way to make code readable.

Well-written code with descriptive names should be self-explanatory in terms of what it's doing at the line-by-line level. If we need to add lots of low-level comments to our code in order to explain what it's doing, then this is likely a sign that our code is not as readable as it ideally should be. Comments that explain *why* code exists or that provide more context, on the other hand, can often be quite useful, as it's not always possible to make this clear with just the code alone.

NOTE: USE COMMON SENSE This section provides some general guidance about how and when to use comments, but these are not hard-and-fast rules. We should use our common sense about what makes the code easiest to understand and maintain. If we have no choice but to include some gnarly bitwise logic or we're having to resort to some clever tricks to optimize our code, then comments explaining what some low-level code does might well be useful.

5.2.1 Redundant comments can be harmful

The code in listing 5.4 produces an ID by joining a first name to a last name using a period. The code uses a comment to explain what it does, but the code is already self-explanatory, so the comment is kind of useless.

Listing 5.4 A comment explaining what code does

```
String generateId(String firstName, String lastName) {
  // Produces an ID in the form "{first name}.{last name}".
  return firstName + "." + lastName;
}
```

Including a redundant comment like this can actually be worse than useless because

- engineers now need to maintain this comment; if someone changes the code, then they also need to remember to update the comment.
- it clutters the code: imagine if every line of code had an associated comment like this. Reading 100 lines of code now turns into reading 100 lines of code plus 100 comments. Given that this comment doesn't add any additional information, it just wastes engineers' time.

It would probably be better to remove this comment and let the code do the explaining.

5.2.2 Comments are a poor substitute for readable code

The code in listing 5.5 again generates an ID by joining a first name to a last name using a period. In this example the code is not self-explanatory because the first and last names are respectively contained within the first and second elements of an array. The code includes a comment that explains this. In this scenario the comment seems useful because the code is not clear on its own, but the real problem here is that the code has not been made as readable as it could be.

Listing 5.5 Unreadable code explained with a comment

```
String generateId(String[] data) {
  // data[0] contains the user's first name, and data[1] contains the user's
  // last name. Produces an ID in the form "{first name}.{last name}".
  return data[0] + "." + data[1];
}
```

Because the comment is only needed because the code itself is not very readable, a better approach would probably be to instead make the code more readable. In this scenario, this can easily be achieved by using some well-named helper functions. This is shown in the following listing.

Listing 5.6 More readable code

```
String generateId(String[] data) {
  return firstName(data) + "." + lastName(data);
}

String firstName(String[] data) {
  return data[0];
}

String lastName(String[] data) {
  return data[1];
}
```

Making code self-explanatory is often preferable to using comments because it reduces the maintenance overhead and removes the chance that comments become out-of-date.

5.2.3 Comments can be great for explaining why code exists

What code is sometimes less good at self-explaining is *why* something is being done. The reason that a certain piece of code exists, or the reason it does what it does, can sometimes be linked to some context or knowledge that would not necessarily be known by another engineer looking at the code. Comments can be very useful when context like this is important for understanding the code or being able to modify it in a safe way. Examples of things that it might be good to comment on to explain why some code exists include the following:

- A product or business decision
- A fix for a weird, nonobvious bug
- Dealing with a counterintuitive quirk in a dependency

Listing 5.7 contains a function to get the ID of a user. There are two different ways of generating an ID depending on when the user signed up. The reason for this would not be obvious from the code alone, so comments are used to explain it. This prevents the code being confusing to other engineers and ensures they know what considerations apply if they need to modify this code.

Listing 5.7 Comment to explain why code exists

```
class User {
  private final Int username;
  private final String firstName;
  private final String lastName;
  private final Version signupVersion;
  ...

  String getUserId() {
    if (signupVersion.isOlderThan("2.0")) {
      // Legacy users (who signed up before v2.0) were assigned
      // IDs based on their name. See issue #4218 for more
      // details.
      return firstName.toLowerCase() + "." +
          lastName.toLowerCase();
    }
    // Newer users (who signed up from v2.0 onwards) are assigned
    // IDs based on their username.
    return username;
  }
  ...
}
```

Comments explaining why some code exists

This does clutter the code slightly, but the benefit outweighs this cost. The code alone, without the comments, could otherwise cause confusion.

5.2.4 Comments can provide useful high-level summaries

We can think of comments and documentation that explain what code does as a bit like a synopsis when reading a book:

- If you pick up a book and every single paragraph on every single page is preceded by a one-sentence synopsis it would be quite an annoying and difficult book to read. This is like low-level comments explaining what code does; it harms readability.
- On the other hand, a synopsis on the back cover of a book (or even at the start of each chapter) that briefly summarizes what the content is about can be incredibly useful. It allows you to quickly gauge whether the book (or chapter) is useful or interesting to you. This is like high-level comments summarizing what a class does. It makes it very easy for an engineer to gauge whether the class is useful to them or what things it might affect.

Some examples where high-level documentation of what code does might be useful are as follows:

- Documentation explaining, at a high level, what a class does and any important details that other engineers should be made aware of
- Documentation explaining what an input parameter to a function is or what it does
- Documentation explaining what a return value from a function represents

It's useful to remember what was said in chapter 3: Documentation is important, but we should be realistic to the fact that engineers often don't read it. It's best not to rely too heavily on it to avoid surprises or prevent our code from being misused (chapters 6 and 7 will respectively cover more robust techniques for this).

Listing 5.8 shows how documentation might be used to summarize what the `User` class as a whole does. It provides some useful high-level details such as the fact that it relates to a user of the "streaming service" and that it can potentially be out of sync with the database.

Listing 5.8 High-level class documentation

```
/**
 * Encapsulates details of a user of the streaming service.
 *
 * This does not access the database directly and is, instead,
 * constructed with values stored in memory. It may, therefore,
 * be out of sync with any changes made in the database after
 * the class is constructed.
 */
class User {
  ...
}
```

Comments and documentation are useful for filling in details that the code alone cannot convey or for summarizing what a larger chunk of code does. The downsides are that they need to be maintained, they can easily become out-of-date, and they can clutter the code. Using them effectively is a balancing act between these pros and cons.

5.3 Don't fixate on number of lines of code

In general, the fewer lines of code in a codebase, the better. Code generally requires some amount of ongoing maintenance, and more lines of code can sometimes be a sign that code is overly complex or not reusing existing solutions. More lines of code can also increase cognitive load on engineers because there are obviously more of them to read.

Engineers sometimes take this to an extreme and argue that minimizing the number of lines of code is more important than any other factors regarding code quality. A complaint that is sometimes made is that a so-called code-quality improvement has turned 3 lines of code into 10 lines of code and that it's, therefore, made the code worse.

It's important to remember, however, that number of lines of code is a proxy measurement for the things we actually care about and, as with most proxy measurements, it's a useful guiding principle but not a hard-and-fast rule. The things we actually care about are ensuring that code is

- easy to understand,
- hard to misunderstand, and
- hard to accidentally break.

Not all lines of code are equal: one extremely hard-to-understand line of code can easily reduce code quality compared to having 10 (or even 20) easy-to-understand lines of code in its place. The next two subsections demonstrate this with an example.

5.3.1 Avoid succinct but unreadable code

To demonstrate how fewer lines of code can be less readable, consider listing 5.9. It shows a function to check if a 16-bit ID is valid. Once you've looked at the code, ask yourself: Is it immediately obvious what the criterion for an ID being valid is? For most engineers the answer to that is no.

Listing 5.9 Succinct but unreadable code

```
Boolean isIdValid(UInt16 id) {
  return countSetBits(id & 0x7FFF) % 2 == ((id & 0x8000) >> 15);
}
```

The code is checking a parity bit, which is a type of error detection sometimes used when transmitting data. The 16-bit ID contains a 15-bit value stored in the least significant 15 bits and a parity bit stored in the most significant bit. The parity bit indicates if an even or odd number of bits are set in the 15-bit value.

The lines of code in listing 5.9 are not very readable or self-explanatory, and, despite being succinct, they contain a lot of assumptions and complexity, such as the following:

- The least significant 15 bits of the ID contain the value.
- The most significant bit of the ID contains the parity bit.
- The parity bit is zero if there are an even number of bits set in the 15-bit value.
- The parity bit is one if there are an odd number of bits set in the 15-bit value.
- 0x7FFF is a bit mask for the least significant 15-bits.
- 0x8000 is a bit mask for the most significant bit.

The problems with compacting all these details and assumptions down into one line of very succinct code are as follows:

- Other engineers have to put a lot of effort and head scratching into figuring out and extracting these details and assumptions from the one line of code. This wastes their time and also increases the chance that they misunderstand something and end up breaking the code.

- These assumptions need to align with some assumptions made elsewhere. There is some code somewhere else that is encoding these IDs. If that code is modified to place the parity bit in the least significant bit (for example), then the code in listing 5.9 would stop functioning correctly. It would be better if subproblems like the location of the parity bit are broken out into a single source of truth that can be reused.

The code in listing 5.9 may be succinct, but it is also near unreadable. Multiple engineers will potentially waste a lot of time trying to understand what it does. The number of nonobvious and undocumented assumptions that the code makes also make it quite fragile and easy to break.

5.3.2 Solution: Make code readable, even if it requires more lines

It would be much better if the assumptions and details of the ID encoding and parity bit are obvious to anyone reading the code, even if this requires using more lines. Listing 5.10 shows how the code could be made a lot more readable. It defines some well-named helper functions and constants. This makes the code a lot easier to understand and ensures that the solutions to subproblems are reusable, but it also results in many more lines of code.

Listing 5.10 Verbose but readable code

```
Boolean isIdValid(UInt16 id) {
  return extractEncodedParity(id) ==
      calculateParity(getIdValue(id));
}

private const UInt16 PARITY_BIT_INDEX = 15;
private const UInt16 PARITY_BIT_MASK = (1 << PARITY_BIT_INDEX);
private const UInt16 VALUE_BIT_MASK = ~PARITY_BIT_MASK;

private UInt16 getIdValue(UInt16 id) {
  return id & VALUE_BIT_MASK;
}

private UInt16 extractEncodedParity(UInt16 id) {
  return (id & PARITY_BIT_MASK) >> PARITY_BIT_INDEX;
}

// Parity is 0 if an even number of bits are set and 1 if
// an odd number of bits are set.
private UInt16 calculateParity(UInt16 value) {
  return countSetBits(value) % 2;
}
```

It's generally good to keep an eye on the number of lines of code being added, as it can be a warning sign that the code is not reusing existing solutions or is overcomplicating something. But it's often more important to ensure that the code is understandable, robust, and unlikely to result in buggy behavior. If it requires more lines of code to effectively do this, then that's fine.

5.4 Stick to a consistent coding style

If we are writing a sentence, there are certain rules that we have to follow if we want to produce something that is grammatically correct. In addition, there are other stylistic guidelines that we should follow to ensure our sentence is readable.

As an example, imagine we are writing something about *software as a service.* Usually if words like *a* and *as* are included in an acronym (or initialism) they are abbreviated using a lowercase character. The most familiar acronym for *software as a service* is therefore written *SaaS.* If we wrote the acronym as *SAAS,* then anyone reading our document might wonder if we are referring to something else, because it's not how they expect *software as a service* to be abbreviated.

The same applies to code. The language syntax and the compiler dictate what is allowed (a bit like grammar rules), but as the engineers writing the code, we have a lot of freedom over what stylistic conventions we adopt.

5.4.1 An inconsistent coding style can cause confusion

Listing 5.11 contains some code from a class to manage a chat between a group of users. This class is used within a server that manages many group chats simultaneously. The class contains an `end()` function that, when called, should end the chat by terminating the connections to all the users in that chat.

A common style convention when writing code is that class names are written in *PascalCase* (first letter capitalized), whereas variable names are written in *camelCase* (first letter in lowercase). Without seeing the whole class definition, an obvious assumption would therefore be that `connectionManager` is an instance variable within the `GroupChat` class. Calling `connectionManager.terminateAll()` should therefore terminate the connections for the given chat but leave other chats being administered by the server unaffected.

Listing 5.11 Inconsistent naming style

```
class GroupChat {
  ...
  end() {
    connectionManager.terminateAll();    <-- We've assumed that connectionManager is an instance variable.
  }
}
```

Unfortunately our assumption is wrong, and this code is very broken. `connectionManager` is not an instance variable; it is in fact a class, and `terminateAll()` is a static function on it. Calling `connectionManager.terminateAll()` terminates all connections for every chat that the server is managing, not just the one associated with that particular instance of the `GroupChat` class. The following listing shows the code for the `connectionManager` class.

Listing 5.12 connectionManager class

```
class connectionManager {
  ...
  static terminateAll() {    <-- Terminates all connections
    ...                          currently being managed
  }                              by the server
}
```

This bug would likely have been spotted (and avoided) if the `connectionManager` class had followed the standard naming convention and instead been called `ConnectionManager`. By not sticking to this convention, the code that uses the `connectionManager` class is easy to misunderstand, and this can result in a serious bug that might go unnoticed.

5.4.2 Solution: Adopt and follow a style guide

As just noted, a common coding style convention is that class names should be written in PascalCase and variable names should be written in camelCase. If this convention were followed then the `connectionManager` class would instead be named `ConnectionManager`. The buggy code from the last section would then look like listing 5.13. It's now very obvious that `ConnectionManager` is a class and not an instance variable within the `GroupChat` class. It's also now obvious that a call like `ConnectionManager.terminateAll()` is probably modifying some global state and likely affecting other parts of the server.

Listing 5.13 Consistent naming style

```
class GroupChat {
  ...
                                          It's obvious that
  end() {                                 ConnectionManager is a class,
    ConnectionManager.terminateAll();  <-- not an instance variable.
  }
}
```

This is just one example of how a consistent coding style can make code more readable and help prevent bugs. Coding styles often cover many more aspects than just how to name things, such as the following:

- Usage of certain language features
- How to indent code
- Package and directory structuring
- How to document code

Most organizations and teams have a coding style guide that they expect engineers to follow, so it's unlikely you need to make any decisions or think too hard about what style to adopt. It's likely just a case of reading and absorbing the style guide that your team mandates, and following it.

If your team doesn't have a style guide and you'd like to align around one, then there are many off-the-shelf ones you can adopt. Google, for example, has published style guides for a number of languages: https://google.github.io/styleguide/.

When a whole team or organization all follow the same coding style, it's akin to them all speaking the same language fluently. The risk of misunderstanding each other is greatly reduced, and this results in fewer bugs and less time wasted trying to understand confusing code.

Linters

There are also tools available that can inform us of any style guide violations that our code might contain. These are called *linters* and are typically specific to whatever language we are using. Some linters do a lot more than just check for style guide violations and can also warn us of code that is error prone or that exhibits some known bad practices.

Linters generally only catch quite simple issues, so they're not a replacement for writing good code in the first place. But running a linter can be a quick and easy way to spot some of the ways in which code can be improved.

5.5 Avoid deeply nesting code

A typical piece of code is made up of blocks that get nested within one another, such as the following:

- A function defines a block of code that runs when the function is called.
- An if-statement defines a block of code that runs when the condition is true.
- A for-loop defines a block of code that runs on each iteration of the loop.

Figure 5.1 illustrates how control-flow logic (such as if-statements and for-loops) can result in blocks of code that are nested within one another. There is usually more than one way to structure a given piece of logic in code. Some forms can result in lots of nesting of blocks of code, while others can result in almost no nesting. It's important to consider how the structure of the code affects readability.

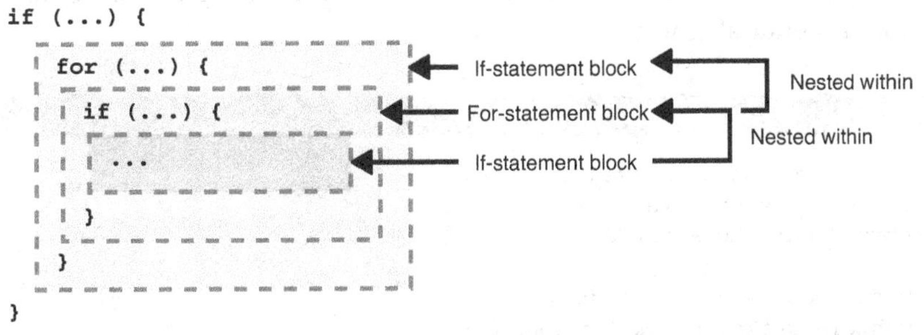

Figure 5.1 Control-flow logic (such as if-statements and for-loops) can often result in blocks of code that are nested within one another.

5.5.1 Deeply nested code can be hard to read

Listing 5.14 contains some code to look up an address for the owner of a vehicle. The code contains several if-statements nested inside one another. This results in code that is quite hard to read, both because it's hard for the eye to follow and because of all the dense if-else logic that needs to be navigated to figure out when certain values are returned.

Listing 5.14 Deeply nested if-statements

```
Address? getOwnersAddress(Vehicle vehicle) {
  if (vehicle.hasBeenScraped()) {
    return SCRAPYARD_ADDRESS;
  } else {
    Purchase? mostRecentPurchase =
        vehicle.getMostRecentPurchase();
    if (mostRecentPurchase == null) {        <-- If-statements nested
      return SHOWROOM_ADDRESS;                   within other
    } else {                                     if-statements
      Buyer? buyer = mostRecentPurchase.getBuyer();
      if (buyer != null) {                   <--
        return buyer.getAddress();
      }
    }
  }
  return null;        <-- It's hard to figure out the scenarios in which this line is reachable.
}
```

Human eyes are not good at keeping track of exactly what level of nesting each line of code has. This can make it difficult for anyone reading the code to understand exactly when different pieces of logic run. Deeply nesting code reduces readability, and it's often better to structure code in a way that minimizes the amount of nesting.

5.5.2 Solution: Restructure to minimize nesting

When we have a function like that in the previous example, it's often quite easy to rearrange the logic to avoid nesting if-statements inside one another. Listing 5.15 shows how this function could be rewritten with no nesting of if-statements. The code is more readable as it's easier for the eye to follow and the logic is presented in a less dense and impenetrable way.

Listing 5.15 Code with minimal nesting

```
Address? getOwnersAddress(Vehicle vehicle) {
  if (vehicle.hasBeenScraped()) {
    return SCRAPYARD_ADDRESS;
  }
  Purchase? mostRecentPurchase =
      vehicle.getMostRecentPurchase();
  if (mostRecentPurchase == null) {
```

```
    return SHOWROOM_ADDRESS;
  }
  Buyer? buyer = mostRecentPurchase.getBuyer();
  if (buyer != null) {
    return buyer.getAddress();
  }
  return null;
}
```

When every branch of nested logic results in a return statement, it's usually quite easy to rearrange the logic to avoid nesting. However, when branches of nesting don't result in return statements, it's usually a sign that a function is doing too much. The next subsection explores this.

5.5.3 Nesting is often a result of doing too much

Listing 5.16 shows a function that does too much by containing both the logic to look up a vehicle owner's address and the logic that makes use of the address to trigger sending a letter. Because of this, it's not straightforward to apply the fix seen in the previous subsection, as returning early from the function would obviously mean that the letter is not sent.

Listing 5.16 A function that does too much

```
SentConfirmation? sendOwnerALetter(
    Vehicle vehicle, Letter letter) {
  Address? ownersAddress = null;             <-- A mutable variable to hold the result of finding the address
  if (vehicle.hasBeenScraped()) {
    ownersAddress = SCRAPYARD_ADDRESS;
  } else {
    Purchase? mostRecentPurchase =
        vehicle.getMostRecentPurchase();
    if (mostRecentPurchase == null) {         <-- If-statements nested within other if-statements
      ownersAddress = SHOWROOM_ADDRESS;
    } else {
      Buyer? buyer = mostRecentPurchase.getBuyer();
      if (buyer != null) {
        ownersAddress = buyer.getAddress();
      }
    }
  }
  if (ownersAddress == null) {
    return null;
  }
  return sendLetter(ownersAddress, letter);   <-- Logic that makes use of the address
}
```

The real problem here is that this function does too much. It contains the nuts-and-bolts logic for finding the address, as well as the logic to trigger sending the letter. We can solve this by breaking the code into smaller functions, which the next subsection will show.

5.5.4 Solution: Break code into smaller functions

The code from the previous subsection can be improved by breaking the logic to find the owner's address out into a different function. It then becomes easy to apply the fix we saw earlier in this section to eliminate the nesting of if-statements. The following listing shows what this would look like.

Listing 5.17 Smaller functions

```
SentConfirmation? sendOwnerALetter(
    Vehicle vehicle, Letter letter) {
  Address? ownersAddress = getOwnersAddress(vehicle);
  if (ownersAddress != null) {
    return sendLetter(ownersAddress, letter);
  }
  return null;
}

Address? getOwnersAddress(Vehicle vehicle) {     <-- Logic to find owner's address in a separate function
  if (vehicle.hasBeenScraped()) {
    return SCRAPYARD_ADDRESS;
  }
  Purchase? mostRecentPurchase = vehicle.getMostRecentPurchase();
  if (mostRecentPurchase == null) {     <-- Nesting of if-statements eliminated
    return SHOWROOM_ADDRESS;
  }
  Buyer? buyer = mostRecentPurchase.getBuyer();
  if (buyer == null) {
    return null;
  }
  return buyer.getAddress();
}
```

Chapter 2 discussed how doing too much inside a single function can lead to poor layers of abstraction, so even without lots of nesting, it's often still a good idea to break large functions up. When there is lots of nesting in the code, breaking a large function up becomes doubly important, because it is often the necessary first step for eliminating the nesting.

5.6 Make function calls readable

If a function is well named, then it should be obvious what it does, but even for a well-named function, it's easy to have unreadable function calls if it's not clear what the arguments are for or what they do.

> **NOTE: LARGE NUMBERS OF PARAMETERS** Function calls tend to get less readable as the number of arguments increases. If a function or constructor has a large number of parameters it can often be a sign of a more fundamental problem with the code, such as not defining appropriate layers of abstraction or not modularizing things enough. Chapter 2 already discussed layers of abstraction, and chapter 8 will cover modularity in more detail.

5.6.1 Arguments can be hard to decipher

Consider the following code snippet that contains a call to a function that sends a message. It's not clear what the arguments in the function call represent. We can guess that `"hello"` is probably the message, but we have no idea what `1` or `true` mean.

```
sendMessage("hello", 1, true);
```

To figure out what the `1` and `true` arguments in the call to `sendMessage()` mean, we'd have to go and look at the function definition. If we did that we'd see that the `1` represents a message priority and the `true` indicates that sending of the message can be retried:

```
void sendMessage(String message, Int priority, Boolean allowRetry) {
  ...
}
```

This gives us the answer to what the values in the function call mean, but we had to find the function definition to figure this out. This might be quite a laborious task as the function definition might well be in a completely different file or hundreds of lines of code away. If we have to refer to a different file or something many lines away to figure out what a given piece of code does, then that code is not very readable. There are a few potential ways to improve this, and the following subsections explore some of these solutions.

5.6.2 Solution: Use named arguments

Named arguments are supported by an increasing number of languages, especially more modern ones. When using named arguments in a function call, arguments are matched based on their name rather than their position within the argument list. If we used named arguments, then the call to the `sendMessage()` function would be very readable, even without ever having seen the function definition:

```
sendMessage(message: "hello", priority: 1, allowRetry: true);
```

Unfortunately not all languages support named arguments, so this is an option only if we are using a language that does. Despite this, there are sometimes ways of faking named arguments. This is quite common in TypeScript (and other forms of JavaScript) using *object destructuring*. Listing 5.18 shows how the `sendMessage()` function could make use of object destructuring if it were written in TypeScript. The function accepts a single object (with the type `SendMessageParams`) as a parameter, but this object is immediately destructured into its constituent properties. Code inside the function can then read these properties directly.

Listing 5.18 Object destructuring in TypeScript

```
interface SendMessageParams {        <-- Interface to define the type
  message: string,                       of the function parameter
  priority: number,
```

```
  allowRetry: boolean,
}

async function sendMessage(
    {message, priority, allowRetry} : SendMessageParams) {
  const outcome = await XhrWrapper.send(
      END_POINT, message, priority);
  if (outcome.failed() && allowRetry) {
    ...
  }
}
```

The function parameter is immediately destructured into its properties.

Properties from the destructured object can be used directly.

The following snippet shows what a call to the `sendMessage()` function would look like. The function is called with an object, meaning each value is associated with a property name. This achieves more or less the same thing as named arguments.

```
sendMessage({
  message: 'hello',
  priority: 1,
  allowRetry: true,
});
```

Argument names are associated with each value.

Using a destructured object to achieve the same benefits as named arguments is relatively common in TypeScript (as well as other forms of JavaScript), so despite being a bit of a work-around, it's usually something that other engineers will be familiar with. There are sometimes ways of faking named arguments in other languages, but they can cause more problems than they solve if they use a language feature that other engineers might be unfamiliar with.

5.6.3 *Solution: Use descriptive types*

Whether the language we're using supports named arguments or not, it can often be a good idea to use more descriptive types when defining a function. In the scenario we saw at the start of this section (repeated again in the following snippet), the author of the `sendMessage()` function used an integer to represent the priority and a Boolean to represent whether retries are allowed.

```
void sendMessage(String message, Int priority, Boolean allowRetry) {
  ...
}
```

Integers and Booleans aren't very descriptive in themselves because they can mean all manner of things depending on the scenario. An alternative would be to use types that describe what they represent when writing the `sendMessage()` function. Listing 5.19 shows two different techniques for achieving this:

- *A class*—The message priority has been wrapped in a class.
- *An enum*—The retry policy now uses an enum with two options instead of a Boolean.

Listing 5.19 Descriptive types in function call

```
class MessagePriority {
  ...
  MessagePriority(Int priority) { ... }
  ...
}

enum RetryPolicy {
  ALLOW_RETRY,
  DISALLOW_RETRY
}

void sendMessage(
    String message,
    MessagePriority priority,
    RetryPolicy retryPolicy) {
  ...
}
```

A call to this function would then be very readable, even without knowing the function definition:

```
sendMessage("hello", new MessagePriority(1), RetryPolicy.ALLOW_RETRY);
```

5.6.4 *Sometimes there's no great solution*

Sometimes there is no particularly good way to ensure that function calls are readable. To demonstrate this, imagine we needed a class to represent a 2D bounding box. We might write code for a `BoundingBox` class similar to that in listing 5.20. The constructor takes four integers to represent the positions of the edges of the box.

Listing 5.20 BoundingBox class

```
class BoundingBox {
  ...
  BoundingBox(Int top, Int right, Int bottom, Int left) {
    ...
  }
}
```

If the language we're using doesn't support named arguments, then a call to this constructor is not very readable because it contains a series of numbers with no hints about what each number represents. Because all the arguments are integers, it's also very easy for an engineer to get confused about the order, make a complete mess of things, and still have code that compiles just fine. The following snippet shows an example of a call to the `BoundingBox` constructor:

```
BoundingBox box = new BoundingBox(10, 50, 20, 5);
```

There's no particularly satisfactory solution in this scenario, and about the best thing that we can do here is to use some inline comments when calling the constructor to explain what each argument is. If we did this, then a call to the constructor would look something like the following:

```
BoundingBox box = new BoundingBox(
    /* top= */ 10,
    /* right= */ 50,
    /* bottom= */ 20,
    /* left= */ 5);
```

The inline comments definitely make the call to the constructor more readable. But they rely on us not having made a mistake when writing them and on other engineers keeping them up to date, so they're not that satisfactory as a solution. There's also an argument to be made for not using these inline comments because of the risk that they become out-of-date; an out-of-date (and therefore incorrect) comment is probably worse than having no comment.

Adding setter functions or using something like the builder pattern (covered in chapter 7) are alternative options, but both have the downside that they make the code easy to misuse by allowing a class to be instantiated with missing values. This would need to be prevented with a runtime check (rather than a compile-time check) to ensure that the code is correct.

5.6.5 What about the IDE?

Some integrated development environments (IDEs) look up function definitions in the background. They then augment the view of the code so that function argument names are displayed at call sites. Figure 5.2 shows what this can look like.

The actual code

```
sendMessage("hello", 1, true);
```

How the code appears in the IDE

```
sendMessage( message: "hello" priority: 1, allowRetry: true) ;
```

Figure 5.2 Some IDEs augment the view of the code to make function calls more readable.

While this can be incredibly useful when editing code, it's usually best not to rely on this to make the code readable. It's probably not guaranteed that every engineer is using an IDE that does this, and there are likely other tools in which the code is viewed that don't have this feature, such as codebase explorer tools, merge tools, and code review tools.

5.7 Avoid using unexplained values

There are many scenarios where a hard-coded value is required. Some common examples are as follows:

- A coefficient for converting one quantity to another
- A number that is a tunable parameter, such as the maximum number of times to retry a certain task if it fails
- A string that represents a template that some values can be populated in

For all these hard-coded values, there are two important pieces of information:

- *What the value is*—The computer needs to know this when it executes the code.
- *What the value means*—An engineer needs to know this in order to understand the code. Without this information, the code is not readable.

It's obviously a given that there's a value or else the code would presumably not compile or function, but it can be easy to forget to make it clear to other engineers what the value actually means.

5.7.1 Unexplained values can be confusing

Listing 5.21 shows some of the functions in a class to represent a vehicle. The function `getKineticEnergyJ()` calculates the current kinetic energy of the vehicle, in joules (J), based on the vehicle's mass and speed. The vehicle's mass is stored in US tons, while the speed is stored in miles per hour (MPH). The equation for calculating kinetic energy in joules ($½ \cdot m \cdot v^2$) requires the mass to be in kilograms and the speed to be in meters per second, so the `getKineticEnergyJ()` contains two conversion coefficients. What these coefficients mean is not obvious from the code; anyone not already familiar with the equation for kinetic energy would likely not know what these constants represent.

Listing 5.21 Vehicle class

```
class Vehicle {
  ...

  Double getMassUsTon() { ... }

  Double getSpeedMph() { ... }

  // Returns the vehicle's current kinetic energy in joules.
  Double getKineticEnergyJ() {
    return 0.5 *
        getMassUsTon() * 907.1847 *          <- Unexplained value that converts US tons to kilograms
        Math.pow(getSpeedMph() * 0.44704, 2);   <- Unexplained value that converts MPH to meters per second
  }
}
```

Having unexplained values like this makes the code less readable because many engineers will not understand why those values are there or what they do. When an engineer has to modify some code that they don't understand, the chance that the code becomes broken is increased.

Imagine an engineer is modifying the vehicle class to get rid of the `getMassUsTon()` function and replace it with a `getMassKg()` function that returns the mass in kilograms. They have to modify the call to `getMassUsTon()` within `getKineticEnergyJ()` to call this new function. But because they don't understand that the value 907.1847 is converting US tons to kilograms, they may not realize that they now also need to remove this too. After their modifications the `getKineticEnergyJ()` function would be broken:

```
...
  // Returns the vehicle's current kinetic energy in joules.
  Double getKineticEnergyJ() {
    return 0.5 *
        getMassKg() * 907.1847 *
        Math.pow(getSpeedMph() * 0.44704, 2);
  }
...
```

907.1847 has not been removed; the function returns the wrong value.

Having an unexplained value in the code can cause confusion and bugs. It's important to ensure that *what the value means* is obvious to other engineers. The following two subsections show different ways in which this can be achieved.

5.7.2 Solution: Use a well-named constant

One simple way to explain values is to give them a name by placing them inside a constant. Instead of using the value directly in the code, the constant is used, meaning its name explains the code. The following listing shows what the `getKineticEnergyJ()` function and surrounding `Vehicle` class would look like if the values are placed inside constants.

Listing 5.22 Well-named constants

```
class Vehicle {
  private const Double KILOGRAMS_PER_US_TON = 907.1847;
  private const Double METERS_PER_SECOND_PER_MPH = 0.44704;
  ...

  // Returns the vehicle's current kinetic energy in joules.
  Double getKineticEnergyJ() {
    return 0.5 *
        getMassUsTon() * KILOGRAMS_PER_US_TON *
        Math.pow(getSpeedMph() * METERS_PER_SECOND_PER_MPH, 2);
  }
}
```

Constant definitions (lines 2–3)

Constants used in code (last two lines of the return statement)

The code is now a lot more readable, and if an engineer modifies the `Vehicle` class to use kilograms instead of US tons, it would likely be obvious to them that multiplying the mass by `KILOGRAMS_PER_US_TON` is no longer correct.

5.7.3 Solution: Use a well-named function

An alternative to using a well-named constant is to use a well-named function. There are two alternative ways in which a function can be used to make the code readable:

- A provider function that returns the constant
- A helper function that does the conversion

A PROVIDER FUNCTION

This is conceptually almost the same as using a constant, just achieved in a slightly different way. The following listing shows the `getKineticEnergyJ()` function and two additional functions to provide the conversion coefficients: `kilogramsPerUsTon()` and `metersPerSecondPerMph()`.

Listing 5.23 Well-named functions to provide values

```
class Vehicle {
  ...
  // Returns the vehicle's current kinetic energy in joules.
  Double getKineticEnergyJ() {
    return 0.5 *
        getMassUsTon() * kilogramsPerUsTon() *
        Math.pow(getSpeedMph() * metersPerSecondPerMph(), 2);
  }

  private static Double kilogramsPerUsTon() {
    return 907.1847;
  }

  private static Double metersPerSecondPerMph() {
    return 0.44704;
  }
}
```

Provider functions called

Provider functions

A HELPER FUNCTION

An alternative would be to treat the conversion of quantities as subproblems that should be solved by dedicated functions. The fact that a value is involved in the particular conversion is an implementation detail that callers don't need to be aware of. The following listing shows the `getKineticEnergyJ()` function and two additional functions that solve the conversion subproblems: `usTonsToKilograms()` and `mphToMetersPerSecond()`.

Listing 5.24 Helper functions to perform conversions

```
class Vehicle {
  ...
  // Returns the vehicle's current kinetic energy in joules.
  Double getKineticEnergyJ() {
    return 0.5 *
        usTonsToKilograms(getMassUsTon()) *
        Math.pow(mphToMetersPerSecond(getSpeedMph()), 2);
  }

  private static Double usTonsToKilograms(Double usTons) {
    return usTons * 907.1847;
  }

  private static Double mphToMetersPerSecond(Double mph) {
    return mph * 0.44704;
  }
}
```

Helper functions called

Helper functions

As the previous examples show, there are three good ways to avoid having unexplained values in our code. It generally requires very little extra work to place a value inside a constant or function and can greatly improve readability.

As a final point, it's also worth considering if other engineers might want to reuse the value or helper function we're defining. If there's a chance that they might, then it's best to place it in a public utility class somewhere rather than just keeping it inside the class that we're using it within.

5.8 Use anonymous functions appropriately

Anonymous functions are functions that don't have a name, and they're typically defined inline in some code at the point that they are needed. The syntax for defining an anonymous function varies between different languages. Listing 5.25 shows a function to get all the pieces of feedback that contain a nonempty comment. It calls the `List.filter()` function using an anonymous function. For completeness, the listing also shows what the filter function on the `List` class might look like. `List.filter()` takes a function as a parameter, and callers can provide an anonymous function here if they want.

Listing 5.25 An anonymous function as an argument

```
class List<T> {
  ...
  List<T> filter(Function<T, Boolean> retainIf) {      <-- Takes a function as a parameter
    ...
  }
}

List<Feedback> getUsefulFeedback(List<Feedback> allFeedback) {
  return allFeedback
      .filter(feedback -> !feedback.getComment().isEmpty());   <-- List.filter() called with an inline, anonymous function
}
```

Most mainstream languages support anonymous functions in some form. Using them for small, self-explanatory things can increase the readability of code, but using them for anything that is big, non–self-explanatory, or that could be reused can cause problems. The following subsections explain why.

> **Functional programming**
>
> Anonymous functions and using functions as parameters are techniques most commonly associated with functional programming and in particular the use of lambda expressions. Functional programming is a paradigm where logic is expressed as calls or references to functions rather than as imperative statements that modify state. There are a number of languages that are "pure" functional programming languages. The languages that this book is most applicable to would not be considered pure functional languages. Most of them do, nonetheless, incorporate features that allow functional-style code to be written in many scenarios.

If you want to learn more about functional programming, the following article contains a more detailed description: http://mng.bz/qewE

5.8.1 Anonymous functions can be great for small things

The code we just saw (repeated in the following snippet) uses an anonymous function to get the pieces of feedback that contain a nonempty comment. This only requires a single statement of code, and because the problem being solved is trivial this single statement is very readable and compact.

```
List<Feedback> getUsefulFeedback(List<Feedback> allFeedback) {
  return allFeedback
      .filter(feedback -> !feedback.getComment().isEmpty());
}
```

Anonymous function to check comment is not empty

In this scenario, using an anonymous function is fine because the logic within it is small, simple, and self-explanatory. The alternative would have been to define a named function for determining if a piece of feedback contains a nonempty comment. Listing 5.26 shows how the code would look if a named function is used instead. It requires more boilerplate to define the named function, which some engineers may find less readable.

Listing 5.26 A named function as an argument

```
List<Feedback> getUsefulFeedback(List<Feedback> allFeedback) {
  return allFeedback.filter(hasNonEmptyComment);
}

private Boolean hasNonEmptyComment(Feedback feedback) {
  return !feedback.getComment().isEmpty();
}
```

Named function used as an argument

A named function

NOTE Even with logic as simple as that in listing 5.26, defining a dedicated named function might still be useful from a code reusability perspective. If there's any chance that someone might need to reuse the logic to check if a piece of feedback has a nonempty comment, then it might be better to put it in a named function rather than an anonymous one.

5.8.2 Anonymous functions can be hard to read

As was covered earlier in this chapter (as well as earlier in the book), function names can be very useful for increasing code readability, as they provide a succinct summary of what the code inside the function does. Because anonymous functions are, by definition, nameless, they don't provide anyone reading the code with this summary. Regardless of how small it is, if the contents of an anonymous function are not self-explanatory then the code is likely not readable.

Listing 5.27 shows the code for a function that takes a list of 16-bit IDs and returns only the valid ones. The format of an ID is a 15-bit value in combination with a parity bit, and an ID is considered valid if it's nonzero and the parity bit is correct. The logic for checking the parity bit is inside an anonymous function, but it's not self-explanatory that this code is checking a parity bit. This means that the code is less readable than it ideally should be.

Listing 5.27 A non–self-explanatory anonymous function

```
List<UInt16> getValidIds(List<UInt16> ids) {
  return ids
      .filter(id -> id != 0)
      .filter(id -> countSetBits(id & 0x7FFF) % 2 ==
          ((id & 0x8000) >> 15));
}
```

Anonymous function to check the parity bit

This is the same succinct but unreadable code seen earlier in the chapter. Logic like this needs explaining because most engineers have no idea what it does. And because anonymous functions offer no explanation beyond the code inside them, this is probably not a good use of one.

5.8.3 *Solution: Use named functions instead*

Anyone reading the `getValidIds()` function from the previous example is probably only interested in knowing the high-level details of how to get valid IDs. In order to do this, they only need to be aware of the two conceptual reasons for an ID being valid:

- It's nonzero.
- The parity bit is correct.

They shouldn't be forced to contend with lower level concepts like bitwise operations in order to understand the high-level reason an ID is or isn't valid. It would be better to use a named function to abstract away the implementation details of checking a parity bit.

Listing 5.28 shows what this might look like. The `getValidIds()` function is now incredibly easy to read; anyone reading it immediately understands that it does two things: filter out nonzero IDs and filter out IDs with an incorrect parity bit. If they want to understand the details of parity bits they can look at the helper function, but they're not forced to contend with these details just to understand the `getValidIds()` function. Another benefit of using a named function is that the logic for checking a parity bit can now be easily reused.

Listing 5.28 Using a named function

```
List<UInt16> getValidIds(List<UInt16> ids) {
  return ids
      .filter(id -> id != 0)
      .filter(isParityBitCorrect);
}
```

Named function used as an argument

```
private Boolean isParityBitCorrect(UInt16 id) {
  ...
}
```

A named function for checking the parity bit

As we saw in chapter 3, looking at the names of things is one of the primary ways in which engineers understand code. The downside of naming things is that it often creates extra verbosity and boilerplate. Anonymous functions are great at reducing verbosity and boilerplate, but with the disadvantage that the function no longer has a name. For small, self-explanatory things this is usually fine, but for anything bigger or more complicated, the benefits of giving a function a name usually outweigh the downsides of the extra verbosity.

5.8.4 Large anonymous functions can be problematic

From personal experience, I find that engineers sometimes conflate *functional*-style programming with the use of inline, anonymous functions. Adopting a functional style of programming has many benefits that can often make code more readable and more robust. As the previous examples in this section show, we can quite easily write functional-style code using named functions; adopting a functional style does not imply that we have to use inline, anonymous functions.

Chapter 2 discussed the importance of keeping functions small and concise so that it's easy for engineers to read, understand, and reuse them. When writing functional-style code, some engineers forget this and produce enormous anonymous functions that contain way too much logic and sometimes even other anonymous functions nested within one another. If an anonymous function starts approaching anything more than two or three lines long, then it's quite likely the code would be more readable if the anonymous function were broken apart and placed into one or more named functions.

To demonstrate this, listing 5.29 shows some code to display a list of pieces of feedback in a UI. The `buildFeedbackListItems()` function contains a very large inline, anonymous function within it. This anonymous function, in turn, contains another anonymous function within it. The amount of logic densely packed together, as well as the amount of nesting and indentation, make this code hard to read. In particular it's quite hard to figure out what information is actually displayed in the UI, as this information is spread all over the place. Once we read all the code, we can see that the UI displays a title, the feedback comment, and some categories, but it is not easy to figure this out.

Listing 5.29 A large anonymous function

```
void displayFeedback(List<Feedback> allFeedback) {
  ui.getFeedbackWidget().setItems(
      buildFeedbackListItems(allFeedback));
}

private List<ListItem> buildFeedbackListItems(
    List<Feedback> allFeedback) {
```

```
  return allFeedback.map(feedback ->          <-- List.map() called with
    new ListItem(                                 an anonymous function
      title: new TextBox(
        text: feedback.getTitle(),                       <-- A title is
        options: new TextOptions(weight: TextWeight.BOLD),   displayed.
      ),
      body: new Column(
        children: [
          new TextBox(                                <-- The comment
            text: feedback.getComment(),                  is displayed.
            border: new Border(style: BorderStyle.DASHED),
          ),
          new Row(
            children: feedback.getCategories().map(category ->   <-- A second anonymous
              new TextBox(                                           function nested
                text: category.getLabel(),                           within the main one
                options: new TextOptions(style: TextStyle.ITALIC),   <-- Some categories
              ),                                                         are displayed.
            ),
          ),
        ],
      ),
    )
  );
}
```

To be fair, many of the problems with the code in listing 5.29 are not totally down to the fact that anonymous functions are being used. Even if all this code were moved to a single, massive named function, it would still be a mess. The real issue is that the function does way too much, which is exacerbated by the use of anonymous functions, but not entirely caused by it. The code would be a lot more readable if it were broken up into smaller named functions.

5.8.5 Solution: Break large anonymous functions into named functions

Listing 5.30 shows what the `buildProductListItems()` function that we just saw looks like if the logic is broken up into a series of well-named helper functions. The code is more verbose but significantly more readable. Importantly, an engineer can now look at the `buildFeedbackItem()` function and immediately see what information is displayed in the UI for each piece of feedback: the title, comment, and categories that the feedback applies to.

Listing 5.30 Smaller named functions

```
private List<ListItem> buildFeedbackListItems(
    List<Feedback> allFeedback) {
  return allFeedback.map(buildFeedbackItem);    <-- List.map() called with
}                                                   a named function

private ListItem buildFeedbackItem(Feedback feedback) {
  return new ListItem(
```

```
    title: buildTitle(feedback.getTitle()),          <-- A title
    body: new Column(                                    is displayed.
      children: [
        buildCommentText(feedback.getComment()),          <-- The comment
        buildCategories(feedback.getCategories()),   <--      is displayed.
      ],
    ),                                                  Some categories
  );                                                    are displayed.
}

private TextBox buildTitle(String title) {
  return new TextBox(
    text: title,
    options: new TextOptions(weight: TextWeight.BOLD),
  );
}

private TextBox buildCommentText(String comment) {
  return new TextBox(
    text: comment,
    border: new Border(style: BorderStyle.DASHED),
  );
}

private Row buildCategories(List<Category> categories) {
  return new Row(
    children: categories.map(buildCategory),       <-- List.map() called
  );                                                   with a named function
}

private TextBox buildCategory(Category category) {
  return new TextBox(
    text: category.getLabel(),
    options: new TextOptions(style: TextStyle.ITALIC),
  );
}
```

Breaking apart large functions that do too much is a great way to improve the readability of code (as well as its reusability and modularity). It's important not to forget this when writing functional-style code: if an anonymous function starts getting big and unwieldy, then it's probably time to move the logic to some named functions instead.

5.9 Use shiny, new language features appropriately

Everyone loves shiny new things, and engineers are no different. Many programming languages are still being actively developed, and every now and again the language designers add a nice, new, shiny feature. When this happens engineers are often eager to make use of this new feature.

Programming language designers think very carefully before adding a new feature, so there are likely many scenarios where the new feature makes code considerably more readable or robust. It's good that engineers get excited about these things because it increases the chance that the new feature gets used to improve code. But if you find yourself eager to use a new or shiny language feature, make sure you're honest with yourself about whether it's really the best tool for the job.

5.9.1 New features can improve code

When Java 8 introduced streams, many engineers got excited, as it provided a way to write much more succinct, functional-style code. To provide an example of how streams can improve code, listing 5.31 shows some traditional Java code that takes a list of strings and filters out any that are empty. The code is quite verbose (for what is a conceptually quite simple task) and requires using a for-loop and instantiating a new list.

Listing 5.31 Traditional Java code to filter a list

```
List<String> getNonEmptyStrings(List<String> strings) {
  List<String> nonEmptyStrings = new ArrayList<>();
  for (String str : strings) {
    if (!str.isEmpty()) {
      nonEmptyStrings.add(str);
    }
  }
  return nonEmptyStrings;
}
```

Using a stream can make this code a lot more succinct and readable. The following listing shows how the same functionality could be implemented using a stream and a filter.

Listing 5.32 Filtering a list with a stream

```
List<String> getNonEmptyStrings(List<String> strings) {
  return strings
      .stream()
      .filter(str -> !str.isEmpty())
      .collect(toList());
}
```

This seems like a good use of this language feature, as the code has become more readable and succinct. Making use of a language feature (instead of hand-rolling something) also increases the chance that the code is optimally efficient and bug-free. Using a language feature when it improves code is generally a good idea (but see the next two subsections).

5.9.2 Obscure features can be confusing

Even if a language feature affords a clear benefit, it's still worth considering how well known the feature is to other engineers. This generally requires thinking about our specific scenario and who will ultimately have to maintain the code.

If we're in a team that maintains only a small amount of Java code, and none of the other engineers are familiar with Java streams, then it might be best to avoid using them. In this scenario, the code improvement we get from using them may be relatively marginal compared to the confusion they might cause.

In general, using a language feature when it improves code is a good idea. But, if the improvement is small or there's a chance others may not be familiar with the feature, it may still be best to avoid using it.

5.9.3 Use the best tool for the job

Java streams are incredibly versatile, and it's possible to solve many problems with them. This doesn't, however, mean that they are always the best way to solve a problem. If we had a map and we needed to lookup a value in it, then the most sensible code to do this would probably be

```
String value = map.get(key);
```

But we could also solve this by getting a stream of the map entries and filtering them based on the key. Listing 5.33 shows what this might look like. Clearly this is not a particularly good way to get a value from a map. Not only is it a lot less readable than calling `map.get()`, but it's also a lot less efficient (because it potentially iterates over every entry in the map).

Listing 5.33 Getting a map value using a stream

```
Optional<String> value = map
    .entrySet()
    .stream()
    .filter(entry -> entry.getKey().equals(key))
    .map(Entry::getValue)
    .findFirst();
```

Listing 5.33 may look like some over-the-top example designed to prove a point, but I've seen code that's more or less identical to this in a real codebase before.

New language features are often added for a reason and can bring great benefits, but as with any code you write, make sure you're using a feature because it's the right tool for the job and not just because it's shiny or new.

Summary

- If code is not readable and easy to understand it can lead to problems such as the following:
  - Other engineers wasting time trying to decipher it
  - Misunderstandings that lead to bugs being introduced
  - Code being broken when other engineers need to modify it
- Making code more readable can sometimes lead to it becoming more verbose and taking up more lines. This is often a worthwhile trade-off.

- Making code readable often requires being empathetic and imagining ways in which others might find something confusing.
- Real-life scenarios are varied and usually present their own set of challenges. Writing readable code nearly always requires an element of applying common sense and using your judgment.

6 Avoid surprises

This chapter covers

- How code can cause surprises
- How surprises can lead to bugs in software
- Ways to ensure that code does not cause surprises

We saw in chapters 2 and 3 how code is often built up in layers, with code in higher layers depending on code in lower ones. When we write code, it's often just one part of a much bigger codebase. We build on top of other pieces of code by depending on them, and other engineers build on top of our code by depending on it. For this to work, engineers need to be able to understand what code does and how they should use it.

Chapter 3 talked about code contracts as a way to think about how other engineers go about understanding how to use a piece of code. In a code contract, things like names, parameter types, and return types are unmistakably obvious, whereas comments and documentation are more like small print and are often overlooked.

Ultimately, an engineer will build a mental model of how to use a piece of code. This will be based on what they notice in the code contract, any prior knowledge they have, and common paradigms that they think might be applicable. If this mental model doesn't match the reality of what the code actually does, then it's likely that a nasty surprise might occur. In the best case this might just result in a bit of wasted engineering time, but in the worst case it could result in a catastrophic bug.

Avoiding surprises is often about being explicit. If a function sometimes returns nothing or there is a special scenario that needs handling then we should make sure other engineers are aware of this. If we don't, then there is a risk that their mental model of what they think the code does will not match the reality. This chapter explores some common ways in which code can cause surprises and some techniques for avoiding these.

6.1 Avoid returning magic values

A *magic value* is a value that fits into the normal return type of a function but which has a special meaning. A very common example of a magic value is returning minus one from a function to indicate that a value is absent (or that an error occurred).

Because a magic value fits into the normal return type of a function, it can be easily mistaken for a normal return value by any callers who are not aware of it and actively vigilant. This section explains how this can cause surprises and how magic values can be avoided.

6.1.1 Magic values can lead to bugs

Returning minus one from a function to indicate that a value is absent is a practice you will no doubt come across from time to time. Some pieces of legacy code do it, and even some built-in language features do it (such as calling `indexOf()` on an array in JavaScript).

In the past, there were some semi-sensible reasons for returning a magic value (like minus one), because more explicit error-signaling techniques or returning a null or an optional were not always available or practical to use. If we are working on some legacy code or have some code that we need to carefully optimize, then some of these reasons may still apply. But in general, returning a magic value carries a risk of causing a surprise, so it's often best to avoid using them.

To demonstrate how a magic value can cause a bug, consider the code in the listing 6.1. It contains a class for storing information about a user. One of the pieces of information stored in the class is the user's age, and this can be accessed by calling the `getAge()` function. The `getAge()` function returns a non-nullable integer, so an engineer looking at this function signature is likely to assume that the age will always be available.

Listing 6.1 User class and getAge() function

```
class User {
  ...
  Int getAge() { ... }    // Returns the user's age. Never returns null.
}
```

Now imagine that an engineer needs to calculate some statistics about all users of a service. One of the statistics they need to calculate is the mean age of the users. They write the code in listing 6.2 to do this. The code works by summing all the ages of the users and then dividing this by the number of users. The code assumes that `user.getAge()` always returns the user's actual age. Nothing in the code looks obviously wrong, and the author and reviewer of this code would likely be satisfied that it works.

Listing 6.2 Calculating mean age of users

```
Double? getMeanAge(List<User> users) {
  if (users.isEmpty()) {
    return null;
  }
  Double sumOfAges = 0.0;
  for (User user in users) {
    sumOfAges += user.getAge().toDouble();    <-- Sums all the return values of user.getAge()
  }
  return sumOfAges / users.size().toDouble();
}
```

In reality this code does not work and often returns an incorrect value for the mean age because not all users have provided their age. When this is the case, the `User.getAge()` function returns minus one. This is mentioned in the code's small print, but unfortunately the author of the `getMeanAge()` function did not realize this (as is often the case with small print buried in a comment). If we take a more detailed look at the `User` class, we see the code in listing 6.3. The fact that `User.getAge()` returns minus one, without making callers explicitly aware of this, has caused a nasty surprise for the author of the `getMeanAge()` function. `getMeanAge()` will return a plausible-looking but incorrect value because some number of minus-one values will likely be included when calculating the mean.

Listing 6.3 More detailed look at User class

```
class User {
  private final Int? age;    <-- The age may not have been provided.
  ...

  // Returns -1 if no age has been provided.    <-- The small print (in a comment) states that getAge() can return minus one.
  Int getAge() {
    if (age == null) {
      return -1;    <-- Returns minus one if no age provided
    }
    return age;
  }
}
```

This might seem like a kind of annoying but not very serious bug, but without knowing exactly where and how this code is being called we can't make that determination.

Imagine if a team compiling statistics for the company's annual report to shareholders reused the `getMeanAge()` function. The reported value of the mean age of users might have a material impact on the company's share price. If the reported value is incorrect, then this could result in severe legal consequences.

Another thing to note is that unit testing may not catch this issue. The author of the `getMeanAge()` function is under the firm (but incorrect) belief that the user's age is always available. There's a high chance that it would not occur to them to write a unit test where the user's age is absent because they're not even aware that this is something that the `User` class supports. Testing is great, but if we write code that can cause a surprise, we are relying on someone else's diligence to not fall into the trap we have set. At some point this will not happen, and someone will fall into it.

6.1.2 Solution: Return null, an optional, or an error

Chapter 3 talked about code contracts and how they contain things that are unmistakably obvious in addition to things that are best described as small print. The problem with returning a magic value from a function is that it requires callers to know the small print of the function's contract. Some number of engineers will not read this small print, or else read it but then forget it. When this happens a nasty surprise can occur.

If a value can be absent, it's much better to make sure this is part of the unmistakably obvious part of the code's contract. One of the easiest ways to do this is to simply return a nullable type if we have null-safety or to return an optional value if we do not. This will ensure that callers are aware that the value might be absent, and they can handle this in an appropriate way.

Listing 6.4 shows the `User` class with the `getAge()` function modified to return null if a value has not been provided. Null safety ensures that callers are aware of the fact that `getAge()` can return null. If the language we are using doesn't have null safety, then returning `Optional<Int>` would achieve the same thing.

Listing 6.4 getAge() modified to return null

```
class User {
  private final Int? age;      // The age may not have been provided (the "?" means age is nullable).
  ...

  Int? getAge() {              // The return type is nullable.
    return age;                // Returns null if no age provided
  }
}
```

The erroneous `getMeanAge()` function (repeated in listing 6.5) now causes a compiler error, which forces the engineer who wrote it to realize that there is a potential bug in their code. In order to make the `getMeanAge()` code compile, the engineer would have to handle the case where `User.getAge()` returns null.

Listing 6.5 Erroneous code doesn't compile

```
Double? getMeanAge(List<User> users) {
  if (users.isEmpty()) {
    return null;
  }
  Double sumOfAges = 0.0;
  for (User user in users) {
    sumOfAges += user.getAge().toDouble();   <-- Causes a compiler error because getAge() can return null
  }
  return sumOfAges / users.size().toDouble();
}
```

From a more organizational and product point of view, returning a nullable type forces the engineer to realize that calculating the mean age of a set of users is not as simple as they had initially thought. They can report this back to their manager or product team, as the requirements may need to be refined based on this information.

A downside of returning null (or an empty optional) is that it doesn't convey any explicit information about why the value is absent: is the user's age null because they didn't provide a value or because some kind of error occurred in our system? If it's useful to differentiate these scenarios, then we should consider using one of the error signaling techniques described in chapter 4.

Doesn't a nullable return type put a burden on the caller?

The short answer to this is often "Yes it does." If a function can return null, then callers often have to write a small amount of extra code to handle the scenario where the value is null. Some engineers cite this as a reason against returning null values or optional types, but it's worth considering what the alternative might be. If a value can be absent and a function doesn't make this sufficiently obvious to callers, then there is a very real risk that we'll end up with buggy code (as we just saw with calculating the mean age of users). In the medium to long term, the effort and expense that goes into dealing with and fixing a bug like this can be orders of magnitude higher than the cost of a few extra lines of code to handle a null return value correctly. Section 6.2 discusses the *null object pattern*, which is sometimes used as an alternative to returning null. But as we'll see, it can be problematic if used inappropriately.

Another reason sometimes cited against returning null is the risk of `NullPointerExceptions`, `NullReferenceExceptions`, or similar. But as discussed in chapter 2 (section 2.1) and in appendix B, the use of null safety or optional types generally eliminates this risk.

6.1.3 Sometimes magic values can happen accidentally

Returning a magic value doesn't always happen because an engineer deliberately means to. It can happen when an engineer doesn't think fully about all the inputs their code might receive and what effect these can have.

To demonstrate this, listing 6.6 contains some code to find the minimum value from a list of integers. The way that the function is implemented means that it returns a magic value (`Int.MAX_VALUE`) if the input list is empty.

Listing 6.6 Finding the minimum value

```
Int minValue(List<Int> values) {
  Int minValue = Int.MAX_VALUE;
  for (Int value in values) {
    minValue = Math.min(value, minValue);
  }
  return minValue;
}
```

If the values list is empty, then Int.MAX_VALUE is returned.

We'd obviously have to ask the engineer who wrote the code, but returning `Int.MAX_VALUE` might not be accidental. A couple of arguments the author of this might give for why this is sensible are as follows:

- It should be obvious to callers that getting the minimum value of an empty list makes no sense, so the value returned in this scenario doesn't really matter.
- `Int.MAX_VALUE` is a sensible value to return, as no integer can be bigger than it. This means that if it's compared against any kind of threshold the code would likely default to some sensible behavior.

The problem with these arguments is that they make assumptions about how the function will be called and how the result will be used. These assumptions could easily be wrong, and if they are it will cause a surprise.

Returning `Int.MAX_VALUE` might not result in some sensible default behavior. An example of this would be using it as part of a *maximin* (maximum minimum) algorithm. Imagine that we're part of the engineering team for a game, and we want to determine which level in the game is the easiest. We decide that for each level we will find the minimum score any player achieved. Whichever level has the highest minimum score will be considered the easiest.

Listing 6.7 shows the code we might write. It makes use of the `minValue()` function we just saw. We run the code, and it outputs that level 14 is the easiest level. In reality, level 14 is so difficult that no one has ever completed it. This means that no scores have ever been recorded for it. When processing level 14, the `minValue()` function is called with an empty list and thus returns `Int.MAX_VALUE`. This then makes level 14 appear to be the runaway winner in terms of having the highest minimum score. But as we just noted, the reality is that there are no scores recorded because it's so difficult that no one has ever completed it.

Listing 6.7 A maximin algorithm

```
class GameLevel {
  ...
  List<Int> getAllScores() { ... }
}
```

Returns an empty list if there are no scores

```
GameLevel? getEasiestLevel(List<GameLevel> levels) {
  GameLevel? easiestLevel = null;
  Int? highestMinScore = null;
  for (GameLevel level in levels) {
    Int minScore = minValue(level.getAllScores());    <-- Resolved to Int.MAX_VALUE if there are no scores
    if (highestMinScore == null || minScore > highestMinScore) {
      easiestLevel = level;
      highestMinScore = minScore;
    }
  }
  return easiestLevel;    <-- If a level has no scores, then it's returned.
}
```

There are a couple of other ways in which `Int.MAX_VALUE` might be problematic:

- `Int.MAX_VALUE` is often specific to the programming language being used. If the `minValue()` function lives inside a Java server, and the response is sent to a client-side application written in JavaScript, then the significance of the value will not be so obvious: `Integer.MAX_VALUE` (in Java) is a very different number to `Number.MAX_SAFE_INTEGER` (in JavaScript).
- If the output of the function were saved to a database, then it might cause a lot of confusion and problems to anyone running queries or to other systems that read the database.

It would be better to just return null, an empty optional, or signal some kind of error from the `minValue()` function so that callers are aware that the value may not be calculable for some inputs. If we go with returning null, this places an extra burden on the caller because they have to write logic to handle it. But it removes another burden from them: having to remember to check if the list is empty before calling `minValue()` and running the risk of buggy code if they don't. The following listing shows what the `minValue()` function might look like if it were to return null for an empty list.

Listing 6.8 Returning a null for an empty list

```
Int? minValue(List<Int> values) {
  if (values.isEmpty()) {
    return null;    <-- If the values list is empty, then null is returned.
  }
  Int minValue = Int.MAX_VALUE;
  for (Int value in values) {
    minValue = Math.min(value, minValue);
  }
  return minValue;
}
```

Returning a magic value is sometimes a conscious decision made by an engineer, but it can also sometimes happen by accident. Regardless of the reason, magic values can easily cause surprises, so it's good to be vigilant for scenarios where they can occur. Returning null, optional, or using an error-signaling technique are simple and effective alternatives.

NOTE: USE AN APPROPRIATE LANGUAGE FEATURE The `minValue()` example is used to demonstrate a general point about returning magic values. If we need to find the minimum value in a list of integers, then there is likely a language feature or existing utility that does this. If there is, then it's probably better to use that rather than hand rolling our own function.

6.2 Use the null object pattern appropriately

The *null object pattern* is an alternative to returning null (or an empty optional) when a value can't be obtained. The idea is that instead of returning null, a valid value is returned that will cause any downstream logic to behave in an innocuous way. The simplest forms of this are returning an empty string or an empty list, while more elaborate forms involve implementing a whole class where every member function either does nothing or returns a default value.

The null object pattern was mentioned briefly in chapter 4 when talking about errors. Chapter 4 showed why it's often a bad idea to use the null object pattern to hide the fact that an error has occurred. Outside of error handling, the null object pattern can be quite useful, but if used inappropriately it can cause nasty surprises and subtle bugs that are hard to find.

The examples in this section contrast the null object pattern with returning null. If you're using a language that doesn't offer null safety, then an optional return type can usually be used in place of a safe null.

6.2.1 Returning an empty collection can improve code

When a function returns a collection (such as a list, a set, or an array), it's sometimes possible that the values in the collection cannot be acquired. This may be because they've not been set or may not be applicable in a given scenario. One approach would be to return a null when this happens.

Listing 6.9 shows some code to check if an HTML element is highlighted. It does this by calling the `getClassNames()` function and checking if the "highlighted" class is in the set of classes on the element. The `getClassNames()` function returns null if the element doesn't have a "class" attribute. This means that the `isElementHighlighted()` function needs to check if the set of class names is null before using it.

Listing 6.9 Returning null

```
Set<String>? getClassNames(HtmlElement element) {
  String? attribute = element.getAttribute("class");
  if (attribute == null) {
    return null;                                  <-- Returns null if no class
  }                                                   attribute on the element
  return new Set(attribute.split(" "));
}
...

Boolean isElementHighlighted(HtmlElement element) {
  Set<String>? classNames = getClassNames(element);
```

```
  if (classNames == null) {
    return false;
  }
  return classNames.contains("highlighted");
}
```

Need to check if classNames is null before using it

Someone might argue that there is a benefit to the `getClassNames()` function returning a nullable type: it distinguishes between the scenario of the "class" attribute not having been set (null returned) and having been explicitly set to nothing (empty set returned). But this is a subtle distinction, which in most cases is probably more confusing than it is useful. The layer of abstraction being provided by the `getClassNames()` function should also be aiming to hide these implementation details about element attributes.

Returning a nullable type also forces every caller of `getClassNames()` to check if the returned value is null before using it. This adds more clutter to the code without much benefit, because it's very unlikely that any caller would care about distinguishing between the class attribute not having been set and it having been set to an empty string.

This is a scenario where the null object pattern can improve the code. The `getClassNames()` function can instead return an empty set if there is no class attribute on the element. This means that callers never have to handle a null value. Listing 6.10 shows the code modified to use the null object pattern by returning an empty set. The `isElementHighlighted()` function is now considerably simpler and more succinct.

Listing 6.10 Returning an empty set

```
Set<String> getClassNames(HtmlElement element) {
  String? attribute = element.getAttribute("class");
  if (attribute == null) {
    return new Set();                          <-- Returns an empty set if no
  }                                                class attribute on the element
  return new Set(attribute.split(" "));
}
...

Boolean isElementHighlighted(HtmlElement element) {
  return getClassNames(element).contains("highlighted");    <-- No need to check
}                                                               for a null
```

This is an example of the null object pattern improving code quality. It simplifies the logic of callers and is very unlikely to cause a nasty surprise. But in more complicated scenarios, the risk of causing a nasty surprise with the null object pattern can start to outweigh the benefits. The following subsections explain why.

> **NOTE: NULL POINTER EXCEPTIONS** A more old-school argument for using the null object pattern is to minimize the chance of causing `NullPointerExceptions`, `NullReferenceExceptions`, and alike. If using a language with unsafe nulls, then returning null always carries a risk because callers may

not bother to check for null before using a value. As long as we are using null safety or optionals (if we don't have null safety), this argument is largely obsolete. But it still has some relevance if we're looking at legacy code that uses unsafe nulls.

6.2.2 Returning an empty string can sometimes be problematic

The previous subsection showed how returning an empty collection instead of a null can improve code quality. Some engineers advocate that this should also apply to strings, whereby an empty string should be returned instead of a null. The appropriateness of this depends on how a string is being used. In some cases a string is nothing more than a collection of characters, and in this scenario returning an empty string instead of a null might well be sensible. When a string has some meaning beyond this, it starts to become less of a good idea. To demonstrate this, consider the following scenarios.

A STRING AS A COLLECTION OF CHARACTERS

When a string is just a collection of characters and has no intrinsic meaning to the code then using the null object pattern when the string is absent is generally fine. In the case of a string, this means returning an empty string instead of returning null when the value is not available. When a string has no intrinsic meaning, the distinction between it being null or an empty string is very unlikely to matter to any caller.

Listing 6.11 demonstrates this with a function to access any free-form comments entered by a user when providing feedback. It is very unlikely that there is any useful distinction to be made between the user having not entered any comments and them having explicitly entered an empty string. The function therefore returns an empty string if no comments have been provided.

Listing 6.11 Returning an empty string

```
class UserFeedback {
  private String? additionalComments;
  ...

  String getAdditionalComments() {
    if (additionalComments == null) {
      return "";                          // Returns an empty string if no comments entered
    }
    return additionalComments;
  }
}
```

A STRING AS AN ID

A string is not always just a collection of characters. It can often have a specific meaning that matters to the code in some way. A common example of this is when a string is used as an ID. In this scenario, it can often be important to know if the string is absent, as this may affect what logic needs to run. It's therefore important to make sure that any callers to a function are made explicitly aware that the string can be absent.

To demonstrate this, listing 6.12 shows a class to represent a payment. It contains a nullable field called `cardTransactionId`. If the payment involved a card transaction, then this field will contain an ID for that transaction. If the payment did not involve a card transaction, then this field will be null. Clearly the `cardTransactionId` string is not just a collection of characters: it has a specific meaning, and it being null signifies something important.

In this code example, the `getCardTransactionId()` function uses the null object pattern by returning an empty string if `cardTransactionId` is null. This is asking for trouble because engineers might see that the field is non-nullable and assume that there is always a link to a card transaction. A business using this code might end up with inaccurate accounting data when engineers fail to properly handle scenarios where payments don't involve card transactions.

Listing 6.12 Returning an empty string for an ID

```
class Payment {
  private final String? cardTransactionId;     // cardTransactionId can be null.
  ...

  String getCardTransactionId() {     // The function signature does not indicate that the ID can be absent.
    if (cardTransactionId == null) {
      return "";     // An empty string is returned if cardTransactionId is null.
    }
    return cardTransactionId;
  }
}
```

It would be much better if the `getCardTransactionId()` function instead returned null when `cardTransactionId` is null. This makes it clear to callers that the payment may not involve a card transaction and avoids surprises. If this were done, then the code would instead look like the following listing.

Listing 6.13 Returning null for an ID

```
class Payment {
  private final String? cardTransactionId;
  ...

  String? getCardTransactionId() {     // The function signature makes it clear that the ID can be absent.
    return cardTransactionId;
  }
}
```

6.2.3 More complicated null objects can cause surprises

Imagine you want to buy a new smartphone. You go to the electronics store and tell the store assistant which model you'd like to buy. They sell you a sealed box that looks exactly like it should contain a shiny new phone inside. You go home, unwrap the cellophane, open the box, and find that there is nothing inside. This is surprising and annoying, and depending on why you need a new phone, this might have even worse ramifications: you might now miss an important work call or message from a friend.

In this scenario, the store had sold out of the phone you wanted. Instead of telling you this and letting you either go to another store or pick a different model, the store assistant kept quiet and sold you an empty box. If we're not careful with how we use the null object pattern, it can easily become analogous to this scenario. We are essentially selling callers of our function an empty box. If there's any chance that they will be surprised or annoyed to receive an empty box, then it's probably best to avoid the null object pattern.

A more complicated form of the null object pattern might involve constructing a whole class with some supposedly innocuous values. Listing 6.14 contains two classes: one to represent a coffee mug and one to represent an inventory of coffee mugs. The `CoffeeMugInventory` class contains a function to get a random coffee mug from the inventory. If there are no coffee mugs in the inventory, then it's obviously impossible to get a random one. When this happens the `getRandomMug()` function constructs and returns a zero-size coffee mug instead of returning null. This is another example of the null object pattern, but in this scenario it could very easily cause surprises for callers. Anyone who calls `getRandomMug()` and receives what looks like a mug will assume they have a valid mug from the inventory, when in fact they may not.

Listing 6.14 A surprising null-object

```
class CoffeeMug {                  <-- CoffeeMug class
  ...
  CoffeeMug(Double diameter, Double height) { ... }

  Double getDiameter() { ... }
  Double getHeight() { ... }
}

class CoffeeMugInventory {
  private final List<CoffeeMug> mugs;
  ...
  CoffeeMug getRandomMug() {
    if (mugs.isEmpty()) {
      return new CoffeeMug(diameter: 0.0, height: 0.0);   <-- Constructs and returns a zero-size coffee mug when no mugs are available
    }
    return mugs[Math.randomInt(0, mugs.size())];
  }
}
```

For some callers, getting a zero-size coffee mug might meet their needs, and it saves them having to check for a null, but for other callers this might cause a serious bug that would occur silently. Imagine if a consulting firm had been paid a large sum of money to produce a report on the distribution of coffee mug sizes and they were using this code. They might report severely incorrect findings due to all these zero-size coffee mugs that appeared in their data set without anyone noticing.

The author of the code in listing 6.14 no doubt has good intentions; they're trying to make life easier for callers of the `getRandomMug()` function by not forcing them to handle a null. But unfortunately this creates a situation that is potentially surprising, because a caller to the function is given the false impression that they will always get a valid `CoffeeMug` back.

It would probably be better to simply return null from `getRandomMug()` when there are no mugs from which to select a random one. This makes it unmistakably obvious in the code's contract that the function may not return a valid mug and leaves no room for surprise when this does in fact happen. The following listing shows what the `getRandomMug()` function looks like if it returns null.

Listing 6.15 Returning null

```
CoffeeMug? getRandomMug(List<CoffeeMug> mugs) {
  if (mugs.isEmpty()) {
    return null;                                    <-- Returns null if a random coffee
  }                                                     mug cannot be acquired
  return mugs[Math.randomInt(0, mugs.size())];
}
```

6.2.4 A null object implementation can cause surprises

Some engineers take the null object pattern a step further and define dedicated null object implementations of interfaces or classes. One of the motivations for this can be when an interface or class has some functions that *do something* rather than just those that return something.

Listing 6.16 contains an interface to represent a coffee mug along with two implementations: `CoffeeMugImpl` and `NullCoffeeMug`. `NullCoffeeMug` is a null object implementation of `CoffeeMug`. It implements all the functions of the `CoffeeMug` interface but returns zero when `getDiameter()` or `getHeight()` are called. In this example `CoffeeMug` now also has a function that does something: `reportMugBroken()`. This can be used to update a record of which mugs are broken. The `NullCoffeeMug` implementation simply does nothing if this function is called.

Listing 6.16 Null-object implementation

```
interface CoffeeMug {                  <-- CoffeeMug
  Double getDiameter();                    interface
  Double getHeight();
  void reportMugBroken();
}
                                                      Normal implementation
class CoffeeMugImpl implements CoffeeMug {      <--  of CoffeeMug
  ...
  override Double getDiameter() { return diameter; }
  override Double getHeight() { return height; }
  override void reportMugBroken() { ... }
}
```

```
class NullCoffeeMug implements CoffeeMug {
  override Double getDiameter() { return 0.0; }
  override Double getHeight() { return 0.0; }
  override void reportMugBroken() {
    // Do nothing
  }
}
```

Null object implementation of CoffeeMug

Functions that should return something return zero.

Functions that should do something instead do nothing.

Listing 6.17 demonstrates what the `getRandomMug()` function (which we previously saw) looks like if it returns a `NullCoffeeMug` when there are no mugs. This achieves more or less the same thing as the previous example that constructed and returned a zero-size coffee mug. And it suffers from the same set of problems and can still easily cause a surprise.

Listing 6.17 Returning NullCoffeeMug

```
CoffeeMug getRandomMug(List<CoffeeMug> mugs) {
  if (mugs.isEmpty()) {
    return new NullCoffeeMug();
  }
  return mugs[Math.randomInt(0, mugs.size())];
}
```

Returns NullCoffeeMug if a random coffee mug cannot be acquired

One slight improvement with returning a `NullCoffeeMug` is that callers can now check if they have a null object by checking if the return value is an instance of `NullCoffeeMug`. This is not much of an improvement though, as it's not at all clear to callers that they might want to check this. Even if the caller is aware, requiring them to check if a value is an instance of `NullCoffeeMug` is kind of clunky and probably worse than just checking for a null (which is a much more common and less surprising paradigm).

The null object pattern can manifest in many forms. It's worth consciously recognizing when we use it or encounter it and thinking about whether it's really appropriate or likely to cause surprises. The rise in popularity of null safety and optionals has made it a lot easier and safer to explicitly signal that a value is absent. And with this, many of the original arguments for using the null object pattern are less compelling these days.

6.3 Avoid causing unexpected side effects

A *side effect* is any state that a function modifies outside of itself when called. If a function has any effects other than just via the value it returns, then it has side effects. Common types of side effects are the following:

- Displaying an output to the user
- Saving something to a file or database
- Causing some network traffic by calling another system
- Updating or invalidating a cache

Side effects are an inevitable part of writing software. A piece of software with no side effects would likely be pointless: at some point it needs to output something to a user, database, or another system. This means that at least some parts of the code need to have side effects. When a side effect is expected and what a caller to a piece of code wants, then it is fine, but when a side effect is unexpected, it can cause a surprise and lead to bugs.

One of the best ways to avoid causing an unexpected side effect is to not cause a side effect in the first place. The examples in this section and section 6.4 will discuss this. But making classes immutable is also a great way to minimize the potential for side effects, and this will be covered in chapter 7. For the cases where a side effect is part of the desired functionality or cannot be avoided, it's important to make sure callers know about it.

6.3.1 *Side effects that are obvious and intentional are fine*

As was just mentioned, side effects are often required at some point in a piece of code. Listing 6.18 shows a class for managing a user display. The `displayErrorMessage()` function causes a side effect: it updates the canvas that is displayed to the user. But given that the class is called `UserDisplay` and the function is called `displayErrorMessage()`, it's completely obvious that this will cause this side effect. There is no room for surprise.

Listing 6.18 An expected side-effect

```
class UserDisplay {
  private final Canvas canvas;
  ...

  void displayErrorMessage(String message) {
    canvas.drawText(message, Color.RED);      <-- Side effect: canvas is updated.
  }
}
```

The `displayErrorMessage()` function is an example of causing an obvious and intentional side effect. Updating the canvas with an error message is the exact thing that a caller wants, and expects, to happen. Functions with side effects that a caller would not necessarily expect or want, on the other hand, can be problematic. The following subsections discuss this.

6.3.2 *Unexpected side effects can be problematic*

When the purpose of a function is to get or read a value, other engineers will generally assume that it won't cause a side effect. Listing 6.19 shows a function to get the color at a particular pixel in a user display. This seems like the kind of thing that should be relatively straightforward and not have any side effects. Unfortunately this is not the case; before reading the pixel color, the `getPixel()` function causes a redraw event on the canvas. This is a side effect, and for anyone not familiar with the implementation of the `getPixel()` function it will be unexpected.

Listing 6.19 An unexpected side effect

```
class UserDisplay {
  private final Canvas canvas;
  ...

  Color getPixel(Int x, Int y) {
    canvas.redraw();                          <-- Triggering a redraw event is a side effect.
    PixelData data = canvas.getPixel(x, y);
    return new Color(
        data.getRed(),
        data.getGreen(),
        data.getBlue());
  }
}
```

There are a few ways in which an unexpected side effect like this can be problematic. The next few subsections will explore some of these.

SIDE EFFECTS CAN BE EXPENSIVE

Calling `canvas.redraw()` is potentially quite an expensive operation and may also cause the display to flicker for the user. An engineer calling `getPixel()` would likely not expect it to be an expensive operation or cause a user-visible issue: nothing about the `getPixel()` function's name suggests this. But if it is expensive and can cause a flicker, then it could cause some quite nasty functionality that most users would interpret as a horrible bug.

Imagine if a feature were added to the application to allow a user to take a screenshot of the display. Listing 6.20 shows how this might be implemented. The `captureScreenshot()` function reads pixels one by one by calling the `getPixel()` function. This causes `canvas.redraw()` to be called for every single pixel in the screenshot. Let's say a single redraw event takes 10 milliseconds and the user display is 400 × 700 pixels (or 280,000 pixels in total). Capturing a screenshot will cause the application to freeze and flicker for 47 minutes. Nearly every user would interpret this as the application having crashed and would likely restart it, potentially losing unsaved work.

Listing 6.20 Capturing a screenshot

```
class UserDisplay {
  private final Canvas canvas;
  ...
  Color getPixel(Int x, Int y) { ... }        <-- Takes approximately 10 ms to run due to the side effect
  ...

  Image captureScreenshot() {
    Image image = new Image(
        canvas.getWidth(), canvas.getHeight());
```

```
    for (Int x = 0; x < image.getWidth(); ++x) {
      for (Int y = 0; y < image.getHeight(); ++y) {
        image.setPixel(x, y, getPixel(x, y));     <-- getPixel() is called
      }                                               many times.
    }
    return image;
  }
}
```

BREAKING AN ASSUMPTION THE CALLER HAS MADE

Even if redrawing the canvas is cheap, a function with the name `captureScreenshot()` doesn't sound like it will cause a side effect, so most engineers calling it will probably assume that it doesn't. The fact that this assumption is wrong could potentially cause a bug.

Listing 6.21 shows a function to capture a redacted screenshot. This deletes any regions of the canvas that contain the user's personal information and then calls `captureScreenshot()`. The function is used to capture an anonymized screenshot whenever a user gives feedback or files a bug report. Deleting areas of the canvas will clear those pixels until the next call to `canvas.redraw()`.

The author of the `captureRedactedScreenshot()` function has assumed that `canvas.redraw()` will not be called by `captureScreenshot()`. Unfortunately this assumption is wrong, because `captureScreenshot()` calls `getPixel()`, which in turn calls `canvas.redraw()`. This means that the redaction functionality is completely broken and personal information will be sent in feedback reports. This is a serious breach of user privacy and a severe bug.

Listing 6.21 Capturing a redacted screenshot

```
class UserDisplay {
  private final Canvas canvas;
  ...                                          Causes a side effect by
                                               calling canvas.redraw()
  Color getPixel(Int x, Int y) { ... }     <--
                                               Indirectly causes a side
  Image captureScreenshot() { ... }        <-- effect by calling getPixel()

  List<Box> getPrivacySensitiveAreas() { ... }  <-- Returns any areas of the canvas
                                                    containing personal user information
  Image captureRedactedScreenshot() {
    for (Box area in getPrivacySensitiveAreas()) {
      canvas.delete(                               Deletes any pixels containing
          area.getX(), area.getY(),                personal user information
          area.getWidth(), area.getHeight());
    }
    Image screenshot = captureScreenshot();      <-- Screenshot
    canvas.redraw();          <--                    is captured
    return screenshot;        Intentional clean-up: the only
  }                           place that the author thinks
}                             canvas.redraw() is being called
```

BUGS IN MULTITHREADED CODE

If a program needs to perform multiple tasks relatively independently of one another, a common way of achieving this is to run each task in its own *thread*. The computer can then quickly switch back and forth between the tasks by repeatedly *preempting* and *resuming* threads in turns. This is known as *multithreading*. Because different threads can often have access to the same data, a side effect caused by one thread can sometimes cause problems for another thread.

Imagine that another piece of functionality in the application allows a user to live-share their screen with a friend. This might be implemented by having another thread that periodically captures a screenshot and sends this to the friend. If more than one thread calls `captureScreenshot()` at the same time, then the screenshots may be broken because one thread might be redrawing the canvas while the other thread is trying to read it. Figure 6.1 illustrates this by showing how two calls to `getPixel()` from two separate threads might interact.

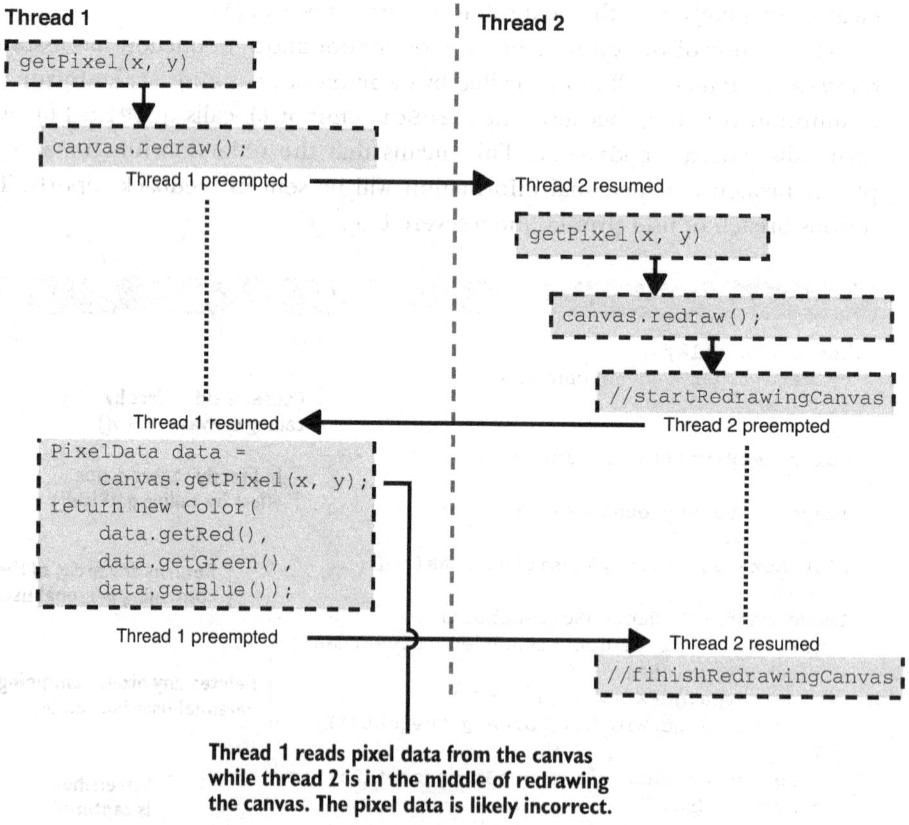

Figure 6.1 Code with side effects can often be problematic if it's ever run in a multithreaded environment and the author has not taken active steps to make it thread safe (such as using a lock).

The chance of a multithreading issue occurring on an individual call to a function is usually quite low. But when a function is being called thousands (or even millions) of times, the cumulative chance of it happening becomes quite high. Bugs related to multithreading issues are also notoriously hard to debug and test for.

An engineer who sees a function named `captureScreenshot()` or `getPixel()`, will not expect either of them to have side effects that might break code running in another thread. Writing code that doesn't behave well in a multithreaded environment can introduce a particularly nasty set of surprises. Debugging and resolving them can waste a lot of engineers' time. It's much better to either avoid side effects or else make them obvious.

6.3.3 Solution: Avoid a side effect or make it obvious

The first question that we should ask is whether calling `canvas.redraw()` before reading a pixel is necessary. This might just be some overly cautious code that hasn't been properly thought through. And not having a side effect in the first place is the best way to avoid causing surprises. If the call to `canvas.redraw()` is not needed, then we should just remove, it meaning the problems go away.

If calling `canvas.redraw()` before reading a pixel is necessary, then the `getPixel()` function should be renamed to make this side effect obvious. A better name would be something like `redrawAndGetPixel()`, so that it's unmistakably obvious that this function has the side effect of causing a redraw event. The following listing shows this.

Listing 6.22 A more informative name

```
class UserDisplay {
  private final Canvas canvas;
  ...

  Color redrawAndGetPixel(Int x, Int y) {    <-- Function name makes side effect obvious
    canvas.redraw();
    PixelData data = canvas.getPixel(x, y);
    return new Color(
        data.getRed(),
        data.getGreen(),
        data.getBlue());
  }
}
```

This is a very simple change to make and emphasizes the power of naming things well. An engineer calling the `redrawAndGetPixel()` function is now forced to notice that it has a side effect and will cause a redraw event. This goes a long way toward solving the three issues we saw in the previous subsection:

- A redraw sounds like the kind of thing that might be expensive, so the author of the `captureScreenshot()` function would probably think twice before calling `redrawAndGetPixel()` thousands of times inside a for-loop. This alerts them that they probably want to implement their function in a different way, such as performing a single redraw and then reading all the pixels in one go.

- If the author of the `captureScreenshot()` function also named it to make the side effect obvious, then they might name it something like `redrawAndCaptureScreenshot()`. It's now quite hard for an engineer to make the erroneous assumption that this doesn't cause a redraw event, since the name of the function directly contradicts this.
- If a function is called `redrawAndCaptureScreenshot()`, then the engineer implementing the screen-sharing feature would immediately be aware of the dangers of calling it from a multithreaded environment. They would obviously have to do some work to make it safe (like using a lock), but this is much better than them being oblivious to this fact and it causing a nasty surprise.

Most functions that get a piece of information don't cause side effects, so an engineer's natural mental model is to assume that such a function will not cause one. The onus is therefore on the author of a function that causes a side effect to make this fact unmistakably obvious to any callers. Not causing a side effect in the first place is the best way to avoid a surprise, but this is not always practical. When a side effect is unavoidable, naming things appropriately can be a very effective way to make it obvious.

6.4 Beware of mutating input parameters

The previous section discussed how unexpected side effects can be problematic. This section discusses a specific type of side effect: a function mutating an input parameter. This can be a particularly common source of surprises and bugs and is thus worthy of a section in its own right.

6.4.1 Mutating an input parameter can lead to bugs

If you lend a book to a friend and they return it with some pages ripped out and notes scribbled all over the margins, you'll probably be quite annoyed. You might be intending to read the book yourself or lend it to another friend, and you'll have a nasty surprise when you eventually realize that the book has been vandalized. A friend who rips pages out and scribbles over the margins of a book that you lend to them is probably a bad friend.

Passing an object to another function as an input is a bit like lending a book to a friend. There's some information within that object that the other function needs, but it's also quite likely that the object might still be needed for other things after this function call. If a function modifies an input parameter there's a real risk that it's doing the code equivalent of ripping pages out and scribbling over the margins. Callers will generally pass the function an object on the understanding that the object is being borrowed. If the function vandalizes the object in the process, it's a bit like a bad friend.

Modifying (or mutating) an input parameter is another example of a side effect because the function is affecting something outside of itself. It's conventional for functions to take (or borrow) inputs via parameters and provide results via return values. To most engineers, mutating an input parameter is therefore an unexpected side effect and is likely to cause a surprise.

Listing 6.23 demonstrates how mutating an input parameter can lead to surprises and bugs. The listing shows some code to process orders for a company selling online services. The company offers a free trial to new users. The `processOrders()` function does two things: sends out billable invoices and then enables the ordered services for each user.

The `getBillableInvoices()` function determines which invoices are billable. An invoice is billable if the user does not have a free trial. Unfortunately, in calculating this, `getBillableInvoices()` mutates one of its input parameters (the `userInvoices` map) by removing all entries for users with a free trial. This causes a bug in the code, because `processOrders()` later reuses the `userInvoices` map to enable the services users have ordered. This means that no services are enabled for any users with a free trial.

Listing 6.23 Mutating an input parameter

```
List<Invoice> getBillableInvoices(
    Map<User, Invoice> userInvoices,
    Set<User> usersWithFreeTrial) {
  userInvoices.removeAll(usersWithFreeTrial);    <-- Mutates userInvoices by removing all entries for users with a free trial
  return userInvoices.values();
}

void processOrders(OrderBatch orderBatch) {
  Map<User, Invoice> userInvoices =
      orderBatch.getUserInvoices();
  Set<User> usersWithFreeTrial =
      orderBatch.getFreeTrialUsers();

  sendInvoices(
      getBillableInvoices(userInvoices, usersWithFreeTrial));    <-- getBillableInvoices() unexpectedly mutates userInvoices.
  enableOrderedServices(userInvoices);    <-- Services will not be enabled for users with a free trial.
}

void enableOrderedServices(Map<User, Invoice> userInvoices) {
  ...
}
```

This bug stems from the fact that the `getBillableInvoices()` function mutates the map of user invoices (a bit like a bad friend ripping pages out of a borrowed book). It would be much better if this function were changed so that it did not modify the input parameter.

6.4.2 *Solution: Copy things before mutating them*

If a set of values contained within an input parameter really need to be mutated, then it's often best to copy them into a new data structure before performing any mutations. This prevents the original object from being changed. The following listing shows what the `getBillableInvoices()` function would look like if it did this.

Listing 6.24 Not mutating an input parameter

```
List<Invoice> getBillableInvoices(
    Map<User, Invoice> userInvoices,
    Set<User> usersWithFreeTrial) {
  return userInvoices
      .entries()
      .filter(entry ->
          !usersWithFreeTrial.contains(entry.getKey()))
      .map(entry -> entry.getValue());
}
```

Gets a list of all key–value pairs in the userInvoices map

filter() copies any values matching the condition into a new list.

Copying values can obviously affect the performance of code (in terms of memory usage, CPU usage, or both). This is often the lesser of two evils when compared to the surprises and bugs that can result from mutating an input parameter. But if a piece of code is likely to handle very large amounts of data or is likely to run on low-end hardware, then mutating an input parameter may become a necessary evil. A common example of this is sorting a list or an array. The number of values could potentially be quite large, and it can be a lot more efficient to sort it in place rather than create a copy. If we do need to mutate an input parameter for a performance reason like this, then it's good to make sure that our function name (and any documentation) make it clear that this will happen.

NOTE: MUTATING PARAMETERS IS SOMETIMES COMMON In some languages and codebases, mutating parameters to a function can be quite commonplace. In C++, a lot of code utilizes the concept of output parameters, as returning class-like objects from functions in an efficient and safe manner used to be tricky. C++ now has features that make output parameters less commonplace in new code (such as the move semantic). Just be aware that in some languages mutating a parameter is more expected than in others.

NOTE: BEING DEFENSIVE This section talked about making sure that the code we write behaves nicely and doesn't "vandalize" objects that belong to other code. The flip side of this is defending objects that our code owns against other code vandalizing them. Chapter 7 will discuss making objects immutable, which can be an effective way to achieve this.

6.5 Avoid writing misleading functions

When an engineer encounters some code that calls a function, they will form an idea of what is happening based on what they see. The unmistakably obvious parts of the code contract (such as names) will often be the main things an engineer notices when glancing at some code.

As we've already seen in this chapter, if things are missing from the unmistakably obvious parts of the code contract, it can cause surprises. What can be even worse, however, is if the unmistakably obvious parts of the code contract are actively misleading. If we see a function named `displayLegalDisclaimer()` we will assume that calling it will display a legal disclaimer. If that's not always the case, it can easily lead to surprising behavior and bugs.

6.5.1 Doing nothing when a critical input is missing can cause surprises

A function can be misleading about what it does if it allows itself to be called with an absent parameter and then does nothing when that parameter is absent. Callers may not be aware of the significance of calling the function without providing a value for that parameter, and anyone reading the code may be misled into thinking that the function call always does something.

Listing 6.25 shows some code to show a legal disclaimer in a user display. The `displayLegalDisclaimer()` function takes some legal text as a parameter and displays this in an overlay. The `legalText` parameter can be null, and when it is, the `displayLegalDisclaimer()` function returns without displaying anything to the user.

Listing 6.25 Nullable but critical parameter

```
class UserDisplay {
  private final LocalizedMessages messages;
  ...

  void displayLegalDisclaimer(String? legalText) {    <-- legalText can be null.
    if (legalText == null) {        <-- When legalText is null, the function
      return;                           returns without displaying anything.
    }
    displayOverlay(
        title: messages.getLegalDisclaimerTitle(),
        message: legalText,
        textColor: Color.RED);
  }
}

class LocalizedMessages {    <-- Contains messages translated into
  ...                            the user's local language
  String getLegalDisclaimerTitle();
  ...
}
```

Why accept null and then do nothing?

You may wonder why anyone would write a function like the one in listing 6.25. The answer is that engineers sometimes do this to avoid callers having to check for a null before calling a function (as demonstrated in the following snippet). Their intentions are good: they are trying to unburden callers, but unfortunately it can result in misleading and surprising code.

```
...
  String? message = getMessage();
  if (message != null) {    <-- If the displayLegalDisclaimer()
                                function doesn't accept a null, then
                                callers must check for a null.
    userDisplay.displayLegalDisclaimer(message);
  }
...
```

To understand why code like this can cause surprises, it's necessary to think about what the code will look like when the `displayLegalDisclaimer()` function is called. Imagine that a company is implementing a user signup flow for a service. There are a couple of very important requirements that the code for this needs to fulfill:

- Before a user can sign up, the company is legally obliged to show them a legal disclaimer in their local language.
- If a legal disclaimer cannot be displayed in the user's local language, then the signup should be aborted. Continuing would potentially break the law.

We'll look at the full implementation in a moment, but first let's concentrate on the function that is meant to ensure these requirements are met: `ensureLegalCompliance()` (shown in the following snippet). An engineer reading this code would likely conclude that a legal disclaimer is always displayed. This is because `userDisplay.displayLegalDisclaimer()` is always called and nothing in the unmistakably obvious part of its contract suggests that it sometimes does nothing.

```
void ensureLegalCompliance() {
  userDisplay.displayLegalDisclaimer(
      messages.getSignupDisclaimer());
}
```

Unlike most engineers reading this code, we happen to be familiar with the implementation details of `userDisplay.displayLegalDisclaimer()` because we saw them earlier (in listing 6.25), so we know that if it's called with a null value it will do nothing. Listing 6.26 shows the full implementation of the signup flow logic. We can now see that `messages.getSignupDisclaimer()` can sometimes return null. This means that, in fact, the `ensureLegalCompliance()` function will not always ensure that all legal requirements have been met. The company using this code might well be breaking the law.

Listing 6.26 Misleading code

```
class SignupFlow {
  private final UserDisplay userDisplay;
  private final LocalizedMessages messages;
  ...

  void ensureLegalCompliance() {
    userDisplay.displayLegalDisclaimer(        // Code appears to always display the
        messages.getSignupDisclaimer());       // disclaimer. In reality it does not.
  }
}

class LocalizedMessages {
  ...
  // Returns null if no translation is available in the
  // user's language, because using a default language
  // for specific legal text may not be compliant.
```

```
  String? getSignupDisclaimer() { ... }    <-- Returns null if no translation
  ...                                          available in the user's language
}
```

A big part of the problem here is that the UserDisplay.displayLegal-Disclaimer() function accepts a nullable value and then does nothing when it is null. Anyone reading a piece of code that calls displayLegalDisclaimer() will think, "Oh great, the disclaimer is definitely displayed." In reality they'd have to know that it's not being called with a null value for that to be true. The next subsection explains how we can avoid a potential surprise like this.

6.5.2 Solution: Make critical inputs required

Making a critical parameter nullable means that callers don't have to check for a null value before calling. This can make the caller's code more succinct, but unfortunately it can also make the caller's code misleading. This is generally not a good trade-off: the caller's code becomes slightly shorter, but in the process the potential for confusion and bugs is greatly increased.

A parameter is critical to a function if the function can't do what it says it does without that parameter. If we have such a parameter, it can often be safer to make it required so that it's impossible to call the function if the value is not available.

Listing 6.27 shows the displayLegalDisclaimer() function modified so that it only accepts a non-null parameter. A call to displayLegalDisclaimer() is now guaranteed to display a legal disclaimer. Any callers of displayLegalDisclaimer() are forced to confront the fact that if they don't have any legal text, they can't display a disclaimer.

Listing 6.27 Required critical parameter

```
class UserDisplay {
  private final LocalizedMessages messages;
  ...

  void displayLegalDisclaimer(String legalText) {    <-- legalText cannot be null.
    displayOverlay(
        title: messages.getLegalDisclaimerTitle(),
        message: legalText,                          <-- A disclaimer will always be displayed.
        textColor: Color.RED);
  }
}
```

The code in the ensureLegalCompliance() function is now forced to be a lot less misleading. The author of the code will realize that they have to handle the scenario where there is no translation. Listing 6.28 shows how the code for the ensureLegal-Compliance() function might now look. It has to now check if the localized legal text is available, and if it is not it signals that compliance could not be ensured by returning false. The function is also annotated with @CheckReturnValue to ensure that the return value is not ignored (as covered in chapter 4).

Listing 6.28 Unambiguous code

```
class SignupFlow {
  private final UserDisplay userDisplay;
  private final LocalizedMessages messages;
  ...

  // Returns false if compliance could not be ensured
  // meaning that signup should be abandoned. Returns true
  // if compliance has been ensured.
  @CheckReturnValue
  Boolean ensureLegalCompliance() {
    String? signupDisclaimer = messages.getSignupDisclaimer();
    if (signupDisclaimer == null) {
      return false;
    }
    userDisplay.displayLegalDisclaimer(signupDisclaimer);
    return true;
  }
}
```

- Ensures that the return value is not ignored (`@CheckReturnValue`)
- Returns a Boolean to indicate if compliance was ensured (`Boolean ensureLegalCompliance()`)
- Returns false if compliance was not ensured (`return false;`)
- A call to displayLegalDisclaimer() will always display a disclaimer. (`userDisplay.displayLegalDisclaimer(signupDisclaimer);`)

Chapter 5 talked about why it's important not to fixate on the total number of lines of code at the expense of other aspects of code quality. Moving an if-null statement to the caller can increase the number of lines of code (especially if there are many callers), but it also reduces the chance of the code being misinterpreted or doing something surprising. The time and effort spent fixing even a single bug caused by some surprising code will likely be orders of magnitude higher than the time spent reading a few extra if-null statements. The benefits of code clarity and being unambiguous often far outweigh the costs of a few extra lines of code.

6.6 Future-proof enum handling

The examples so far in this chapter have concentrated on ensuring that callers of our code are not surprised by something it does or returns, in other words ensuring that code which depends on our code is correct and bug free. However, surprises can also occur if we make brittle assumptions about code that we depend on. This section demonstrates an example of this.

Enums cause some amount of disagreement among software engineers. Some argue that they are a great, simple way to provide type safety and avoid invalid inputs to functions or systems. Others argue that they prevent clean layers of abstraction because the logic for how to handle a specific enum value ends up being spread all over the place. Engineers in this latter group often argue that polymorphism is a better approach: encapsulate information and behaviors for each value inside a class dedicated to that value and then have all these classes implement a common interface.

Regardless of your personal opinions about enums, the likelihood is that you will come across them and have to handle them at some point. This might be because

- you have to consume the output of someone else's code and they really love enums for whatever reason, or

- you are consuming the output provided by another system. Enums can often be the only practical option in an over-the-wire data format.

When you do have to handle an enum, it's often important to remember that more values may be added to the enum in the future. If you write code that ignores this fact, then you may cause some nasty surprises for yourself or other engineers.

6.6.1 *Implicitly handling future enum values can be problematic*

Sometimes engineers look at the current set of values within an enum and think, "Oh great, I can handle that with an if-statement." This might work for the set of values that the enum currently has, but it's often not robust to more values being added in the future.

To demonstrate this, imagine a company has developed a model to predict what will happen if it pursues a given business strategy. Listing 6.29 contains the definition of the enum that indicates the prediction from the model. The listing also contains a function that consumes a model prediction and then indicates if it's a safe outcome. If `isOutcomeSafe()` returns true, then an automated system downstream of this will initiate the business strategy. If it returns false the business strategy will not be initiated.

Currently the `PredictedOutcome` enum contains only two values: `COMPANY_WILL_GO_BUST` and `COMPANY_WILL_MAKE_A_PROFIT`. The engineer writing the `isOutcomeSafe()` function has noticed that one of these outcomes is safe and the other is not and has thus decided to handle the enum using a simple if-statement. `isOutcomeSafe()` explicitly handles the `COMPANY_WILL_GO_BUST` case as not safe and implicitly handles all other enum values as being safe.

Listing 6.29 Implicit handling of enum values

```
enum PredictedOutcome {
  COMPANY_WILL_GO_BUST,            // Two enum values
  COMPANY_WILL_MAKE_A_PROFIT,
}

...

Boolean isOutcomeSafe(PredictedOutcome prediction) {
  if (prediction == PredictedOutcome.COMPANY_WILL_GO_BUST) {   // COMPANY_WILL_GO_BUST explicitly handled as not safe
    return false;
  }
  return true;                     // All other enum values implicitly handled as safe
}
```

The code in the previous listing works while there are only the two enum values. But things could go horribly wrong if someone were to introduce a new enum value. Imagine that the model and enum are now updated with a new potential outcome: `WORLD_WILL_END`. As the name suggests, this enum value indicates that the model predicts that the entire world will end if the company initiates the given business strategy. The enum definition now looks like the following listing.

Listing 6.30 A new enum value

```
enum PredictedOutcome {
  COMPANY_WILL_GO_BUST,
  COMPANY_WILL_MAKE_A_PROFIT,
  WORLD_WILL_END,                    <-- Value indicating that the
}                                        world is predicted to end
```

The isOutcomeSafe() function definition could be many hundreds of lines of code away from the enum definition or be in a completely different file or package. They may also be maintained by completely different teams. It's therefore not safe to assume that any engineer adding an enum value to PredictedOutcome would be aware of the need to also update the isOutcomeSafe() function.

If the isOutcomeSafe() function (repeated again in the following snippet) is not updated it will return true for the WORLD_WILL_END prediction, indicating that it's a safe outcome. Obviously WORLD_WILL_END is not a safe outcome, and it would be disastrous if the downstream system initiated any business strategy with this predicted outcome.

```
Boolean isOutcomeSafe(PredictedOutcome prediction) {
  if (prediction == PredictedOutcome.COMPANY_WILL_GO_BUST) {
    return false;
  }
  return true;              <-- Returns true if prediction
}                               is WORLD_WILL_END
```

The author of the isOutcomeSafe() function has ignored the fact that more enum values might be added in the future. As a result the code contains a brittle and unreliable assumption that could lead to a catastrophic outcome. It's unlikely that a real scenario would result in the world ending, but the consequences for an organization could still be severe if customer data were mismanaged or the wrong automated decisions were made.

6.6.2 Solution: Use an exhaustive switch statement

The problem with the code in the previous subsection is that the isOutcomeSafe() function is implicitly handling some enum values instead of doing it explicitly. A better approach would be to handle all known enum values explicitly and then ensure that either the code stops compiling or a test fails if a new unhandled enum value is added.

A common way to achieve this is using an exhaustive switch statement. Listing 6.31 shows what the isOutcomeSafe() function looks like if it uses this approach. If the switch statement ever completes without one of the cases matching, this indicates that an unhandled enum value has been encountered. If this happens, it means that there is a programming error: an engineer has failed to update the code in the isOutcomeSafe() function to handle the new enum value. This is signaled by throwing an unchecked exception to ensure that the code fails fast and fails loudly (as discussed in chapter 4).

Listing 6.31 An exhaustive switch statement

```
enum PredictedOutcome {
  COMPANY_WILL_GO_BUST,
  COMPANY_WILL_MAKE_A_PROFIT,
}

...

Boolean isOutcomeSafe(PredictedOutcome prediction) {
  switch (prediction) {
    case COMPANY_WILL_GO_BUST:              <-- Each enum value is
      return false;                             explicitly handled.
    case COMPANY_WILL_MAKE_A_PROFIT:        <--
      return true;
  }
  throw new UncheckedException(
      "Unhandled prediction: " + prediction);   <-- An unhandled enum value is a
}                                                   programming error, so an
                                                    unchecked exception is thrown.
```

This can be combined with a unit test that performs a call to the function with each potential enum value. If an exception is thrown for any value, then the test will fail, and an engineer adding a new value to `PredictedOutcome` will be made aware of the need to update the `isOutcomeSafe()` function. The following listing shows what this unit test might look like.

Listing 6.32 Unit testing all enum values

```
testIsOutcomeSafe_allPredictedOutcomeValues() {
  for (PredictedOutcome prediction in
      PredictedOutcome.values()) {           <-- Iterates through every
    isOutcomeSafe(prediction);     <--           value in the enum
  }                                     If an exception is thrown due to an
}                                       unhandled value, the test will fail.
```

Assuming that the `PredictedOutcome` enum definition and the `isOutcomeSafe()` function are part of the same codebase and that there are sufficient presubmit checks, the engineer is prevented from submitting their code until they update the `isOutcomeSafe()` function. This forces the engineer to notice the problem, and they will update the function to explicitly handle the `WORLD_WILL_END` value. The following listing shows the updated code.

Listing 6.33 Handling the new enum

```
Boolean isOutcomeSafe(PredictedOutcome prediction) {
  switch (prediction) {
    case COMPANY_WILL_GO_BUST:
```

```
    case WORLD_WILL_END:                    <-- WORLD_WILL_END enum
      return false;                             value explicitly handled
    case COMPANY_WILL_MAKE_A_PROFIT:
      return true;
  }
  throw new UncheckedException(
      "Unhandled prediction: " + prediction);
}
```

With the updated code, the `testIsOutcomeSafe_allPredictedOutcomeValues()` test passes again. If the engineer is doing their job properly, then they will also add an additional test case to ensure the `isOutcomeSafe()` function returns false for the `WORLD_WILL_END` prediction.

By using an exhaustive switch statement in combination with a unit test, a nasty surprise and a potentially catastrophic bug in the code have been avoided.

> **NOTE: COMPILE-TIME SAFETY** In some languages (e.g., C++), the compiler can produce a warning for a switch statement that doesn't exhaustively handle every enum value. If your team's build setup is configured so that warnings are treated as errors, then this can be a very effective way of immediately identifying an error like this. It's often still advisable to throw an exception (or fail fast in some way) for an unhandled value if it can come from another system. This is because that other system may be running a more up-to-date release of the code that includes a new enum value while the current release of your code may be old and not contain the updated switch statement logic.

6.6.3 Beware of the default case

Switch statements generally support a *default* case, which is a catch-all for any unhandled values. Adding one of these to a switch statement that handles an enum can lead to future enum values being implicitly handled and potentially cause surprises and bugs.

If a default case were added to the `isOutcomeSafe()` function, then it would look like listing 6.34. The function now defaults to returning false for any new enum values. This means that any business strategy with a prediction that is not explicitly handled is regarded as nonsafe and is not initiated. This might seem like a sensible default, but this is not necessarily true. A new prediction outcome might be `COMPANY_WILL_AVOID_LAWSUIT`, in which case defaulting to false is definitely not sensible. Using a default case causes new enum values to be implicitly handled, and as we established earlier in this section, this can cause surprises and bugs.

Listing 6.34 A default case

```
Boolean isOutcomeSafe(PredictedOutcome prediction) {
  switch (prediction) {
    case COMPANY_WILL_GO_BUST:
      return false;
    case COMPANY_WILL_MAKE_A_PROFIT:
```

```
      return true;
    default:                  // Defaults to returning false
      return false;           // for any new enum values
  }
}
```

THROWING AN ERROR FROM THE DEFAULT CASE

Another way in which a default case is sometimes used is to throw an exception that indicates an enum value is unhandled. Listing 6.35 shows this. The code is only subtly different from the version we saw earlier in listing 6.33: the `throw new Unchecked-Exception()` statement is now in a default case rather than being outside the switch statement. This might seem like an inconsequential, stylistic choice, but in some languages, it can make the code slightly more error prone in a subtle way.

Some languages (e.g., C++) can display a compiler warning when a switch statement does not exhaustively handle all values. This is a very useful warning to have. Even if we have a unit test that should detect an unhandled enum value, it really doesn't hurt to have the extra layer of protection that the compiler warning offers. A compiler warning might be noticed before a test failure so it saves engineers time. And there is always some risk that a test might be accidentally deleted or turned off. By adding a default case to the switch statement (as in listing 6.35), the compiler will now determine that the switch statement handles all values, even if new ones are added to the enum in the future. This means that the compiler will not output a warning, and the extra layer of protection is lost.

Listing 6.35 Exception in default case

```
Boolean isOutcomeSafe(PredictedOutcome prediction) {
  switch (prediction) {
    case COMPANY_WILL_GO_BUST:
      return false;
    case COMPANY_WILL_MAKE_A_PROFIT:
      return true;
    default:          // A default case means that the compiler will always think all values are handled.
      throw new UncheckedException(
          "Unhandled prediction: " + prediction);   // Exception thrown from the default case
  }
}
```

To ensure that the compiler still outputs a warning for unhandled enum values, it can be better to place the `throw new UncheckedException()` statement after the switch statement. The code we saw earlier in this section (within listing 6.31) that demonstrates this is repeated in the following listing.

Listing 6.36 Exception after the switch statement

```
Boolean isOutcomeSafe(PredictedOutcome prediction) {
  switch (prediction) {
    case COMPANY_WILL_GO_BUST:
```

```
        return false;
      case COMPANY_WILL_MAKE_A_PROFIT:
        return true;
    }
    throw new UncheckedException(
        "Unhandled prediction: " + prediction);
}
```

Exception thrown after the switch-statement

6.6.4 Caveat: Relying on another project's enum

Sometimes our code may rely on an enum that is owned by a different project or organization. How we should handle that enum will depend on the nature of our relationship with that other project, as well as our own development and release cycle. If the other project is likely to add new enum values without warning and this would immediately break our code, we may have no choice but to be more permissive in how we handle new values. As with many things, we need to use our judgment.

6.7 Can't we just solve all this with testing?

An argument sometimes made against code quality efforts that concentrate on avoiding surprises is that it's a waste of time because tests should catch all these issues. From my experience, this is a somewhat idealistic argument that does not work out in reality.

At the point you write some code, you probably have control over how you test that code. You may be extremely diligent and knowledgeable about testing and write a near perfect set of tests that lock in all the correct behaviors and assumptions for your code. But avoiding surprises is not only about the technical correctness of your own code. It's also about trying to ensure that the code other engineers write, which calls your code, functions correctly. Testing alone may not be enough to ensure this for the following reasons:

- Other engineers may not be so diligent about testing, meaning they don't test enough scenarios or corner cases to reveal that an assumption they made about your code is wrong. This can be especially true if an issue would only reveal itself in certain scenarios or for very large inputs.
- Tests don't always accurately simulate the real world. An engineer testing their code may be forced to mock out one of the dependencies. If this happens they will program the mock to behave how they *think* the mocked out code behaves. If the real code behaves in a surprising way and the engineer does not realize this, then they will likely not program the mock correctly. If this happens, a bug caused by the surprising behavior may never surface during testing.
- Some things are very hard to test. The section about side effects showed how they can be problematic for multithreaded code. Bugs related to multithreading issues are notoriously hard to test for because they often occur with a low probability and reveal themselves only when the code is run at scale.

These same points apply with regard to making code hard to misuse (covered in chapter 7).

To reiterate, testing is extremely important. No amount of code structuring or worrying about code contracts will ever replace the need for high-quality and thorough testing. But in my experience the reverse is also true; testing alone does not make up for unintuitive or surprising code.

Summary

- The code we write will often be depended on by code that other engineers write.
  - If other engineers misinterpret what our code does, or fail to spot special scenarios they need to handle, then it's likely that code built on top of ours will be buggy.
  - One of the best ways to avoid causing surprises for callers of a piece of code is to ensure that important details are in the unmistakably obvious part of the code's contract.
- Another source of surprises can occur if we make brittle assumptions about code we depend on.
  - An example of this is failing to anticipate new values being added to an enum.
  - It's important to ensure that either our code stops compiling or a test fails if code we depend on breaks one of our assumptions.
- Testing alone does not make up for code that does surprising things: if another engineer misinterprets our code, they may also misinterpret what scenarios they need to test.

7 Make code hard to misuse

This chapter covers

- How the misuse of code can lead to bugs
- Common ways code can be easy to misuse
- Techniques for making code hard to misuse

Chapter 3 discussed how the code we write is often just one piece of the jigsaw in a much larger piece of software. For a piece of software to function correctly the different pieces of code have to fit together and work. If a piece of code is easy to misuse, then the chances are sooner or later it will get misused and the software will not function correctly.

Code is often easy to misuse when there are assumptions baked in that are unintuitive or ambiguous and other engineers are not prevented from doing the wrong thing. Some common ways code can be misused are as follows:

- Callers providing invalid inputs
- Side effects from other pieces of code (such as them modifying input parameters)

- Callers not calling functions at the correct times or in the correct order (as seen in chapter 3)
- A related piece of code being modified in a way that breaks an assumption

Writing documentation and providing usage instructions for code can help mitigate against these. But as we saw in chapter 3, these are like small print in the code contract and can often be overlooked and become out of date. It's therefore important to design and write code in a way that makes it hard to misuse. This chapter shows some common ways code can be easy to misuse and demonstrates techniques for instead making it hard to misuse.

Hard to misuse

The idea of avoiding problems by making things hard (or impossible) to misuse is a well-established principle in design and manufacturing. An example of this is the lean manufacturing concept of *poka yoke*[a] coined by Shigeo Shingo in the 1960s in the context of reducing defects during car manufacturing. More generally, it is a common feature of *defensive design* principles. Some real-world examples of making things hard to misuse are the following:

- Many designs of food processors will only operate when the lid is properly attached. This prevents the blades from being accidentally spun while someone might have their fingers near them.
- Different sockets and plugs have different shapes; for example a power plug can't be plugged into an HDMI socket (this example was used in chapter 1).
- The pull handle to operate an ejection seat in a fighter jet is positioned sufficiently far away from the other aircraft controls that it minimizes the chance of it being accidentally operated. In older designs of ejection seats (with an overhead pull handle), the position of the handle also meant that the act of reaching for it made the occupant straighten their back[b] (reducing the risk of injury during ejection), so the handle position simultaneously served two functions in terms of making misuse difficult.

In the world of software engineering, this principle is sometimes captured by the statement that APIs and interfaces should be "easy to use and hard to misuse," which is sometimes abbreviated EUHM.

[a] https://tulip.co/ebooks/poka-yoke/
[b] http://mng.bz/XYM1

7.1 Consider making things immutable

Something is *immutable* if its state cannot be changed after it's created. To understand why immutability is desirable, it's important to consider how the opposite, *mutability*, can cause problems. Some of the problems with things being mutable have already cropped up in this book:

- In chapter 3 we saw how having a mutable class with setup functions made it easy to misconfigure, which results in it being in an invalid state.
- In chapter 6 we saw how a function that mutates an input parameter can cause a nasty surprise.

On top of these, there are even more reasons mutability can cause problems, including the following:

- *Mutable code can be harder to reason about.* To illustrate this, let's consider a real-world scenario that is somewhat analogous. If you buy a carton of juice from a shop, it will likely have a tamper-proof seal. This lets you know that the content of the carton has not been mutated between leaving the factory and you buying it. It's very easy for you to know, with a high degree of confidence, what is inside the carton (juice) and who put it there (the manufacturer). Now imagine there is a carton of juice in the shop with no seal: who knows what might have happened to that carton? It might have picked up some dirt or someone nefarious might have added something to it. It's very hard to reason about what exactly is in the carton and who might have put it there. When writing code, if an object is immutable, then it's a bit like having a tamper-proof seal that no one can ever break. You can pass the object all over the place and know with certainty that no one has altered it or added anything to it.
- *Mutable code can cause issues with multithreading.* We saw in chapter 6 how side effects can cause problems in multithreaded code. If an object is mutable, then multithreaded code using that object can be particularly susceptible to issues. If one thread is in the middle of reading from an object, while another is modifying it, then an error might occur. An example of this might be if one thread is just about to read the last element in a list while another thread is removing that element from the list.

It's not always possible or appropriate to make things immutable. There are inevitably some parts of our code that have to keep track of changing state, and these will obviously require some kinds of mutable data structures to do this. But, as was just explained, having mutable objects can increase the complexity of the code and lead to problems, so it can often be a good idea to take the default stance that things should be as immutable as possible and make things mutable only where it's necessary.

7.1.1 Mutable classes can be easy to misuse

One of the most common ways a class is made mutable is by providing setter functions. Listing 7.1 shows an example of this. The `TextOptions` class contains styling information about how to render some text. Both the font and the font size can be set by calling the `setFont()` and `setFontSize()` functions, respectively.

In this example, there's no limit on who can call the `setFont()` and `setFontSize()` functions, so any code that has access to an instance of `TextOptions` can change the font or the font size. This can make it very easy to misuse an instance of the `TextOptions` class.

Listing 7.1 A mutable class

```
class TextOptions {
  private Font font;
  private Double fontSize;

  TextOptions(Font font, Double fontSize) {
    this.font = font;
    this.fontSize = fontSize;
  }

  void setFont(Font font) {          <-- The font can be
    this.font = font;                    changed at any time
  }                                      by calling setFont().

  void setFontSize(Double fontSize) {   <-- The font size can be
    this.fontSize = fontSize;               change at any time by
  }                                         calling setFontSize().

  Font getFont() {
    return font;
  }

  Double getFontSize() {
    return fontSize;
  }
}
```

Listing 7.2 demonstrates how an instance of `TextOptions` might be misused. The `sayHello()` function creates an instance of `TextOptions` with some default styling information. It passes this instance to `messageBox.renderTitle()` and then to `messageBox.renderMessage()`. Unfortunately `messageBox.renderTitle()` mutates the `TextOptions` by setting the font size to 18. This means that `messageBox.renderMessage()` is called with `TextOptions` that specify a font size of 18 (instead of the intended value of 12).

We saw in chapter 6 how mutating an input parameter is often bad practice, so the `messageBox.renderTitle()` function is probably not great code. But despite being discouraged, code like this might still exist in the codebase, and currently the `TextOptions` class does nothing to defend itself against this kind of misuse.

Listing 7.2 A bug due to mutability

```
class UserDisplay {
  private final MessageBox messageBox;
  ...                                                  Creates an instance
                                                       of TextOptions
  void sayHello() {
    TextOptions defaultStyle = new TextOptions(Font.ARIAL, 12.0);   <--
    messageBox.renderTitle("Important message", defaultStyle);
    messageBox.renderMessage("Hello", defaultStyle);
  }
}                                 Passes instance to messageBox.renderTitle()
                                  and then to messageBox.renderMessage()
```

```
...

class MessageBox {
  private final TextField titleField;
  private final TextField messageField;
  ...

  void renderTitle(String title, TextOptions baseStyle) {
    baseStyle.setFontSize(18.0);
    titleField.display(title, baseStyle);
  }

  void renderMessage(String message, TextOptions style) {
    messageField.display(message, style);
  }
}
```

The instance of TextOptions is mutated by changing the font size.

Because the `TextOptions` class is mutable, any code that passes an instance of it to some other code runs the risk that it might get misused by changing things. It would be much better if code could freely pass an instance of `TextOptions` around and know that it's not going to be mutated. Just like the juice carton, we want the `TextOptions` class to have a tamper-proof seal. The next two subsections demonstrate some ways we could achieve this.

7.1.2 Solution: Set values only at construction time

We can make a class immutable (and prevent it being misused) by ensuring that all the values are provided at construction time and that they cannot be changed after this. Listing 7.3 shows the `TextOptions` class with the setter functions removed. This prevents any code outside of the class ever modifying the `font` and `fontSize` member variables.

When defining a variable within a class, it's often possible to prevent it from being reassigned even by code within the class. How to do this can vary between languages but common keywords are `const`, `final`, or `readonly`. The pseudocode convention in this book uses the keyword `final` for this concept. The `font` and `fontSize` variables have been marked as final. This prevents anyone accidentally adding code to the class to reassign them, and it makes it explicitly clear that they will not (and should not) ever change.

Listing 7.3 Immutable TextOptions class

```
class TextOptions {
  private final Font font;
  private final Double fontSize;

  TextOptions(Font font, Double fontSize) {
    this.font = font;
    this.fontSize = fontSize;
  }
```

Member variables marked as final

Member variables set at construction time only

```
  Font getFont() {
    return font;
  }

  Double getFontSize() {
    return fontSize;
  }
}
```

This now makes it impossible for other code to misuse the `TextOptions` object by mutating it. But this is not the whole story because the `MessageBox.renderTitle()` function that we saw earlier needs a way to override just the font size of some `TextOptions`. For this we can use the copy-on-write pattern. This will be covered in the next subsection, but the end result is that the `MessageBox.renderTitle()` function would end up looking like the following listing.

Listing 7.4 TextOptions not mutated

```
class MessageBox {
  private final TextField titleField;
  ...

  void renderTitle(String title, TextOptions baseStyle) {
    titleField.display(
        title,
        baseStyle.withFontSize(18.0));     <-- Returns a copy of baseStyle but with
  }                                            the font size changed. The original
  ...                                          baseStyle object is unchanged.
}
```

In the `TextOptions` example we just saw, all the text option values are required. But if some were instead optional, it might be better to use either the builder pattern or the copy-on-write pattern (both covered in the next subsection). Using named arguments in conjunction with optional parameters can also be a good approach, but, as noted in chapter 5, not all languages support named arguments.

> **NOTE: CONST MEMBER VARIABLES IN C++** In C++, the equivalent of marking a member variable as `final` is to use the `const` keyword. In C++ code, marking a member variable as `const` can be a bad idea because it can cause issues with move semantics. For a fuller explanation, this blog post goes into the details: http://mng.bz/y9Xo.

7.1.3 Solution: Use a design pattern for immutability

Removing the setter functions from a class and marking the member variables as `final` can avoid bugs by preventing the class from being mutated. But as was just noted, it can also make the class impractical to use. If some values are optional or if mutated versions of the class need to be created, it can often be necessary to implement the class in a more versatile way. Two design patterns that can often be useful for this are the following:

- The builder pattern
- The copy-on-write pattern

THE BUILDER PATTERN

When some values that a class can be constructed with are optional, it can become quite unwieldy to specify them all in the constructor. Rather than making the class mutable by adding setter functions, it can often be better to use the builder pattern.[1]

The builder pattern effectively splits a class into two classes:

- A builder class that allows values to be set one by one
- An immutable, read-only version of the class that is built from the builder

When constructing a class, it will often be the case that some values are required and some are optional. To demonstrate how the builder pattern can handle this, we will assume that for the `TextOptions` class the font is a required value and the font size is an optional value. Listing 7.5 shows the `TextOptions` class along with a builder class for it.

An important thing to note is that the `TextOptionsBuilder` class takes the required font value as a parameter to its constructor (not via a setter function). This makes it impossible to write code that builds an invalid object. If the font were specified with a setter function, we would require a runtime check to ensure the object is valid, which is generally inferior to a compile time check (as discussed in chapter 3).

Listing 7.5 The builder pattern

```
class TextOptions {
  private final Font font;
  private final Double? fontSize;

  TextOptions(Font font, Double? fontSize) {
    this.font = font;
    this.fontSize = fontSize;
  }

  Font getFont() {                    <--
    return font;
  }                                      The TextOptions class
                                         contains only read-only
  Double? getFontSize() {             <--  getter functions.
    return fontSize;
  }
}
```

[1] A form of the builder pattern was popularized by Erich Gamma, Richard Helm, Ralph Johnson, and John Vlissides in the book *Design Patterns: Elements of Reusable Object-Oriented Software* (Addison-Wesley, 1994).

```
class TextOptionsBuilder {
  private final Font font;
  private Double? fontSize;

  TextOptionsBuilder(Font font) {
    this.font = font;
  }

  TextOptionsBuilder setFontSize(Double fontSize) {
    this.fontSize = fontSize;
    return this;
  }

  TextOptions build() {
    return new TextOptions(font, fontSize);
  }
}
```

The builder takes any required values in its constructor.

The builder takes any optional values via setter functions.

Setter returns this to allow chaining of function calls.

Once all the values have been specified, a caller calls build to get a TextOptions object.

Figure 7.1 illustrates the relationship between the `TextOptions` class and the `TextOptionsBuilder` class.

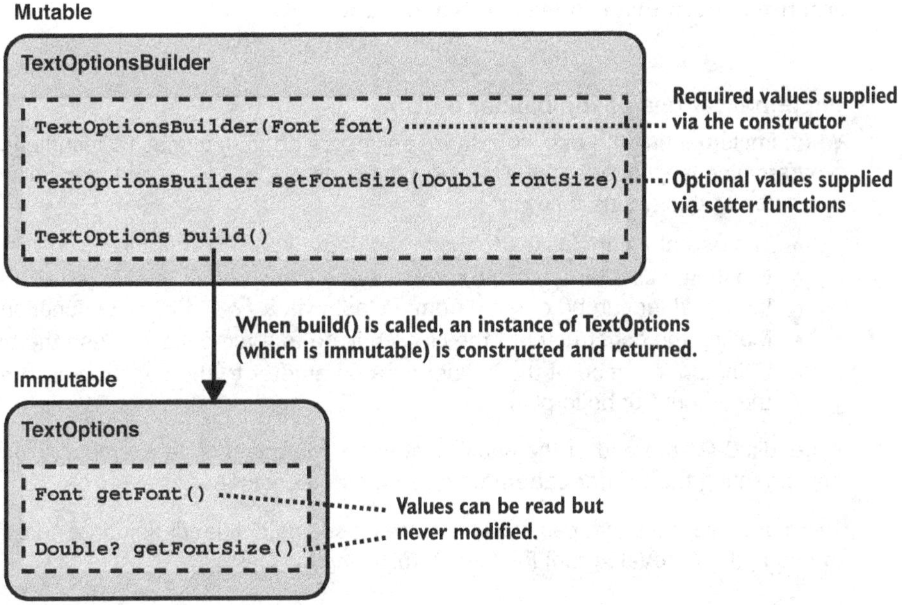

Figure 7.1 The builder pattern effectively splits a class into two. The builder class can be mutated in order to set values. A call to the `build()` function then returns an instance of an immutable class containing the configured values.

The following snippet shows an example of building an instance of `TextOptions` where both the required font value and the optional font size value are specified:

```
TextOptions getDefaultTextOptions() {
  return new TextOptionsBuilder(Font.ARIAL)
      .setFontSize(12.0)
      .build();
}
```

The following snippet shows an example of building an instance of `TextOptions` where only the required font value is specified:

```
TextOptions getDefaultTextOptions() {
  return new TextOptionsBuilder(Font.ARIAL)
      .build();
}
```

The builder pattern can be a very useful way of creating an immutable class when some (or all) of the values are optional. If we need to get a slightly modified copy of an instance of a class after construction, then there are ways to make this work with the builder pattern (by providing a function to create a prepopulated builder from a class), but this can become a little cumbersome. The next subsection discusses an alternative pattern that can make this a lot easier.

Implementations of the builder pattern

When implementing the builder pattern, engineers often use specific techniques and programming language features to make the code easier to use and maintain. Some examples of this are as follows:

- The use of inner classes to make the name spacing a bit nicer
- Creating a circular dependency between a class and its builder so a prepopulated builder can be created from a class (via a `toBuilder()` function)
- Making the constructor of the class private to force callers to use the builder
- Using an instance of the builder as a parameter to the constructor to reduce the amount of boilerplate

Appendix C (at the end of the book) contains a more complete example (in Java) of implementing the builder pattern using all these techniques.

There are also tools that can auto-generate class and builder definitions. An example of this is the AutoValue tool for Java: http://mng.bz/MgPD.

THE COPY-ON-WRITE PATTERN

Sometimes it's necessary to get a modified version of an instance of a class. An example of this is the `renderTitle()` function we saw earlier (repeated in the following snippet). It needs to retain all the styles from `baseStyle` but modify only the font size. Unfortunately allowing this to happen by making `TextOptions` mutable can cause issues, as we saw earlier:

```
void renderTitle(String title, TextOptions baseStyle) {
  baseStyle.setFont(18.0);
  titleField.display(title, baseStyle);
}
```

A way to support this use case, while also ensuring that `TextOptions` is immutable is the *copy-on-write* pattern. Listing 7.6 shows what the `TextOptions` class looks like with two copy-on-write functions added. The `withFont()` and `withFontSize()` functions both return a new `TextOptions` object with only the font or font size changed (respectively).

In addition to a public constructor that takes the required font value, the `TextOptions` class also has a private constructor that takes every value (required and optional). This allows the copy-on-write functions to create a copy of the `TextOptions` with only one of the values changed.

Listing 7.6 Copy-on-write pattern

```
class TextOptions {
  private final Font font;
  private final Double? fontSize;

  TextOptions(Font font) {          // Public constructor that takes any required values
    this(font, null);               // Calls the private constructor
  }

  private TextOptions(Font font, Double? fontSize) {   // Private constructor that takes all values (required and optional)
    this.font = font;
    this.fontSize = fontSize;
  }

  Font getFont() {
    return font;
  }

  Double? getFontSize() {
    return fontSize;
  }

  TextOptions withFont(Font newFont) {
    return new TextOptions(newFont, fontSize);   // Returns a new TextOptions object with only the font changed
  }

  TextOptions withFontSize(Double newFontSize) {
    return new TextOptions(font, newFontSize);   // Returns a new TextOptions object with only the font size changed
  }
}
```

Figure 7.2 illustrates how the copy-on-write implementation of the `TextOptions` class works.

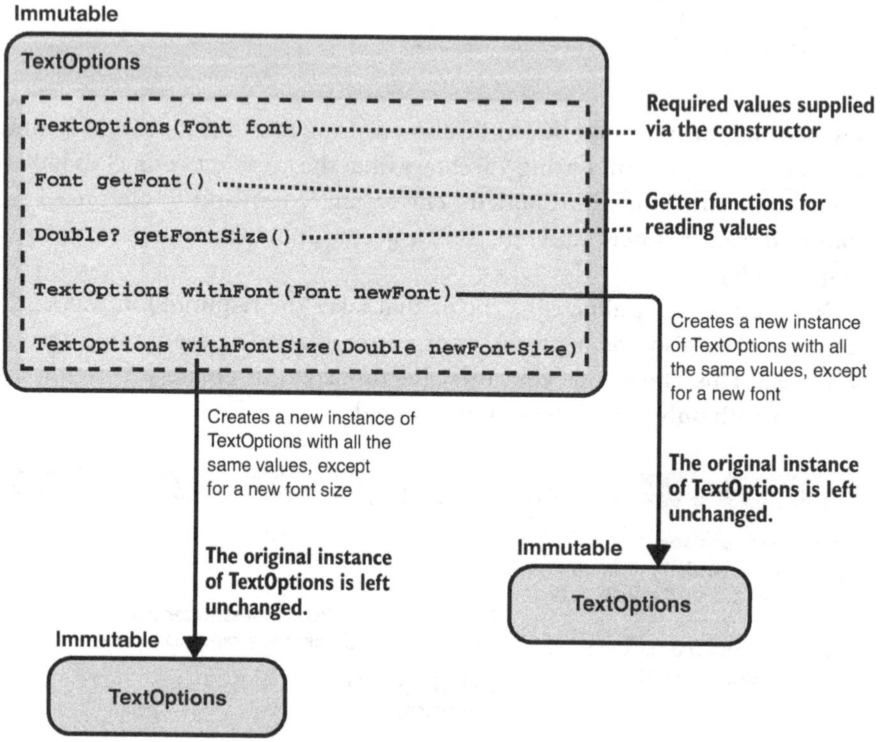

Figure 7.2 With the copy-on-write pattern, any change to a value results in a new instance of the class being created, which contains the desired change. The existing instance of the class is never modified.

An instance of `TextOptions` can be constructed using the constructor and calls to the copy-on-write functions:

```
TextOptions getDefaultTextOptions() {
  return new TextOptions(Font.ARIAL)
      .withFontSize(12.0);
}
```

When some code like the `renderTitle()` function needs a mutated version of a `TextOptions` object, it can easily acquire a mutated copy without affecting the original object:

```
void renderTitle(String title, TextOptions baseStyle) {
  titleField.display(
      title,
      baseStyle.withFontSize(18.0));   <-- A new, modified version of baseStyle
}                                         is created by calling withFontSize().
```

Making classes immutable can be a great way to minimize the chance that they get misused. Sometimes this can be as simple as removing setter methods and providing values only at construction time. In other scenarios it can be necessary to use an appropriate design pattern. Even with these approaches, mutability can still creep into the code in deeper ways; the next section discusses this.

7.2 Consider making things deeply immutable

Engineers are very often aware of the benefits of immutability and follow the advice in section 7.1. But it can be easy to overlook more subtle ways a class can inadvertently become mutable. A common way a class can accidentally become mutable is due to *deep mutability*. This can happen when a member variable is of a type that is itself mutable and other code somehow has access to it.

7.2.1 Deep mutability can lead to misuse

If the `TextOptions` class (from section 7.1) stored a font family instead of a single font, it might use a list of fonts as a member variable. The following listing shows what the `TextOptions` class looks like with this change.

Listing 7.7 A deeply mutable class

```
class TextOptions {
  private final List<Font> fontFamily;      // fontFamily is a list of fonts.
  private final Double fontSize;

  TextOptions(List<Font> fontFamily, Double fontSize) {
    this.fontFamily = fontFamily;
    this.fontSize = fontSize;
  }

  List<Font> getFontFamily() {
    return fontFamily;
  }

  Double getFontSize() {
    return fontSize;
  }
}
```

This can inadvertently make the class mutable, as the class doesn't have complete control over the list of fonts. To appreciate why, it's important to remember that the `TextOptions` class does not contain a list of fonts; it instead contains a *reference* to a list of fonts (as shown in figure 7.3). If another piece of code also has a reference to this same list of fonts, then any changes it makes to the list will affect the `TextOptions` class too, because they are both referring to the same exact list.

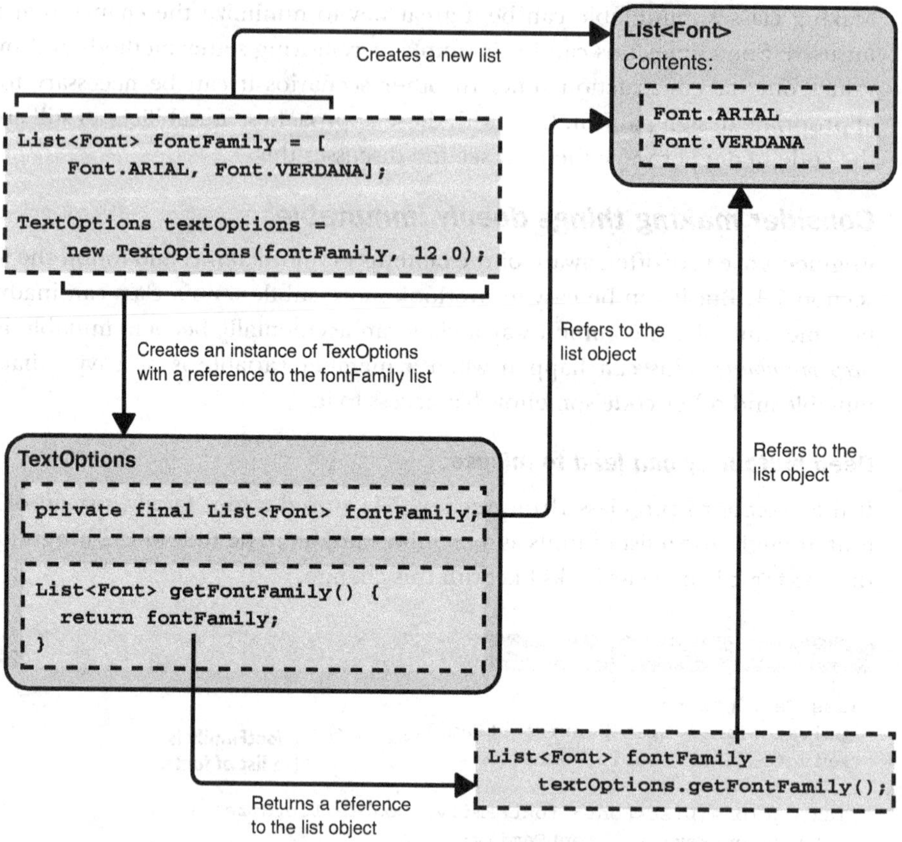

Figure 7.3 Objects are often held by reference, meaning multiple pieces of code can all be referring to the same object. This can be a cause of deep mutability.

As figure 7.3 shows, there are two scenarios in which other code might have a reference to the same list of fonts that the `TextOptions` class contains:

- *Scenario A*—The code that constructs the `TextOptions` class might hold on to a reference to the list of fonts and make changes at some later time.
- *Scenario B*—Code that calls `TextOptions.getFontFamily()` is given a reference to the list of fonts. It can use this reference to modify the contents of the list.

SCENARIO A CODE EXAMPLE

Listing 7.8 demonstrates scenario A. The code creates a list of fonts containing `Font.ARIAL` and `Font.VERDANA`. It then constructs an instance of `TextOptions` with this list. After this, the list is cleared and `Font.COMIC_SANS` is added. Because the code in the listing and the instance of `TextOptions` are both referring to the same list, the `fontFamily` within the instance of `TextOptions` is now also set to `Font.COMIC_SANS`.

Listing 7.8 List modified after construction

```
...
List<Font> fontFamily = [Font.ARIAL, Font.VERDANA];

TextOptions textOptions =
    new TextOptions(fontFamily, 12.0);    <-- A reference to the fontFamily list is
                                              passed to the TextOptions constructor.

fontFamily.clear();                        The fontFamily list is modified. This is the
fontFamily.add(Font.COMIC_SANS);           same list that textOptions has a reference to.
...
```

Scenario B code example

Listing 7.9 demonstrates scenario B. An instance of `TextOptions` is constructed with a font list containing `Font.ARIAL` and `Font.VERDANA`. Some code then gets a reference to this list by calling `textOptions.getFontFamily()`. The code then mutates the referenced list by clearing it and adding `Font.COMIC_SANS`. This means that the font family within the instance of `TextOptions` is now also set to `Font.COMIC_SANS`.

Listing 7.9 List modified by caller

```
...
TextOptions textOptions =
    new TextOptions([Font.ARIAL, Font.VERDANA], 12.0);   Gets a reference to the
                                                          same list that textOptions
List<Font> fontFamily = textOptions.getFontFamily();  <-- has a reference to
fontFamily.clear();
fontFamily.add(Font.COMIC_SANS);          Modifies exactly the
...                                       same list that textOptions
                                          has a reference to
```

Making code mutable in these ways can very easily lead to it being misused. When an engineer calls a function like `textOptions.getFontFamily()` the list might be passed around several times as other functions or constructors are called. It can be quite easy to lose track of where it came from and whether it's safe to modify it. Sooner or later some code might modify the list, and it will cause a weird bug that is extremely hard to track down. It can be much better to make the class deeply immutable and avoid this kind of problem in the first place. The next subsections demonstrate a couple of ways this can be achieved.

7.2.2 Solution: Defensively copy things

As we just saw, problems with deep mutability can occur when a class holds a reference to an object that another piece of code may also hold a reference to. This can be avoided by ensuring that the object the class refers to is one that only it knows about and that no other code can ever get a reference to.

This can be achieved by making defensive copies of objects both when the class is constructed and also whenever an object is returned from a getter function. This isn't necessarily the best solution (as this subsection and next one will explain), but it does work and can be a simple way to make things deeply immutable.

Listing 7.10 shows what the `TextOptions` class would look like if it made defensive copies of the `fontFamily` list. The constructor creates a copy of the `fontFamily` list and stores a reference to this copy (solving scenario A). And the `getFontFamily()` function creates a copy of the `fontFamily` and returns a reference to this copy (solving scenario B).

Listing 7.10 Defensive copying

```
class TextOptions {
  private final List<Font> fontFamily;
  private final Double fontSize;

  TextOptions(List<Font> fontFamily, Double fontSize) {
    this.fontFamily = List.copyOf(fontFamily);
    this.fontSize = fontSize;
  }

  List<Font> getFontFamily() {
    return List.copyOf(fontFamily);
  }

  Double getFontSize() {
    return fontSize;
  }
}
```

- A copy of the fontFamily list that only this class has a reference to
- The constructor copies the list and stores a reference to that copy.
- A copy of the list is returned.

Defensively copying things can be quite effective at making a class deeply immutable, but it has some obvious drawbacks:

- Copying things can be expensive. In the case of the `TextOptions` class this is probably fine because we don't expect there to be too many fonts in a font family, and the constructor and `getFontFamily()` function probably won't be called that many times. But if there were hundreds of fonts in a font family, and the `TextOptions` class was used extensively, then all this copying could become a big problem for performance.
- It often doesn't protect against changes from within the class. In most programming languages, marking a member variable as `final` (or `const` or `readonly`) doesn't prevent deep mutations. Even with the `fontFamily` list marked as final, an engineer could add code within the class that calls `fontFamily.add (Font.COMIC_SANS)`. If an engineer accidentally did this, the code would still compile and run, so just copying things is usually not a complete guarantee of deep mutability.

Luckily, in many scenarios, there is often a more efficient and robust way of making classes deeply immutable. The next subsection discusses this.

Pass by value

In languages like C++, the programmer has a lot more control over how objects are passed into a function or returned. There is the distinction between *pass by reference* (or *pointer*) and *pass by value*. Pass by value will mean that a copy of the object is created rather than just a reference (or pointer) to it. This prevents code from mutating the original object but still incurs the downsides of copying things.

C++ also has the idea of const correctness (mentioned in the next subsection), which can often be a better way to keep things immutable.

7.2.3 Solution: Use immutable data structures

Making things immutable is a widely accepted good practice, and, as a result, many utilities have been built that provide immutable versions of common types or data structure. The benefit of these is that once they are constructed no one can modify their contents. This means that they can be passed around without the need to make defensive copies.

Depending on which language we're using, some appropriate immutable data structure choices for the `fontFamily` list might be the following:

- *Java*—The `ImmutableList` class from the Guava library (http://mng.bz/aK09)
- *C#*—The `ImmutableList` class from System.Collections.Immutable (http://mng.bz/eMWG)
- *JavaScript-based language*—A couple of options are the following:
  - The List class from the Immutable.js module (http://mng.bz/pJAR)
  - A JavaScript array, but with the Immer module used to make it immutable (https://immerjs.github.io/immer/)

These libraries contain a whole host of different immutable types, such as sets, maps, and many more, so we can often find an immutable version of whatever standard data type we might need.

Listing 7.11 shows what the `TextOptions` class looks like if it's changed to use an `ImmutableList`. There is no need to defensively copy anything, as it doesn't matter if other code has a reference to the same list (because it's immutable).

Listing 7.11 Using ImmutableList

```
class TextOptions {
  private final ImmutableList<Font> fontFamily;
  private final Double fontSize;

  TextOptions(ImmutableList<Font> fontFamily, Double fontSize) {
    this.fontFamily = fontFamily;
    this.fontSize = fontSize;
  }
```

Even code within this class cannot modify the contents of the ImmutableList.

There is no way that the caller of the constructor can modify the list at some later time.

```
  ImmutableList<Font> getFontFamily() {
    return fontFamily;
  }

  Double getFontSize() {
    return fontSize;
  }
}
```

The ImmutableList is returned, safe in the knowledge that callers cannot modify it.

Using immutable data structures is one of the best ways to ensure that classes are deeply immutable. They avoid the downsides of defensively copying things and ensure that even code within the class can't inadvertently cause mutations.

> **Const correctness in C++**
>
> C++ has quite advanced support for immutability at the compiler level. When defining a class, engineers can indicate which member functions don't cause mutations by marking them as `const`. If a function returns a reference (or pointer) to an object that is marked as `const`, then the compiler will ensure that this can only be used to call nonmutable member functions on that object.
>
> This can often negate the need for separate classes to represent an immutable version of something. More information on const correctness in C++ can be found at https://isocpp.org/wiki/faq/const-correctness.

7.3 Avoid overly general data types

Simple data types like integers, strings, and lists are some of the most fundamental building blocks of code. They are incredibly general and versatile and can represent all manner of different things. The flip side of being very general and versatile is that they are not very descriptive and are also quite permissive in terms of which values they can contain.

Just because something *can* be represented by a type like an integer or a list doesn't necessarily mean that it's a *good* way to represent that thing. The lack of descriptiveness and the amount of permissiveness can make code too easy to misuse.

7.3.1 Overly general types can be misused

A certain piece of information can often require more than one value to fully represent it. An example of this is a location on a 2D map: it requires a value for both the latitude and the longitude to fully describe it.

If we're writing some code to process locations on a map, then we'll likely need a data structure for representing a location. The data structure needs to contain values for both the location's latitude and its longitude. A quick and simple way of doing this might be to use a list (or an array), where the first value in the list represents the latitude and the second value represents the longitude. This means that a single location would have the type `List<Double>` and a list of multiple locations would have the type `List<List<Double>>`. Figure 7.4 shows what this looks like.

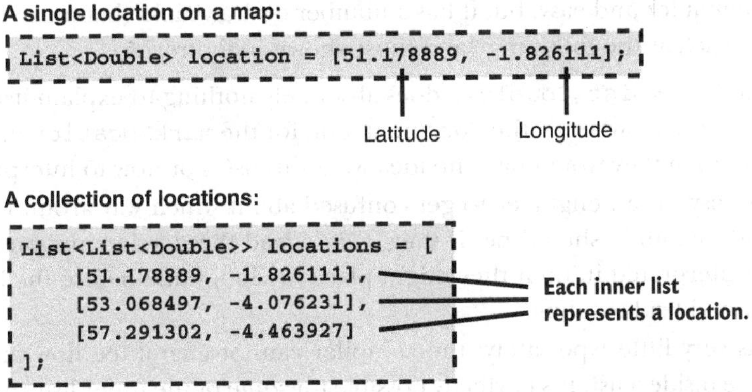
A single location on a map:
List<Double> location = [51.178889, -1.826111];
Latitude
Longitude
A collection of locations:
List<List<Double>> locations = [
[51.178889, -1.826111],
[53.068497, -4.076231],
[57.291302, -4.463927]
];
Each inner list represents a location.

Figure 7.4 A very general data type like a list can be used to represent a location on a map (a latitude and longitude pair). But just because it *can* represent it doesn't necessarily mean it's a *good* way to represent it.

Unfortunately, a list is an incredibly general data type, and using it in this way could make the code easy to misuse. To demonstrate this, listing 7.12 contains a class for displaying locations on a map. The `markLocationsOnMap()` function takes a list of locations and for each location marks it on the map. As seen in figure 7.4, each location is represented by a `List<Double>`, meaning the collection of all locations to mark on the map is of the type `List<List<Double>>`. This gets kind of complicated, and documentation is required to explain how the input parameter should be used.

Listing 7.12 Overly general data type

```
class LocationDisplay {
  private final DrawableMap map;
  ...

  /**
   * Marks the locations of all the provided coordinates
   * on the map.
   *
   * Accepts a list of lists, where the inner list should
   * contain exactly two values. The first value should
   * be the latitude of the location and the second value
   * the longitude (both in degrees).
   */
  void markLocationsOnMap(List<List<Double>> locations) {
    for (List<Double> location in locations) {
      map.markLocation(location[0], location[1]);
    }
  }
}
```

Semi-complicated documentation is required to explain the input parameter.

The first and second items are read from each inner list.

This might seem quick and easy, but it has a number of drawbacks that make the code easy to misuse, such as the following (and those shown in figure 7.5).

- The type List<List<Double>> does absolutely nothing to explain itself: if an engineer weren't aware of the documentation for the markLocationsOnMap() function, then they would have no idea what this list is or how to interpret it.
- It's very easy for an engineer to get confused about which way around the latitude and longitude should be. If they hadn't read the documentation fully, or had misinterpreted it, then they might place the longitude before the latitude, which would lead to a bug.
- There is very little type safety: the compiler cannot guarantee how many elements are inside a list. It's perfectly possible for some of the inner lists to contain the wrong number of values (as shown in figure 7.5). If this happens then the code will compile fine and the problem will be noticed only at runtime (if at all).

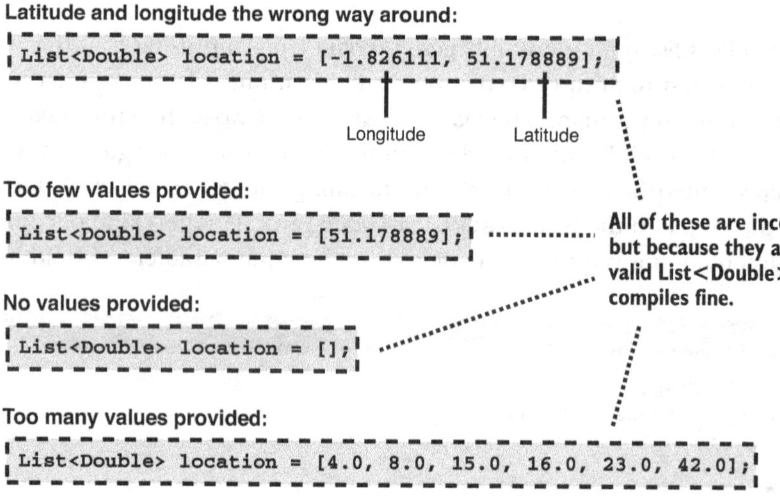

Figure 7.5 Representing something specific like a latitude–longitude pair using a list of doubles can make code very easy to misuse.

In summary, it's almost impossible to call the markLocationsOnMap() function correctly without having detailed knowledge of (and correctly following) the small print in the code contract. Given that small print is often not a very reliable way to guarantee that other engineers do something, this makes it highly likely that the markLocationsOnMap() function will be misused at some point, which could obviously lead to bugs.

PARADIGMS HAVE A HABIT OF SPREADING

The shelf analogy in chapter 1 explained how doing one thing in a slightly hacky way can often force more stuff to be done in a hacky way. This could easily happen with this List<Double> representation of a map location. Imagine that another engineer is implementing a class to represent a feature on a map and an output from that class has to be fed into the markLocationsOnMap() function. They are pushed down the path of also using the List<Double> representation of a location so their code can interact easily with the markLocationsOnMap() function.

Listing 7.13 shows the code they might write. The getLocation() function returns a List<Double> containing the latitude and longitude. Notice how another chunk of semi-complicated documentation is required to explain the return type of the function. This, in itself, should worry us a bit: the instructions about how to store the latitude and longitude in a list are now encoded and documented in two separate places (the MapFeature class and the LocationDisplay class). This is an example of there being two *sources of truth* instead of a single source of truth. This can lead to bugs and will be discussed more in section 7.6.

Listing 7.13 Other code adopts the paradigm

```
class MapFeature {
  private final Double latitude;
  private final Double longitude;
  ...

  /*
   * Returns a list with 2 elements in it. The first value
   * represents the latitude and the second value represents
   * the longitude (both in degrees).
   */
  List<Double> getLocation() {
    return [latitude, longitude];
  }
}
```

Semi-complicated documentation is required to explain the return type.

The author of the original LocationDisplay.markLocationsOnMap() function probably knows that using a List<Double> is a kind of hacky way to represent a map location. But they may have justified it on the basis that it was only one function and is therefore unlikely to cause too much damage to the codebase as a whole. The problem is that slightly hacky things like this have a habit of spreading, as it becomes hard for other engineers to interact with them without also resorting to doing something slightly hacky. And this can spread quite quickly and quite far: if yet another engineer needs to use the MapFeature class for something else, they may be forced to adopt the List<Double> representation for that other thing too. Before we know it, the List<Double> representation is pervasive and very hard to get rid of.

7.3.2 Pair types are easy to misuse

Many programming languages have a *pair* data type. This is sometimes part of the standard libraries, and when it's not, there is often an add-on library somewhere that provides an implementation of it.

The point of a pair is that it stores two values that can be of the same or different types. The values are referred to as first and second. A simple implementation of a pair data type would look something like the following listing.

Listing 7.14 Pair data type

```
class Pair<A, B> {                          <-- Generics (or templating) allow
  private final A first;                        Pair to store any types.
  private final B second;

  Pair(A first, B second) {
    this.first = first;
    this.second = second;
  }

  A getFirst() {                            <--
    return first;                               Values referred to as
  }                                             "first" and "second"

  B getSecond() {                           <--
    return second;
  }
}
```

If a `Pair<Double, Double>` were used to represent a location on a map (instead of a `List<Double>`), then the `markLocationsOnMap()` function would look like listing 7.15. Note that semi-complicated documentation is still required to explain the input parameter, and the input parameter type (`List<Pair<Double, Double>>`) is still not very self-descriptive.

Listing 7.15 Usage of Pair for location

```
class LocationDisplay {
  private final DrawableMap map;
  ...

  /**
   * Marks the locations of all the provided coordinates
   * on the map.
   *
   * Accepts a list of pairs, where each pair represents a
   * location. The first element in the pair should be the
   * latitude and the second element in the pair should be
   * the longitude (both in degrees).
   */
  void markLocationsOnMap(List<Pair<Double, Double>> locations) {
    for (Pair<Double, Double> location in locations) {
      map.markLocation(
          location.getFirst(),
          location.getSecond());
    }
  }
}
```

Semi-complicated documentation is required to explain the input parameter.

Using `Pair<Double, Double>` instead of `List<Double>` solves some of the problems we noted in the previous subsection: the pair has to contain exactly two values, so it prevents callers from accidentally providing too few or too many values. But it does not solve the other problems:

- The type `List<Pair<Double, Double>>` still does very little to explain itself.
- It's still easy for an engineer to get confused about which way around the latitude and longitude should be.

An engineer still requires detailed knowledge of the small print in the code contract to call `markLocationsOnMap()` correctly, so using `Pair<Double, Double>` is still not a great solution in this scenario.

7.3.3 Solution: Use a dedicated type

Chapter 1 explained how taking shortcuts often actually slows us down in the mid- to long-term. Using an overly general data type (like a list or pair) for a very specific thing can often be an example of such a shortcut. It can seem like a lot of effort or overkill to define a new class (or struct) to represent something, but it's usually less effort than it might seem and will save engineers a lot of head scratching and potential bugs further down the line.

For the case of representing a 2D location of a map, a simple way to make the code less easy to misuse and misinterpret is to define a dedicated class for representing a latitude and longitude. Listing 7.16 shows what this new class might look like. It's an incredibly simple class and is unlikely to take more than a few minutes to code and test.

Listing 7.16 LatLong class

```
/**
 * Represents a latitude and longitude in degrees.
 */
class LatLong {
  private final Double latitude;
  private final Double longitude;

  LatLong(Double latitude, Double longitude) {
    this.latitude = latitude;
    this.longitude = longitude;
  }

  Double getLatitude() {
    return latitude;
  }

  Double getLongitude() {
    return longitude;
  }
}
```

Using this new `LatLong` class, the `markLocationsOnMap()` function looks like listing 7.17. It now requires no documentation to explain the intricacies of the input parameter, as it's completely self-explanatory. There is now good type safety, and it's extremely hard to confuse the latitude with the longitude.

Listing 7.17 Usage of LatLong

```
class LocationDisplay {
  private final DrawableMap map;
  ...

  /**
   * Marks the locations of all the provided coordinates
   * on the map.
   */
  void markLocationsOnMap(List<LatLong> locations) {
    for (LatLong location in locations) {
      map.markLocation(
          location.getLatitude(),
          location.getLongitude());
    }
  }
}
```

Using very general, off-the-shelf data types can sometimes seem like a quick and easy way to represent something. But when we need to represent a specific thing it can often be better to put in a small amount of extra effort to define a dedicated type for it. In the mid- to long-run, this usually saves time because the code becomes a lot more self-explanatory and hard to misuse.

Data objects

Defining simple objects that just group data together is a reasonably common task, and as such a number of languages have features (or add-on utilities) that make this even easier:

- Kotlin has the concept of data classes, which make it possible to define a class for containing data using a single line of code: http://mng.bz/O15j.
- In more recent versions of Java, records can be used: https://openjdk.java.net/jeps/395. For older versions of Java, an alternative is the AutoValue tool: http://mng.bz/YAaj.
- In various languages (such as C++, C#, Swift, and Rust) it's possible to define structs, which can sometimes be more succinct to define than a class.
- In TypeScript it's possible to define an interface and then use it to provide compile-time safety for which properties an object must contain: http://mng.bz/G6PA.

> Proponents of a more traditional take on object-oriented programming sometimes consider defining data-only objects a bad practice. They argue that data and any functionality that requires that data should be encapsulated together in the same class.
>
> If some data is tightly coupled to a specific piece of functionality, this makes a lot of sense. But many engineers also recognize that there are scenarios where it's useful to group some data together without having to tie it to some specific functionality. And in this scenario data-only objects can be incredibly useful.

7.4 Dealing with time

The previous section discussed how using overly general data types to represent specific things can lead to code that is easy to misuse. One specific example of this, which often crops up, is representing time-based concepts.

Time might seem like a simple thing, but the representation of time is actually quite nuanced:

- Sometimes we refer to an instant in time, which can be absolute, such as "02:56 UTC July 21, 1969," or relative, such as "in five minutes' time."
- Sometimes we refer to an amount of time, such as "bake in the oven for 30 minutes." Amounts of time can be expressed in one of any number of different units, such as hours, seconds, or milliseconds.
- To make things even more complicated we also have concepts like time zones, daylight saving time, leap years, and even leap seconds.

The room for confusion and misusing code when dealing with time is enormous. This section discusses how we can avoid confusion and misuse by using appropriate data types and language constructs when dealing with time-based concepts.

7.4.1 Representing time with integers can be problematic

A common way of representing time is to use an integer (or a long integer), which represents a number of seconds (or milliseconds). This is often used for representing both instants in time as well as amounts of time:

- An instant in time is often represented as a number of seconds (ignoring leap seconds) since the unix epoch (00:00:00 UTC on 1 January 1970).
- An amount of time is often represented as a number of seconds (or milliseconds).

An integer is a very general type and can thus make code easy to misuse when used to represent time like this. We'll now look at three common ways this can happen.

AN INSTANT IN TIME OR AN AMOUNT OF TIME?

Consider the code in listing 7.18. The `sendMessage()` function has an integer parameter named `deadline`. The documentation for the function explains what the deadline parameter does and that the units are in seconds, but it forgets to mention what the deadline value actually represents. It's not clear what should be provided as an argument to the deadline parameter when the function is called. A couple of plausible options might be the following:

- The parameter represents an absolute instant in time, and we should provide a number of seconds since the unix epoch.
- The parameter represents an amount of time. When the function is called, it will start a timer and the deadline will be passed when this timer hits the specified number of seconds.

Listing 7.18 Instant in time or amount of time?

```
/**
 * @param message The message to send
 * @param deadline The deadline in seconds. If the message
 *     has not been sent by the time the deadline is exceeded,
 *     then sending will be aborted
 * @return true if the message was sent, false otherwise
 */
Boolean sendMessage(String message, Int64 deadline) {
  ...
}
```

Explains what the parameter does and the units but not what the value represents

The documentation is obviously not great if it leaves this much ambiguity. Improving the documentation would be one way to improve this, but that would pile more stuff into the small print of the code contract. Small print is not a particularly reliable way to prevent code from being misused. And considering that this parameter already requires three lines of documentation to explain it, adding yet more to explain what the number represents is probably not ideal.

MISMATCHING UNITS

As mentioned at the start of this section, there are many different units for measuring time. The most common units used in code are usually milliseconds and seconds, but others (like microseconds) also get used, depending on the context.

An integer type does absolutely nothing to indicate which units the value is in. We can indicate the units using a function name, parameter name, or documentation, but this can often still leave it relatively easy to misuse some code.

Listing 7.19 shows two different parts of a codebase. The UiSettings.getMessageTimeout() function returns an integer representing a number of seconds. The showMessage() function has a parameter called timeoutMs that represents a number of milliseconds.

Listing 7.19 Mismatch in time units

```
class UiSettings {
  ...

  /**
   * @return The number of seconds that UI messages should be
   *     displayed for.
   */
  Int64 getMessageTimeout() {
    return 5;
  }
}

...

/**
 * @param message The message to display
 * @param timeoutMs The amount of time to show the message for
 *     in milliseconds.
 */
void showMessage(String message, Int64 timeoutMs) {
  ...
}
```

This part of the code uses seconds.

This part of the code uses milliseconds.

Despite the documentation (and "Ms" suffix on the `timeoutMs` parameter name), it's quite easy for an engineer to make a mistake when they are plugging these two bits of code together. The function call in the following snippet doesn't look obviously wrong, but it would cause the warning to be displayed for five milliseconds rather than five seconds. This means that the message will disappear before a user has even noticed it.

```
showMessage("Warning", uiSettings.getMessageTimeout());
```

MISHANDLING TIME ZONES

A common way to represent an instant in time is as a number of seconds (ignoring leap seconds) since the unix epoch. This is often referred to as a timestamp and is a very exact way of identifying precisely when some event has occurred (or will occur). But, as humans, we often find it desirable to talk about an event in time in a less exact way.

An example of this is when talking about birthdays. If someone was born on the 2nd of December 1990, we don't particularly care about the exact instant in time they were born. Instead, we just care that the calendar day was the 2nd of December and every year we wish them happy birthday and eat some cake on that day.

The difference between a date and an instant in time can be a subtle one, but if we're not careful to treat them differently it can lead to problems. Figure 7.6 illustrates how this can go wrong. If a user enters a date (like their birthday) and this is interpreted as being a date and time within a local time zone, this can lead to a different date being displayed when a user in a different time zone accesses the information.

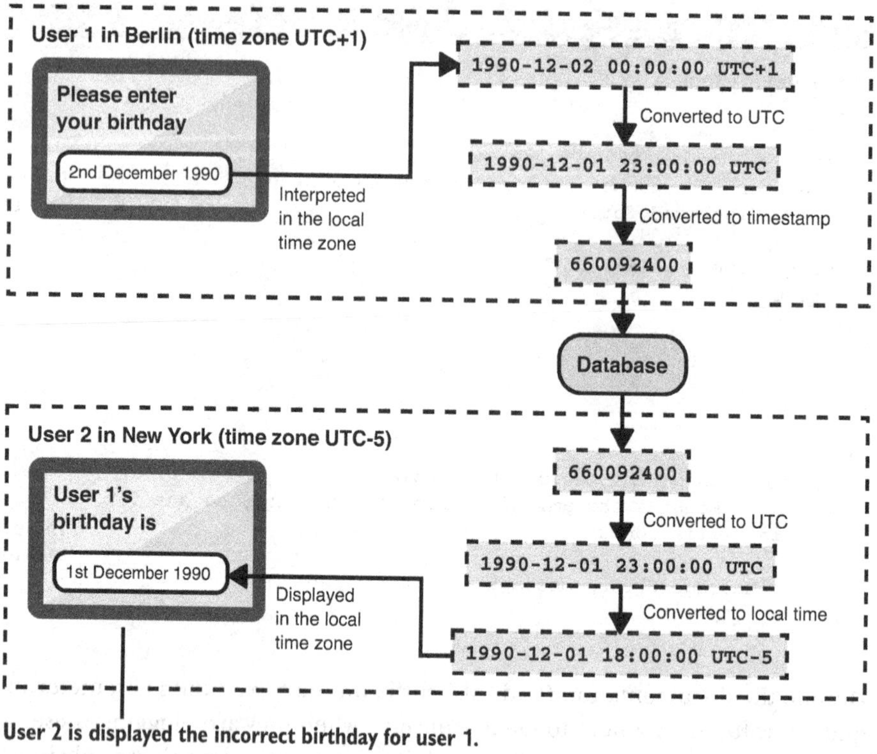

Figure 7.6 Not handling time zones properly can easily lead to bugs.

A problem similar to that described in figure 7.6 can also happen in purely server-side logic if servers are running in different locations and have their systems set to different time zones. For example a server in California might save a date value that a different server in Europe ends up processing.

Time-based concepts like instants in time, amounts of time, and dates can be tricky things to work with at the best of times. But we make our own lives and other engineers' lives even harder when we try to represent them using a very general type like an integer. Integers convey very little information about what they mean or represent, and this can make them very easy to misuse. The next subsection explains how using more appropriate types can improve code that deals with time.

7.4.2 Solution: Use appropriate data structures for time

As we can see, dealing with time is complicated and nuanced and provides lots of room for confusion. Most programming languages have some built-in libraries for handling time, but unfortunately some of these have drawbacks or design issues that can make them quite error prone. Luckily, for most programming languages with poor in-built support for time-based concepts, people have built third-party, open-source libraries to provide a more robust set of utilities. This means there is usually a way to handle time-based concepts in a robust way, but it's often necessary to put some effort into finding the best library for the language we're using. Some examples of options that are available are as follows:

- In Java, the classes in the java.time package can be used (http://mng.bz/0rPE).
- In C#, the Noda Time library provides a number of utilities for dealing with time in a robust way (https://nodatime.org).
- In C++, the chrono library can be used (https://en.cppreference.com/w/cpp/header/chrono).
- In JavaScript, there are a number of third-party libraries to choose from. One example is the js-joda library (https://js-joda.github.io/js-joda/).

These libraries make the problems discussed in the previous subsection a lot easier to handle. The following subsections explain some of the ways these libraries can improve code.

DIFFERENTIATING AN INSTANT IN TIME FROM AN AMOUNT OF TIME

The java.time, Noda Time, and js-joda libraries all provide a class called `Instant` (for representing an instant in time) and a separate class called `Duration` (for representing an amount of time). Similarly, the C++ chrono library provides a class called `time_point` and a separate class called `duration`.

Using one of these means that the type of a function parameter dictates whether it represents an instant in time or an amount of time. For example the `sendMessage()` function we saw earlier would look like listing 7.20 if it used a `Duration` type. It's now unmistakably obvious that the value represents an amount of time and not an instant in time.

Listing 7.20 Using Duration type

```
/**
 * @param message The message to send
 * @param deadline If the message has not been sent by the time
 *     the deadline is exceeded, then sending will be aborted
 * @return true if the message was sent, false otherwise
 */
Boolean sendMessage(String message, Duration deadline) {
  ...
}
```

The Duration type makes it clear what the deadline represents.

NO MORE CONFUSION ABOUT UNITS

The other thing that types like `Instant` and `Duration` achieve is that the units are encapsulated within the type. This means that there is no need for small print in the contract to explain which units are expected, and it becomes impossible to accidentally provide a value with the incorrect ones. The following snippet demonstrates how different factory functions can be used to create a `Duration` using different units. Regardless of which units are used to create the `Duration`, it can later be read back as a number of milliseconds. This allows each part of the code to use whichever units it likes without there being a risk of them mismatching when the different pieces of code interact.

```
Duration duration1 = Duration.ofSeconds(5);
print(duration1.toMillis()); // Output: 5000

Duration duration2 = Duration.ofMinutes(2);
print(duration2.toMillis()); // Output: 120000
```

The following listing shows how the problems with the `showMessage()` function can be eliminated by using `Duration` types instead of integers to handle the amount of time after which the message should timeout.

Listing 7.21 Units encapsulated in Duration type

```
class UiSettings {
  ...

  /**
   * @return The duration for which the UI messages should be
   *     displayed.
   */
  Duration getMessageTimeout() {
    return Duration.ofSeconds(5);
  }
}

...

/**
 * @param message The message to display
 * @param timeout The amount of time to show the message for.
 */
void showMessage(String message, Duration timeout) {
  ...
}
```

The Duration type fully encapsulates the units.

BETTER HANDLING OF TIME ZONES

In the example of representing a birthday we don't actually care what the time zone is. But if we want to represent a birthday by linking it to an exact instant in time (using a timestamp), then we are forced to think carefully about time zones. Luckily, libraries for handling time often provide a way to represent a date (and time) without having to link it to an exact instant in time like this. The java.time, Noda Time, and js-joda libraries all provide a class called `LocalDateTime`, which achieves exactly this.

As this section shows, dealing with time can be tricky, and if we're not careful we can end up with code that's too easy to misuse and introduce bugs. Luckily we're not the first engineers to face these challenges, and as a result, many libraries already exist to make dealing with time a lot more robust. We can improve our code by making use of them.

7.5 Have single sources of truth for data

More often than not code deals with data of some kind, be it numbers, strings, or streams of bytes. Data can often come in two forms:

- *Primary data*—Things that need to be supplied to the code. There is no way that the code could work this data out without being told it.
- *Derived data*—Things that the code can calculate based on the primary data.

An example of this might be the data required to describe the state of a bank account. There are two pieces of primary data: the amount of credit and the amount of debit. A piece of derived data that we might want to know is the account balance, which is the amount of credit minus the amount of debit.

Primary data usually provides the source of truth for a program. The values for the credit and debit fully describe the state of an account and are the only things that need to be stored to keep track of it.

7.5.1 Second sources of truth can lead to invalid states

In the case of the bank account, the value of the account balance is fully constrained by the two pieces of primary data. It makes no sense to say that the balance is $10 if the credit is $5 and the debit is $2; it's logically incorrect. This is a case of having two sources of "truth" that disagree with one another: the credit and debit values state one thing (that the balance is $3), while the provided balance value says something else ($10).

When writing code that deals with both primary and derived data, there can often be the potential for logically incorrect states like this. If we write code that allows these logically incorrect states to occur, then it can make it too easy for the code to be misused.

Listing 7.22 demonstrates this. The `UserAccount` class is constructed with values for the credit, debit, and account balance. As we just saw, the account balance is redundant information because it can be derived from the credit and debit, so this class allows callers to instantiate it in a logically incorrect state.

Listing 7.22 Second source of truth for balance

```
class UserAccount {
  private final Double credit;
  private final Double debit;
  private final Double balance;

  UserAccount(Double credit, Double debit, Double balance) {
    this.credit = credit;
    this.debit = debit;
    this.balance = balance;
  }

  Double getCredit() {
    return credit;
  }
```

The credit, debit, and balance are all provided to the constructor.

```
    Double getDebit() {
      return debit;
    }

    Double getBalance() {
      return balance;
    }
  }
```

The following snippet shows an example of how the `UserAccount` class might be instantiated in an invalid state. An engineer has accidentally calculated the balance as debit minus credit instead of credit minus debit.

```
UserAccount account =
    new UserAccount(credit, debit, debit - credit);   <-- Balance provided as debit minus credit, which is incorrect
```

We'd hope that testing would spot a bug like this, but if it didn't it could lead to some nasty bugs. The bank might end up sending out statements with incorrect balances. Or internal systems might start doing unpredictable things because of the logically incorrect values.

7.5.2 Solution: Use primary data as the single source of truth

Because the account balance can be fully derived from the credit and debit, it would be much better to just calculate it as and when it's needed. Listing 7.23 shows what the `UserAccount` class looks like with this change. The balance is no longer taken as a constructor parameter and is not even stored in a member variable. The `getBalance()` function simply calculates it on the fly whenever the function is called.

Listing 7.23 Calculating balance on the fly

```
class UserAccount {
  private final Double credit;
  private final Double debit;

  UserAccount(Double credit, Double debit) {
    this.credit = credit;
    this.debit = debit;
  }

  Double getCredit() {
    return credit;
  }

  Double getDebit() {
    return debit;
  }

  Double getBalance() {
    return credit - debit;     <-- The balance is calculated from the credit and debit.
  }
}
```

The example of the bank account balance is pretty simple, and most engineers would likely spot the fact that providing the balance is redundant given that it can be derived from the credit and debit. But more complicated situations that are analogous to this can often crop up and be harder to spot. It's well worth taking the time to think about any data models we might be defining and whether they allow any logically incorrect states to exist.

WHEN DERIVING DATA IS EXPENSIVE

Calculating an account balance from the credit and debit is trivially simple and not at all computationally expensive. But sometimes it can be a lot more expensive to calculate a derived value. Imagine that instead of having single values for the credit and debit, we instead have a list of transactions. Now the list of transactions is the primary data and the total credit and debit are derived data. But calculating this derived data is now quite expensive because it requires traversing a whole list of transactions.

If calculating a derived value is expensive like this, it can often be a good idea to calculate it *lazily* and cache the result. Calculating something lazily means that we put off doing the work until we absolutely have to (just like being lazy in real life). Listing 7.24 shows what the `UserAccount` class looks like with these changes. The `cachedCredit` and `cachedDebit` member variables start off as null but are populated with values if and when the `getCredit()` and `getDebit()` functions are called respectively.

The `cachedCredit` and `cachedDebit` member variables store derived information, so they are in effect a second source of truth. In this situation this is OK, because this second source of truth is fully contained within the `UserAccount` class and the class and list of transactions are both immutable. This means we know that the `cachedCredit` and `cachedDebit` variables will be in agreement with the transactions list and that this will never change.

Listing 7.24 Lazy calculation and caching

```
class UserAccount {
  private final ImmutableList<Transaction> transactions;

  private Double? cachedCredit;        // Member variables to store cached
  private Double? cachedDebit;         // values for the credit and debit

  UserAccount(ImmutableList<Transaction> transactions) {
    this.transactions = transactions;
  }

  ...

  Double getCredit() {
    if (cachedCredit == null) {
      cachedCredit = transactions
          .map(transaction -> transaction.getCredit())
          .sum();
    }
    return cachedCredit;
  }
```

(Annotation: Credit is calculated (and cached) if it's not already cached.)

```
  Double getDebit() {
    if (cachedDebit == null) {
      cachedDebit = transactions
          .map(transaction -> transaction.getDebit())
          .sum();
    }
    return cachedDebit;
  }

  Double getBalance() {
    return getCredit() - getDebit();
  }
}
```

Debit is calculated (and cached) if it's not already cached.

Calculates the balance using potentially cached values

If a class is not immutable, then things get a lot more complicated: we have to make sure the cache variables are reset to null whenever the class is mutated. This can get quite fiddly and error prone, so this is another strong argument for making things immutable.

7.6 Have single sources of truth for logic

Sources of truth don't just apply to data provided to the code; they apply to the logic within the code as well. There are many scenarios where something that one piece of code does needs to match something that another piece of code does. If the two pieces of code don't match one another, the software will stop functioning properly. It's therefore important to ensure that there is a single source of truth for logic like this.

7.6.1 Multiple sources of truth for logic can lead to bugs

Listing 7.25 shows a class that can be used to log some integer values and then save them to a file. There are two important details in this code about how the values are stored in the file:

1. Each value is converted into a string format (using a base-10 radix).
2. The strings for each value are then joined together with a comma separating them.

Listing 7.25 Code to serialize and save values

```
class DataLogger {
  private final List<Int> loggedValues;
  ...

  saveValues(FileHandler file) {
    String serializedValues = loggedValues
        .map(value -> value.toString(Radix.BASE_10))
        .join(",");
    file.write(serializedValues);
  }
}
```

The values are converted to strings using a base-10 radix.

The values are joined together with comma separation.

It's very likely that there is some other code, somewhere else, that is used to read files and parse integers from them (the reverse process of what `DataLogger.saveValues()` does). Listing 7.26 shows the code that does this. This code is in a completely different file (and potentially a different part of the codebase) to the `DataLogger` class, but the logic needs to match. In particular, to successfully parse the values from the contents of a file, the following steps need to be performed:

1. The string needs to be split into a list of strings on the comma character.
2. Each string in the list needs to be parsed into an integer (using a base-10 radix).

Listing 7.26 Code to read and deserialize values

```
class DataLoader {
  ...

  List<Int> loadValues(FileHandler file) {
    return file.readAsString()
        .split(",")                                        <-- File contents are split into a list of strings.
        .map(str -> Int.parse(str, Radix.BASE_10));        <-- Each string is parsed into an integer using a base-10 radix.
  }
}
```

NOTE: ERROR HANDLING There are obviously considerations around error handling when it comes to writing data to a file or reading and parsing data from a file. Listings 7.25 and 7.26 omit these for the sake of brevity, but in real life we'd probably want to consider using one of the techniques discussed in chapter 4 to signal when writing to or reading from a file fails, or when strings cannot be parsed into integers.

In this scenario, the format in which values are stored in a file is a critical piece of logic, but there are two sources of truth for what this format is. Both the `DataLogger` and `DataLoader` classes independently contain logic that specify the format. When the classes both contain the same logic everything works fine, but if one is modified and the other is not, problems will arise.

Some potential changes that an engineer might make to the logic are as follows. If the engineer made one of these changes to the `DataLogger` class but not the `DataLoader` class, then things would go wrong.

- An engineer decides that it would be better to store values using hexadecimal instead of base-10 to save space (meaning the file would contain strings like "7D" instead of "125").
- An engineer decides that it would be better to separate values using a new line instead of a comma to make the files more human readable.

Having two sources of truth for logic can easily cause problems whenever an engineer modifies one of them without realizing that they also need to modify the other.

7.6.2 Solution: Have a single source of truth

Chapter 2 discussed how a given piece of code will usually solve a high-level problem by breaking it down into a series of subproblems. The `DataLogger` and `DataLoader` classes both solve a high-level problem: logging data and loading data respectively. But in doing so they both need to solve the subproblem of what format should be used to store a list of serialized integers in a file.

Figure 7.7 illustrates how the `DataLogger` and `DataLoader` classes are both solving one of the same subproblems (the format for storing serialized integers). But rather than solving this problem once and both making use of that single solution, each class contains its own logic for solving it.

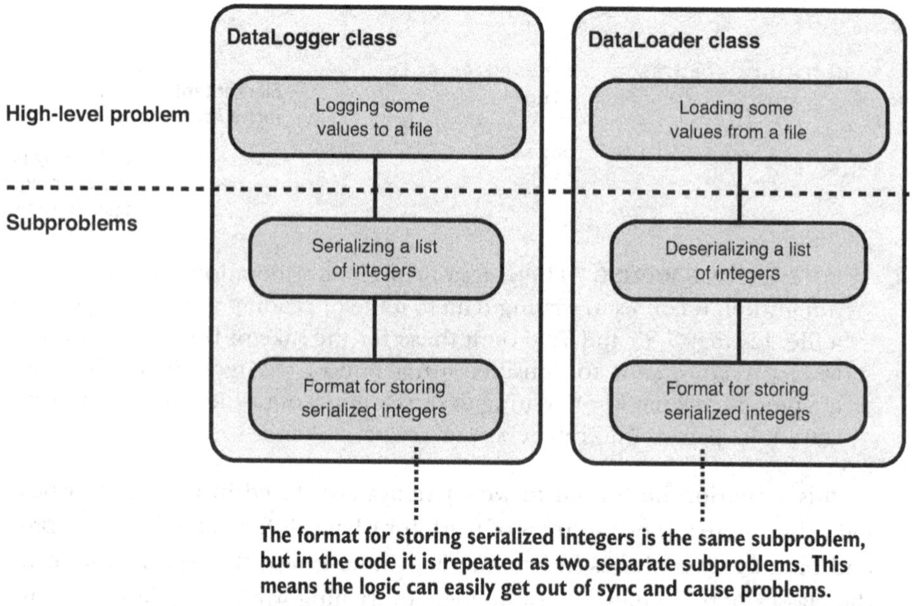

Figure 7.7 The format for storing serialized integers is a subproblem that is common to both the `DataLogger` and `DataLoader` classes. But rather than sharing the same solution, they each contain their own logic to solve it.

We could make the code more robust and less likely to be broken by having a single source of truth for the format for storing serialized integers. We can achieve this by making the serialization and deserialization of a list of integers be a single, reusable layer of code.

Listing 7.27 shows one way of doing this by defining a class called `IntList-Format`, which contains two functions: `serialize()` and `deserialize()`. All the logic related to the format for storing serialized integers is now contained within a single class that provides a single source of truth. Another detail to notice is that the comma delimiter and radix are each specified once in a constant so that there is a single source of truth for these, even within the class.

Listing 7.27 IntListFormat class

```
class IntListFormat {
  private const String DELIMITER = ",";
  private const Radix RADIX = Radix.BASE_10;

  String serialize(List<Int> values) {
    return values
        .map(value -> value.toString(RADIX))
        .join(DELIMITER);
  }

  List<Int> deserialize(String serialized) {
    return serialized
      .split(DELIMITER)
      .map(str -> Int.parse(str, RADIX));
  }
}
```

The delimiter and radix are specified in constants.

Listing 7.28 shows what the `DataLogger` and `DataLoader` classes now look like if they both make use of the `IntListFormat` class to do the serialization and deserialization. All the details of how to serialize and deserialize a list of integers to and from a string are now handled by the `IntListFormat` class.

Listing 7.28 DataLogger and DataLoader

```
class DataLogger {
  private final List<Int> loggedValues;
  private final IntListFormat intListFormat;
  ...
  saveValues(FileHandler file) {
    file.write(intListFormat.serialize(loggedValues));
  }
}

...

class DataLoader {
  private final IntListFormat intListFormat;
  ...
  List<Int> loadValues(FileHandler file) {
    return intListFormat.deserialize(file.readAsString());
  }
}
```

IntListFormat class used to solve the subproblem

Figure 7.8 illustrates how the high-level problems and subproblems are now broken up between the layers of code. We can see that the `IntListFormat` class now provides the single source of truth for the format for storing serialized integers. This almost entirely eliminates the risk that an engineer might change the format used by the `DataLogger` class and inadvertently forget to change the one used by the `DataLoader` class.

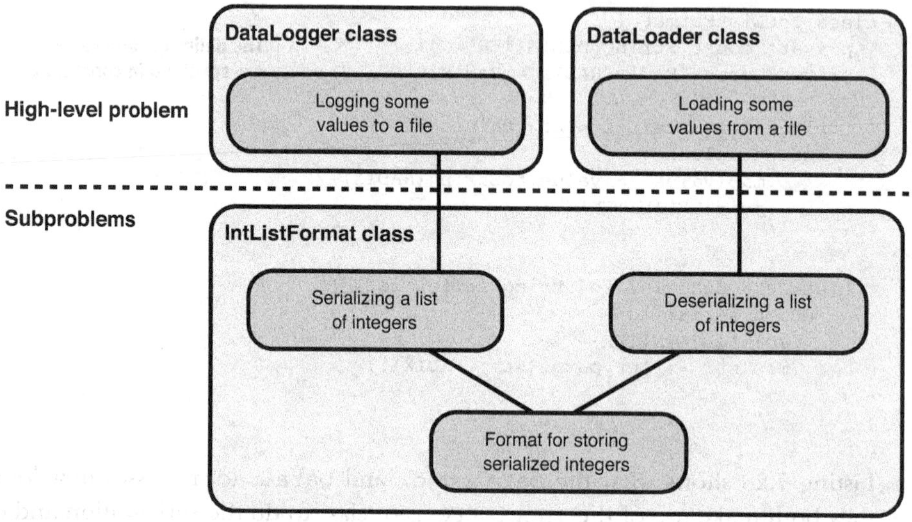

Figure 7.8 The `IntListFormat` class provides a single source of truth for the format for storing serialized integers.

When the logic performed by two different pieces of code need to match, we shouldn't leave it to chance that they do. Engineers working on one part of the codebase may not be aware of an assumption made by some code in another part of the codebase. We can make code a lot more robust by ensuring that important pieces of logic have a single source of truth. This almost entirely eliminates the risk of bugs caused by different pieces of code getting out of sync with one another.

Summary

- If code is easy to misuse, then there is a high chance that at some point it will be misused. This can lead to bugs.
- Some common ways in which code can be misused are the following:
  - Callers providing invalid inputs
  - Side effects from other pieces code
  - Callers not calling functions at the correct times or in the correct order
  - A related piece of code being modified in a way that breaks an assumption
- It's often possible to design and structure code in a way that makes it hard or impossible to misuse. This can greatly reduce the chance of bugs and save engineers a lot of time in the mid- to long-term.

8 Make code modular

This chapter covers

- The benefits of modular code
- Common ways code can be less modular than is ideal
- How to make code more modular

Chapter 1 discussed how requirements often evolve over the lifetime of a piece of software. In many cases they evolve even before the software is released, so it's not uncommon to write some code and then have to adapt it only a few weeks or months later. Trying to predict exactly how requirements will evolve is usually a waste of time, because it's near impossible to do this with any accuracy. But we can usually be more or less certain that they will evolve in some way.

One of the main aims of modularity is to create code that can be easily adapted and reconfigured, without having to know exactly how it will need to be adapted or reconfigured. A key goal in achieving this is that different pieces of functionality (or requirements) should map to distinct parts of the codebase. If we achieve this, and later on one of the software requirements changes, we should need to make nontrivial changes to only the single place in the codebase that relates to that requirement or feature.

This chapter builds heavily on the idea of clean layers of abstraction (which was discussed in chapter 2). Making code modular often comes down to ensuring that the nuts-and-bolts details of solutions to subproblems are each self-contained and not tightly coupled to one another. In addition to making code more adaptable, this also tends to make software systems easier to reason about. And as we'll see in chapters 9, 10, and 11, it also tends to make code more reusable and more testable, so making code modular has a number of benefits.

8.1 Consider using dependency injection

It's common for classes to depend on other classes. Chapter 2 showed how code often solves a high-level problem by breaking it down into subproblems. In well-structured code, each of these subproblems is often solved by a dedicated class. There is not always a single solution to a subproblem however, so it can be useful to structure code in a way that allows solutions to subproblems to be reconfigured. Dependency injection can help us achieve this.

8.1.1 Hard-coded dependencies can be problematic

Listing 8.1 shows some of the code in a class that implements a route planner for car journeys. The `RoutePlanner` class depends on an instance of `RoadMap`. `RoadMap` is an interface with potentially many different implementations (one for each geographical region). But in this example, the `RoutePlanner` class constructs a `NorthAmericaRoadMap` in its constructor, meaning it has a hard-coded dependency on a specific implementation of `RoadMap`. This means that the `RoutePlanner` class can be used only for planning journeys in North America. It's completely useless for planning journeys in any other part of the world.

Listing 8.1 A hard-coded dependency

```
class RoutePlanner {
  private final RoadMap roadMap;            <-- RoutePlanner depends on RoadMap.

  RoutePlanner() {
    this.roadMap = new NorthAmericaRoadMap();   <-- RoutePlanner class constructs
  }                                              a NorthAmericaRoadMap.

  Route planRoute(LatLong startPoint, LatLong endPoint) {
    ...
  }
}
                                   RoadMap is
interface RoadMap {           <--  an interface.
  List<Road> getRoads();
  List<Junction> getJunctions();
}                                                  NorthAmericaRoadMap is one
                                                   of potentially many
class NorthAmericaRoadMap implements RoadMap {  <-- implementations of RoadMap.
  ...
  override List<Road> getRoads() { ... }
  override List<Junction> getJunctions() { ... }
}
```

Baking in a dependency on a specific implementation of `RoadMap` makes it impossible to reconfigure the code with a different implementation. But this is not the only problem with hard coding a dependency like this. Imagine if the `NorthAmericaRoadMap` class were modified and now required some constructor parameters. Listing 8.2 shows what the `NorthAmericaRoadMap` class now looks like. It accepts two parameters to its constructor:

- The `useOnlineVersion` parameter controls whether the class will try to connect to a server to get the most up-to-date version of the map.
- The `includeSeasonalRoads` parameter controls whether the map includes roads that are open only at certain times of the year.

Listing 8.2 A configurable dependency

```
class NorthAmericaRoadMap implements RoadMap {
  ...

  NorthAmericaRoadMap(
      Boolean useOnlineVersion,
      Boolean includeSeasonalRoads) { ... }

  override List<Road> getRoads() { ... }
  override List<Junction> getJunctions() { ... }
}
```

The knock-on effect of this is that the `RoutePlanner` class can't construct an instance of `NorthAmericaRoadMap` without providing these values. This forces the `RoutePlanner` class to now handle concepts specific to the `NorthAmericaRoadMap` class: whether to connect to a server to get an up-to-date map and whether to include seasonal roads. This starts to make the layers of abstraction messy and can even further limit the adaptability of the code. Listing 8.3 shows what the `RoutePlanner` class might now look like. It now hard codes that the map will use an online version and that it won't include seasonal roads. These are kind of arbitrary decisions and make the scenarios in which the `RoutePlanner` class can be used even more limited. It's now useless whenever there isn't an internet connection or whenever seasonal roads are required.

Listing 8.3 Configuring a hard-coded dependency

```
class RoutePlanner {
  private const Boolean USE_ONLINE_MAP = true;
  private const Boolean INCLUDE_SEASONAL_ROADS = false;

  private final RoadMap roadMap;

  RoutePlanner() {
    this.roadMap = new NorthAmericaRoadMap(
        USE_ONLINE_MAP, INCLUDE_SEASONAL_ROADS);
  }
```

Constructor arguments for NorthAmericaRoadMap are baked in.

```
  Route planRoute(LatLong startPoint, LatLong endPoint) {
    ...
  }
}
```

The RoutePlanner class has one thing going for it: it's very easy to construct. Its constructor takes no parameters, and as such, callers don't have to worry about providing any configuration. The downside, however, is that the RoutePlanner class is not very modular and not very versatile. It's hard coded to use a road map of North America, will always try to connect to an online version of the map, and will always exclude seasonal roads. This is probably not ideal, as we're quite likely to have some users outside of North America, and we might also want our application to work even when the user is offline.

8.1.2 Solution: Use dependency injection

We can make the RoutePlanner class a lot more modular and versatile if we allow it to be constructed with different road maps. We can achieve this by *injecting* a RoadMap by providing it via a parameter in the constructor. This removes the need for the RoutePlanner class to have a hard-coded dependency on a particular road map and means that we can configure it with any road map we like. The following listing shows how the RoutePlanner class looks with this change.

Listing 8.4 Dependency injection

```
class RoutePlanner {
  private final RoadMap roadMap;

  RoutePlanner(RoadMap roadMap) {    <-- A RoadMap is injected via the constructor.
    this.roadMap = roadMap;
  }

  Route planRoute(LatLong startPoint, LatLong endPoint) {
    ...
  }
}
```

Now engineers can construct an instance of RoutePlanner using any road map they like. Some examples of how engineers might now use the RoutePlanner class are the following:

```
RoutePlanner europeRoutePlanner =
    new RoutePlanner(new EuropeRoadMap());

RoutePlanner northAmericaRoutePlanner =
    new RoutePlanner(new NorthAmericaRoadMap(true, false));
```

The downside of injecting the RoadMap like this is that the RoutePlanner class is now more complicated to construct. An engineer now has to construct an instance of RoadMap before they can construct a RoutePlanner. We can make this a lot easier by providing some factory functions that other engineers can use. Listing 8.5 shows what these might look like. The `createDefaultNorthAmericaRoutePlanner()` function constructs a `RoutePlanner` with a `NorthAmericaRoadMap` using some "sensible" default values. This can make it easy for engineers to quickly create a `RoutePlanner` that probably does what they need, but without preventing anyone with a different use case from using `RoutePlanner` with a different road map, so for the default use case `RoutePlanner` is almost as easy to use as it was in the previous subsection, but it is now adaptable to other use cases too.

Listing 8.5 Factory functions

```
class RoutePlannerFactory {
  ...

  static RoutePlanner createEuropeRoutePlanner() {
    return new RoutePlanner(new EuropeRoadMap());
  }

  static RoutePlanner createDefaultNorthAmericaRoutePlanner() {
    return new RoutePlanner(
        new NorthAmericaRoadMap(true, false));
  }
}
```

Constructs a NorthAmericaRoadMap with some "sensible" defaults

An alternative to manually writing factory functions is to use a *dependency injection framework*.

DEPENDENCY INJECTION FRAMEWORKS

We've seen that dependency injection can make classes more configurable, but that it can also have the downside of making them more complicated to construct. We can use manually coded factory functions to alleviate this, but if we end up with a lot of these it can get a bit laborious and lead to a lot of boilerplate code.

We can make life easier by using a dependency injection framework, which automates a lot of the work. There are many different dependency injection frameworks around, and whichever language you are using, you will probably have more than a few to choose from. Because there are so many, and because they are so language specific, we won't go into too many details here. The main point to take away is that dependency injection frameworks can enable us to create very modular and versatile code without drowning in loads of factory function boilerplate. It's well worth looking up what options are available for the language you're using and deciding if it's something that could be useful.

As a note of caution, even engineers who love dependency injection are not always fans of dependency injection frameworks. If not used carefully, they can result in code that can be hard to reason about. This can be because it becomes hard to figure out which pieces of configuration for the framework apply to which pieces of the code. If you do choose to use a dependency injection framework, then it's worth reading up on the best practices to avoid any potential pitfalls.

8.1.3 Design code with dependency injection in mind

When writing code, it can often be beneficial to consciously consider that we might want to use dependency injection. There are ways of writing code that make it near impossible to use dependency injection, so if we know we might want to inject a dependency, it's best to avoid these.

To demonstrate this, let's consider another way an engineer might implement the `RoutePlanner` and road map example. Listing 8.6 shows this. The `NorthAmericaRoadMap` class now contains static functions (rather than ones that are called via an instance of the class). This means that the `RoutePlanner` class doesn't depend on an instance of the `NorthAmericaRoadMap` class; it instead depends directly on the static functions `NorthAmericaRoadMap.getRoads()` and `NorthAmericaRoadMap.getJunctions()`. This exhibits the same problem that we saw at the start of this section: there's no way to use the `RoutePlanner` class with anything other than a North American road map. But the problem is now even worse because we can't solve this by modifying the `RoutePlanner` class to use dependency injection even if we want to.

Previously, when the `RoutePlanner` class was creating an instance of `NorthAmericaRoadMap` in its constructor, we were able to improve the code by using dependency injection to instead inject an implementation of `RoadMap`. But now we can't do this, because the `RoutePlanner` class doesn't depend on an instance of `RoadMap`; it instead depends directly on the static functions within the `NorthAmericaRoadMap` class.

Listing 8.6 Depending on static functions

```
class RoutePlanner {

  Route planRoute(LatLong startPoint, LatLong endPoint) {
    ...
    List<Road> roads = NorthAmericaRoadMap.getRoads();
    List<Junction> junctions =
        NorthAmericaRoadMap.getJunctions();
    ...
  }
}
```

Calls to static functions on the NorthAmericaRoadMap class

```
class NorthAmericaRoadMap {
  ...
  static List<Road> getRoads() { ... }

  static List<Junction> getJunctions() { ... }
}
```

Static functions

When we're writing code to solve a subproblem it can be easy to assume that it's the only solution to the problem that anyone would ever want. If we're in this mind-set, it can often seem that the most obvious thing to do is simply create a static function. For really fundamental subproblems with only one solution this is usually fine. But for subproblems that higher layers of code might want to reconfigure, this can be problematic.

NOTE: STATIC CLING An overreliance of static functions (or variables) is often referred to as *static cling*. The potential problems with this are well known and well documented. It can be especially problematic when unit testing code because it can make it impossible to use test doubles (covered in chapter 10).

Chapter 2 discussed how it's often good to define an interface if there is more than one potential solution to a subproblem. In this case, the road map solves a subproblem, and it's not hard to imagine that code (or tests) might sometimes want different solutions to that subproblem for different geographical areas (or different test scenarios). Because we can foresee this as a likely eventuality, it's probably better to define an interface for a road map and make the `NorthAmericaRoadMap` a class that implements it (which also means making the functions non-static). If we do this, we end up with the code we saw earlier (repeated in listing 8.7). This means that anyone using a `RoadMap` can use dependency injection and make their code adaptable if they want to.

Listing 8.7 An instantiable class

```
interface RoadMap {                        <-- RoadMap is an interface.
  List<Road> getRoads();
  List<Junction> getJunctions();
}

class NorthAmericaRoadMap implements RoadMap {   <-- NorthAmericaRoadMap is one
  ...                                                of potentially many
  override List<Road> getRoads() { ... }             implementations of RoadMap.
  override List<Junction> getJunctions() { ... }
}
```

Dependency injection can be an excellent way to make code modular and ensure that it can be adapted to different use cases. Whenever we're dealing with subproblems that might have alternative solutions, this can be particularly important. Even when this isn't the case, dependency injection can still be useful. Chapter 9 will show how it can help us avoid global state. And chapter 11 will explore how it can make code more testable.

8.2 Prefer depending on interfaces

The previous section demonstrated the benefits of using dependency injection: it allows the `RoutePlanner` class to be more easily reconfigured. But this is only possible because all the different road map classes implement the same `RoadMap` interface, meaning the `RoutePlanner` class can depend on this. This allows any implementation of `RoadMap` to be used, making the code considerably more modular and adaptable.

This leads us to a more general technique for making code more modular and easy to adapt: if we're depending on a class that implements an interface and that interface captures the functionality that we need, then it's usually better to depend on that interface rather than directly on the class. The previous section already hinted at this, but we'll now look at it more explicitly.

8.2.1 Depending on concrete implementations limits adaptability

Listing 8.8 shows what the `RoutePlanner` class (from the previous section) would look like if it used dependency injection but depended directly on the `NorthAmericaRoadMap` class rather than the `RoadMap` interface.

We still get some of the benefits of dependency injection: the `RoutePlanner` class doesn't have to know anything about how to construct a `NorthAmericaRoadMap`. But we miss out on one of the major advantages of using dependency injection: we can't use the `RoutePlanner` class with other implementations of `RoadMap`.

Listing 8.8 Depending on a concrete class

```
interface RoadMap {                          // The RoadMap interface
  List<Road> getRoads();
  List<Junction> getJunctions();
}

class NorthAmericaRoadMap implements RoadMap {     // NorthAmericaRoadMap implements the RoadMap interface.
  ...
}

class RoutePlanner {
  private final NorthAmericaRoadMap roadMap;       // Depends directly on the NorthAmericaRoadMap class

  RoutePlanner(NorthAmericaRoadMap roadMap) {
    this.roadMap = roadMap;
  }

  Route planRoute(LatLong startPoint, LatLong endPoint) {
    ...
  }
}
```

We already established in the previous section how it's highly likely that we might have some users outside of North America, so having a `RoutePlanner` class that doesn't work in any other geographical location is less than ideal. It would be better if the code could work with any road map.

8.2.2 Solution: Depend on interfaces where possible

Depending on concrete implementation classes often limits adaptability compared to depending on an interface. We can think of an interface as providing a layer of abstraction for solving a subproblem. A concrete implementation of that interface provides a less abstract and more implementation-focused solution to the subproblem. Depending on the more abstract interface will usually achieve cleaner layers of abstraction and better modularity.

In the case of the RoutePlanner class, this means that we depend on the RoadMap interface instead of directly on the NorthAmericaRoadMap class. If we do this, then we arrive back at the same code we had in section 8.1.2 (repeated in listing 8.9). Engineers can now construct an instance of RoutePlanner with any road map they like.

Listing 8.9 Depending on an interface

```
class RoutePlanner {
  private final RoadMap roadMap;

  RoutePlanner(RoadMap roadMap) {          <-- Depends on the
    this.roadMap = roadMap;                    RoadMap interface
  }

  Route planRoute(LatLong startPoint, LatLong endPoint) {
    ...
  }
}
```

Chapter 2 talked about the usage of interfaces, and in particular how it's often useful to define an interface when there might be more than one way of solving the given subproblem. It's exactly for scenarios like the one in this section that this advice exists. If a class implements an interface and that interface captures the behavior we need, then it's a strong hint that other engineers might want to use our code with different implementations of that interface. Depending on the interface rather than a specific class is rarely any more effort but makes the code considerably more modular and adaptable.

> **NOTE: THE DEPENDENCY INVERSION PRINCIPLE** The idea that it's better to depend on abstractions as opposed to more concrete implementations is central to the *dependency inversion principle*.[1] A more detailed description of this design principle can be found at https://stackify.com/dependency-inversion-principle/.

8.3 Beware of class inheritance

One of the defining features of most object-oriented programming languages is that they allow one class to inherit from another. A somewhat canonical example of this is modeling a hierarchy of vehicles using classes (figure 8.1). Both cars and trucks are a type of vehicle, so we might define a Vehicle class to provide functionality common to all vehicles and then define Car and Truck classes that both inherit from the Vehicle class. In turn, any class representing a specific type of car might inherit from the Car class. This forms a *class hierarchy*.

[1] The dependency inversion principle is often associated with Robert C. Martin. It's one of the five SOLID design principles promoted by Martin (SOLID is an acronym coined by Michael Feathers, and the D stands for dependency inversion principle). See http://mng.bz/K4Pg.

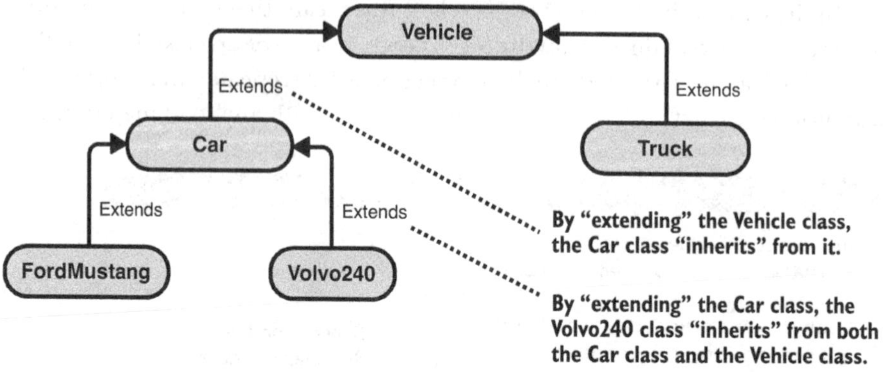

Figure 8.1 Classes can inherit from one another, forming a class hierarchy.

Class inheritance certainly has its uses and is sometimes the right tool for the job. When two things have a genuine *is-a* relationship (e.g., a car *is a* vehicle) this can be a sign that inheritance might be appropriate (although see the caveats in section 8.3.3). Inheritance is a powerful tool, but it can also have several drawbacks and be quite unforgiving in terms of the problems it causes, so it's usually worth thinking carefully before writing code where one class inherits from another.

In many scenarios, an alternative to using inheritance is to use *composition*. This means that we *compose* one class out of another by containing an instance of it rather than extending it. This can often avoid some of the pitfalls of inheritance and result in code that is more modular and more robust. This section demonstrates some of the problems that inheritance can cause and how composition can be a better alternative.

8.3.1 Class inheritance can be problematic

The vehicle and car example shows what we mean by class inheritance, but it's a bit too abstract to demonstrate some of the pitfalls that engineers usually encounter, so we'll consider a more realistic scenario where an engineer might be tempted to use class inheritance. Let's assume that we have been asked to write a class that will read integers one by one from a file that contains comma-separated values. We think about this and identify the following subproblems:

- We must read data from a file.
- We must split the comma-separated contents of the file into individual strings.
- We must parse each of these strings into an integer.

NOTE: ERRORS We'll ignore error scenarios for the sake of this example (such as the file not being accessible or containing invalid data). In real life we'd probably want to consider these and use one of the techniques from chapter 4.

We notice that the first two of these subproblems have already been solved by an existing class called `CsvFileHandler` (shown in listing 8.10). This class opens a file and allows us to read the comma-separated strings one by one from it. The `CsvFileHandler` class implements two interfaces: `FileValueReader` and `FileValueWriter`. We need only the functionality captured by the `FileValueReader` interface, but as we'll see in a moment, class inheritance doesn't allow us to depend on an interface like this.

Listing 8.10 Class that reads a CSV file

```
interface FileValueReader {
  String? getNextValue();
  void close();
}

interface FileValueWriter {
  void writeValue(String value);
  void close();
}

/**
 * Utility for reading and writing from/to a file containing
 * comma-separated values.
 */
class CsvFileHandler
    implements FileValueReader, FileValueWriter {
  ...

  CsvFileReader(File file) { ... }

  override String? getNextValue() { ... }    <- Reads the comma-separated
                                                strings from the file one by one
  override void writeValue(String value) { ... }

  override void close() { ... }
}
```

In order to use the `CsvFileHandler` class to help us solve our high-level problem, we have to incorporate it into our code somehow. Listing 8.11 shows how our code might look if we used inheritance to do this. Some things to notice about the code are as follows:

- The `IntFileReader` class *extends* the `CsvFileHandler` class, meaning that `IntFileReader` is a *subclass* of `CsvFileHandler`, or to put it another way, `CsvFileHandler` is a *superclass* of `IntFileReader`.
- The `IntFileReader` constructor has to instantiate the `CsvFileHandler` superclass by calling its constructor. It does this by calling `super()`.
- Code within the `IntFileReader` class has access to functions from the `CsvFileHandler` superclass as though they were part of the `IntFileReader` class, so a call to `getNextValue()` from within the `IntFileReader` class calls this function on the superclass.

Listing 8.11 Class inheritance

```
/**
 * Utility for reading integers from a file one by one. The
 * file should contain comma-separated values.
 */
class IntFileReader extends CsvFileHandler {
  ...

  IntFileReader(File file) {
    super(file);
  }

  Int? getNextInt() {
    String? nextValue = getNextValue();
    if (nextValue == null) {
      return null;
    }
    return Int.parse(nextValue, Radix.BASE_10);
  }
}
```

- IntFileReader (subclass) extends CsvFileHandler (superclass).
- The IntFileReader constructor calls the superclass constructor.
- Calls the getNextValue() function from the superclass

One of the key features of inheritance is that a subclass will inherit all the functionality provided by the superclass, so any code that has an instance of `IntFileReader` can call any of the functions provided by `CsvFileHandler`, such as the `close()` function. An example usage of the `IntFileReader` class might look like this:

```
IntFileReader reader = new IntFileReader(myFile);
Int? firstValue = reader.getNextInt();
reader.close();
```

As well as having access to the `close()` function, any code with an instance of `IntFileReader` will also have access to all the other functions from `CsvFileHandler`, such as `getNextValue()` and `writeValue()`, which, as we will see in a moment, can be problematic.

INHERITANCE CAN PREVENT CLEAN LAYERS OF ABSTRACTION

When one class extends another class it inherits all the functionality of the superclass. This is sometimes useful (as in the case of the `close()` function) but can also end up exposing more functionality than we'd ideally like to. This can lead to messy layers of abstraction and the leaking of implementation details.

To demonstrate this, let's consider what the API for the `IntFileReader` class looks like if we explicitly show both the functions it provides as well as those that it inherits from the `CsvFileHandler` superclass. Listing 8.12 shows what the API of `IntFileReader` effectively looks like. We can see that any users of the `IntFileReader` class can call the `getNextValue()` and `writeValue()` functions if they want to. For a class that claims to just read integers from a file, these are very strange functions to have in the public API.

Listing 8.12 The public API of IntFileReader

```
class IntFileReader extends CsvFileHandler {
  ...

  Int? getNextInt() { ... }

  String? getNextValue() { ... }
  void writeValue(String value) { ... }
  void close() { ... }
}
```

Functions inherited from superclass

If a class's API exposes some functionality, then we should expect that at least some engineers will make use of this functionality. After a few months or years, we may find that the `getNextValue()` and `writeValue()` functions are being called in multiple places through the codebase. This will make it very difficult to ever change the implementation of the `IntFileReader` class in the future. The use of `CsvFileHandler` should really be an implementation detail, but by using inheritance we've accidentally made it part of the public API.

Inheritance can make code hard to adapt

When we implemented the `IntFileReader` class, the problem we'd been asked to solve was reading integers from a file containing comma-separated values. Imagine that there is now a requirement that, in addition to this, we now also need to provide a way to read integers from files containing semicolon-separated values.

Once again we notice that there is already a solution for reading strings from a file containing semicolon-separated values. An engineer has already implemented a class called `SemicolonFileHandler` (shown in listing 8.13). This class implements exactly the same interfaces as the `CsvFileHandler` class: `FileValueReader` and `FileValueWriter`.

Listing 8.13 Class that reads a semicolon-separated file

```
/**
 * Utility for reading and writing from/to a file containing
 * semicolon-separated values.
 */
class SemicolonFileHandler
    implements FileValueReader, FileValueWriter {
  ...

  SemicolonFileHandler(File file) { ... }

  override String? getNextValue() { ... }

  override void writeValue(String value) { ... }

  override void close() { ... }
}
```

Implements the same interfaces as the CsvFileHandler class

The problem we need to solve is almost identical to the problem that we've already solved, but with one tiny difference: we sometimes need to use `SemicolonFileHandler` instead of `CsvFileHandler`. We would hope that such a small change in requirements would result in only a small change in the code, but unfortunately if we use inheritance this might not be the case.

The requirement is that in *addition* to handling comma-separated file contents, we need to *also* handle semicolon-separated contents, so we can't simply switch `IntFileReader` to inherit from `SemicolonFileHandler` instead of `CsvFileHandler` because this would break that existing functionality. Our only option is to write a new, separate version of the `IntFileReader` class that inherits from `SemicolonFileHandler`. Listing 8.14 shows what this would look like. The new class is named `SemicolonIntFileReader`, and it's a near duplicate of the original `IntFileReader` class. Code duplication like this is usually not good because it increases maintenance overhead as well as the chances of bugs (as discussed in chapter 1).

Listing 8.14 SemicolonIntFileReader class

```
/**
 * Utility for reading integers from a file one by one. The
 * file should contain semicolon-separated values.
 */
class SemicolonIntFileReader extends SemicolonFileHandler {
  ...

  SemicolonIntFileReader(File file) {
    super(file);
  }

  Int? getNextInt() {
    String? nextValue = getNextValue();
    if (nextValue == null) {
      return null;
    }
    return Int.parse(nextValue, Radix.BASE_10);
  }
}
```

The fact that we have to duplicate so much code is particularly frustrating when we consider that both the `CsvFileHandler` and `SemicolonFileHandler` classes implement the `FileValueReader` interface. This interface provides a layer of abstraction for reading values without having to know the file format. But because we used inheritance, we're not able to make use of this layer of abstraction. We'll see in a moment how composition can solve this.

8.3.2 Solution: Use composition

Our original motivation for using inheritance was that we wanted to reuse some of the functionality from the `CsvFileHandler` class to help us implement the `IntFileReader` class. Inheritance is one way to achieve this, but as we just saw, it can have several drawbacks. An alternative way to reuse the logic from `CsvFileHandler` would be to use composition. This means that we *compose* one class out of another by containing an instance of it rather than extending it.

Listing 8.15 shows how our code might look if we use composition. Some things to notice about the code are as follows:

- As mentioned previously, the `FileValueReader` interface captures the functionality we care about, so rather than using the `CsvFileHandler` class directly, we use the `FileValueReader` interface. This ensures cleaner layers of abstraction and makes the code easier to reconfigure.
- Instead of extending the `CsvFileHandler` class, the `IntFileReader` class holds an instance of `FileValueReader`. In this sense the `IntFileReader` class is composed of an instance of the `FileValueReader` (thus why we call it *composition*).
- An instance of `FileValueReader` is dependency injected via the `IntFileReader` class's constructor (this was covered in section 8.1).
- Because the `IntFileReader` class no longer extends the `CsvFileHandler` class, the `IntFileReader` class no longer inherits the `close()` method from it. To allow users of the `IntFileReader` class to close the file, we manually add a `close()` function to the class, which just calls the `close()` function on the instance of `FileValueReader`. This is called *forwarding* because the `IntFileReader.close()` function is forwarding the instruction to close the file to the `FileValueReader.close()` function.

Listing 8.15 A class that uses composition

```
/**
 * Utility for reading integers from a file one-by-one.
 */
class IntFileReader {
  private final FileValueReader valueReader;          <-- IntFileReader holds an instance of FileValueReader.

  IntFileReader(FileValueReader valueReader) {        <-- An instance of FileValueReader is dependency injected.
    this.valueReader = valueReader;
  }

  Int? getNextInt() {
    String? nextValue = valueReader.getNextValue();
    if (nextValue == null) {
      return null;
    }
    return Int.parse(nextValue, Radix.BASE_10);
  }

  void close() {
    valueReader.close();       The close() function forwards to valueReader.close().
  }
}
```

> **Delegation**
>
> Listing 8.15 demonstrates how the `IntFileReader.close()` function forwards to the `FileValueReader.close()` function. When we only need to forward a single function, this isn't much of a bother. But there can be scenarios where it's necessary to forward many functions to a composing class, and it can become extremely tedious to manually write all of these.
>
> This is a recognized problem, and as such some languages have either built-in or add-on support for delegation, which can make this a lot easier. This generally makes it possible for one class to expose some functions from a composing class in a controlled way. A couple of language specific examples are as follows:
>
> - Kotlin has built-in support for delegation: https://kotlinlang.org/docs/reference/delegation.html
> - In Java, Project Lombok provides an add-on `Delegate` annotation that can be used to delegate methods to a composing class: https://projectlombok.org/features/Delegate.html

The use of composition gives us the benefits of code reuse but avoids the problems with inheritance that we saw earlier in this section. The following subsections explain why.

CLEANER LAYERS OF ABSTRACTION

When using inheritance, a subclass inherits and exposes any functionality from the superclass. This meant that our `IntFileReader` class ended up exposing functions from the `CsvFileHandler` class. This resulted in a very strange public API, which allowed callers to read strings and even write values. If we use composition instead, then none of the functionality of the `CsvFileHandler` class is exposed (unless the `IntFileReader` class explicitly exposes it using forwarding or delegation).

To demonstrate how much cleaner the layer of abstraction is, listing 8.16 shows how the API of the `IntFileReader` class looks now that we're using composition. Only the `getNextInt()` and `close()` functions are exposed, and callers can no longer read strings or write values.

Listing 8.16 The public API of IntFileReader

```
class IntFileReader {
  ...

  Int? getNextInt() { ... }
  void close() { ... }
}
```

MORE ADAPTABLE CODE

Let's consider the requirement change we saw previously: we need to also support files that use semicolon-separated values. Because the `IntFileReader` class now depends on the `FileValueReader` interface, and because this is dependency injected, this requirement is very easy to support. The `IntFileReader` class can be constructed with any implementation of `FileValueReader`, so it's trivially easy to configure it with either a `CsvFileHandler` or a `SemicolonFileHandler` without duplicating any code. We could make this especially easy by providing two factory functions to create suitably configured instances of the `IntFileReader` class. The following listing shows what these might look like.

Listing 8.17 Factory functions

```
class IntFileReaderFactory {

  IntFileReader createCsvIntReader(File file) {
    return new IntFileReader(new CsvFileHandler(file));
  }

  IntFileReader createSemicolonIntReader(File file) {
    return new IntFileReader(new SemicolonFileHandler(file));
  }
}
```

The `IntFileReader` class is relatively straightforward, so using composition may not seem like a massive win in terms of making the code adaptable and avoiding duplication, but this is a deliberately simple example. In real life, classes can often contain more code and functionality than this, so the costs of having code that can't be adapted to even small changes in requirements can become quite high.

8.3.3 What about genuine is-a relationships?

The start of this section mentioned that inheritance can make sense when two classes have a genuine *is-a* relationship: a Ford Mustang is a car, so we might make a `FordMustang` class extend a `Car` class. The example of the `IntFileReader` and `CsvFileHandler` classes clearly doesn't follow this relationship: an `IntFileReader` is not intrinsically a `CsvFileHandler`, so this is quite a clear-cut scenario where composition is almost certainly better than inheritance. But when there is a genuine is-a relationship, it can be less clear-cut as to whether inheritance is a good approach. Unfortunately, there is no one answer to this, and it will depend on the given scenario and the code we're working on. But it's worth being aware that even when there is a genuine is-a relationship, inheritance can still be problematic. Some things to watch out for are as follows:

- *The fragile base class problem*—If a subclass inherits from a superclass (sometimes called a base class), and that superclass is later modified, this can sometimes break the subclass. This can make it very hard to reason about whether a certain code change is safe.
- *The diamond problem*—Some languages support *multiple inheritance* (a class extending more than one superclass). This can lead to issues if multiple superclasses provide versions of the same function, because it can be ambiguous as to which superclass the function should be inherited from.

- *Problematic hierarchies*—Many languages do not support multiple inheritance, meaning a class can only directly extend a maximum of one other class. This is called *single inheritance* and can cause another type of problem. Imagine we have a class called `Car`, which all classes representing a type of car should extend. In addition to this, imagine we also have a class called `Aircraft`, which all classes representing a type of aircraft should extend. Figure 8.2 shows what our class hierarchy looks like. Now imagine someone invents a flying car; what do we do? There's no sensible way to fit this into our class hierarchy because the `FlyingCar` class can either extend the `Car` class or the `Aircraft` class, but not both.

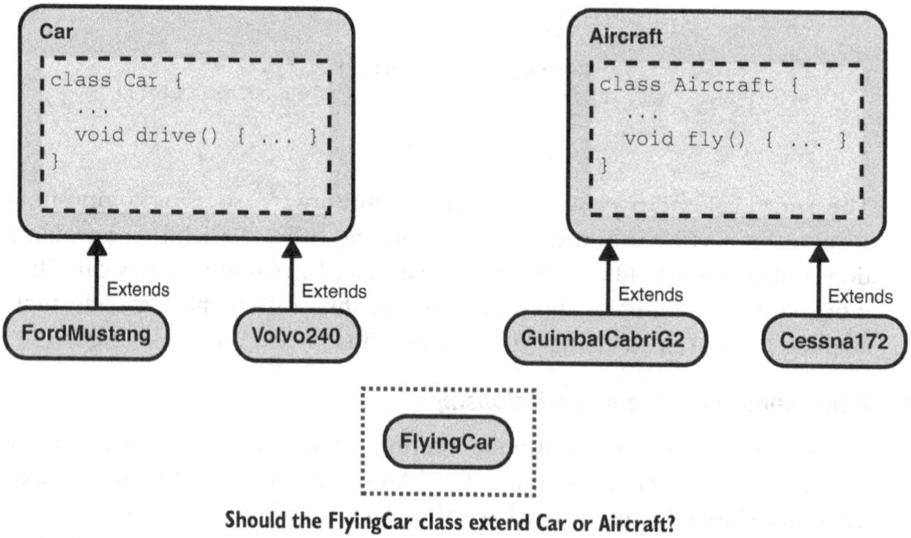

Figure 8.2 Many languages support only single inheritance. This can lead to problems when a class logically belongs in more than one hierarchy.

Sometimes there is an inescapable need for a hierarchy of objects. To achieve this, while avoiding many of the pitfalls of class inheritance, engineers often do the following:

- Use interfaces to define a hierarchy of objects.
- Use composition to achieve reuse of code.

Figure 8.3 shows how the car and aircraft hierarchies look if `Car` and `Aircraft` are interfaces. To achieve reuse of the code that is common between all cars, each car class is composed of an instance of `DrivingAction`. Similarly, classes for aircraft are composed of an instance of `FlyingAction`.

There are enough pitfalls with class inheritance that it's good to be wary of it. Many engineers go as far as to make a point of avoiding it whenever they can. Luckily, the use of composition and interfaces can often achieve many of the benefits of inheritance without suffering the drawbacks.

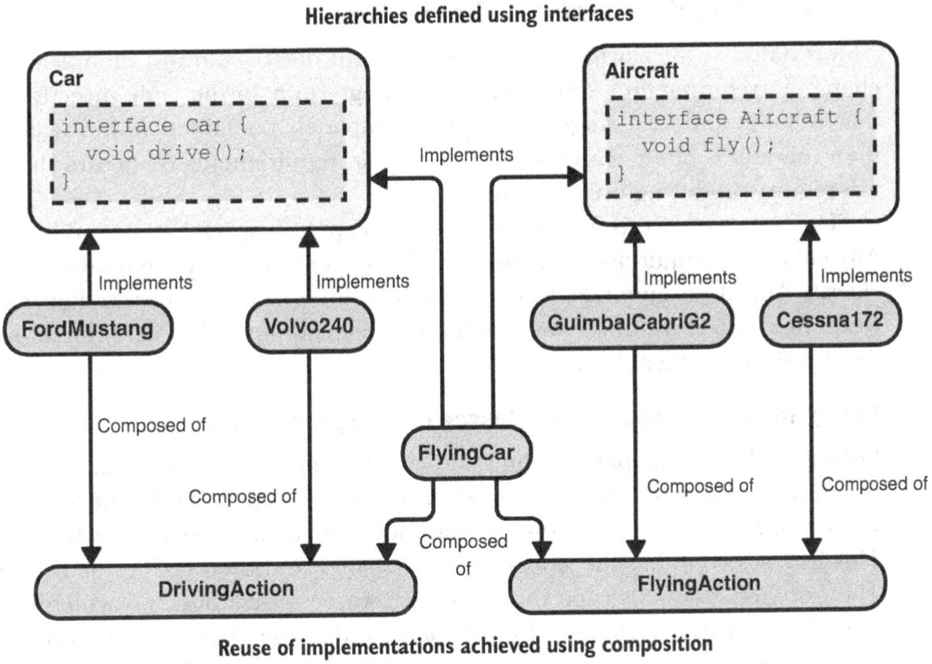

Figure 8.3 Hierarchies can be defined using interfaces, while code reuse can be achieved using composition.

> ### Mixins and traits
>
> Mixins and traits are features supported in some languages. They allow pieces of functionality to be added to (and shared between) classes without having to use traditional class inheritance. The exact definitions of mixin and trait and the distinction between them varies from language to language. How to implement them can also vary a lot between different languages.
>
> Mixins and traits help overcome some of the issues with multiple inheritance and problematic class hierarchies. But, similar to class inheritance, they can still lead to code that doesn't have clean layers of abstraction and that isn't very adaptable, so it's usually still a good idea to apply care and consideration when thinking about using mixins and traits. Some language-specific examples of mixins and traits are as follows:
>
> - *Mixins*—The Dart programming language supports mixins and provides a practical example of how they can be used: http://mng.bz/9NPq. The use of mixins is also relatively common in TypeScript: http://mng.bz/jBl8.
> - *Traits*—The Rust programming language supports traits: http://mng.bz/Wryl. And the inclusion of default interface methods in more recent versions of Java and C# provide a way of implementing traits in those languages.

8.4 Classes should care about themselves

As was stated at the start of this chapter, one of the key aims of modularity is that a change in requirements should require changes only in the code directly related to that requirement. If a single concept is completely contained within a single class, then this aim is often achieved. Any change in requirements related to that concept will require modifying only that single class.

The opposite of this is when a single concept gets spread across multiple classes. Any change in requirements related to that concept will require modifying multiple classes. And if an engineer forgets to modify one of these classes, then this might result in a bug. A common way this can happen is when a class cares too much about the details of another class.

8.4.1 Caring too much about other classes can be problematic

Listing 8.18 contains part of the code for two separate classes. The first class represents a book and the second represents a chapter within a book. The `Book` class provides a `wordCount()` function for counting how many words are within the book. This involves counting the words in each chapter and then taking the sum of these. The `Book` class contains the function `getChapterWordCount()`, which counts the number of words in a chapter. Despite being within the `Book` class, this function cares about things to do with only the `Chapter` class. This means that a lot of details about the `Chapter` class are now hard coded into the `Book` class. For example, the `Book` class assumes that a chapter will contain only a prelude and a list of sections.

Listing 8.18 Book and chapter classes

```
class Book {
  private final List<Chapter> chapters;
  ...

  Int wordCount() {
    return chapters
        .map(getChapterWordCount)
        .sum();
  }

  private static Int getChapterWordCount(Chapter chapter) {
    return chapter.getPrelude().wordCount() +
        chapter.getSections()
            .map(section -> section.wordCount())
            .sum();
  }
}

class Chapter {
  ...

  TextBlock getPrelude() { ... }

  List<TextBlock> getSections() { ... }
}
```

This function cares only about the Chapter class.

Placing the `getChapterWordCount()` function within the `Book` class makes the code less modular. If a requirement changes and a chapter is now meant to have a summary at the end, then the `getChapterWordCount()` function would need to be updated to also count the words in the summary. This means that changes in requirements that relate only to chapters will affect more than just the `Chapter` class. And if an engineer adds support for a summary to the `Chapter` class, but then forgets to update the `Book.getChapterWordCount()` function, the logic for counting the words in the book would be broken.

8.4.2 Solution: Make classes care about themselves

To keep code modular and to ensure that changes to one thing affect only one part of the code, we should ensure that the `Book` and `Chapter` classes care only about themselves as much as possible. The `Book` class obviously needs some knowledge of the `Chapter` class (because a book contains chapters). But we can minimize the amount these classes care about each other's details by moving the logic within the `getChapterWordCount()` function to the `Chapter` class.

Listing 8.19 shows what the code now looks like. The `Chapter` class now has a member function named `wordCount()`, and the `Book` class makes use of this function. The `Book` class now only cares about itself rather than also caring about details of the `Chapter` class. If a requirement changed and chapters were meant to have a summary at the end, then only the `Chapter` class would need to be modified.

Listing 8.19 Improved book and chapter classes

```
class Book {
  private final List<Chapter> chapters;
  ...

  Int wordCount() {
    return chapters
        .map(chapter -> chapter.wordCount())
        .sum();
  }
}

class Chapter {
  ...

  TextBlock getPrelude() { ... }

  List<TextBlock> getSections() { ... }

  Int wordCount() {
    return getPrelude().wordCount() +
        getSections()
            .map(section -> section.wordCount())
            .sum();
  }
}
```

Logic to count words within a chapter is fully contained within the Chapter class

The Law of Demeter

The Law of Demeter[a] (sometimes abbreviated LoD) is a software engineering principle that states that one object should make as few assumptions as possible about the content or structure of other objects. In particular, the principle advocates that an object should interact only with other objects that it's immediately related to.

In the context of the example in this section, the Law of Demeter would advocate that the `Book` class should interact only with instances of the `Chapter` class and not with any objects within the `Chapter` class (such as the `TextBlocks` that represent the prelude and sections). The original code in listing 8.18 clearly breaks this with a line like `chapter.getPrelude().wordCount()`, so the Law of Demeter could have been used to spot the problem with the original code in this scenario.

With any software engineering principle, it's important to consider the reasoning behind it and the advantages as well as disadvantages that it might provide in different scenarios. The Law of Demeter is no different, so if you want to find out more about it, I'd encourage you to read the differing arguments around it and form a well-grounded opinion. To this end, the following articles may be useful:

- An article that explains the principle in more detail and presents some of the advantages: http://mng.bz/8WP5
- An article that presents some of the disadvantages: http://mng.bz/EVPX

[a] The Law of Demeter was proposed by Ian Holland in the 1980s.

One of the key aims of making code modular is that a change in requirements should result in changes only to those parts of the code that directly relate to that requirement. Classes often need some amount of knowledge of one another, but it's often worth minimizing this as much as possible. This can help keep code modular and can greatly improve adaptability and maintainability.

8.5 Encapsulate related data together

Classes allow us to group things together. Chapter 2 cautioned about the problems that can be caused when we try to group too many things together into one class. We should be cautious of this, but in doing so we shouldn't lose sight of the benefits of grouping things together when it makes sense.

Sometimes different pieces of data are inescapably related to one another and a piece of code needs to pass them around together. In this scenario it often makes sense to group them together into a class (or similar structure). Doing this allows code to deal with the higher level concept that the group of items represent rather than always having to deal with the nuts-and-bolts details. This can make code more modular and keep changes in requirements more isolated.

8.5.1 Unencapsulated data can be difficult to handle

Consider the code in listing 8.20. The `TextBox` class represents an element within a user interface and the `renderText()` function displays some text within this element. The `renderText()` function has four parameters that are related to what styling the text should have.

Listing 8.20 Class and function to render text

```
class TextBox {
  ...

  void renderText(
      String text,
      Font font,
      Double fontSize,
      Double lineHeight,
      Color textColor) {
    ...
  }
}
```

The `TextBox` class is likely a relatively low-level piece of code, so the `renderText()` function is probably called by a function, which is in turn called by another function, and so on. This means that the values related to styling the text potentially have to be passed from one function to the next several times. Listing 8.21 shows a simplified version of this. In this scenario the `UiSettings` class is the source of the text styling values. The `UserInterface.displayMessage()` function reads these values from `uiSettings` and passes them along to the `renderText()` function.

The `displayMessage()` function doesn't actually care about any of the specifics of text styling. All it cares about is the fact that `UiSettings` provides some styling and `renderText()` needs these. But because the text styling options are not encapsulated together, the `displayMessage()` function is forced to have detailed knowledge of the nuts-and-bolts details of text styling.

Listing 8.21 UiSettings and UserInterface classes

```
class UiSettings {
  ...

  Font getFont() { ... }
  Double getFontSize() { ... }
  Double getLineHeight() { ... }
  Color getTextColor() { ... }
}


class UserInterface {
  private final TextBox messageBox;
  private final UiSettings uiSettings;

  void displayMessage(String message) {
```

```
    messageBox.renderText(
        message,
        uiSettings.getFont(),
        uiSettings.getFontSize(),
        uiSettings.getLineHeight(),
        uiSettings.getTextColor());
  }
}
```

The displayMessage() function contains nuts-and-bolts details of text styling.

In this scenario the `displayMessage()` function is a bit like a courier delivering some information from the `UiSettings` class to the `renderText()` function. In real life, a courier will often not care exactly what is inside a package. If you post a box of chocolates to a friend, the courier doesn't need to know whether you're posting caramel truffles or pralines. But in this scenario the `displayMessage()` class has to know exactly what it is relaying.

If a requirement changes and it's now necessary to define a font style (e.g., italic) for the `renderText()` function, we'll have to modify the `displayMessage()` function to relay this new piece of information. As we saw earlier, one of the aims of modularity is to ensure a change in a requirement only affects parts of the code directly related to that requirement. In this case only the `UiSettings` and `TextBox` classes actually deal with text styling, so it's not ideal that the `displayMessage()` function should also need to be modified.

8.5.2 Solution: Group related data into objects or classes

In this scenario the font, font size, line height, and text color are intrinsically linked to one another: to know how to style some text, we need to know all of them. Given that they are linked like this, it makes sense to encapsulate them together into a single object that can then be passed around. The following listing shows a class called `TextOptions`, which does exactly this.

Listing 8.22 TextOptions encapsulating class

```
class TextOptions {
  private final Font font;
  private final Double fontSize;
  private final Double lineHeight;
  private final Color textColor;

  TextOptions(Font font, Double fontSize,
      Double lineHeight, Color textColor) {
    this.font = font;
    this.fontSize = fontSize;
    this.lineHeight = lineHeight;
    this.textColor = textColor;
  }

  Font getFont() { return font; }
  Double getFontSize() { return fontSize; }
  Double getLineHeight() { return lineHeight; }
  Color getTextColor() { return textColor; }
}
```

> **Alternative to data objects**
>
> Encapsulating data together (like the `TextOptions` class does) can be another use case for data objects, which were discussed in the previous chapter in section 7.3.3.
>
> As was said in the previous chapter, proponents of a more traditional take on object-oriented programming sometimes consider data-only objects bad practice, so it's worth noting that another approach in this scenario might be to bundle the styling information and the logic that implements text styling into the same class. If we did this, then we'd likely end up with a `TextStyler` class that we pass around. The general point about encapsulating related data together still applies though.

Using the `TextOptions` class, we can now encapsulate text styling information together and just pass around an instance of `TextOptions` instead. Listing 8.23 shows what the code from the previous subsection now looks like. The `displayMessage()` function now has no knowledge of the specifics of text styling. If we did need to add a font style, then we wouldn't need to make any changes to the `displayMessage()` function. It's become more like a good courier: it diligently delivers the package without caring too much about what's inside.

Listing 8.23 Passing encapsulating object around

```
class UiSettings {
  ...

  TextOptions getTextStyle() { ... }
}


class UserInterface {
  private final TextBox messageBox;
  private final UiSettings uiSettings;

  void displayMessage(String message) {
    messageBox.renderText(
        message, uiSettings.getTextStyle());
  }
}


class TextBox {
  ...

  void renderText(String text, TextOptions textStyle) {
    ...
  }
}
```

The displayMessage() function has no specific knowledge of text styling.

Deciding when to encapsulate things together can require a bit of thought. Chapter 2 demonstrated how problems can occur when too many concepts are bundled together into the same class, so it pays to be a bit cautious. But when different pieces of data are inescapably related to one another, and there's no practical scenario in which someone would want some of the pieces of data without wanting all of them, then it usually makes sense to encapsulate them together.

8.6 Beware of leaking implementation details in return types

Chapter 2 established the importance of creating clean layers of abstraction. In order to have clean layers of abstraction, it's necessary to ensure that layers don't leak implementation details. If implementation details are leaked, this can reveal things about lower layers in the code and can make it very hard to modify or reconfigure things in the future. One of the most common ways code can leak an implementation detail is by returning a type that is tightly coupled to that detail.

8.6.1 Leaking implementation details in a return type can be problematic

Listing 8.24 shows some code that can be used to look up the profile picture for a given user. The `ProfilePictureService` is implemented using an `HttpFetcher` to fetch the profile picture data from a server. The fact that `HttpFetcher` is used is an implementation detail, and as such, any engineer using the `ProfilePictureService` class should ideally not have to concern themselves with this piece of information.

Even though the `ProfilePictureService` class does not directly leak the fact that `HttpFetcher` is used, it unfortunately leaks it indirectly via a return type. The `getProfilePicture()` function returns an instance of `ProfilePictureResult`. If we look inside the `ProfilePictureResult` class we see that it uses `HttpResponse.Status` to indicate if the request was successful and `HttpResponse.Payload` to hold the image data for the profile picture. These both leak the fact that the `ProfilePictureService` uses an HTTP connection to fetch the profile picture.

Listing 8.24 Implementation details in a return type

```
class ProfilePictureService {
  private final HttpFetcher httpFetcher;
  ...

  ProfilePictureResult getProfilePicture(Int64 userId) { ... }
}

class ProfilePictureResult {
  ...

  /**
   * Indicates if the request for the profile picture was
   * successful or not.
   */
  HttpResponse.Status getStatus() { ... }

  /**
   * The image data for the profile picture if it was successfully
   * found.
   */
  HttpResponse.Payload? getImageData() { ... }
}
```

- ProfilePictureService is implemented using an HttpFetcher. (annotates `private final HttpFetcher httpFetcher;`)
- Returns an instance of ProfilePictureResult (annotates `getProfilePicture`)
- Data types specific to an HTTP response (annotates `getStatus()` and `getImageData()`)

Chapter 2 emphasized the importance of not leaking implementation details, so from that point of view we can probably immediately see that this code is less than ideal. But to really see how harmful this code could be, let's drill into some of the consequences, such as the following:

- Any engineer using the `ProfilePictureService` class has to deal with a number of concepts specific to an `HttpResponse`. To understand if a profile picture request was successful and why it may have failed, an engineer has to interpret an `HttpResponse.Status` enum value. This requires knowing about HTTP status codes and which specific HTTP status codes the server might actually be utilizing. An engineer might guess that they need to check for `STATUS_200` (which indicates success) and `STATUS_404` (which indicates that the resource could not be found). But what about the other 50-plus HTTP status codes that sometimes get used?
- It's very hard to ever change the implementation of `ProfilePictureService`. Any code that calls `ProfilePictureService.getProfilePicture()` has to deal with the `HttpResponse.Status` and `HttpResponse.Payload` types to make sense of the response, so layers of code built on top of `ProfilePictureService` are relying on the fact that it returns types specific to an `HttpResponse`. Imagine there is a change in requirements meaning that our application should be able to fetch profile pictures using a WebSocket connection (for example). Because so much code relies on the usage of types specific to an `HttpResponse`, it will require a lot of code changes in a lot of places to support any change in requirements like this.

It would be better if the `ProfilePictureService` didn't leak implementation details like this. A better approach would be if it returned a type that was appropriate to the layer of abstraction it aims to provide.

8.6.2 Solution: Return a type appropriate to the layer of abstraction

The problem that the `ProfilePictureService` class solves is that of fetching a profile picture for a user. This dictates the layer of abstraction that this class should ideally be providing, and any return types should reflect this. We should try to keep the number of concepts that we expose to engineers using the class to a minimum. In this scenario the minimal set of concepts that we need to expose are the following:

- A request may succeed, or it may fail for one of the following reasons:
  - The user does not exist.
  - Some kind of transient error occurred (like the server being unreachable).
- The bytes of data that represent the profile picture.

Listing 8.25 shows how we might implement the `ProfilePictureService` and `ProfilePictureResult` classes if we try to keep the number of concepts we expose to this minimal set. The important changes we've made are as follows:

- Instead of using the `HttpResponse.Status` enum, we have defined a custom enum that contains only the set of statuses that an engineer using this class actually needs to care about.

- Instead of returning `HttpResponse.Payload`, we return a list of bytes.

Listing 8.25 Return type matches layer of abstraction

```
class ProfilePictureService {
  private final HttpFetcher httpFetcher;
  ...

  ProfilePictureResult getProfilePicture(Int64 userId) { ... }
}

class ProfilePictureResult {
  ...

  enum Status {
    SUCCESS,
    USER_DOES_NOT_EXIST,
    OTHER_ERROR,
  }

  /**
   * Indicates if the request for the profile picture was
   * successful or not.
   */
  Status getStatus() { ... }

  /**
   * The image data for the profile picture if it was successfully
   * found.
   */
  List<Byte>? getImageData() { ... }
}
```

A custom enum to define just the statuses we require

Returns custom enum

Returns a list of bytes

> **Enums**
>
> As was mentioned in chapter 6, enums cause some amount of disagreement among engineers. Some like using them, and others consider polymorphism a better approach (creating different classes that implement a common interface).
>
> Whether you like enums or not, the key take-away here is to use a type that is appropriate to the layer of abstraction (be that an enum or class).

In general, reusing code is good, so at a first glance it might have seemed like a good idea to reuse the `HttpResponse.Status` and `HttpResponse.Payload` types in the `ProfilePictureResult` class. But when we think about it more, we realize that these types are not appropriate to the layer of abstraction we're providing, so defining our own types that capture the minimal set of concepts and using these instead results in cleaner layers of abstraction and more modular code.

8.7 Beware of leaking implementation details in exceptions

The previous section showed how leaking implementation details in return types can cause problems. A return type is in the unmistakably obvious part of the code contract, so (while being problematic) it's usually quite easy to spot when we might be doing this, which can make it easier to avoid. Another common way in which implementation details can be leaked is via the types of exceptions that we throw. In particular, chapter 4 discussed how unchecked exceptions are in the small print of the code contract, and sometimes not even in the written contract at all, so if we're using unchecked exceptions for errors that callers might want to recover from, then leaking implementation details in them can be particularly problematic.

8.7.1 Leaking implementation details in exceptions can be problematic

One of the defining features of unchecked exceptions is that the compiler does not enforce anything about where and when they may be thrown, or about where (or if) code catches them. Knowledge about unchecked exceptions is either conveyed in the small print of the code contract or else not conveyed in the written contract at all if engineers forget to document them.

Listing 8.26 contains the code for two adjacent layers of abstraction. The lower layer is the `TextImportanceScorer` interface, and the upper layer is the `TextSummarizer` class. In this scenario, `ModelBasedScorer` is a concrete implementation that implements the `TextImportanceScorer` interface, but `ModelBasedScorer.isImportant()` can throw the unchecked exception `PredictionModelException`.

Listing 8.26 Exception leaking implementation detail

```
class TextSummarizer {
  private final TextImportanceScorer importanceScorer;   <-- Depends on the TextImportanceScorer interface
  ...

  String summarizeText(String text) {
    return paragraphFinder.find(text)
        .filter(paragraph =>
            importanceScorer.isImportant(paragraph))
        .join("\n\n");
  }
}

interface TextImportanceScorer {
  Boolean isImportant(String text);
}

class ModelBasedScorer implements TextImportanceScorer {   <-- An implementation of the TextImportanceScorer interface
  ...
  /**
   * @throws PredictionModelException if there is an error   <-- An unchecked exception that can be thrown
   *     running the prediction model.
   */
  override Boolean isImportant(String text) {
    return model.predict(text) >= MODEL_THRESHOLD;
  }
}
```

An engineer using the `TextSummarizer` class will likely notice sooner or later that their code sometimes crashes due to a `PredictionModelException`, and they may well want to handle this error scenario gracefully and recover from it. To do so, they would have to write something like the code in listing 8.27. The code catches a `PredictionModelException` and displays an error message to the user. In order to make the code work, the engineer has had to become aware of the fact that the `TextSummarizer` class can use model-based predictions (an implementation detail).

Not only does this break the concept of layers of abstraction, but it can also be unreliable and error prone. The `TextSummarizer` class depends on the `TextImportanceScorer` interface, and as such can be configured with any implementation of this interface. `ModelBasedScorer` is just one such implementation, but it's likely not the only one. `TextSummarizer` might be configured with a different implementation of `TextImportanceScorer` that throws a completely different type of exception. If this happens then the catch statement won't catch the exception, and the program would either crash or the user would see a potentially less helpful error message from a higher level in the code.

Listing 8.27 Catching implementation-specific exception

```
void updateTextSummary(UserInterface ui) {
  String userText = ui.getUserText();
  try {
    String summary = textSummarizer.summarizeText(userText);
    ui.getSummaryField().setValue(summary);
  } catch (PredictionModelException e) {
    ui.getSummaryField().setError("Unable to summarize text");
  }
}
```

PredictionModelException caught and handled

The risk of leaking implementation details is not unique to unchecked exceptions, but in this instance their use exacerbates the problem. It's too easy for engineers to not document what unchecked exceptions might be thrown, and classes that implement an interface are not forced to only throw errors that the interface dictates.

8.7.2 Solution: Make exceptions appropriate to the layer of abstraction

In order to prevent implementation details being leaked, each layer in the code should ideally reveal only error types that reflect the given layer of abstraction. We can achieve this by wrapping any errors from lower layers into error types appropriate to the current layer. This means that callers are presented with an appropriate layer of abstraction while also ensuring that the original error information is not lost (because it's still present within the wrapped error).

Listing 8.28 demonstrates this. A new exception type called `TextSummarizerException` has been defined to signal any errors to do with summarizing text. Similarly, a `TextImportanceScorerException` has been defined to signal any errors to do with scoring text (regardless of which implementation of the interface is being used). Finally, the code has been modified to use an explicit error-signaling technique. In this example, this is achieved with checked exceptions.

An obvious downside is that there are now more lines of code, as we've had to define some custom exception classes and catch, wrap, and rethrow various exceptions. On a first glance at the code it may seem "more complex," but this is not really true if we consider the software as a whole. An engineer using the `TextSummarizer` class now has only one type of error they will ever have to deal with, and they know for sure which type this is. The downsides of the extra error handling boilerplate within the code are likely outweighed by the benefits of improved modularity and the more predictable behavior of the `TextSummarizer` class.

Recap: Alternatives to checked exceptions

Checked exceptions are just one type of explicit error-signaling technique and (among mainstream programming languages) are more or less unique to Java. Chapter 4 covered this in detail and demonstrated some alternative explicit techniques that can be used in any language (such as result types and outcomes). Checked exceptions are used in listing 8.28 to keep the code more easily comparable to the code in listing 8.26.

Another thing that chapter 4 discussed is how error signaling and handling is a divisive topic, and in particular how engineers disagree about the usage of unchecked exceptions versus more explicit error-signaling techniques for errors that a caller might want to recover from. But even if we work on a codebase where the use of unchecked exceptions is encouraged for this, it's still often important to ensure that they don't leak implementation details (as the previous subsection showed).

An approach sometimes favored by engineers using unchecked exceptions is to prefer standard exception types (like `ArgumentException` or `StateException`), because it's more likely that other engineers will predict that these might be thrown, and handle them appropriately. A downside of this is that it can limit the ability to distinguish between different error scenarios (this was also discussed in chapter 4, section 4.5.2).

Listing 8.28 Exceptions appropriate to layers

```
class TextSummarizerException extends Exception {
  ...
  TextSummarizerException(Throwable cause) { ... }
  ...
}

class TextSummarizer {
  private final TextImportanceScorer importanceScorer;
  ...

  String summarizeText(String text)
      throws TextSummarizerException {
```

- Exception for signaling an error to do with summarizing text
- Constructor accepts another exception to wrap (Throwable is a superclass of Exception)

```
    try {
      return paragraphFinder.find(text)
          .filter(paragraph =>
              importanceScorer.isImportant(paragraph))
          .join("\n\n");
    } catch (TextImportanceScorerException e) {
      throw new TextSummarizerException(e);
    }
  }
}

class TextImportanceScorerException extends Exception {
  ...
  TextImportanceScorerException(Throwable cause) { ... }
  ...
}

interface TextImportanceScorer {
  Boolean isImportant(String text)
      throws TextImportanceScorerException;
}

class ModelBasedScorer implements TextImportanceScorer {
  ...
  Boolean isImportant(String text)
      throws TextImportanceScorerException {
    try {
      return model.predict(text) >= MODEL_THRESHOLD;
    } catch (PredictionModelException e) {
      throw new TextImportanceScorerException(e);
    }
  }
}
```

TextImportanceScorerException is wrapped in a TextSummarizerException and rethrown.

Exception for signaling an error to do with scoring text

The interface defines the error types exposed by the layer of abstraction.

PredictionModelException is wrapped in a TextImportanceScorerException and rethrown.

An engineer using the `TextSummarizer` class would now need to handle only the `TextSummarizerException`. This means that they don't have to be aware of any implementation details, and it also means that their error handling will keep working regardless of how the `TextSummarizer` class has been configured or is changed in the future. This is shown in the following listing.

Listing 8.29 Catching layer-appropriate exception

```
void updateTextSummary(UserInterface ui) {
  String userText = ui.getUserText();
  try {
    String summary = textSummarizer.summarizeText(userText);
    ui.getSummaryField().setValue(summary);
  } catch (TextSummarizerException e) {
    ui.getSummaryField().setError("Unable to summarize text");
  }
}
```

If we know for sure that an error is not one any caller would ever want to recover from, then leaking implementation details is not a massive issue, as higher layers probably won't try to handle that specific error anyway. But whenever we have an error that a caller might want to recover from, it's often important to ensure that the type of the error is appropriate to the layer of abstraction. Explicit error-signaling techniques (like checked exceptions, results, and outcomes) can make it easier to enforce this.

Summary

- Modular code is often easier to adapt to changing requirements.
- One of the key aims of modularity is that a change in a requirement should only affect parts of the code directly related to that requirement.
- Making code modular is highly related to creating clean layers of abstraction.
- The following techniques can be used to make code modular:
  - Using dependency injection
  - Depending on interfaces instead of concrete classes
  - Using interfaces and composition instead of class inheritance
  - Making classes care about themselves
  - Encapsulating related data together
  - Ensuring that return types and exceptions don't leak implementation details

9 Make code reusable and generalizable

This chapter covers

- How to write code that can be safely reused
- How to write code that can generalize to solve different problems

Chapter 2 discussed how, as engineers, we often solve a high-level problem by breaking it down into a series of subproblems. As we do this on one project after another, we often find that the same subproblems come up again and again. If we or other engineers have already solved a given subproblem, then it makes sense to reuse that solution. It saves us time and reduces the chance of bugs (because the code is already tried and tested).

Unfortunately, just because a solution to a subproblem already exists, it doesn't always mean that we can reuse it. This can happen if the solution makes assumptions that don't fit our use case, or if it's bundled together with some other logic that we don't need. It's therefore worth actively considering this and deliberately writing and structuring code in a way that will allow it to be reused in the future.

This can require a bit more upfront effort (although often not much more) but will usually save us and our teammates time and effort in the long run.

This chapter is highly related to creating clean layers of abstraction (chapter 2) and making code modular (chapter 8). Creating clean layers of abstraction and making code modular tend to result in the solutions to subproblems being broken up into distinct pieces of code that are only loosely coupled. This usually makes code much easier and safer to reuse and generalize. But the things we discussed in chapters 2 and 8 aren't the only considerations that go into making code reusable and generalizable. This chapter covers some additional things to think about.

9.1 Beware of assumptions

Making assumptions can sometimes result in code that is simpler, more efficient, or both. But assumptions also tend to result in code that is more fragile and less versatile, which can make it less safe to reuse. It's incredibly hard to keep track of exactly which assumptions have been made in which parts of the code, so they can easily turn into nasty traps that other engineers will inadvertently fall into. What might have initially seemed like an easy way to improve the code might actually have the opposite effect when bugs and weird behavior manifest as soon as the code is reused.

Given this, it's worth thinking through the costs and benefits before baking an assumption into the code. If the apparent gains in code simplification or efficiency are marginal, then it might be best to avoid making the assumption, because the costs from increased fragility might outweigh these. The following subsections explore this.

9.1.1 Assumptions can lead to bugs when code is reused

Consider the code in listing 9.1. The `Article` class represents an article on a news website that users can read. The `getAllImages()` function returns all the images contained within the article. To do this, it iterates through the sections within the article until it finds one that contains images and then returns the images from that section. The code makes the assumption that there will be only one section that contains images. This assumption is commented within the code, but this is unlikely to be something that any caller of the code notices.

By making this assumption, the code is very marginally more performant because it can exit the for-loop as soon as the image-containing section is found, but this gain is probably so small that it's of no real consequence. What might well be of consequence, however, is the fact that the `getAllImages()` function won't return all the images if it's ever used with an article that contains images in more than one section. This could well be an accident waiting to happen, and when it does happen it will likely cause a bug.

Listing 9.1 Code containing an assumption

```
class Article {
  private List<Section> sections;
  ...

  List<Image> getAllImages() {
    for (Section section in sections) {
      if (section.containsImages()) {
        // There should only ever be a maximum of one
        // section within an article that contains images.
        return section.getImages();
      }
    }
    return [];
  }
}
```

Assumption commented within the code

Returns images only from the first image-containing section

The assumption that there will be only one image section was no doubt correct for the original use case that the author had in mind. But it could quite easily become incorrect if the `Article` class is ever reused for something else (or if the placement of images within articles ever changes). And because this assumption is buried deep within the code, it's very unlikely that callers will be aware of it. They'll see a function called `getAllImages()` and assume that it returns "all" the images. Unfortunately this is true only if the hidden assumption is true.

9.1.2 *Solution: Avoid unnecessary assumptions*

The cost–benefit trade-off of assuming that there is only one image section suggests that it's probably not a worthwhile assumption to make. On the one hand, there is a marginal performance gain (which will likely not be noticeable), but on the other hand there is a real likelihood of bugs being introduced if anyone reuses the code or if a requirement changes. Given this, it's probably better to just get rid of this assumption: its presence introduces risk with no appreciable reward.

Premature optimization

The desire to avoid premature optimizations is a well-established concept within software engineering and computer science. Optimizing code generally has a cost associated with it: it often takes more time and effort to implement an optimized solution, and the resulting code is often less readable, harder to maintain, and potentially less robust (if assumptions are introduced). In addition to this, optimizations usually only have an appreciable benefit when made in pieces of code that run many thousands or millions of times within a program.

Therefore, in most scenarios, it's better to concentrate on making code readable, maintainable, and robust rather than chasing marginal gains in performance. If a piece of code ends up being run many times and it would be beneficial to optimize it, this can be done later at the point this becomes apparent.

Listing 9.2 shows what the code looks like if we remove the assumption by modifying the `getAllImages()` function to return images from all sections (instead of just the first one that contains images). This makes the function a lot more versatile and robust to different use cases. The downside is that it results in the for-loop potentially running for a few more iterations, but, as was just noted, it's unlikely that this would have a noticeable effect on performance.

Listing 9.2 Code with assumption removed

```
class Article {
  private List<Section> sections;
  ...

  List<Image> getAllImages() {
    List<Image> images = [];
    for (Section section in sections) {
      images.addAll(section.getImages());
    }
    return images;
  }
}
```

Collects and returns images from all sections

When writing code, we're often very alert to things like the performance costs of running a line of code more times than necessary. But it's important to remember that assumptions also carry an associated cost in terms of fragility. If making a particular assumption results in a big performance gain or enormously simplified code, then it might well be a worthwhile one to make. But if the gains are marginal, then the costs associated with baking an assumption into the code might well outweigh the benefits.

9.1.3 Solution: If an assumption is necessary, enforce it

Sometimes making an assumption is necessary, or simplifies the code to such an extent that the benefits outweigh the costs. When we do decide to make an assumption in the code, we should still be mindful of the fact that other engineers might not be aware of it, so to ensure that they don't inadvertently get caught out by our assumption, we should enforce it. There are generally two approaches we can take to achieve this:

1. *Make the assumption "impossible to break"*—If we can write the code in such a way that it won't compile if an assumption is broken, then this will ensure that the assumption always holds. This was covered in chapters 3 and 7.
2. *Use an error-signaling technique*—If it's not feasible to make the assumption impossible to break, then we can write code to detect it being broken and use an error-signaling technique to fail fast. This was covered in chapter 4 (and the end of chapter 3).

A POTENTIALLY PROBLEMATIC, UNENFORCED ASSUMPTION

To demonstrate how an unenforced assumption can be problematic, let's consider another function that the `Article` class might contain, one that returns the image section. Listing 9.3 shows what this function might look like if it doesn't enforce an assumption. It finds the sections that contain images and then returns the first one or null if no section contains images. This code again makes the assumption that an article will only ever contain a maximum of one image section. If this assumption is broken and the article contains multiple image sections, then the code won't fail or produce any kind of warning. Instead, it will just return the first such section and carry on as though everything is fine (the opposite of failing fast).

Listing 9.3 Code containing an assumption

```
class Article {
  private List<Section> sections;
  ...

  Section? getImageSection() {
    // There should only ever be a maximum of one
    // section within an article that contains images.
    return sections
        .filter(section -> section.containsImages())
        .first();
  }
}
```

Returns the first image-containing section or null if there are none

The `getImageSection()` function is called by one of the pieces of code that renders articles to display them to users. This is shown in listing 9.4. The template that this code renders articles within has space for only a single image section. The assumption that an article has a maximum of only one image section is therefore necessary for this particular use case.

Listing 9.4 A caller that relies on the assumption

```
class ArticleRenderer {
  ...

  void render(Article article) {
    ...
    Section? imageSection = article.getImageSection();
    if (imageSection != null) {
      templateData.setImageSection(imageSection);
    }
    ...
  }
}
```

The article template can only handle a maximum of one image-containing section.

If anyone creates an article with multiple image sections and then tries to render it using this code, things will behave in a weird and unexpected way. Everything will seem to work (in that no errors or warnings occur), but in reality a load of the images will be missing from the article. Depending on the nature of the article, this might result in it being misleading or completely nonsensical.

ENFORCING THE ASSUMPTION

As noted in chapter 4, it's usually best to ensure that failures and errors don't go unnoticed. In this scenario, trying to render an article with multiple image sections is not supported and is therefore an error scenario. It would probably be better if the code failed fast in this scenario rather than trying to limp on. We can modify the code to do this by enforcing the assumption using an error-signaling technique.

Listing 9.5 shows what the `Article.getImageSection()` function might look like if it uses an assertion to enforce the assumption that there is a maximum of one image section. The function has also been renamed to `getOnlyImageSection()` to better convey to any callers of this function that they are making the assumption there is only one image section. This makes it unlikely that any callers who do not wish to make this assumption will call it.

Listing 9.5 Enforcing the assumption

```
class Article {
  private List<Section> sections;
  ...

  Section? getOnlyImageSection() {
    List<Section> imageSections = sections
        .filter(section -> section.containsImages());

    assert(imageSections.size() <= 1,
        "Article contains multiple image sections");

    return imageSections.first();
  }
}
```

- Function name conveys the assumption that callers are making
- Assertion enforces the assumption
- Returns the first item in the imageSections list or null if it's empty

> **Error-signaling techniques**
>
> Chapter 4 discussed different error-signaling techniques in detail, in particular how the choice of technique often depends on whether a caller might want to recover from the error.
>
> Listing 9.5 uses an assertion, which is appropriate if we're sure that no caller would want to recover from the error. If the article is generated internally within our program, then breaking the assumption implies a programming error, meaning an assertion is probably appropriate. But if the article is supplied by an external system or a user, then it's likely that some callers will want to catch the error and handle it in a more graceful way. In this scenario, an explicit error-signaling technique might be more appropriate.

As we've seen, assumptions tend to have an associated cost in terms of increased fragility. When the costs of a given assumption outweigh the benefits, it's probably best to avoid making it. If an assumption is necessary, then we should do our best to ensure that other engineers don't get caught by it; we can achieve this by enforcing the assumption.

9.2 Beware of global state

A piece of *global state* (or a *global variable*) is one that is shared between all contexts within a given instance of a program. Some common ways of defining a global variable are as follows:

- Marking a variable as `static` in languages like Java or C# (this is the paradigm used in the pseudocode in this book)
- Defining a file-level variable (outside of a class or function) in languages like C++
- Defining properties on the global window object in JavaScript-based languages

To demonstrate what is meant by a variable being global, consider the code in listing 9.6. Some things to notice about the code are as follows:

- a is an instance variable. Each instance of `MyClass` will have its own dedicated a variable. One instance of the class modifying this variable will not affect any other instance of the class.
- b is a static variable (meaning it's a global variable). It's therefore shared between all instances of `MyClass` (and can even be accessed without having an instance of `MyClass`; explained in the next bullet point).
- The `getBStatically()` function is marked `static`, meaning it can be called without needing an instance of the class using a call like: `MyClass.getBStatically()`. A static function like this can access any static variables defined in the class, but it can never access any instance variables.

Listing 9.6 A class with a global variable

```
class MyClass {
  private Int a = 3;                    // An instance variable
  private static Int b = 4;             // A global variable (because it's marked static)

  void setA(Int value) { a = value; }
  Int getA() { return a; }

  void setB(Int value) { b = value; }
  Int getB() { return b; }

  static Int getBStatically() { return b; }   // A static function
}
```

The following snippet demonstrates how the instance variable a applies to individual instances of the class, while the global variable `b` is shared between all instances of the class (as well as static contexts):

```
MyClass instance1 = new MyClass();
MyClass instance2 = new MyClass();

instance1.setA(5);
instance2.setA(7);
print(instance1.getA())  // Output: 5
print(instance2.getA())  // Output: 7
```

Each instance of MyClass has its own separate "a" variable.

```
instance1.setB(6);
instance2.setB(8);
print(instance1.getB())  // Output: 8
print(instance2.getB())  // Output: 8
print(MyClass.getBStatically())  // Output: 8
```

The global "b" variable is shared between all instances of MyClass.

"b" can also be accessed statically without needing an instance of MyClass.

> **NOTE: DON'T CONFUSE GLOBALNESS WITH VISIBILITY** Whether or not a variable is global shouldn't be confused with the visibility of a variable. The visibility of a variable refers to whether it is public or private, which dictates what other parts of the code can see and access it. A variable can be public or private regardless of whether it's global. The point is that a global variable is shared between all contexts in the program instead of each instance of a class or function having its own version of it.

Because global variables affect every context within a program, using them often makes the implicit assumption that no one would ever want to reuse the code for a slightly different purpose. As we saw in the previous section, assumptions come with an associated cost. Global state tends to make code extremely fragile and completely unsafe to reuse, so the costs usually outweigh the benefits. The following subsections explain why and provide an alternative.

9.2.1 *Global state can make reuse unsafe*

When there is some state that different parts of a program need to access, it can seem tempting to put it into a global variable somewhere. This makes it very easy for any piece of code to access the state. But, as was just mentioned, it also often has the effect of making the code impossible to safely reuse. To demonstrate why, let's imagine that we're building an online shopping application. In our application, users can browse items, add them to their basket, and then check out at the end.

In this scenario, the contents of the user's shopping basket constitute state that many different parts of the application all need to access, such as any code that adds items to it, the screen where users review the contents of their basket, and the code that handles the checkout. Because so many parts of the application need access to this shared state, we might be tempted to store the contents of the user's basket in a global variable. Listing 9.7 shows what the code for the shopping basket might look like if we use global state. Some things to notice about the code are as follows:

- The `items` variable is marked with the word `static`. This means that this variable is not associated with a specific instance of the `ShoppingBasket` class, making it a global variable.
- The functions `addItem()` and `getItems()` are also both marked `static`. This means they can be called from anywhere in the code (without needing an instance of `ShoppingBasket`) like so: `ShoppingBasket.addItem(...)` and `ShoppingBasket.getItems()`. When called, they access the `items` global variable.

Listing 9.7 ShoppingBasket class

```
class ShoppingBasket {
  private static List<Item> items = [];      <-- Marked static, making
                                                 it a global variable
  static void addItem(Item item) {       <--
    items.add(item);                         | Functions
  }                                          | marked static
                                             |
  static void List<Item> getItems() {    <--
    return List.copyOf(items);
  }
}
```

Anywhere in the code that needs to access the user's shopping basket can easily do this. Some examples are shown in listing 9.8. The `ViewItemWidget` allows users to add the viewed item to their basket. This is achieved by calling `ShoppingBasket.addItem()`. The `ViewBasketWidget` allows users to view the contents of their basket. The contents of the basket are accessed by calling `ShoppingBasket.getItems()`.

Listing 9.8 Classes using ShoppingBasket

```
class ViewItemWidget {
  private final Item item;

  ViewItemWidget(Item item) {
    this.item = item;
  }
  ...

  void addItemToBasket() {
    ShoppingBasket.addItem(item);      <-- Modifies the
  }                                        global state
}

class ViewBasketWidget {
  ...
  void displayItems() {
    List<Item> items = ShoppingBasket.getItems();    <-- Reads the
    ...                                                  global state
  }
}
```

Modifying and reading the contents of the basket is trivially easy, and this is why it can seem so tempting to use global state in this way. But in using global state like this, we have created code that will break and do potentially weird things if anyone ever tries to reuse it. The following subsection explains why.

WHAT HAPPENS WHEN SOMEONE TRIES TO REUSE THIS CODE?

Whether we realized it or not, our implicit assumption when writing this code was that there would be only one basket needed per running instance of our piece of software.

If our shopping application runs on only the user's device, then for basic functionality this assumption will hold and things will work correctly. But there are many reasons this assumption might be broken, meaning it's quite brittle. Some potential scenarios that would result in this assumption being broken are as follows:

- We decide to back-up the contents of users' baskets in our server, so we start using the `ShoppingBasket` class in our server-side code. A single instance of our server will handle many requests from many different users, so we now have many baskets per running instance of our piece of software (the server in this case).
- We add a feature that allows a user to save the contents of their basket for later. This means that the client-side application now has to handle several different baskets: all of the saved-for-later ones in addition to the active one.
- We start selling fresh produce in addition to our normal stock. This uses a completely different set of suppliers and delivery mechanism so has to be handled as a separate shopping basket.

We could probably sit here all day dreaming up different scenarios that break our original assumption. Whether any of them will actually happen is anyone's guess. But the point is that there are enough plausible-sounding scenarios that break our original assumption that we should probably realize that it's brittle and quite likely to be broken in one way or another at some point.

When our original assumption gets broken, things will go wrong with the software. If two different pieces of code are both using the `ShoppingBasket` class, they will interfere with one another (figure 9.1). If one of them adds an item, this item will then be in the basket for all other pieces of code using it. In any of the scenarios that were just listed, this would probably result in buggy behavior, so the `ShoppingBasket` class is basically impossible to reuse in a safe way.

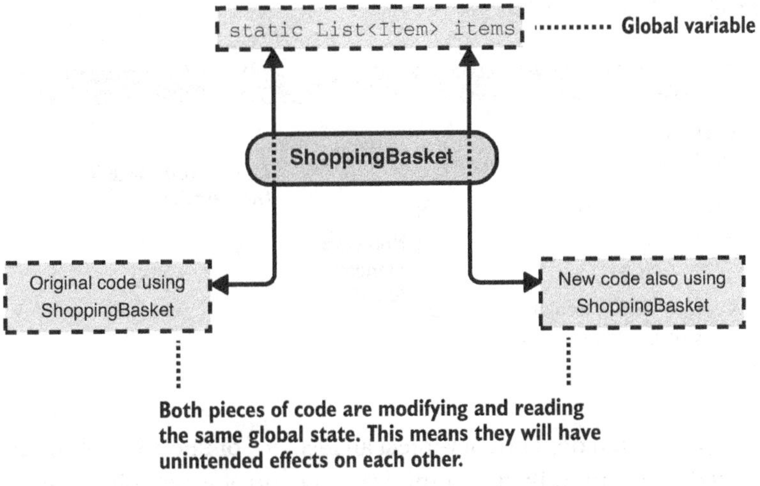

Figure 9.1 Using global state can make code reuse unsafe.

In the best-case scenario an engineer would realize that reusing the `ShoppingBasket` class is unsafe and write new, completely separate code for their new use case. In the worst-case scenario, they might not realize that reusing it is unsafe and the software will end up containing bugs. These bugs could be quite catastrophic if customers end up ordering items they don't want, or if we breach their privacy by revealing the items in their baskets to others. To summarize, in the best case, we end up with a load of near-duplicate code that engineers now need to maintain, and in the worst case we end up with some nasty bugs. Neither of these is particularly desirable, so it would probably be much better to avoid using global state. The next subsection discusses an alternative.

9.2.2 Solution: Dependency-inject shared state

The previous chapter discussed the technique of dependency injection. This means that we construct a class by "injecting" its dependencies rather than making it have a hard-coded dependency on them. Dependency injection is also a great way to share state between different classes in a more controlled way than using global state.

The `ShoppingBasket` class that we saw in the previous subsection used a static variable and static functions, meaning that state was global, so the first step is to change this by making the `ShoppingBasket` class one that needs to be instantiated and ensuring that each instance of the class has its own distinct state. Listing 9.9 shows what this would look like. Some things to notice about the code are as follows:

- The `items` variable is no longer static. It's now an instance variable, meaning it's associated with a specific instance of the `ShoppingBasket` class, so if we create two instances of the `ShoppingBasket` class, they will both have different and separate lists of items contained within them.
- The `addItem()` and `getItems()` functions are no longer static. This means that they can only be accessed via an instance of the `ShoppingBasket` class, so calls like `ShoppingBasket.addItem(...)` or `ShoppingBasket.getItems()` no longer work.

Listing 9.9 Modified ShoppingBasket class

```
class ShoppingBasket {
  private final List<Item> items = [];      // An instance variable (non-static)

  void addItem(Item item) {                 // Non-static member functions
    items.add(item);
  }

  void List<Item> getItems() {              // Non-static member functions
    return List.copyOf(items);
  }
}
```

The second step is to then dependency-inject an instance of `ShoppingBasket` into any classes that need access to it. By doing this we can control which pieces of code share the same basket and which pieces of code use a different basket. Listing 9.10 shows what the ViewItemWidget and ViewBasketWidgets look like if a ShoppingBasket is dependency-injected via their constructors. Calls to addItem() and getItems() are now on the specific instance of ShoppingBasket that was injected.

Listing 9.10 ShoppingBasket dependency-injected

```
class ViewItemWidget {
  private final Item item;
  private final ShoppingBasket basket;

  ViewItemWidget(Item item, ShoppingBasket basket) {
    this.item = item;
    this.basket = basket;
  }
  ...

  void addItemToBasket() {
    basket.addItem(item);
  }
}


class ViewBasketWidget {
  private final ShoppingBasket basket;

  ViewBasketWidget(ShoppingBasket basket) {
    this.basket = basket;
  }

  void displayItems() {
    List<Item> items = basket.getItems();
    ...
  }
}
```

ShoppingBasket dependency-injected

Called on specific instance of ShoppingBasket that was injected

To demonstrate how we can now safely reuse the ShoppingBasket code, listing 9.11 creates two ShoppingBaskets: one for normal products and one for fresh products. It also creates two ViewBasketWidgets: one for each basket. The two baskets are completely independent of one another and will never interfere with each other. And each ViewBasketWidget will display only items from the basket that it was constructed with.

Listing 9.11 Separate ShoppingBasket instances

```
ShoppingBasket normalBasket = new ShoppingBasket();
ViewBasketWidget normalBasketWidget =
    new ViewBasketWidget(normalBasket);


ShoppingBasket freshBasket = new ShoppingBasket();
ViewBasketWidget freshBasketWidget =
    new ViewBasketWidget(freshBasket);
```

Figure 9.2 illustrates how the internal structure of the code now looks. Instead of everything sharing the same global state for which items are in the basket, each instance of `ShoppingBasket` is now self-contained.

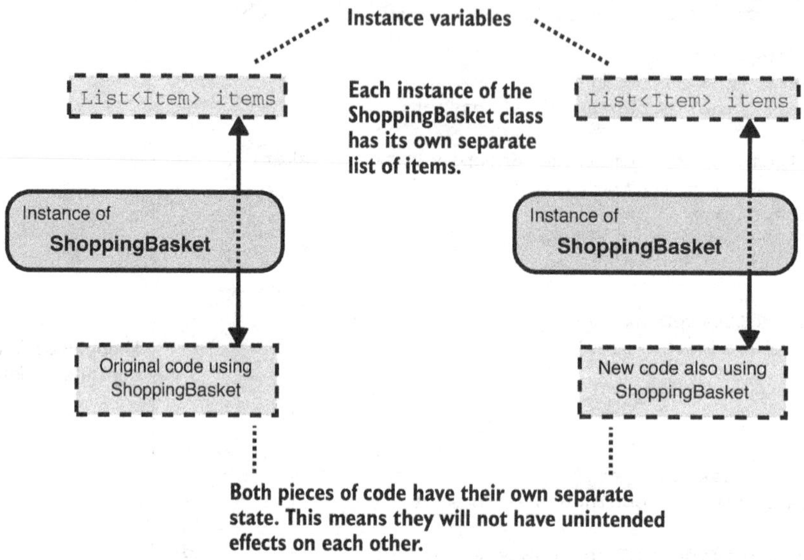

Figure 9.2 By keeping state encapsulated within instances of classes, code reuse becomes safe.

Global state is one of the most well-known and well-documented coding pitfalls. It can be very tempting to use it because it can seem like a quick and easy way to share information between different parts of a program. But using global state can make code reuse completely unsafe. The fact that global state is used might not be apparent to another engineer, so if they do try to reuse the code, this might result in weird behavior and bugs. If we need to share state between different parts of a program, it's usually safer to do this in a more controlled way using dependency injection.

9.3 Use default return values appropriately

Using sensible default values can be an excellent way to make software more user friendly. Imagine if, upon opening a word-processing application, we are always forced to choose exactly which font, text size, text color, background color, line spacing, and line height we want before we can type a single word. The software would be infuriating to use, and we'd likely just switch to an alternative.

In reality, most word-processing applications provide a set of sensible defaults. Upon opening the application, it's configured with default choices for things like the font, text size, and background color. This means we can start typing straight away and edit these settings only if and when we want to.

Even in a piece of software that is not user-facing, default values can still be useful. If a given class can be configured using 10 different parameters, then it makes callers' lives easier if they don't have to provide all these values. The class might therefore provide some default values for anything they don't provide.

Providing a default value often requires making two assumptions:

- What default value is sensible
- That higher layers of code don't care if they're getting a default value or a value that was explicitly set

As we saw earlier, it's worth considering the costs as well as the benefits when making an assumption. Making assumptions like these in high-level code tends to have a lower cost than making them in lower level code. Higher level code tends to be more tightly coupled to a specific use case, meaning it's easier to choose a default value that suits all uses of the code. Lower level code, on the other hand, tends to solve more fundamental subproblems and therefore be reused more broadly for multiple use cases. This makes it a lot harder to pick a default value that will suit all uses of the code.

9.3.1 *Default return values in low-level code can harm reusability*

Let's imagine we are building a word-processing application. We just established that a likely requirement is that we have some default choices for text styling to allow a user to get going straight away. If the user wants to override these then they can. Listing 9.12 shows one way we might implement this for the choice of font. The `UserDocumentSettings` class stores the user's preferences for a particular document, one of which is the font they would like to use. If they've not specified a font, then the `getPreferredFont()` function returns a default of `Font.ARIAL`.

This achieves the requirement that we just stated, but if anyone ever wants to reuse the `UserDocumentSettings` class for a scenario where they don't want Arial as the default font, then they will have a hard time. It's impossible to distinguish between the case where a user specifically chose Arial and the case where they didn't provide a preference (meaning the default was returned).

Listing 9.12 Returning a default value

```
class UserDocumentSettings {
  private final Font? font;
  ...

  Font getPreferredFont() {
    if (font != null) {
      return font;
    }
    return Font.ARIAL;    <-- Default of Font.ARIAL returned if no user preference
  }
}
```

This approach also harms adaptability: if the requirements around defaults ever change it will be problematic. One example is that we start selling our word-processing application to large organizations who want to be able to specify an organization-wide default font. This is hard to implement because the `UserDocumentSettings` class doesn't allow us to determine when there is no user-provided preference (and thus when the organization-wide default might apply).

By bundling a default return value into the `UserDocumentSettings` class, we've made an assumption about every potential layer of code above: that Arial is a sensible default font. This will probably be fine initially, but if other engineers want to reuse our code, or if requirements change, then this assumption can easily become problematic. Figure 9.3 shows how an assumption like this affects layers of code above. The lower the level in the code that we define a default value, the more layers above we're making an assumption about.

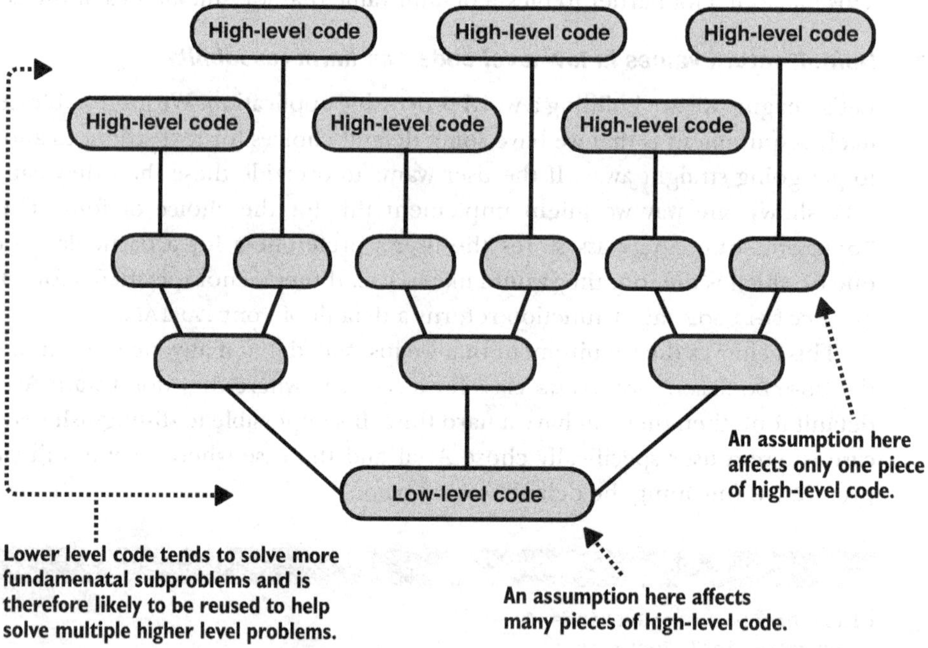
High-level code
High-level code
High-level code
High-level code
High-level code
High-level code
Low-level code
An assumption here affects only one piece of high-level code.
Lower level code tends to solve more fundamenatal subproblems and is therefore likely to be reused to help solve multiple higher level problems.
An assumption here affects many pieces of high-level code.

Figure 9.3 Assumptions affect layers of code above. Returning a default value in low-level code makes an assumption that will tend to affect many pieces of high-level code.

Chapter 2 emphasized the benefits of clean layers of abstraction. One of the key ways of achieving this is to ensure that we separate distinct subproblems into distinct pieces of code. The `UserDocumentSettings` class goes against this: retrieving some user preferences and defining some sensible defaults for our application are two separate subproblems. But the `UserDocumentSettings` class bundles these together in a way that makes them completely inseparable. This forces anyone using the `UserDocumentSettings` class to also use our implementation of default values. It would be better if we made these distinct subproblems so that higher layers of code can handle defaults in whatever way is appropriate to them.

9.3.2 Solution: Provide defaults in higher level code

To remove the decision about a default value from the `UserDocumentSettings` class, the simplest thing to do is just return null when there is no user-provided value. The following listing shows what the class looks like with this change.

Listing 9.13 Returning null

```
class UserDocumentSettings {
  private final Font? font;
  ...

  Font? getPreferredFont() {
    return font;
  }
}
```

Null returned if no user preference

This makes the provisioning of default values a distinct subproblem from that of handling user settings. This means that different callers can solve this subproblem in whatever way they want, making the code more reusable. In our higher level code, we might now choose to define a dedicated class for solving the subproblem of provisioning default values (as shown in the following listing).

Listing 9.14 Class for encapsulating defaults

```
class DefaultDocumentSettings {
  ...

  Font getDefaultFont() {
    return Font.ARIAL;
  }
}
```

We might then define a `DocumentSettings` class that handles the logic to choose between a default value and a user-provided value. Listing 9.15 shows this. The `DocumentSettings` class provides a clean layer of abstraction to higher levels of code that just want to know which settings to use. It hides all the implementation details about default and user-provided values, but at the same time also ensures that these implementation details are reconfigurable (by using dependency injection). This ensures that the code is reusable and adaptable.

Listing 9.15 Layer of abstraction for settings

```
class DocumentSettings {
  private final UserDocumentSettings userSettings;
  private final DefaultDocumentSettings defaultSettings;

  DocumentSettings(
      UserDocumentSettings userSettings,
      DefaultDocumentSettings defaultSettings) {
    this.userSettings = userSettings;
    this.defaultSettings = defaultSettings;
  }
  ...

  Font getFont() {
    Font? userFont = userSettings.getPreferredFont();
    if (userFont != null) {
      return userFont;
    }
    return defaultSettings.getFont();
  }
}
```

User settings and default values are dependency injected.

In listing 9.15, handling the null value using an if-statement is, admittedly, a little clunky. In many languages (such as C#, JavaScript, and Swift) we can use the *null coalescing operator* to make the code a lot less clunky. In most languages, this is written as `nullableValue ?? defaultValue`, which will evaluate to the `nullableValue` if it's not null and the `defaultValue` otherwise. So in C#, for example, we could write the `getFont()` function as follows:

```
Font getFont() {
  return userSettings.getPreferredFont() ??
      defaultSettings.getFont();
}
```

?? is the null coalescing operator.

Default return value parameters

Shifting the decision about what default value to use to the caller tends to make code more reusable. But by returning null in languages that don't support the null coalescing operator, we also force callers to write boilerplate code to handle this.

One approach that some pieces of code employ is to use a default return value parameter. The `Map.getOrDefault()` function in Java is an example of this. If the map contains a value for the key, then it will be returned. If the map does not contain a value for the key, then the specified default value will be returned. A call to this function looks like the following:

```
String value = map.getOrDefault(key, "default value");
```

This achieves the aim of allowing the caller to decide what default value is appropriate, but without requiring the caller to handle a null value.

Default values can make code (and software) much easier to use, so they can be well worth including. But it pays to be careful about where they are incorporated into the code. Returning a default value makes an assumption about all of the layers of code above that use the value and can thus limit code reuse and adaptability. Returning default values from low-level code can be particularly problematic. It can often be better to simply return null and implement default values at a higher level, where assumptions are more likely to hold.

9.4 Keep function parameters focused

In chapter 8 we saw the example of encapsulating various text styling options together. We defined the `TextOptions` class to do this (repeated in the following listing).

Listing 9.16 TextOptions class

```
class TextOptions {
  private final Font font;
  private final Double fontSize;
  private final Double lineHeight;
  private final Color textColor;

  TextOptions(
      Font font,
      Double fontSize,
      Double lineHeight,
      Color textColor) {
    this.font = font;
    this.fontSize = fontSize;
    this.lineHeight = lineHeight;
    this.textColor = textColor;
  }

  Font getFont() { return font; }
  Double getFontSize() { return fontSize; }
  Double getLineHeight() { return lineHeight; }
  Color getTextColor() { return textColor; }
}
```

Encapsulates multiple styling options together

In scenarios where a function needs all the pieces of information contained within a data object or class, it makes sense for that function to take an instance of the object or class as a parameter. It reduces the number of function parameters and saves intermediate code from having to deal with the nuts-and-bolts details of the encapsulated data. But in scenarios where a function only needs one or two pieces of information, using an instance of the object or class as a parameter can harm the reusability of the code. The following subsections explain why and demonstrate a simple alternative.

9.4.1 A function that takes more than it needs can be hard to reuse

Listing 9.17 shows part of the code for a text box widget that can be used within a user interface. Some things to notice about the code are as follows:

- There are two public functions that the `TextBox` class exposes: `setTextStyle()` and `setTextColor()`. Both these functions take an instance of `TextOptions` as a parameter.
- The `setTextStyle()` function makes use of all of the information within `TextOptions`, so for this function it makes perfect sense to have this as the parameter.

- The `setTextColor()` function only makes use of the text color information from `TextOptions`. In this sense the `setTextColor()` function takes more than it needs because it doesn't need any of the other values within `TextOptions`.

Currently the `setTextColor()` function is only called from the `setTextStyle()` function, so this doesn't cause too many problems. But if anyone ever wants to reuse the `setTextColor()` function, they might have a hard time, as we'll see in a moment.

Listing 9.17 A function that takes more than it needs

```
class TextBox {
  private final Element textContainer;
  ...

  void setTextStyle(TextOptions options) {
    setFont(...);
    setFontSize(...);
    setLineHight(...);
    setTextColor(options);          <-- Calls the setTextColor() function
  }

  void setTextColor(TextOptions options) {   <-- Takes an instance of TextOptions as a parameter
    textContainer.setStyleProperty(
        "color", options.getTextColor().asHexRgb());   <-- Makes use of only the text color
  }
}
```

Now imagine that an engineer needs to implement a function that will style a `TextBox` to be a warning. The requirement for this function is that it sets the text color to red but leaves all other styling information unchanged. The engineer will most likely want to reuse the `TextBox.setTextColor()` function to do this, but because that function takes an instance of `TextOptions` as its parameter, this is not straightforward.

Listing 9.18 shows the code that the engineer ends up writing. All they want to do is set the text color to red, but they've had to construct an entire instance of `TextOptions` with various irrelevant, made-up values in order to do this. This code is very confusing: if we glance at it, we might be left with the impression that in addition to setting the color to red, it also sets the font to Arial, the size to 12, and the line height to 14. This is not the case, but we have to know details about the `TextBox.setTextColor()` function for this to be apparent.

Listing 9.18 Calling a function that takes too much

```
void styleAsWarning(TextBox textBox) {
  TextOptions style = new TextOptions(
      Font.ARIAL,
      12.0,          Irrelevant,
      14.0           made-up values
      Color.RED);
  textBox.setTextColor(style);
}
```

The whole point in the `TextBox.setTextColor()` function is that it sets just the color of the text. It's therefore unnecessary for it to take an entire instance of `TextOptions` as a parameter. And beyond being unnecessary, it becomes actively harmful when anyone wants to reuse the function for a slightly different scenario. It would be better if the function takes only what it needs.

9.4.2 Solution: Make functions take only what they need

The only thing that the `TextBox.setTextColor()` function reads from the `TextOptions` is the text color. So instead of the function taking an entire instance of `TextOptions`, it can just take an instance of `Color` as a parameter. The following listing shows how the code for the `TextBox` class looks with this change.

Listing 9.19 A function that only takes what it needs

```
class TextBox {
  private final Element textElement;
  ...

  void setTextStyle(TextOptions options) {
    setFont(...);
    setFontSize(...);
    setLineHight(...);
    setTextColor(options.getTextColor());      <-- Calls setTextColor() with just the text color
  }
                                               <-- Takes an instance of Color as a parameter
  void setTextColor(Color color) {
    textElement.setStyleProperty("color", color.asHexRgb());
  }
}
```

The `styleAsWarning()` function now becomes a lot simpler and less confusing. There is no need to construct an instance of `TextOptions` with irrelevant, made-up values:

```
void styleAsWarning(TextBox textBox) {
  textBox.setTextColor(Color.RED);
}
```

In general, making functions take only what they need results in code that is more reusable and easier to understand. It's still good to apply your judgment, though. If we have a class that encapsulates 10 things together and a function that needs 8 of them, then it might still make sense to pass the entire encapsulating object into the function. The alternative of passing 8, unencapsulated values around can harm modularity (as we saw in the previous chapter). As with many things, there is no one answer that applies to every situation, but it's good to be conscious of the tradeoffs we're making and the consequences they might have.

9.5 Consider using generics

Classes often contain (or reference) instances of other types or classes. An obvious example of this is a list class. If we have a list of strings, then the list class contains instances of the string class. Storing things in a list is a very general subproblem: in some scenarios we might want a list of strings, but in other scenarios we might want a list of integers. It would be quite annoying if we needed completely separate list classes for storing strings and integers.

Luckily many languages support *generics* (sometimes called *templates*). These allow us to write a class without having to concretely specify all the types that it references. In the case of a list, this allows us to easily use the same class to store any type we want. Some examples of using a list to store different types are as follows:

```
List<String> stringList = ["hello", "world"];

List<Int> intList = [1, 2, 3];
```

If we're writing some code that references another class, but we don't particularly care what that other class is, then it's often a sign that we should consider using generics. Doing this is often very little extra work but makes our code considerably more generalizable. The following subsections provide a worked example.

9.5.1 Depending on a specific type limits generalizability

Imagine we're creating a word guessing game. A group of players each submit words and then take it in turns to act out one word at a time so that the other players can guess it. One of the subproblems we need to solve is that of storing the collection of words. In addition, we need to be able to select words one by one at random and also be able to return a word to the collection if it couldn't be guessed within the time limit of each turn.

We decide that we can solve this subproblem by implementing a randomized queue. Listing 9.20 shows the code for the `RandomizedQueue` class that we implement. It stores a collection of strings. We can add new strings by calling `add()`, and we can get and remove a random string from the collection by calling `getNext()`. The `RandomizedQueue` class has a hard dependency on `String`, and as such it can never be used to store any other type.

Listing 9.20 Hard-coded use of String type

```
class RandomizedQueue {
  private final List<String> values = [];

  void add(String value) {
    values.add(value);
  }

  /**
   * Removes a random item from the queue and returns it.
   */
  String? getNext() {
    if (values.isEmpty()) {
      return null;
    }
```

Hard-coded dependency on String

```
    Int randomIndex = Math.randomInt(0, values.size());
    values.swap(randomIndex, values.size() - 1);
    return values.removeLast();
  }
}
```

This implementation of `RandomizedQueue` solves our very specific use case of storing words (which can be represented as strings), but it doesn't generalize to solve the same subproblem for other types. Imagine that another team within our company is developing an almost identical game, where instead of players submitting words, they submit pictures. Many of the subproblems between the two games are almost identical, yet because we hard coded our solutions to use strings, none of them generalize to solve the subproblems the other team faces. It would be a lot better if the code generalized to solve almost identical subproblems.

9.5.2 Solution: Use generics

In the case of the `RandomizedQueue` class, it's trivially easy to make the code generalizable using generics. Instead of having a hard-coded dependency on `String`, we can instead specify a placeholder (or template) for a type that can then be dictated later when the class is used. Listing 9.21 shows how the `RandomizedQueue` class looks with the use of generics. The class definition begins with `class RandomizedQueue<T>`. The `<T>` tells the compiler that we will use `T` as a placeholder for a type. We can then use `T` throughout the class definition as though it were a real type.

Listing 9.21 Use of a generic type

```
class RandomizedQueue<T> {        <-- T is specified as the placeholder for the generic type.
  private final List<T> values = [];

  void add(T value) {
    values.add(value);
  }

  /**
   * Removes a random item from the queue and returns it.
   */
  T? getNext() {        <-- The type placeholder can be used throughout the class.
    if (values.isEmpty()) {
      return null;
    }
    Int randomIndex = Math.randomInt(0, values.size());
    values.swap(randomIndex, values.size() - 1);
    return values.removeLast();
  }
}
```

The `RandomizedQueue` class can now be used to store anything we want, so in our version of the game that uses words, we can define one to store strings as follows:

```
RandomizedQueue<String> words = new RandomizedQueue<String>();
```

And the other team who wants to use it to store pictures can easily define one to store pictures as follows:

```
RandomizedQueue<Picture> pictures =
    new RandomizedQueue<Picture>();
```

> **Generics and nullable types**
>
> In listing 9.21, the `getNext()` function returns null if the queue is empty. This is fine as long as no one wants to store null values in the queue, which is probably a reasonable assumption. (Although we may want to consider enforcing this assumption using a check or an assertion, as discussed in chapter 3.)
>
> If someone did want to store null values in the queue by creating something like a `RandomizedQueue<String?>`, then this might be problematic. This is because it would be impossible to distinguish between `getNext()` returning a null value from within the queue and it signaling that the queue is empty. If we did want to support this use case, then we could provide a `hasNext()` function that can be called to check if the queue is nonempty before calling `getNext()`.

As we break a high-level problem down into subproblems, we will often encounter some that are quite fundamental and that might apply to all sorts of different use cases. When the solution to a subproblem could easily apply to any data type, it's often very little effort to use generics instead of depending on a specific type. This can be an easy win in terms of making code more generalizable and reusable.

Summary

- The same subproblems often crop up again and again, so making code reusable can save your future self and your teammates considerable time and effort.
- Try to identify fundamental subproblems and structure the code in a way that will allow others to reuse the solutions to specific subproblems even if they're solving a different high-level problem.
- Creating clean layers of abstraction and making code modular often result in code that is a lot easier and safer to reuse and generalize.
- Making an assumption often has a cost in terms of making the code more fragile and less reusable.
  - Make sure the benefits of an assumption outweigh the costs.
  - If an assumption does need to be made, then make sure it's in an appropriate layer of the code and enforce it if possible.
- Using global state often makes a particularly costly assumption that results in code that is completely unsafe to reuse. In most scenarios, global state is best avoided.

Part 3

Unit testing

Testing is an essential part of creating code and software that work correctly (and that keep working correctly). As discussed in chapter 1, there are different levels of testing, but unit testing is usually the one engineers interact with most in their everyday lives. This part on unit testing may be at the end of the book, but please don't infer from this that unit testing is an add-on consideration to be addressed only after writing the code. As we saw in previous chapters, testing and testability are things we often need to consider at all times when writing code. And, as we'll see in chapter 10, some schools of thought even go as far as to advocate that the tests should be written before writing the code.

This part of the book is split into two chapters. Chapter 10 covers some of the foundational principles of unit testing: what we're trying to achieve, and some fundamental concepts like test doubles. Chapter 11 expands on this with a series of more practical considerations and techniques that can help us achieve the goals we identified in chapter 10.

10 Unit testing principles

This chapter covers

- The basics of unit testing
- What makes a good unit test
- Test doubles, including when and how to use them
- Testing philosophies

Every time an engineer modifies a line of code there is a risk that they might inadvertently break something or make a mistake. Even extremely small, innocent-looking changes can have bad consequences: "It's just a one line change" are famous last words before a system crash. Because every change is risky, we need a way to reassure ourselves that the code is working, both initially and whenever it's modified. Tests are often the main thing that give us this reassurance.

As engineers, we usually concentrate on writing automated tests. This means we write test code that exercises the "real" code in order to check that it's working correctly. Chapter 1 described how there are different levels of testing, and in particular, how unit testing is the level of testing that engineers typically deal with most often in their everyday coding. We'll therefore concentrate on unit testing in these two final chapters.

At this point, it would probably be useful to provide a precise definition of exactly what we mean by *unit testing*. But it's unfortunately not a precisely defined term. Unit testing is concerned with testing distinct units of code in a relatively isolated manner. What exactly we mean by a *unit of code* can vary, but it often refers to a specific class, function, or file of code. What we mean by *in a relatively isolated manner* can also vary and be open to interpretation. Most pieces of code do not live in isolation; they depend on a number of other pieces of code. As we'll see in section 10.4.6, some engineers make a point of trying to isolate code from its dependencies in unit tests, while others prefer to include them.

Unit testing may not be a precisely defined term, but this is usually not too much of a problem. It's best to not get too hung up on exactly what constitutes a unit test and whether the tests we're writing accurately fit a contrived definition for it. What ultimately matters is that we ensure our code is well tested and that we do this in a way that is maintainable. This chapter covers some of the key principles of unit testing that can help us achieve this. Chapter 11 will build on this to discuss a number of practical techniques.

10.1 Unit testing primer

If you've never written software in a professional environment, then you may have never come across unit testing before. If this is the case, then this section should quickly give you the important details that will be needed for this chapter and the next to make sense.

When it comes to unit testing, some important concepts and terminology to remember are as follows:

- *Code under test*—Sometimes referred to as "the real code." This refers to the piece of code we are trying to test.
- *Test code*—This refers to the code that forms our unit tests. The test code will typically be in a file separate from the "real code," but there is often a one-to-one mapping between files of real code and files of test code, so if we have some real code in a file called `GuestList.lang`, then we might put the unit test code in a file called `GuestListTest.lang`. Sometimes real code and test code are kept next to each other in the same directory and sometimes test code is kept in a completely different part of the codebase. This varies from language to language and from team to team.
- *Test case*—Each file of test code is typically divided into multiple test cases, where each test case tests a specific behavior or scenario. At a practical level, a test case is usually just a function, and for anything other than the simplest of test cases, it's common to divide the code within each of them into three distinct sections as follows:
  - *Arrange*—It's often necessary to perform some setup before we can invoke the specific behavior we want to test. This could involve defining some test values, setting up some dependencies, or constructing a correctly configured instance of the code under test (if it's a class). This is often placed in a distinct block of code at the start of the test case.

  - *Act*—This refers to the lines of code that actually invoke the behavior that is being tested. This typically involves calling one or more of the functions provided by the code under test.
  - *Assert*—Once the behavior being tested has been invoked, the test needs to check that the correct things actually happened. This typically involves checking that a return value is equal to an expected value or that some resultant state is as expected.
- *Test runner*—As the name suggests, a test runner is a tool that actually runs the tests. Given a file of test code (or several files of test code), it will run each test case and output details of which pass and which fail.

Figure 10.1 illustrates how some of these concepts fit together.

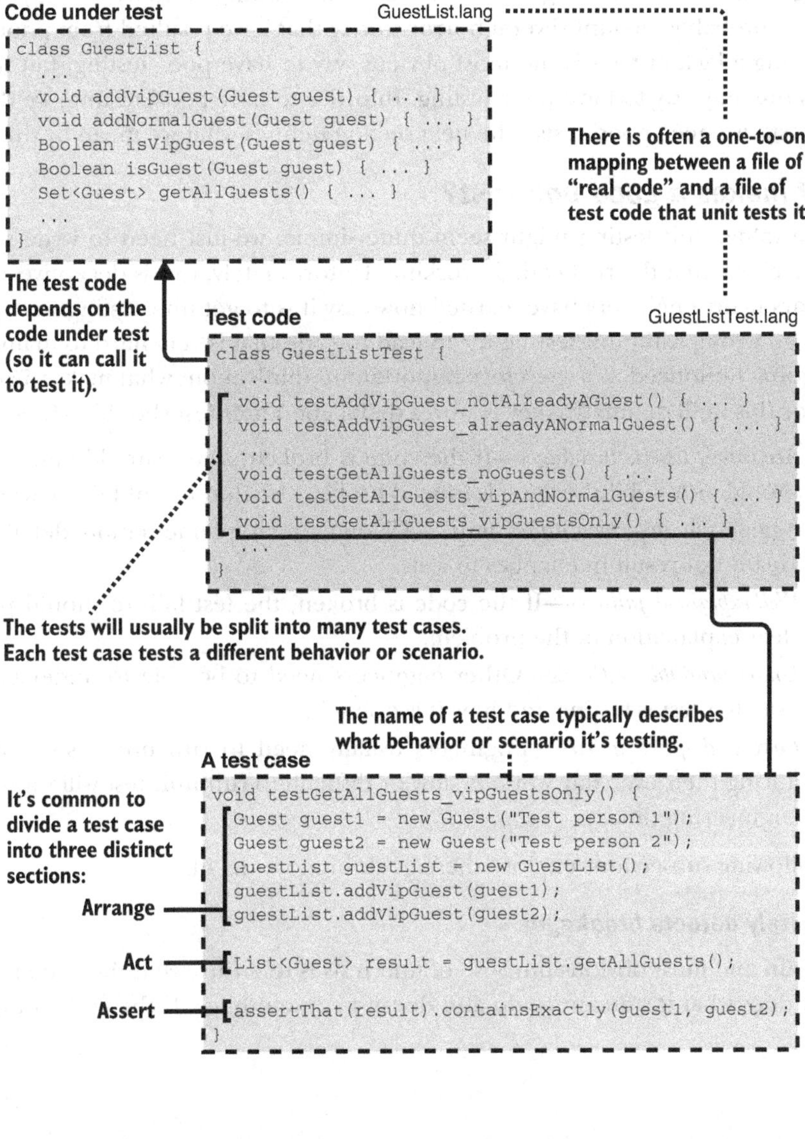

Figure 10.1 How various unit testing concepts fit together

> **NOTE: GIVEN, WHEN, THEN** Some engineers prefer the terms *given*, *when*, and *then* over *arrange*, *act*, and *assert*. There are some nuances around which testing philosophies advocate these different sets of terms, but in the context of the code within a test case, they are equivalent.

The importance of testing is so often stated that it can start to sound like a cliché. Cliché or not, testing is important. In most professional software engineering environments these days, pretty much every piece of "real code" is expected to have an accompanying unit test. And every behavior that the "real code" exhibits is expected to have an accompanying test case. This is the ideal and it's what we should strive for.

You'll quickly discover that not every piece of existing code lives up to this ideal, and in some codebases, testing can be particularly poor. But this is no excuse for lowering our own standards away from the ideal. Bad or inadequate testing is often an accident waiting to happen. Most engineers who've been building software for any length of time can probably recount several horror stories that have resulted from poor testing.

Having a lack of tests is the most obvious way to have poor testing, but it's by no means the only way to have poor testing. In order to have good testing, we don't just need tests, we need good tests. The next section defines what we mean by this.

10.2 What makes a good unit test?

At face value, unit testing might seem quite simple: we just need to write some test code to check that the real code is working. Unfortunately, this is deceptive, and over the years many engineers have learned how easy it is to get unit testing wrong. When things go wrong with unit testing it can lead to code that is very hard to maintain and bugs going unnoticed. It's therefore important to think about what makes a good unit test. For this we'll define five key features that a good unit test should exhibit:

- *Accurately detects breakages*—If the code is broken, a test should fail. And a test should only fail if the code is indeed broken (we don't want false alarms).
- *Agnostic to implementation details*—Changes in implementation details should ideally not result in changes to tests.
- *Well-explained failures*—If the code is broken, the test failure should provide a clear explanation of the problem.
- *Understandable test code*—Other engineers need to be able to understand what exactly a test is testing and how it is doing it.
- *Easy and quick to run*—Engineers usually need to run unit tests quite often during their everyday work. A slow or difficult-to-run unit test will waste a lot of engineering time.

The following subsections explore these goals in more detail.

10.2.1 Accurately detects breakages

The main and most obvious purpose of unit tests is to ensure that the code is not broken: it does what it's meant to do and doesn't contain bugs. If the code under test is broken in any way, it should either not compile or a test should fail. This serves two very important roles:

- *It gives us initial confidence in the code.* Regardless of how carefully we code, it's almost impossible to avoid making some number of mistakes. By writing a thorough set of tests alongside any new code or code changes we create, it's likely that we'll discover and fix many of these mistakes before the code is even submitted to the codebase.
- *It protects against future breakage.* Chapter 3 discussed how a codebase is often a busy place, with multiple engineers constantly making changes. It's highly likely that at some point another engineer will make a change that inadvertently breaks our code. Our only effective defenses against this are to ensure that either the code stops compiling or a test starts failing when this occurs. It's not possible to engineer everything so that the code stops compiling when something is broken, so making sure that all the correct behaviors are locked in with tests is absolutely vital. A piece of functionality being broken by a code change (or some other event), is known as a *regression*. Running tests with the aim of detecting any such regressions is known as *regression testing*.

It's also important to consider another aspect of accuracy: a test should only fail if the code under test is genuinely broken. It might seem like this would naturally follow from what we just discussed, but in practice it often doesn't. As anyone with experience of logical fallacies will appreciate, "a test will definitely fail if the code is broken" does not necessarily imply that "a test will fail only if the code is broken."

A test that sometimes passes and sometimes fails despite the code under test being fine is referred to as *flakey*. This is usually a result of indeterministic behavior in the test, such as randomness, timing-based race conditions, or depending on an external system. The most obvious downside of flakey tests is that they waste engineers' time because they end up having to investigate failures that turn out to be nothing. But flakey tests are actually much more dangerous than they might initially seem. Anyone who's familiar with the fable "The Boy Who Cried Wolf" will appreciate why: if a test keeps giving a false alarm that the code is broken, then engineers will learn to ignore it. They might even go as far as turning the test off if it's really annoying. If no one pays attention to test failures anymore, then it's no different to the situation where there are no tests. There is then very little protection against future breakages, and the chances of bugs being introduced becomes high. Ensuring that tests fail when something is broken, and only when something is broken, is incredibly important.

10.2.2 Agnostic to implementation details

Broadly speaking there are two kinds of changes an engineer might make to a codebase:

- *A functional change*—This modifies the externally visible behavior of a piece of code. Examples of this are adding a new feature, fixing a bug, or handling an error scenario in a different way.

- *A refactoring*—This is a structural change to the code, such as splitting a large function into smaller ones or moving some utility code from one file to another so it's easier to reuse. In theory, if a refactoring is done correctly, then it should not modify any of the externally visible behaviors (or functional attributes) of the code.

The first of these (a functional change) is very much something that affects anyone using our code, and as such any callers of our code need to be carefully considered before we make this kind of change. Because a functional change modifies the behavior of our code, we would hope and expect that it will also require modifying the tests. If it doesn't, that probably suggests that our original tests were insufficient.

The second of these (a refactoring) is something that should not affect anyone using our code. We're changing implementation details, but not any behaviors that anyone else should care about. However, modifying code is always risky, and refactoring is no different. Our intention is to modify just the structure of the code, but how do we know for sure that we're not inadvertently modifying a behavior of the code in the process?

To help answer this, let's consider two approaches that we might have taken when we were writing the original unit tests for our code (long before we decided to do this refactoring):

- *Approach A*—As well as locking in all the behaviors of our code, the tests also lock in various implementation details. We test several private functions by making them visible to tests, we simulate state by directly manipulating private member variables and dependencies, and we also verify the state of various member variables after the code under test has run.
- *Approach B*—Our tests lock in all the behaviors but no implementation details. We make a point of using the code's public API to set up state and to verify behaviors wherever we can. And we never manipulate or verify anything using private variables or functions.

Now let's consider what happens when we come along several months later and refactor the code. If we perform the refactoring correctly, then only implementation details should be changed, and no externally visible behaviors should be affected. If externally visible behaviors are affected, then we have made a mistake. Let's consider what happens if we'd used the different testing approaches:

- *Approach A*—Regardless of whether we performed the refactoring correctly, the tests will start failing, and we'll need to make lots of changes to them to make them pass again. We now have to test different private functions, set up state in different private member variables and dependencies, and verify a different set of member variables after the code under test has run.
- *Approach B*—If we did the refactoring correctly, the tests should still pass (without us having to modify them). If a test does fail, then we clearly made a

mistake, because this means we've inadvertently changed an externally visible behavior.

With approach A, it's very hard to have any confidence about whether we've made a mistake when we refactor the code. The tests fail and need modifying either way, and figuring out which of these modifications to the tests are to be expected and which are not is likely not an easy task. With approach B, it's incredibly easy to have confidence in our refactoring: if the tests still pass then everything is fine; if a test fails then we made a mistake.

Don't mix functional changes and refactorings

When making a change to the codebase, it's usually best to either make a functional change or do a refactoring but not to do both at the same time.

A refactoring should not change any behaviors, whereas a functional change should. If we make both a functional change and do a refactoring at the same time, it can become hard to reason about which changes in behavior are the expected ones from the functional change and which might be due to a mistake we've made in the refactoring. It's usually better to do the refactoring and then make the functional change separately. This makes it a lot easier to isolate the cause of any potential problems.

Code is very often refactored. In mature codebases, the amount of refactoring can often exceed the amount of new code written, so ensuring that code does not break when it's refactored is of paramount importance. By making tests agnostic to implementation details, we can ensure that there is a reliable and clean signal that anyone refactoring code can use to see if they made a mistake.

10.2.3 Well-explained failures

As we saw a couple of subsections ago, one of the main purposes of tests is to protect against future breakages. A common scenario is that another engineer makes a change that inadvertently breaks someone else's code. A test then starts failing, which alerts the engineer that they have broken something. That engineer will then go and look at the test failure to figure out what is wrong. The engineer might be quite unfamiliar with the code that they have inadvertently broken, so if the test failure does not indicate what is broken, then they will likely waste a lot of time trying to figure it out.

To ensure that tests clearly and precisely explain what is broken, it's necessary to think about what kind of failure message the test will produce when something is wrong and whether this will be useful to another engineer. Figure 10.2 shows two potential failure messages we might see when a test fails. The first of these flags that *something* is wrong with getting events but gives us absolutely no information about *what* exactly is wrong. The second message, on the other hand, gives quite a clear description of what is wrong. We can see that the problem is that events are not being returned in chronological order.

A poorly explained test failure

Name of test case doesn't indicate which behavior is being tested

```
Test case testGetEvents failed:
Expected: [Event@ea4a92b, Event@3c5a99da]
But was actually: [Event@3c5a99da, Event@ea4a92b]
```

Failure message is hard to decipher.

A well-explained test failure

Name of test case makes it clear which behavior is being tested

```
Test case testGetEvents_inChronologicalOrder failed:
Contents match, but order differs
Expected:
  [<Spaceflight, April 12, 1961>, <Moon Landing, July 20, 1969>]
But was actually:
  [<Moon Landing, July 20, 1969>, <Spaceflight, April 12, 1961>]
```

Failure message is clear.

Figure 10.2 A test failure that clearly explains *what* is wrong is a lot more useful than one that just indicates that *something* is wrong.

One of the best ways to ensure that test failures are well explained is to test one thing at a time and use descriptive names for each test case. This often results in many small test cases that each lock in one specific behavior rather than one large test case that tries to test everything in one go. When a test starts failing, it's quite easy to see exactly which behaviors have been broken by checking the names of the test cases that fail.

10.2.4 Understandable test code

Up until this point, we've assumed that a test failing indicates that the code is broken. But this is not entirely true; to be more precise, a test failing indicates that the code now behaves in a different way. Whether the fact that it behaves in a different way actually constitutes it being broken (or not) depends on the circumstance. Another engineer might be deliberately modifying the functionality of the code to meet a new requirement, for example. In this case, the change in behavior is intentional.

The engineer making this change will obviously have to be careful, but once they've done their diligence and made sure the change is safe, they'll need to update the tests to reflect the new functionality. As we've seen before, modifying code is risky, and this also applies to the test code itself. Let's say a piece of code has three behaviors that are locked in by the tests. If an engineer is making intentional changes to only one of these behaviors, then ideally they should need to make changes to only test cases that test that behavior. Test cases that test the other two behaviors should ideally be left untouched.

For an engineer to have any confidence that their change is affecting only the desired behavior, they need to be able to know which parts of the test they're affecting and whether it's expected that they should need updating. For this to be the case they need to understand the tests, both what different test cases are testing and how they are testing them.

As we'll see in the next chapter, two of the most common ways this can go wrong are testing too many things at once and using too much shared test setup. Both of these can lead to tests that are very hard to understand and reason about. This makes future modifications to the code under test much less safe, because engineers will struggle to understand whether specific changes they're making are safe.

Another reason to strive for making test code understandable is that some engineers like to use the tests as a kind of instruction manual for the code. If they're wondering how to use a particular piece of code or what functionality it provides, then reading through the unit tests can be a good way to find this out. If the tests are difficult to understand, they won't make a very useful instruction manual.

10.2.5 Easy and quick to run

Most unit tests are run quite frequently. One of the most important functions of a unit test is to prevent broken code from being submitted to the codebase. Many codebases, therefore, will employ presubmit checks that ensure that any relevant tests pass before a change can be submitted. If the unit tests take an hour to run, this will slow every engineer down, because submitting a code change will take a minimum of an hour regardless of how small or trivial it is. In addition to being run before submitting changes to the codebase, engineers often run unit tests numerous times while developing the code, so this is another way that slow unit tests slow engineers down.

Another reason to keep tests fast and easy to run is to maximize the chance that engineers actually test stuff. When tests are slow, testing becomes painful, and if testing is painful, engineers tend to do less of it. This is probably not something that many self-respecting engineers would readily admit to, but from experience it seems to be a reality. Making tests as easy and quick to run as possible not only makes engineers more efficient, but it also tends to result in more extensive and more thorough testing.

10.3 Focus on the public API but don't ignore important behaviors

We just discussed why it's important for unit tests to be agnostic to implementation details. Chapter 2 stated that the different aspects of a piece of code can be split into two distinct parts: the public API and implementation details. If one of our aims is to avoid testing implementation details, this implies that we should try to test a piece of code using only its public API.

"Test using only the public API" is, in fact, a very common piece of advice with regard to unit testing. If you already have some knowledge of the subject, then you will likely have heard this before. By focusing on the public API, it forces us to concentrate on the behaviors that users of a piece of code ultimately care about rather than details that are just a means to an end. This helps ensure that we test the things that actually matter, and in the process also tends to keep tests agnostic to implementation details.

To demonstrate the benefits of focusing on the public API when testing, consider the function in the following snippet for calculating kinetic energy (in joules). The thing that anyone calling this function cares about is that it returns the correct value for the given mass (in kilograms) and speed (in meters per second). The fact that the function calls `Math.pow()` is an implementation detail. We could replace `Math.pow(speedMs, 2.0)` with `speedMs * speedMs` and the function would behave in exactly the same way as far as anyone calling it is concerned:

```
Double calculateKineticEnergyJ(Double massKg, Double speedMs) {
  return 0.5 * massKg * Math.pow(speedMs, 2.0);
}
```

By concentrating on the public API, we're forced to write tests that lock in the behaviors that callers actually care about. We might, therefore, write a series of test cases that check that the expected value is returned for given inputs. The following snippet shows one such test case. *(Note that because the return value is a double, we check that it's within a certain range rather than checking for exact equality.)*

```
void testCalculateKineticEnergy_correctValueReturned() {
  assertThat(calculateKineticEnergyJ(3.0, 7.0))
      .isWithin(1.0e-10)
      .of(73.5);
}
```

Assert that the value is within 0.0000000001 of 73.5.

If we felt the temptation to write a test that checked that the `calculateKineticEnergyJ()` function calls `Math.pow()`, then the principle of "test using only the public API" would guide us away from this. This prevents us from coupling our tests to implementation details and ensures that we concentrate on testing the things that callers actually care about. With a simple example like this, it seems quite clear-cut. But things can get more convoluted when we have more complicated pieces of code to test.

10.3.1 Important behaviors might be outside the public API

The `calculateKineticEnergyJ()` function we just saw is quite self-contained. The only inputs it takes are via parameters, and the only effect it has is to return an answer. In reality, code is rarely so self-contained. It often depends on numerous other pieces of code and testing can become more nuanced if some of these dependencies provide external inputs to the code or if the code causes side effects in them.

In such scenarios, what exactly is meant by "the public API" can be subjective, and I've encountered situations where engineers quote "test using only the public API" as justification for leaving important behaviors untested. Their argument is that if a behavior can't be triggered or checked using what they consider the public API, then it shouldn't be tested. This is where it becomes important to use common sense and think pragmatically.

The definition of *implementation details* given in chapter 2 is too simplistic when it comes to unit testing. Whether something is an implementation detail or not is in fact somewhat context specific. Chapter 2 discussed this from the perspective of layers of abstraction, where pieces of code depend on one another. In that scenario all that one piece of code needs to know about another are the things in the public API, so everything else is an implementation detail. But when it comes to testing, there may be other things that the test code needs to know about that are not considered part of the public API. To better explain this, let's consider an analogy.

Figure 10.3 A coffee vending machine has a public API, but we can't fully test the machine using only the public API.

Imagine that we work for a company that runs a network of coffee vending machines. Figure 10.3 shows one of the models of machine that our company makes and deploys. Our task is to test it to check that it works correctly. What constitutes the public API of this machine is open to some amount of interpretation, but an engineer might define it as "the way in which a customer buying a cup of coffee is expected to interact with the machine." If we take this definition, then the public API is quite simple: a customer taps their credit card on the reader, selects which drink they would like, and the machine returns the chosen drink in a cup. There are also some error scenarios that the public API might need to signal to the customer, such as their credit card being declined or the machine being out of service.

At first glance, it seems like we can test the main behaviors of the vending machine using what we've defined to be the public API: paying for and selecting a drink and checking that the machine returns the correct choice. But this isn't entirely true, and from our point of view as testers of the machine, we need to consider more than just the public API. For starters, the vending machine has some dependencies that we need to set up. We can't test the machine until we've plugged it into a power socket, filled up the water tank, and put some beans in the bean hopper. To a customer, all these things are implementation details, but to us testers, there's no feasible way we could test the machine without first setting up these things.

There may also be behaviors that we need to test that are not part of the public API and that a customer would consider implementation details. This vending machine happens to be a "smart" vending machine. It's connected to the internet and will automatically notify a technician whenever the water or coffee beans are running low. (This is an example of an intentional side effect that the vending machine can cause.) Customers probably aren't aware of this feature, and even if they were they would consider it an implementation detail. But it is, nonetheless, an important behavior that the vending machine exhibits and is therefore something that we need to test.

On the other hand, there are many things that are definitely implementation details to both customers and us testers. An example of this is how the machine heats water in order to make coffee: does it use a thermoblock or a boiler? This is not something we should test, because it's an internal detail of the machine, which doesn't directly matter. A coffee connoisseur might argue that it does matter because a boiler produces better tasting coffee. But if we unpack their argument, it still suggests that the method of heating the water is an implementation detail. What the connoisseur ultimately cares about is the taste of the coffee, and the method of heating the water is just a means to that end, so if we are worried about connoisseurs complaining, we should make sure that the taste of the coffee is something we test (not the method of heating the water). Figure 10.4 illustrates the different dependencies that the vending machine has and how tests might need to interact with them.

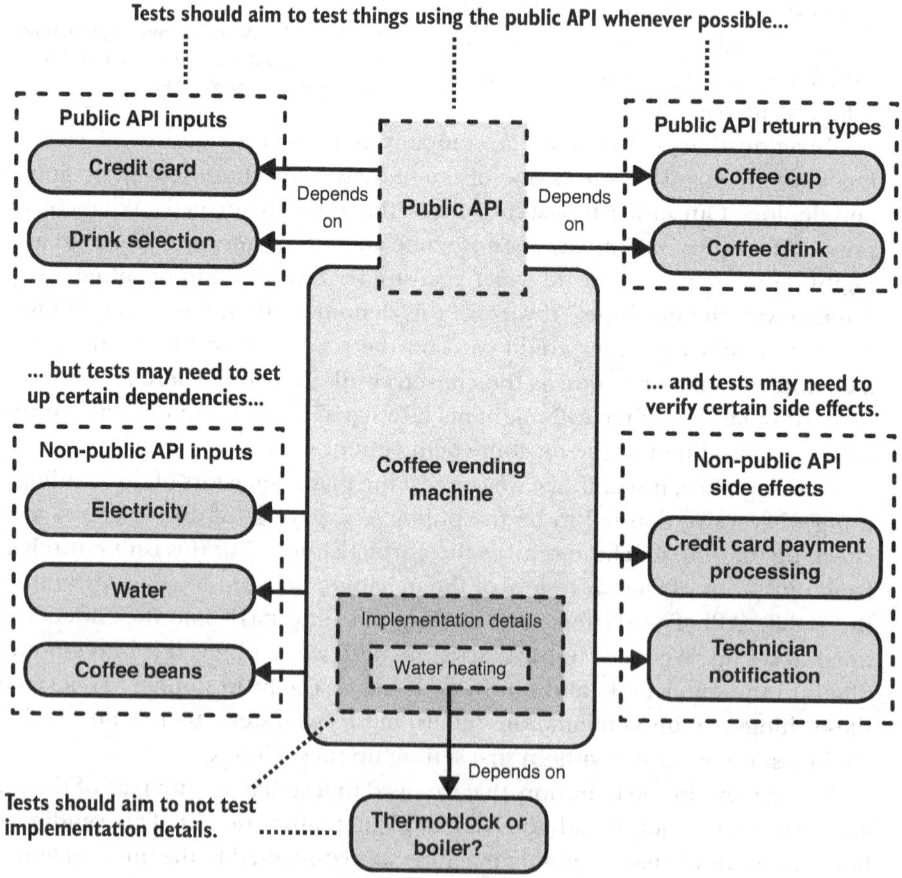

Figure 10.4 Tests should aim to test things using the public API whenever possible. But it can often be necessary for tests to interact with dependencies that are not part of the public API in order to perform setup and to verify desired side effects.

Testing the vending machine is analogous to unit testing a piece of code. To demonstrate this with an example, consider listing 10.1. The `AddressBook` class allows a caller to look up the email address for a user. It achieves this by fetching the email address from a server. It also caches any previously fetched email addresses to prevent overloading the server with repeat requests. As far as anyone using this class is concerned, they call `lookupEmailAddress()` with a user ID and get back an email address (or null if there is no email address), so it would be reasonable to say that the `lookupEmailAddress()` function is the public API of this class. This means that the fact that it depends on the `ServerEndPoint` class and caches email addresses are both implementation details as far as users of the class are concerned.

Listing 10.1 AddressBook class

```
class AddressBook {
  private final ServerEndPoint server;                 // Implementation details as far as
  private final Map<Int, String> emailAddressCache;    // users of the class are concerned
  ...

  String? lookupEmailAddress(Int userId) {             // The public API
    String? cachedEmail = emailAddressCache.get(userId);
    if (cachedEmail != null) {
      return cachedEmail;
    }
    return fetchAndCacheEmailAddress(userId);
  }

  private String? fetchAndCacheEmailAddress(Int userId) {    // More implementation details
    String? fetchedEmail = server.fetchEmailAddress(userId);
    if (fetchedEmail != null) {
      emailAddressCache.put(userId, fetchedEmail);
    }
    return fetchedEmail;
  }
}
```

The public API reflects the most important behavior of the class: looking up an email address given a user ID. But we can't test this unless we set up (or simulate) a `ServerEndPoint`. In addition to this, another important behavior is that repeated calls to `lookupEmailAddress()` with the same user ID don't result in repeated calls to the server. This is not part of the public API (as we defined it), but it's still an important behavior because we don't want our server to get overloaded, and we should therefore test it. Note that the thing we actually care about (and should test) is that repeat requests are not sent to the server. The fact that the class achieves this using a cache is just a means to this end and is, therefore, an implementation detail even to tests. Figure 10.5 illustrates the dependencies of the `AddressBook` class and how tests might need to interact with them.

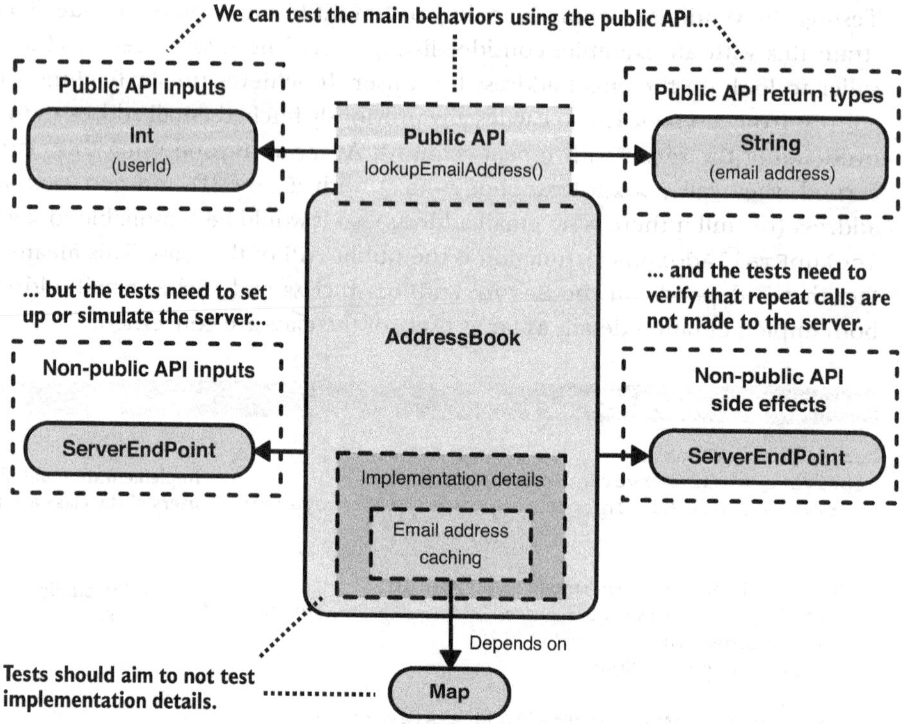

Figure 10.5 We can't fully test all the important behaviors of the `AddressBook` class using what we defined as the public API.

Where possible we should test the code's behaviors using the public API. This is likely to be applicable for any behaviors that occur purely via public function parameters, return values, or error signaling. But depending on how we choose to define the public API of our code, there may be scenarios where it's not possible to test all behaviors using only the public API. This might happen if it's necessary to set up various dependencies or verify that certain side effects have or haven't occurred. Some examples of this might be as follows:

- *Code that interacts with a server.* In order to test the code, it might be necessary to set up or simulate the server so that it can provide the necessary inputs. We might also want to verify what side effects the code has on the server, such as how frequently it calls it and that requests are in a valid format.
- *Code that saves values to, or reads values from, a database.* We might need to test the code with several different values in the database to exercise all the behaviors. And we'll likely want to check what values the code saves to the database (a side effect).

"Test using only the public API" and "don't test implementation details" are both excellent pieces of advice, but we need to appreciate that they are guiding principles and that the definitions of "public API" and "implementation details" can be subjective and context specific. What ultimately matters is that we properly test all the important behaviors of the code, and there may be occasions where we can't do this using only what we consider the public API. But we should still stay alert to the desire to keep tests agnostic to implementation details as much as possible, so we should stray away from the public API only when there really is no alternative.

10.4 Test doubles

It was said at the start of this chapter that unit tests aim to test a unit of code in a "relatively isolated manner." But as we've just seen, code tends to depend on other things, and to fully test all the behaviors of the code we often need to set up inputs and verify side effects. But, as we'll see in a moment, it's not always feasible or desirable to use real dependencies in tests.

An alternative to using a real dependency is to use a *test double*. A test double is an object that simulates a dependency, but in a way that makes it more suitable to use in tests. We'll start off by exploring some of the reasons for using a test double. We'll then look at three specific kinds of test double: mocks, stubs, and fakes. Along the way, we'll see how mocks and stubs can be problematic and why using a fake is often preferable if one is available.

10.4.1 Reasons for using a test double

Three common reasons why we might want to use a test double are as follows:

- *Simplifying a test*—Some dependencies are tricky and painful to use in tests. A dependency might require lots of configuration or might require us to also configure loads of its sub-dependencies. If this is the case, our tests may become complicated and tightly coupled to implementation details. Using a test double instead of the real dependency might simplify things.
- *Protecting the outside world from the test*—Some dependencies have real-world side effects. If one of the code's dependencies sends requests to a real server or writes values to a real database, this might have bad consequences for users or business-critical processes. In such scenarios, we might use a test double to protect our systems in the outside world from the actions of the test.
- *Protecting the test from the outside world*—The outside world can be indeterministic. If one of the code's dependencies reads a value from a real database that other systems are writing to, then the returned value might change over time. This could result in our tests being flakey. A test double, on the other hand, can be configured to always behave in the same deterministic way.

The following subsections explore these reasons in more detail and illustrate how a test double might be used in these scenarios.

SIMPLIFYING A TEST

Some dependencies can require a lot of effort to set up. The dependency itself might require us to specify lots of parameters, or it might have many sub-dependencies that all require configuring. In addition to setting things up, it may also be necessary for our tests to verify desired side effects in sub-dependencies. In a situation like this, things can get out of hand. We might end up with a mountain of setup code within our tests, and they may also end up being tightly coupled to a lot of implementation details (figure 10.6).

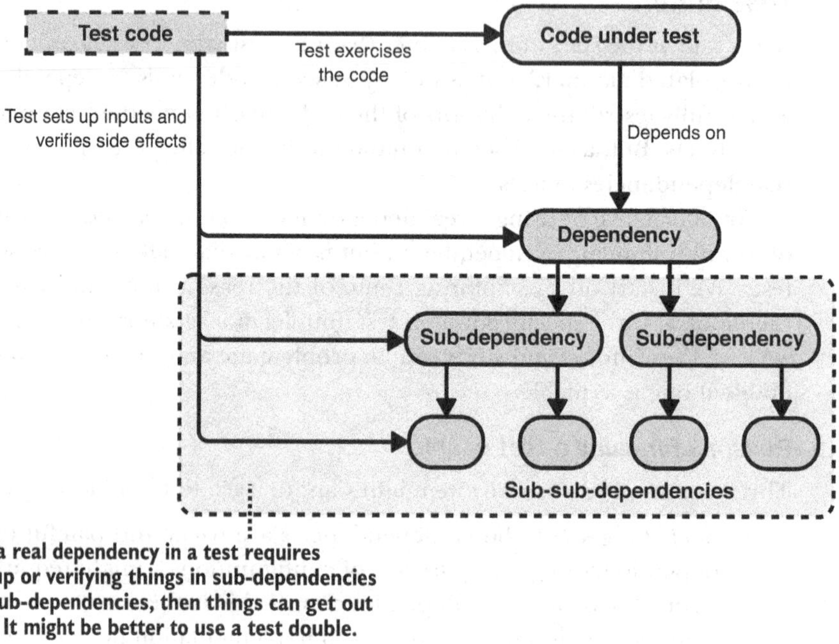
Test code
Code under test
Test exercises the code
Test sets up inputs and verifies side effects
Depends on
Dependency
Sub-dependency
Sub-dependency
Sub-sub-dependencies
If using a real dependency in a test requires setting up or verifying things in sub-dependencies or sub-sub-dependencies, then things can get out of hand. It might be better to use a test double.

Figure 10.6 It can sometimes be impractical to use real dependencies in tests. This can be the case if a dependency has lots of sub-dependencies that would also need to be interacted with.

In contrast, if we use a test double, then we bypass the need to set up the real dependency or to verify things in its sub-dependencies. The test code needs to interact with only the test double to set things up and verify side effects (which should both be relatively simple). Figure 10.7 illustrates how much simpler the test becomes.

Another motivation for simplifying things might be to make the tests run faster; this might be applicable if one of the dependencies invokes a computationally expensive algorithm or requires lots of slow setup.

As we'll explore in later sections, there are scenarios where using a test double can actually make a test more coupled to implementation details. And setting up a test double can also sometimes be more complicated than using a real dependency, so the arguments for and against using a test double to simplify a test need to be considered on a case-by-case basis.

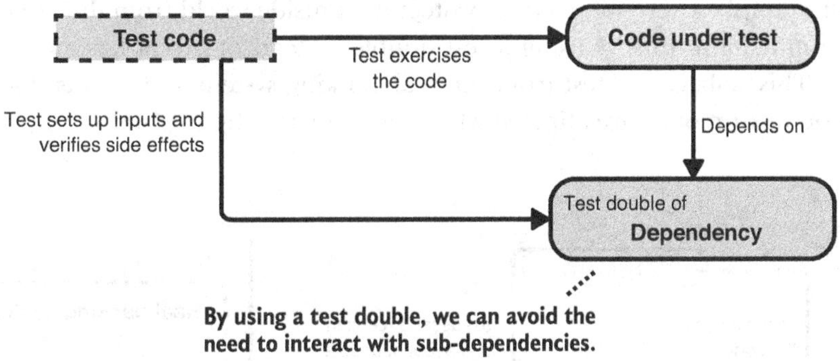

Figure 10.7 A test double can simplify the test by removing the need to worry about sub-dependencies.

PROTECTING THE OUTSIDE WORLD FROM THE TEST

In addition to the desire to test code in a relatively isolated manner, there may also be inescapable reasons that mean we have to test it in isolation. Imagine we work on a system that handles payments and we're unit testing a piece of code that debits money from a customer's bank account. When the code runs in the real world, one of the side effects will be to take real money out of a real customer's account. The code achieves this by depending on a class called `BankAccount`, which in turn interacts with the real-world banking system. If we use an instance of the `BankAccount` class in our test, then real money will be taken from a real account whenever the test runs (figure 10.8). This is almost certainly not a good idea, because there may be bad consequences, such as affecting real people's money or corrupting the company's auditing and accounting.

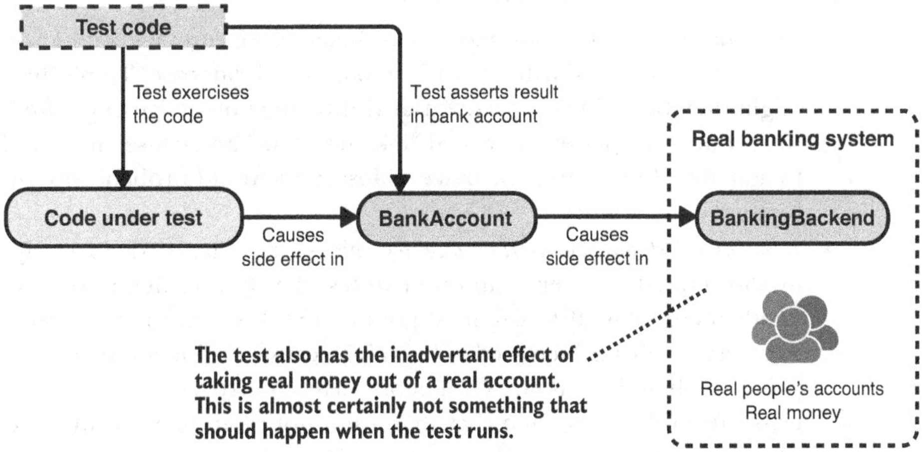

Figure 10.8 If a dependency causes real-world side effects, we'll likely want to use a test double instead of using the real dependency.

This is an example where we need to protect the outside world from the effects of the test. We can achieve this by using a test double instead of a real instance of `BankAccount`. This isolates the test from the real banking system and means that no real bank accounts or money are affected when the test runs (figure 10.9).

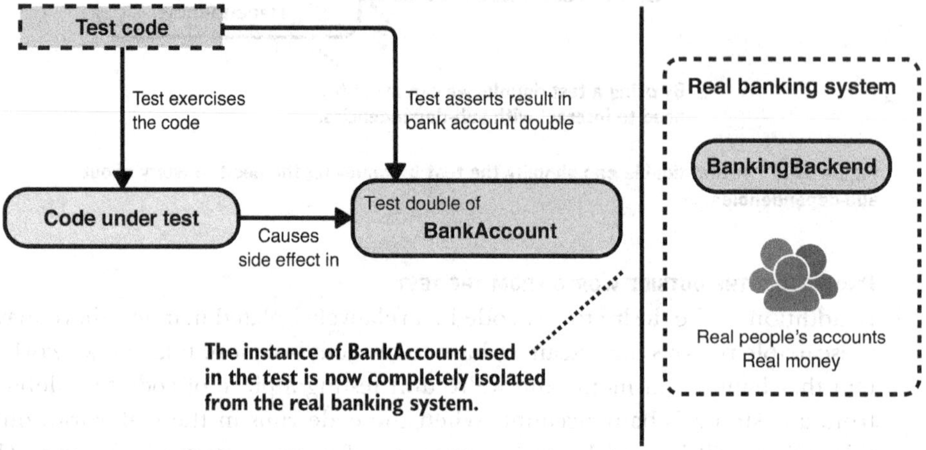

Figure 10.9 A test double can protect real systems in the outside world from side effects.

A test that has the side effect of taking real money from a real bank account is perhaps an extreme example, but the point that it demonstrates is widely applicable. A more likely scenario might be a test that has the side effect of sending requests to a real server or writing values to a real database. While these might not be catastrophic, they could lead to problems such as the following:

- *Users seeing weird and confusing values*—Imagine we run an ecommerce business and one of our tests writes records to our actual database. These "test" records might then be visible to users. A user visiting the homepage might find that half the products displayed are called "fake test item" and cause an error if they try to add any of them to their basket. Most users would probably not find this to be a good experience.
- *It might affect our monitoring and logging*—A test might deliberately send an invalid request to a server in order to test that the resultant error response is handled correctly. If this request goes to a real server, then the error rate for that server will be increased. This might cause engineers to think there is a problem when there is not. Or if people learn to expect this baseline number of errors from the tests, then they might not notice an increase in the error rate when real errors occur in the system.

It's important that tests don't cause side effects in customer-facing or business-critical systems. These systems need to be protected from the tests, and a test double can be an effective way to achieve this by keeping the test isolated.

PROTECTING THE TEST FROM THE OUTSIDE WORLD

In addition to protecting the outside world from the test, another reason to use a test double might be the reverse of this: to protect the test from the outside world. Real dependencies can have nondeterministic behaviors. Examples of this might be a real dependency reading a regularly changing value from a database or generating something like an ID using a random number generator. Using a dependency like this in a test might result in the test being flakey, and as we saw previously, this is probably something we want to avoid.

To demonstrate this and how a test double can help, let's consider another thing that a piece of code might want to do with a bank account: read the balance. The balance of a real bank account potentially changes quite often, as the owner of the account pays money in and takes money out. Even if we create a special account that we use just for testing, the balance might still change as interest gets paid in or an account fee is deducted every month, so if a test makes use of a real bank account and the code under test reads the balance, the test might end up being flakey (figure 10.10).

The solution is to isolate the test from the real banking system, and once again this is something we can do with a test double. If we use a test double for the `BankAccount`, then the test code can configure it with a predetermined value for the account balance (figure 10.11). This means that the account balance will always be the same deterministic value every time the test runs.

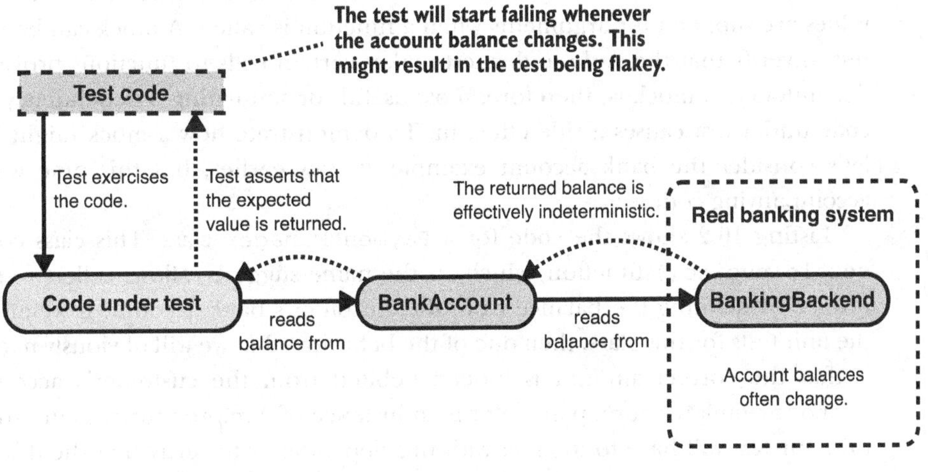

Figure 10.10 If a dependency behaves in an indeterministic manner it can cause tests to be flakey.

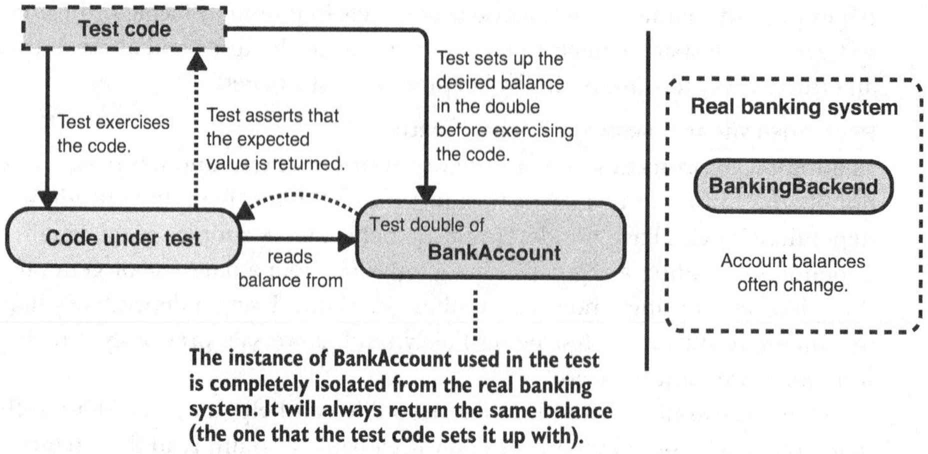

Figure 10.11 A test double can protect the test from any indeterministic behavior that a real dependency might exhibit.

As we've seen, there are a few reasons we might decide that it's not desirable or feasible to use a real dependency. Once we've determined that we'd rather use a test double, we need to decide which kind of test double to use. The following subsections will discuss three of the most common choices: mocks, stubs, and fakes.

10.4.2 Mocks

A *mock* simulates a class or interface by providing no functionality other than just recording what calls are made to member functions. In doing so, it also records what values are supplied for arguments when a function is called. A mock can be used in a test to verify that the code under test makes certain calls to functions provided by a dependency. A mock is, therefore, most useful for simulating a dependency that the code under test causes a side effect in. To demonstrate how a mock might be used, let's consider the bank account example we saw earlier, but this time with some accompanying code.

Listing 10.2 shows the code for a `PaymentManager` class. This class contains a `settleInvoice()` function, which, as the name suggests, allows callers to settle an invoice by debiting the balance from the customer's bank account. If we are writing the unit tests for this class, then one of the behaviors that we will obviously need to test is that the correct amount is indeed debited from the customer's account. The `customerBankAccount` parameter is an instance of `BankAccount`, so in order to do this, our test will have to interact with this dependency to verify that the desired side effect is caused.

Listing 10.2 Code that depends on BankAccount

```
class PaymentManager {
  ...

  PaymentResult settleInvoice(
      BankAccount customerBankAccount,       <-- Takes an instance of BankAccount as a parameter
      Invoice invoice) {
    customerBankAccount.debit(invoice.getBalance());   <-- The debiting of the balance from the account is one of the behaviors we need to test.
    return PaymentResult.paid(invoice.getId());
  }
}
```

BankAccount is an interface and the class that implements it is called BankAccount-Impl. Listing 10.3 shows the BankAccount interface alongside the BankAccount-Impl class. We can see that the BankAccountImpl class depends on Banking-Backend, which connects to the real banking system. As we saw previously, this means that we can't use an instance of BankAccountImpl in our test, because this would result in moving real money around in real accounts (we need to protect the outside world from the test).

Listing 10.3 BankAccount interface and implementation

```
interface BankAccount {
  void debit(MonetaryAmount amount);
  void credit(MonetaryAmount amount);
  MonetaryAmount getBalance();
}

class BankAccountImpl implements BankAccount {
  private final BankingBackend backend;     <-- Depends on BankingBackend, which affects real money in real bank accounts
  ...

  override void debit(MonetaryAmount amount) { ... }
  override void credit(MonetaryAmount amount) { ... }
  override MonetaryAmount getBalance() { ... }
}
```

An alternative to using BankAccountImpl is to use a mock of the BankAccount interface and then check that the debit() function is called with the correct arguments. Listing 10.4 shows the code for the test case that checks that the account is debited with the correct amount. Some things to notice about the code are as follows:

- A mock of the bank account interface is created by calling createMock(Bank-Account).
- The mockAccount is passed to the settleInvoice() function (the code under test).
- The test verifies that mockAccount.debit() was called once with the expected amount (in this case the invoice balance).

Listing 10.4 A test case that uses a mock

```
void testSettleInvoice_accountDebited() {
  BankAccount mockAccount = createMock(BankAccount);      <-- Mock of BankAccount created
  MonetaryAmount invoiceBalance =
      new MonetaryAmount(5.0, Currency.USD);
  Invoice invoice = new Invoice(invoiceBalance, "test-id");
  PaymentManager paymentManager = new PaymentManager();

  paymentManager.settleInvoice(mockAccount, invoice);     <-- The code under test is called with mockAccount.

  verifyThat(mockAccount.debit)                 The test asserts that
      .wasCalledOnce()                          mockAccount.debit() is called
      .withArguments(invoiceBalance);           with expected arguments.
}
```

The use of a mock has allowed us to test the `PaymentManager.settleInvoice()` function without having to use the `BankAccountImpl` class. This has successfully protected the outside world from the test, but as we'll see in section 10.4.4, there is a real risk that the test might now be unrealistic and not catch important bugs.

10.4.3 Stubs

A *stub* simulates a function by returning predefined values whenever the function is called. This allows tests to simulate dependencies by stubbing certain member functions that the code under test will call and use the return values from. Stubs are therefore useful for simulating dependencies that code takes an input from.

Although there is a clear difference between mocks and stubs, in casual conversation, many engineers just use the word *mock* to refer to both. And in many testing tools that provide stubbing functionality, it's necessary to create what the tool refers to as a mock, even if we only want to use it to stub certain member functions. The code examples in this subsection demonstrate this.

Let's imagine that we now need to modify the `PaymentManager.settleInvoice()` function to check if the bank account has a sufficient balance before it tries to debit the bank account. This will help minimize the number of declined transactions, which might otherwise affect a customer's credit rating with their bank. The following listing shows what the code looks like after we make this change.

Listing 10.5 Code that calls getBalance()

```
class PaymentManager {
  ...

  PaymentResult settleInvoice(
      BankAccount customerBankAccount,
      Invoice invoice) {
    if (customerBankAccount.getBalance()            <-- The code relies on the value returned by customerBankAccount.getBalance().
        .isLessThan(invoice.getBalance())) {
      return PaymentResult.insufficientFunds(invoice.getId());
    }
    customerBankAccount.debit(invoice.getBalance());
    return PaymentResult.paid(invoice.getId());
  }
}
```

The new functionality that we've added to the `PaymentManager.settleInvoice()` function means that there are now more behaviors that we need to add test cases for, such as the following:

- That an "insufficient funds" `PaymentResult` is returned if the funds are insufficient
- That no attempt is made to debit the account if the funds are insufficient
- That the account is debited when the funds are sufficient

It's clear that we need to write some unit test cases that will be dependent on the bank account balance. If we use `BankAccountImpl` in the test, then the code under test will be reading the balance of a real bank account and, as we established earlier, this is liable to change from time to time, so using `BankAccountImpl` would introduce indeterminism into our tests and potentially make them flakey.

This is a scenario where we need to protect the tests from the outside world. We can do this by using a stub for the `BankAccount.getBalance()` function. We can configure the stub to return a predetermined value whenever it is called. This allows us to test that the code behaves correctly while also ensuring that the tests are deterministic and non-flakey.

Listing 10.6 shows the test case for the first of the behaviors just mentioned (that an "insufficient funds" `PaymentResult` is returned if the funds are insufficient). Some things to notice about the code are as follows:

- As mentioned earlier, with many testing tools it's necessary to create what the tool refers to as a mock even if we want to use it only to create stubs, so we create a `mockAccount`, but then stub the `getBalance()` function rather than actually making use of any mocking functionality.
- The `mockAccount.getBalance()` stub is configured to return the predetermined value of $9.99.

Listing 10.6 A test case that uses a stub

```
void testSettleInvoice_insufficientFundsCorrectResultReturned() {
  MonetaryAmount invoiceBalance =
      new MonetaryAmount(10.0, Currency.USD);
  Invoice invoice = new Invoice(invoiceBalance, "test-id");
  BankAccount mockAccount = createMock(BankAccount);
  when(mockAccount.getBalance())
      .thenReturn(new MonetaryAmount(9.99, Currency.USD));
  PaymentManager paymentManager = new PaymentManager();

  PaymentResult result =
      paymentManager.settleInvoice(mockAccount, invoice);

  assertThat(result.getStatus()).isEqualTo(INSUFFICIENT_FUNDS);
}
```

The BankAccount interface is "mocked" even though we only want to create a stub.

The mockAccount .getBalance() function is stubbed and configured to always return $9.99.

The test asserts that an "insufficient funds" result is returned.

The use of a stub has allowed us to protect the test from the outside world and prevent flakiness. This (and the previous subsection) demonstrates how mocks and stubs can help us isolate our tests by simulating dependencies that might otherwise be problematic. Sometimes this is necessary, but there are also downsides to using mocks and stubs. The next subsection explains two of the main drawbacks.

10.4.4 Mocks and stubs can be problematic

There are different schools of thought regarding the usage of mocks and stubs, which we'll look at in section 10.4.6. Before we discuss these different schools of thought (and before we look at fakes), it's important to discuss some of the problems that mocks and stubs can cause. Two of the main downsides of using them are as follows:

- They can lead to tests that are unrealistic if a mock or a stub is configured to behave in a way that is different to the real dependency.
- They can cause tests to become tightly coupled to implementation details, which, as we saw earlier, can make refactoring difficult.

The next two subsections explore these in more detail.

MOCKS AND STUBS CAN LEAD TO UNREALISTIC TESTS

Whenever we mock or stub a class or function we (as the engineers writing the test) have to decide how that mock or stub will behave. There's a real risk that we make it behave in a way that differs from how the class or function behaves in real life. If we do this, our test might pass and we'll think that everything is working, but when our code then runs in real life it may behave in an incorrect or buggy way.

Earlier, when we used a mock to test the `PaymentManager.settleInvoice()` function, we tested the scenario where the invoice has a positive balance of $5, meaning that the customer owes the company $5. But invoices can also have negative balances, for example, if a customer receives a refund or compensation for something, so this is also a scenario that we should test. At face value, this might seem quite easy. We just copy the code for the previous test case we saw and use a value of minus $5 for the invoice balance. Listing 10.7 shows the code we end up with for our test case. The test passes, so our conclusion is that the `PaymentManager.settleInvoice()` function can handle negative balance invoices fine. Unfortunately, as we'll see in a moment, this is not the case.

Listing 10.7 Testing a negative invoice balance

```
void testSettleInvoice_negativeInvoiceBalance() {
  BankAccount mockAccount = createMock(BankAccount);
  MonetaryAmount invoiceBalance =
      new MonetaryAmount(-5.0, Currency.USD);          <-- A negative invoice balance
  Invoice invoice = new Invoice(invoiceBalance, "test-id");
  PaymentManager paymentManager = new PaymentManager();

  paymentManager.settleInvoice(mockAccount, invoice);

  verifyThat(mockAccount.debit)
      .wasCalledOnce()
      .withArguments(invoiceBalance);
}
```

The test asserts that mockAccount.debit() is called with the expected negative amount.

Our test case asserts that our code calls `mockAccount.debit()` with the correct invoice balance (in this case a negative one). But this doesn't mean that calling `BankAccountImpl.debit()` with a negative value will actually do what we expect it to in real life. While writing the `PaymentManager` class, we've made the implicit assumption that debiting a negative amount from a bank account will result in money being added to the account. By using a mock, we then repeated this assumption in our test. This means that the validity of this assumption never actually gets tested, and it's basically a tautology that the test will pass, regardless of whether the code actually works in real life.

In reality, our assumption is unfortunately not valid. If we look more closely at the `BankAccount` interface, we see the following documentation indicating that an `ArgumentException` will be thrown if either `debit()` or `credit()` are called with a negative value:

```
interface BankAccount {
  /**
   * @throws ArgumentException if called with a negative amount
   */
  void debit(MonetaryAmount amount);

  /**
   * @throws ArgumentException if called with a negative amount
   */
  void credit(MonetaryAmount amount);

  ...
}
```

Clearly there is a bug in the `PaymentManager.settleInvoice()` function, but because we used a mock in our test, it didn't reveal this bug. This is one of the major drawbacks of using a mock. The engineer writing the test has to decide how the mock will behave, and if they made a mistake in understanding how the real dependency works, then they will likely make the same mistake when they configure the mock.

This same problem can apply to the usage of stubs. Using a stub will test that our code behaves how we want it to when a dependency returns a certain value. But it tests nothing about whether that is actually a realistic value for that dependency to return. In the previous subsection we used a stub to simulate the `BankAccount.getBalance()` function, but we might have failed to properly consider the code contract of this function. Imagine we look more closely at the `BankAccount` interface and discover the following documentation. This is something we overlooked when configuring our stub:

```
interface BankAccount {
  ...

  /**
   * @return the bank account balance rounded down to the
   *     nearest multiple of 10. E.g. if the real balance is
   *     $19, then this function will return $10. This is for
   *     security reasons, because exact account balances are
```

```
     * sometimes used by the bank as a security question.
     */
    MonetaryAmount getBalance();
  }
```

NOTE: ROUNDING DOWN A BALANCE The example of `getBalance()` returning a rounded value is to illustrate how it can be easy to overlook certain details when stubbing a function. In reality, rounding an account balance down is probably not a particularly robust security feature. There are still ways an attacker could figure out the exact balance, for example by repeatedly crediting the account with $0.01 until the value returned by `getBalance()` changes.

MOCKS AND STUBS CAN CAUSE TIGHT COUPLING BETWEEN TESTS AND IMPLEMENTATION DETAILS

In the previous subsection, we saw how calling `customerBankAccount.debit()` doesn't work if the invoice has a negative balance, and how using a mock meant that this bug went unnoticed during testing. If an engineer does eventually notice this bug, they might solve it by introducing an if-statement into the `settleInvoice()` function, such as the one in the following snippet. This calls `customerBankAccount.debit()` if the balance is positive and `customerBankAccount.credit()` if it's negative:

```
PaymentResult settleInvoice(...) {
  ...
  MonetaryAmount balance = invoice.getBalance();
  if (balance.isPositive()) {
    customerBankAccount.debit(balance);
  } else {
    customerBankAccount.credit(balance.absoluteAmount());
  }
  ...
}
```

If the engineer uses mocks to test this code, then they will end up with various test cases where they verify that `customerBankAccount.debit()` is called and others where they verify that `customerBankAccount.credit()` is called:

```
void testSettleInvoice_positiveInvoiceBalance() {
  ...
  verifyThat(mockAccount.debit)
      .wasCalledOnce()
      .withArguments(invoiceBalance);
}
...
void testSettleInvoice_negativeInvoiceBalance() {
  ...
  verifyThat(mockAccount.credit)
      .wasCalledOnce()
      .withArguments(invoiceBalance.absoluteAmount());
}
```

This tests that the code calls the expected functions, but it doesn't directly test the behavior that someone using the class actually cares about. The behavior they care about is that the `settleInvoice()` function transfers the correct amount of money to or from the account. The exact mechanics of this is just a means to an end, so whether the `credit()` or `debit()` function is called is an implementation detail.

To emphasize this, let's consider a refactoring that an engineer might decide to perform. They notice that several pieces of code in different parts of the codebase contain this clunky if-else statement to switch between calling `debit()` and `credit()`. To improve the code, they decide to move this functionality into the `BankAccountImpl` class where it can be reused. This means that a new function is added to the `BankAccount` interface called `transfer()`:

```
interface BankAccount {
  ...

  /**
   * Transfers the specified amount to the account. If the
   * amount is negative, then this has the effect of transferring
   * money from the account.
   */
  void transfer(MonetaryAmount amount);
}
```

The `settleInvoice()` function is then refactored to call the new `transfer()` function as follows:

```
PaymentResult settleInvoice(...) {
  ...
  MonetaryAmount balance = invoice.getBalance();
  customerBankAccount.transfer(balance.negate());
  ...
}
```

This refactoring hasn't changed any behaviors; it's changed only an implementation detail. But many of the tests now fail because they are using mocks that expect a call to either `debit()` or `credit()`, which now no longer occurs. This is the opposite of the goal we stated in section 10.2.2: that tests should be agnostic to implementation details. The engineer who performed the refactoring will have to modify many test cases to make them pass again, so it's hard for them to have confidence that their refactoring didn't inadvertently modify any behaviors.

As mentioned earlier, there are different schools of thought around the usage of mocks and stubs, but in my opinion it's best to keep use of them to a minimum. If there's no feasible alternative, then using a mock or a stub in a test is better than not having a test. But if it's feasible to use a real dependency or a fake (which we'll discuss in the next subsection), then this is usually preferable in my opinion.

10.4.5 Fakes

A *fake* is an alternative implementation of a class (or interface) that can safely be used in tests. A fake should accurately simulate the public API of the real dependency, but the implementation is typically simplified. This can often be achieved by storing state in a member variable within the fake instead of communicating with an external system.

The whole point in a fake is that its code contract is identical to the real dependency, so if the real class (or interface) doesn't accept a certain input, then the fake shouldn't either. This typically means that a fake should be maintained by the same team that maintains the code for the real dependency, because if the code contract of the real dependency ever changes, then the code contract of the fake will also need to be updated.

Let's consider the `BankAccount` interface and `BankAccountImpl` class that we saw earlier. If the team that maintains these implements a fake bank account, it might look something like listing 10.8. Some things to notice about the code are as follows:

- `FakeBankAccount` implements the `BankAccount` interface, so during testing it can be used in any code that requires an implementation of `BankAccount`.
- Instead of communicating with the banking backend system, the fake just keeps track of the account balance using a member variable.
- The fake throws an `ArgumentException` if either of `debit()` or `credit()` are called with a negative amount. This enforces the code contract and means that the fake behaves in exactly the same way as real implementations of `BankAccount`. Details like this are what make fakes so useful. If an engineer writes code that erroneously calls either of these functions with a negative value, then a test using a mock or a stub may not catch it, whereas a test using this fake will catch a bug like that.
- The `getBalance()` function returns the balance rounded down to the nearest 10, because this is what the code contract states and it's how real implementations of `BankAccount` behave. Again, this maximizes the chance that any bugs resulting from this slightly surprising behavior will be caught during testing.
- In addition to implementing all the functions in the `BankAccount` interface, the fake also provides a `getActualBalance()` function that tests can use to verify the actual balance of the fake account. This is important because the `getBalance()` function rounds the balance down, meaning that tests can't use it to accurately verify the state of the account.

Listing 10.8 A fake BankAccount

```
class FakeBankAccount implements BankAccount {       <-- Implements the BankAccount interface
  private MonetaryAmount balance;                    <-- Keeps track of state using member variables

  FakeBankAccount(MonetaryAmount startingBalance) {
    this.balance = startingBalance;
  }

  override void debit(MonetaryAmount amount) {
    if (amount.isNegative()) {
      throw new ArgumentException("Amount can't be negative");   <-- ArgumentException thrown if amount negative
    }
    balance = balance.subtract(amount);
  }
```

```
  override void credit(MonetaryAmount amount) {
    if (amount.isNegative()) {
      throw new ArgumentException("Amount can't be negative");
    }
    balance = balance.add(amount);
  }

  override void transfer(MonetaryAmount amount) {
    balance.add(amount);
  }

  override MonetaryAmount getBalance() {
    return roundDownToNearest10(balance);
  }

  MonetaryAmount getActualBalance() {
    return balance;
  }
}
```

ArgumentException thrown if amount negative

Returns the balance rounded down to the nearest 10

Additional function to allow tests to check the actual (unrounded) balance

Using a fake instead of a mock or a stub can avoid the problems we identified in the previous subsection, as we'll now see.

FAKES CAN RESULT IN MORE REALISTIC TESTS

In the previous subsection, we saw the example of a test case that aimed to verify that the `PaymentManager.settleInvoice()` function correctly handled an invoice with a negative balance. In that example, the test case used a mock to verify that `BankAccount.debit()` was called with the correct negative amount. This resulted in a test that passed even though the code was broken (because, in reality, `debit()` doesn't accept negative amounts). If we'd used a fake in the test case instead of a mock, then this bug would have been revealed.

If we rewrite the negative invoice balance test case using a `FakeBankAccount`, then it would look like listing 10.9. When `paymentManager.settleInvoice()` is called, the subsequent call to `FakeBankAccount.debit()` with a negative amount will throw an exception and cause the test to fail. This will make us immediately aware that there is a bug in the code and prompt us to fix it before submitting anything to the codebase.

Listing 10.9 Negative invoice balance test using a fake

```
void testSettleInvoice_negativeInvoiceBalance() {
  FakeBankAccount fakeAccount = new FakeBankAccount(
      new MonetaryAmount(100.0, Currency.USD));
  MonetaryAmount invoiceBalance =
      new MonetaryAmount(-5.0, Currency.USD);
  Invoice invoice = new Invoice(invoiceBalance, "test-id");
  PaymentManager paymentManager = new PaymentManager();

  paymentManager.settleInvoice(fakeAccount, invoice);

  assertThat(fakeAccount.getActualBalance())
      .isEqualTo(new MonetaryAmount(105.0, Currency.USD));
}
```

Fake account created with an initial balance of $100

Invoice balance of minus $5

Code under test called with fakeAccount

The test asserts that new balance is $105.

The main reason for tests is that they should fail when there is a bug in the code, so the test case is now useful because it does exactly this.

FAKES CAN DECOUPLE TESTS FROM IMPLEMENTATION DETAILS

Another benefit of using a fake instead of a mock or a stub is that it tends to result in the test being less tightly coupled to implementation details. We saw earlier how using a mock led to tests failing when an engineer performed a refactoring. This was because the tests using a mock verified that specific calls were made to either `debit()` or `credit()` (which is an implementation detail). In contrast, if the test uses a fake, then instead of verifying these implementation details, it will instead assert that the final account balance is correct:

```
...
  assertThat(fakeAccount.getActualBalance())
       .isEqualTo(new MonetaryAmount(105.0, Currency.USD));
...
```

The code under test can transfer money into or out of the account using whatever function calls it likes, but as long as the end result is the same, the test will pass. This makes the test much more agnostic to implementation details; a refactoring that doesn't change any behaviors will not result in the tests failing.

Not every dependency will have an equivalent fake. It depends on whether the team that maintains the real dependency has created one and whether they are willing to maintain it. But we can be proactive; if our team owns a certain class or interface and we know that it would be unsuitable to use the real thing in a test, it might well be worth us implementing a fake for it. This will likely make our own testing better and may also benefit numerous other engineers who depend on our code.

If it's not feasible to use a real dependency in a test, then it might be necessary to use a test double. If this is the case and a fake exists, then, in my opinion, it's preferable to use that fake rather than a mock or a stub. I say "in my opinion" because there are different schools of thought around mocking and stubbing, which we'll briefly discuss in the next subsection.

10.4.6 Schools of thought on mocking

Broadly speaking there are two schools of thought around the usage of mocks (and stubs) in unit tests:

- *Mockist*—Sometimes referred to as the "London school of thought." Proponents argue that engineers should avoid using real dependencies in tests and instead use mocks. Avoiding the usage of real dependencies and using lots of mocks often also implies the need to use stubs for any parts of dependencies that provide inputs, so using a mockist approach often also involves stubbing as well as mocking.

- *Classicist*—Sometimes referred to as the "Detroit school of thought." Proponents argue that the usage of mocks and stubs should be kept to a minimum and that engineers should prefer using real dependencies in tests. When it's not feasible to use a real dependency, then using a fake is the next preference. Mocks and stubs should only be used as a last resort when it's not feasible to use either the real dependency or a fake.

One of the main practical differences between tests written using these two approaches is that mockist tests tend to test interactions, while classicist tests tend to test the resultant state in the code and its dependencies. In this sense, a mockist approach tends to lock in *how* the code under test does something, while a classicist approach tends to lock in *what* the end result of running the code is (without necessarily caring how this is achieved).

Some arguments in favor of a mockist approach are as follows:

- *It keeps unit tests more isolated.* Using a mock means that a test doesn't also end up testing things about dependencies. This means that a breakage in a particular piece of code will cause test failures only in the unit tests for that code and not the tests for other code that depends on it.
- *It can make tests easier to write.* Using real dependencies requires figuring out which of them are needed for the test and how to correctly configure and verify things in them. A mock or a stub, on the other hand, is often trivial to set up because it can be done without needing to actually construct a dependency and worry about configuration of sub-dependencies.

Some arguments in favor of using a classicist approach and against using a mockist approach are as follows (both these were discussed in the preceding subsections):

- A mock tests that the code makes a particular call, but it doesn't test that the call is actually valid. Using lots of mocks (or stubs) can result in tests that pass even though the code is completely broken.
- A classicist approach can result in tests that are more agnostic to implementation details. With a classicist approach, the emphasis is on testing an end result: what the code returns or the resultant state. And as far as the test is concerned, it doesn't matter how the code achieves this. This means that the tests fail only when behaviors change, and not when implementation details change.

If I'm honest, in my early days as a software engineer, I had no idea that these two approaches existed as formalized schools of thought. Without knowing it at the time, I seemed to naturally adopt more of a mockist approach and would write unit tests where the majority of dependencies were mocked or stubbed out. Admittedly, I hadn't really put much thought into this at the time, and my main reason for using what turned out to be a mockist approach was just that it seemed to make my life easier. But

I came to regret this, as it resulted in tests that didn't properly test that things actually worked and made refactoring the code very difficult.

Having tried both approaches, my preference is now firmly in favor of the classicist school of thought, and the content in this chapter reflects that. But it's important to emphasize that this is an opinion and not every engineer would agree with it. If you're interested in reading a more detailed description of mockist and classicist schools of thought, then the second half of this article by Martin Fowler discusses the topic in lots of detail: http://mng.bz/N8Pv.

10.5 Pick and choose from testing philosophies

As you may have already discovered, there are multiple philosophies and methodologies around testing, and they will sometimes be presented as an all-or-nothing kind of thing: you either subscribe to every part of a philosophy or none of the parts. In reality, life isn't like this, and we're free to pick and choose from different philosophies as we see fit.

One example of a testing philosophy is *test-driven development (TDD)*. The most famous part of this philosophy states that engineers should write tests before they write any implementation code. While many recognize the theoretical benefits of this, I don't often meet engineers who actually do this in practice; it's just not how they choose to work. This doesn't mean that they completely ignore everything that the TDD philosophy has to say; it just means they don't fully subscribe to it. Many of them still aim to achieve a lot of other things prescribed under TDD, such as keeping tests isolated, keeping them focused, and not testing implementation details.

Some examples of testing philosophies and methodologies are as follows:

- *Test-driven development*[1]—TDD advocates a process whereby a test case is written before writing any real code; a bare minimum of real code is then written to make the test case pass, and the code is then refactored to improve the structure or remove duplication. Engineers are encouraged to repeat these steps in small iterations. As just mentioned, TDD proponents usually also advocate various other best practices such as keeping test cases isolated and focused and not testing implementation details.
- *Behavior-driven development*[2]—BDD can mean slightly different things to different people, but the essence of it is a focus on identifying behaviors (or functionality) that the software should exhibit (often from the point of view of a user, a customer, or the business). These desired behaviors are captured and recorded in a

---

[1] Some argue that TDD can trace its origins back to the 1960s, but the more modern, formalized philosophy most often associated with the term is widely credited to Kent Beck in the 1990s. (Beck famously claims to have "rediscovered" TDD rather than having invented it.)

[2] The idea of behavior-driven development is widely attributed to Daniel Terhorst-North in the 2000s. A copy of the article in which Terhorst-North introduced the idea can be found here: https://dannorth.net/introducing-bdd/.

format that the software can then be developed against. Tests should reflect these desired behaviors rather than attributes of the software itself. Exactly how these behaviors are captured and recorded, which stakeholders are involved in the process, and how formalized it is can vary a lot from one organization to another.

- *Acceptance test–driven development*—Again, ATDD can mean slightly different things to different people, and the degree to which it overlaps with (or fits alongside) BDD varies between definitions. ATDD involves identifying behaviors (or functionality) that the software should exhibit (often from a customer's point of view) and creating automated *acceptance tests* that will verify if the software as a whole is functioning as required. Similar to TDD, these tests should be created before implementing the real code. In theory, once the acceptance tests all pass, the software is complete and is ready to be accepted by the customer.

Testing philosophies and methodologies tend to document ways of working that some engineers have found to be effective. But at the end of the day the goal we're ultimately trying to achieve matters more than the method of working we chose to get there. The important thing is to ensure that we write good, thorough tests and produce high-quality software. Different people work in different ways; if you work most effectively by following a given philosophy or methodology to the letter, then great, but if you work more effectively another way, then that's absolutely fine.

Summary

- Pretty much every piece of "real code" submitted to the codebase should have an accompanying unit test.
- Every behavior that the "real code" exhibits should have an accompanying test case that exercises it and checks the result. For anything other than the simplest of test cases, it's common to divide the code within each of them into three distinct sections: arrange, act, and assert.
- The key features of a good unit test are as follows:
  - Accurately detects breakages
  - Is agnostic to implementation details
  - Has well-explained failures
  - Has understandable test code
  - Is easy and quick to run
- Test doubles can be used in a unit test when it's infeasible or impractical to use a real dependency. Some examples of test doubles are the following:
  - Mocks
  - Stubs
  - Fakes

- Mocks and stubs can result in tests that are unrealistic and that are tightly coupled to implementation details
- There are different schools of thought on the usage of mocks and stubs. My opinion is that real dependencies should be used in tests where possible. Failing that, a fake is the next best option, while mocks and stubs should be used only as a last resort.

11 Unit testing practices

This chapter covers

- Effectively and reliably unit testing all the behaviors of a piece of code
- Ensuring that tests are understandable and that failures are well explained
- Using dependency injection to ensure that code is testable

Chapter 10 identified a number of principles that can be used to guide us toward writing effective unit tests. This chapter builds on these principles to cover a number of practical techniques that we can apply in our everyday coding.

Chapter 10 described the key features that good unit tests should exhibit. The motivation for many of the techniques described in this chapter directly follow from these, so as a reminder, the key features are as follows:

- *Accurately detects breakages*—If the code is broken, a test should fail. And a test should fail only if the code is indeed broken (we don't want false alarms).
- *Agnostic to implementation details*—Changes in implementation details should ideally not result in changes to tests.

- *Well-explained failures*—If the code is broken, the test failure should provide a clear explanation of the problem.
- *Understandable test code*—Other engineers need to be able to understand what exactly a test is testing and how it is doing it.
- *Easy and quick to run*—Engineers usually need to run unit tests quite often during their everyday work. A slow or difficult-to-run unit test will waste a lot of engineering time.

It's by no means a given that the tests we write will exhibit these features, and it's all too easy to end up with tests that are ineffective and unmaintainable as a result. Luckily there are a number of practical techniques that we can apply to maximize the chance that our tests do exhibit these features. The following sections cover some of the main ones.

11.1 Test behaviors not just functions

Testing a piece of code is a bit like working through a to-do list. There are a number of things that the code under test does (or will do if we're writing the tests before writing the code), and we need to write a test case to test each of these. But as with any to-do list, a successful outcome is contingent on the correct things actually being on the list.

A mistake that engineers sometimes make is to look at a piece of code and add only function names to their to-do list of things to test, so if a class has two functions, then an engineer might write only two test cases (one for each function). We established in chapter 10 that we should test all the important behaviors that a piece of code exhibits. The problem with concentrating on testing each function is that a function can often exhibit more than one behavior and a behavior can sometimes span across multiple functions. If we write only one test case per function, it's likely that we might miss some important behaviors. It's better to fill our to-do list with all the behaviors we care about rather than just the function names we see.

11.1.1 One test case per function is often inadequate

Imagine we work for a bank maintaining a system that automatically assesses mortgage applications. The code in listing 11.1 shows the class that makes the decision of whether a customer can get a mortgage and, if so, how much they can borrow. There are quite a few things going on in the code, such as the following:

- The `assess()` function calls a private helper function to determine whether the customer is eligible for a mortgage. A customer is eligible if they
  - have a good credit rating,
  - have no existing mortgage, and
  - are not banned by the company.
- If the customer is eligible, then another private helper function is called to determine the maximum loan amount for the customer. This is calculated as their yearly income minus their yearly outgoings, multiplied by 10.

Listing 11.1 Mortgage assessment code

```
class MortgageAssessor {
  private const Double MORTGAGE_MULTIPLIER = 10.0;

  MortgageDecision assess(Customer customer) {
    if (!isEligibleForMortgage(customer)) {
      return MortgageDecision.rejected();
    }
    return MortgageDecision.approve(getMaxLoanAmount(customer));
  }

  private static Boolean isEligibleForMortgage(Customer customer) {
    return customer.hasGoodCreditRating() &&
        !customer.hasExistingMortgage() &&
        !customer.isBanned();
  }

  private static MonetaryAmount getMaxLoanAmount(Customer customer) {
    return customer.getIncome()
        .minus(customer.getOutgoings())
        .multiplyBy(MORTGAGE_MULTIPLIER);
  }
}
```

Application rejected if the customer is ineligible

Private helper function to determine if customer is eligible

Private helper function to determine max loan amount

Now imagine we go and look at the tests for this code and see only a single test case that tests the `assess()` function. Listing 11.2 shows this single test case. This tests some of the things that the `assess()` function does, such as the following:

- A mortgage being approved for a customer with a good credit rating, no existing mortgage, and who isn't banned.
- The max loan amount being the customer's income minus their outgoings, multiplied by 10.

But it also clearly leaves a lot of things untested, such as all the reasons a mortgage might be rejected. This is clearly an inadequate amount of testing: we could modify the `MortgageAssessor.assess()` function to approve mortgages even for banned customers and the tests would still pass!

Listing 11.2 Mortgage assessment test

```
testAssess() {
  Customer customer = new Customer(
      income: new MonetaryAmount(50000, Currency.USD),
      outgoings: new MonetaryAmount(20000, Currency.USD),
      hasGoodCreditRating: true,
      hasExistingMortgage: false,
      isBanned: false);
  MortgageAssessor mortgageAssessor = new MortgageAssessor();

  MortgageDecision decision = mortgageAssessor.assess(customer);

  assertThat(decision.isApproved()).isTrue();
  assertThat(decision.getMaxLoanAmount()).isEqualTo(
      new MonetaryAmount(300000, Currency.USD));
}
```

The problem here is that the engineer writing the tests has concentrated on testing functions not behaviors. The `assess()` function is the only function in the public API of the `MortgageAssessor` class, so they wrote only one single test case. Unfortunately this one test case is nowhere near sufficient to fully ensure that the `MortgageAssessor.assess()` function behaves in the correct way.

11.1.2 Solution: Concentrate on testing each behavior

As the previous example demonstrates, there is often not a one-to-one mapping between functions and behaviors. If we concentrate on testing just functions, then it is very easy to end up with a set of test cases that do not verify all the important behaviors that we actually care about. In the example of the `MortgageAssessor` class there are several behaviors that we care about, including the following:

- That a mortgage application is rejected for any customers that at least one of the following applies to:
  - They don't have a good credit rating.
  - They already have an existing mortgage.
  - They are banned by the company.
- If a mortgage application is accepted, then the maximum loan amount is the customer's income minus their outgoings, multiplied by 10.

Each one of these behaviors should be tested, which requires writing a lot more than one single test case. To increase our level of confidence in the code, it also makes sense to test different values and boundary conditions, so we would probably want to include test cases such as the following:

- A few different values for incomes and outgoings to ensure that the arithmetic in the code is correct
- Some extreme values, such as zero income or outgoings, as well as very large amounts of income or outgoings

It's not unlikely that we'll end up with 10 or more different test cases to fully test the `MortgageAssessor` class. This is completely normal and expected: it's not uncommon to see 300 lines of test code for a 100-line piece of real code. It's actually sometimes a warning sign when the amount of test code doesn't exceed the amount of real code, as this can suggest that not every behavior is being tested properly.

The exercise of thinking up behaviors to test is also a great way to spot potential problems with the code. For example, as we're thinking of behaviors to test, we'll probably end up wondering what will happen if a customer's outgoings exceed their income. Currently the `MortgageAssessor.assess()` function will approve such an application with a negative maximum loan amount. This is kind of weird functionality, so this realization would probably prompt us to revisit the logic and handle this scenario a bit more gracefully.

DOUBLE-CHECK THAT EVERY BEHAVIOR HAS BEEN TESTED

A good way to gauge whether a piece of code is tested properly is to think about how someone could theoretically break the code and still have the tests pass. Some good questions to ask while looking over the code are as follows. If the answer to any of them is yes, then this suggests that not all the behaviors are being tested.

- Are there any lines of code that could be deleted and still result in the code compiling and the tests passing?
- Could the polarity of any if-statements (or equivalent) be reversed and still result in the tests passing (e.g., swapping `if (something) {` with `if (!something) {`)?
- Could any logical or arithmetic operators be replaced with alternatives and still result in the tests passing? Examples of this might be swapping a `&&` with a `||` or swapping a `+` with a `-`.
- Could the values of any constants or hard-coded values be changed and still result in the tests passing?

The point is that each line of code, if-statement, logical expression, or value in the code under test should exist for a reason. If it genuinely is superfluous code, then it should be removed. If it's not superfluous, then that means that there must be some important behavior that is somehow dependent on it. If there is an important behavior that the code exhibits, then there should be a test case to test that behavior, so any change in functionality to the code should result in at least one test case failing. If it doesn't, then not all the behaviors are being tested.

The only real exception to this is code that defensively checks for programming errors. For example, we might have a check or assertion within the code to ensure that a particular assumption is valid. There may be no way to exercise this in a test because the only way to test the defensive logic would be to break the assumption by breaking the code.

Checking that changes in functionality result in a test failure can sometimes be automated to some extent using *mutation testing*. A mutation testing tool will create versions of the code with small things mutated. If the tests still pass after the code has been mutated, this is a sign that not every behavior is tested properly.

DON'T FORGET ABOUT ERROR SCENARIOS

Another important set of behaviors that can be easy to overlook is how the code behaves when error scenarios occur. These can seem a bit like edge cases because we don't necessarily expect errors to occur that often. But how a piece of code handles and signals different error scenarios are nonetheless important behaviors that we (and callers of our code) care about. They should therefore be tested.

To demonstrate this, consider listing 11.3. The `BankAccount.debit()` function throws an `ArgumentException` if it's called with a negative amount. The function being called with a negative amount is an error scenario, and the fact that it throws an `ArgumentException` when this happens is an important behavior. It should therefore be tested.

Listing 11.3 Code that handles an error

```
class BankAccount {
  ...
  void debit(MonetaryAmount amount) {
    if (amount.isNegative()) {
      throw new ArgumentException("Amount can't be negative");
    }
    ...
  }
}
```

Throws an ArgumentException if the amount is negative

Listing 11.4 shows how we might test the behavior of the function in this error scenario. The test case asserts that an `ArgumentException` is thrown when `debit()` is called with an amount of -$0.01. It also asserts that the thrown exception contains the expected error message.

Listing 11.4 Testing error handling

```
void testDebit_negativeAmount_throwsArgumentException {
  MonetaryAmount negativeAmount =
      new MonetaryAmount(-0.01, Currency.USD);
  BankAccount bankAccount = new BankAccount();

  ArgumentException exception = assertThrows(
      ArgumentException,
      () -> bankAccount.debit(negativeAmount));
  assertThat(exception.getMessage())
      .isEqualTo("Amount can't be negative");
}
```

Asserts that an ArgumentException is thrown when debit() is called with a negative amount

Asserts that the thrown exception contains the expected error message

A piece of code tends to exhibit many behaviors, and it's quite often the case that even a single function can exhibit many different behaviors depending on the values it's called with or the state that the system is in. Writing just one test case per function rarely results in an adequate amount of testing. Instead of concentrating on functions, it's usually more effective to identify all the behaviors that ultimately matter and ensure that there is a test case for each of them.

11.2 Avoid making things visible just for testing

A class (or unit of code) usually has some number of functions that are visible to code outside; we often refer to these as being *public* functions. This set of public functions typically forms the public API of the code. In addition to public functions, it's quite common for code to also have some number of *private* functions. These are only visible to code within the class (or unit of code). The following snippet demonstrates this distinction:

```
class MyClass {

  String publicFunction() { ... }
```

Visible to code outside of the class

```
  private String privateFunction1 { ... }
  private String privateFunction2 { ... }
}
```

Visible only to code within the class

Private functions are implementation details, and they're not something that code outside the class should be aware of or ever make direct use of. Sometimes it can seem tempting to make some of these private functions visible to the test code so that they can be directly tested. But this is often not a good idea, as it can result in tests that are tightly coupled to implementation details and that don't test the things we ultimately care about.

11.2.1 Testing private functions is often a bad idea

In the previous section, we established that it's important to test all the behaviors of the `MortgageAssessor` class (repeated in listing 11.5). The public API of this class is the `assess()` function. In addition to this publicly visible function, the class also has two private helper functions: `isEligibleForMortgage()` and `getMaxLoanAmount()`. These are not visible to any code outside of the class and are therefore implementation details.

Listing 11.5 Class with private helper functions

```
class MortgageAssessor {
  ...

  MortgageDecision assess(Customer customer) { ... }

  private static Boolean isEligibleForMortgage(
      Customer customer) { ... }

  private static MonetaryAmount getMaxLoanAmount(
      Customer customer) { ... }
}
```

Public API

Private helper functions

Let's concentrate on one of the behaviors of the `MortgageAssessor` class that we need to test: that a mortgage application is rejected if the customer has a bad credit rating. One common way engineers can end up testing the wrong thing is to conflate the desired end result with an intermediate implementation detail. If we look more closely at the `MortgageAssessor` class, we see that the private `isEligibleFor-Mortgage()` helper function returns false if the customer has a bad credit rating. This can make it tempting to make the `isEligibleForMortgage()` function visible to test code so it can be tested. Listing 11.6 shows what the class would look like if an engineer makes the `isEligibleForMortgage()` function visible like this. By making it publicly visible, it's visible to all other code (not just the test code). The engineer has added a "Visible only for testing" comment to warn other engineers not to call it from anything other than test code. But as we've seen already throughout this book, small print like this is very easily overlooked.

Listing 11.6 Private function made visible

```
class MortgageAssessor {
  private const Double MORTGAGE_MULTIPLIER = 10.0;

  MortgageDecision assess(Customer customer) {          <-- Public API
    if (!isEligibleForMortgage(customer)) {             <-- Which helper functions are called
      return MortgageDecision.rejected();                   is an implementation detail.
    }
    return MortgageDecision.approve(getMaxLoanAmount(customer));
  }

  /** Visible only for testing */                                 Made publicly visible only
  static Boolean isEligibleForMortgage(Customer customer) {       so it can be directly tested
    return customer.hasGoodCreditRating() &&
        !customer.hasExistingMortgage() &&
        !customer.isBanned();
  }

  ...
}
```

After having made the `isEligibleForMortgage()` function visible, the engineer would then likely write a bunch of test cases that call it and test that it returns true or false in the correct scenarios. Listing 11.7 shows one such test case. It tests that `isEligibleForMortgage()` returns false if a customer has a bad credit rating. As we'll see in a moment, there are a number of reasons testing a private function like this can be a bad idea.

Listing 11.7 Testing a private function

```
testIsEligibleForMortgage_badCreditRating_ineligible() {
  Customer customer = new Customer(
      income: new MonetaryAmount(50000, Currency.USD),
      outgoings: new MonetaryAmount(25000, Currency.USD),
      hasGoodCreditRating: false,
      hasExistingMortgage: false,
      isBanned: false);                              Directly tests the "private"
                                                     isEligibleForMortgage() function
  assertThat(MortgageAssessor.isEligibleForMortgage(customer))     <--
      .isFalse();
}
```

The problem with making a private function visible and testing it like this is three-fold:

- The test is not actually testing the behavior we care about. We said a few moments ago that the outcome we care about is that a mortgage application is rejected if the customer has a bad credit rating. What the test case in listing 11.7 is actually testing is that there is a function called `isEligibleForMortgage()`

that returns false when called with a customer with a bad credit rating. This doesn't guarantee that a mortgage application will ultimately be rejected in such a scenario. An engineer might inadvertently modify the `assess()` function to call `isEligibleForMortgage()` incorrectly (or to not call it at all). The test case in listing 11.7 would still pass, despite the `MortgageAssessor` class being badly broken.

- It makes the test non-agnostic to implementation details. The fact that there is a private function called `isEligibleForMortgage()` is an implementation detail. Engineers might want to refactor the code, for example renaming this function or moving it to a separate helper class. Ideally, any refactoring like that shouldn't cause any of the tests to fail. But because we're directly testing the `isEligibleForMortgage()` function, a refactoring like that will cause the tests to fail.
- We've effectively changed the public API of the `MortgageAssessor` class. A comment like "Visible only for testing" is very easily overlooked (it's small print in the code contract), so we might find that other engineers start calling the `isEligibleForMortgage()` function and relying on it. Before we know it we'll be unable to ever modify or refactor this function because so much other code is depending on it.

A good unit test should test the behaviors that ultimately matter. This maximizes the chance that the test will accurately detect breakages, and it tends to keep the test agnostic to implementation details. These are two of the key features of a good unit test that were identified in chapter 10. Testing a private function often goes against both these aims. As we'll see in the next two subsections, we can often avoid testing private functions by either testing via the public API or by ensuring that our code is broken into appropriate layers of abstraction.

11.2.2 Solution: Prefer testing via the public API

In the previous chapter we discussed the guiding principle of "test using only the public API." This principle aims to guide us toward testing the behaviors that actually matter and not implementation details. Whenever we find ourselves making an otherwise private function visible so that tests can call it, it's usually a red flag that we're breaking this guiding principle.

In the case of the `MortgageAssessor` class, the behavior that actually matters is that a mortgage application is rejected for a customer with a bad credit rating. We can test this behavior using only the public API by calling the `MortgageAssessor.assess()` function. Listing 11.8 shows how the test case might look if we did this. The test case now tests the behavior that actually matters rather than an implementation detail and we no longer need to make any of the otherwise private functions in the `MortgageAssessor` class visible.

Listing 11.8 Testing via the public API

```
testAssess_badCreditRating_mortgageRejected() {
  Customer customer = new Customer(
      income: new MonetaryAmount(50000, Currency.USD),
      outgoings: new MonetaryAmount(25000, Currency.USD),
      hasGoodCreditRating: false,
      hasExistingMortgage: false,
      isBanned: false);
  MortgageAssessor mortgageAssessor = new MortgageAssessor();

  MortgageDecision decision = mortgageAssessor.assess(customer);     <- Behavior tested via the public API

  assertThat(decision.isApproved()).isFalse();
}
```

> **Be pragmatic**
>
> Making a private function visible for testing is almost always a red flag that implementation details are being tested, and there's usually a better alternative. But when applying the principle of "test using only the public API" to other things (such as dependencies), it's important to remember the advice in chapter 10 (section 10.3). The definition of the "public API" can be open to some amount of interpretation, and some important behaviors (such as side effects) may fall outside of what engineers consider the public API. But, if a behavior is important and is something that we ultimately care about, then it should be tested.

For relatively simple classes (or units of code), it's often very easy to test all the behaviors using only the public API. Doing this results in better tests that will more accurately detect breakages and not be tied to implementation details. But when a class (or unit of code) is more complicated or contains a lot of logic, testing everything via the public API can start to get tricky. This is often a sign that the layer of abstraction is too thick and that the code might benefit from being split into smaller units.

11.2.3 Solution: Split the code into smaller units

In the previous two subsections, the logic for determining if a customer has a good credit rating was relatively simple: it just involved calling `customer.hasGoodCreditRating()`, so it wasn't too difficult to fully test the `MortgageAssessor` class using only the public API. In reality, the temptation to make a private function visible for testing more often occurs when a private function involves more complicated logic.

To demonstrate this, imagine that determining whether a customer has a good credit rating involves calling an external service and processing the result. Listing 11.9 shows what the `MortgageAssessor` class might look like if this were the case. The logic for checking the customer's credit rating is now considerably more complicated, as noted by the following:

- The `MortgageAssessor` class now depends on `CreditScoreService`.
- `CreditScoreService` is queried with the customer ID in order to look up the customer's credit score.

- A call to `CreditScoreService.query()` can fail, so the code needs to handle this error scenario.
- If the call succeeds, then the returned score is compared to a threshold to determine whether the customer's credit rating is good.

Testing all this complexity and all these corner cases (such as error scenarios) via the public API now seems quite daunting and not at all easy. This is when engineers most often resort to making an otherwise private function visible in order to make the testing easier. In listing 11.9, the `isCreditRatingGood()` function has been made "visible only for testing" for this reason. This still incurs all the same problems that we saw earlier, but the solution of testing via the public API no longer seems so feasible due to how complicated the logic is. But, as we'll see in a moment, there's a more fundamental problem here: the `MortgageAssessor` class is doing too much stuff.

Listing 11.9 More complicated credit rating check

```
class MortgageAssessor {
  private const Double MORTGAGE_MULTIPLIER = 10.0;
  private const Double GOOD_CREDIT_SCORE_THRESHOLD = 880.0;

  private final CreditScoreService creditScoreService;
  ...

  MortgageDecision assess(Customer customer) {
    ...
  }

  private Result<Boolean, Error> isEligibleForMortgage(
      Customer customer) {
    if (customer.hasExistingMortgage() || customer.isBanned()) {
      return Result.ofValue(false);
    }
    return isCreditRatingGood(customer.getId());
  }

  /** Visible only for testing */
  Result<Boolean, Error> isCreditRatingGood(Int customerId) {
    CreditScoreResponse response = creditScoreService
        .query(customerId);
    if (response.errorOccurred()) {
      return Result.ofError(response.getError());
    }
    return Result.ofValue(
        response.getCreditScore() >= GOOD_CREDIT_SCORE_THRESHOLD);
  }

  ...
}
```

The MortgageAssessor class depends on CreditScoreService.

isCreditRatingGood() function made visible for testing

The CreditScoreService service is queried.

The error scenario of a call to the service failing is signaled via a Result type.

The score is compared to a threshold.

Figure 11.1 illustrates the relationship between the test code (`MortgageAssessorTest`) and the code under test (`MortgageAssessor`).

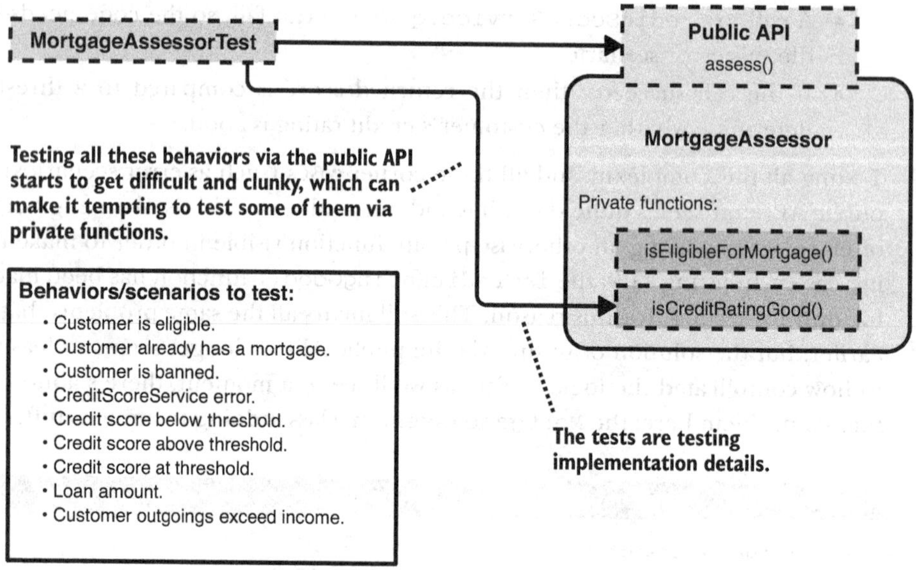

Figure 11.1 When a class does too much, it can be difficult to test everything using only the public API.

In chapter 2, when discussing layers of abstraction, we saw how it's often best not to place too many different concepts into a single class. The `MortgageAssessor` class contains a lot of different concepts, so in the language of chapter 2, the layer of abstraction it provides is "too thick." This is the real reason it seems hard to fully test everything using the public API.

The solution here is to split the code up into thinner layers. One way we might achieve this is to move the logic for determining if a customer has a good credit rating into a separate class. Listing 11.10 shows what this class might look like. The `CreditRatingChecker` class solves the subproblem of determining if a customer has a good credit rating. The `MortgageAssessor` class depends on `CreditRatingChecker`, meaning it's greatly simplified, as it no longer contains all the nut-and-bolts logic for solving subproblems.

Listing 11.10 Code split into two classes

```
class CreditRatingChecker {
  private const Double GOOD_CREDIT_SCORE_THRESHOLD = 880.0;

  private final CreditScoreService creditScoreService;
  ...

  Result<Boolean, Error> isCreditRatingGood(Int customerId) {
    CreditScoreService response = creditScoreService
        .query(customerId);
    if (response.errorOccurred()) {
      return Result.ofError(response.getError());
    }
```

A separate class to contain the logic for checking if a credit rating is good

```
    return Result.ofValue(
        response.getCreditScore() >= GOOD_CREDIT_SCORE_THRESHOLD);
  }
}

class MortgageAssessor {
  private const Double MORTGAGE_MULTIPLIER = 10.0;

  private final CreditRatingChecker creditRatingChecker;
  ...

  MortgageDecision assess(Customer customer) {
    ...
  }

  private Result<Boolean, Error> isEligibleForMortgage(
      Customer customer) {
    if (customer.hasExistingMortgage() || customer.isBanned()) {
      return Result.ofValue(false);
    }
    return creditRatingChecker
        .isCreditRatingGood(customer.getId());
  }
  ...
}
```

MortgageAssessor depends on CreditRating-Checker.

Both the `MortgageAssessor` and `CreditRatingChecker` classes deal with a much more manageable number of concepts. This means that both can be easily tested using their respective public APIs, as shown in figure 11.2.

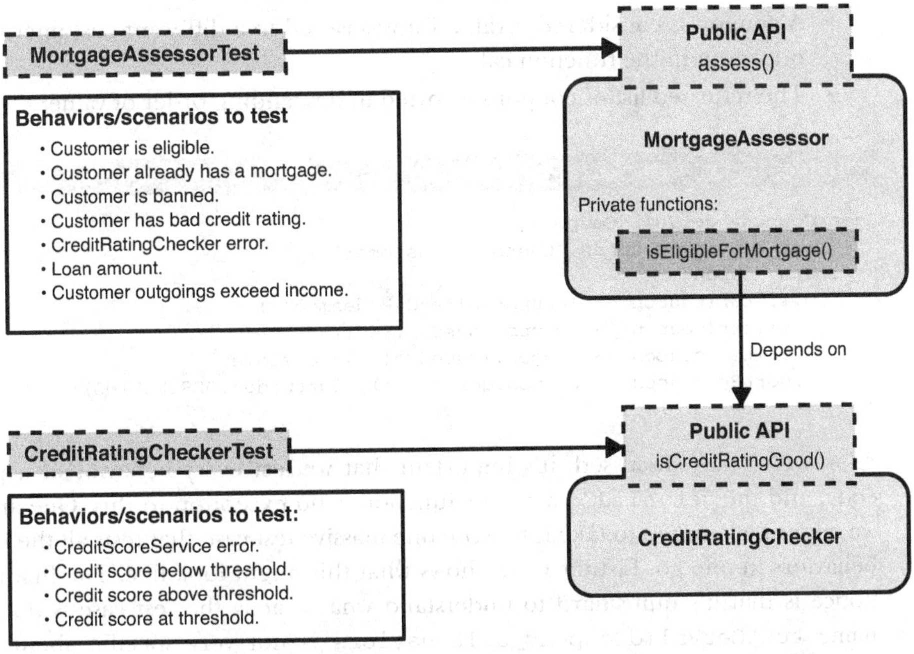

Figure 11.2 Splitting a big class into smaller classes can make the code more testable.

When we find ourselves making a private function visible so that we can test the code, it's usually a warning sign that we're not testing the behaviors that we actually care about. It's nearly always better to test the code using the already public functions. If this is infeasible, then it's often a sign that the class (or unit of code) is too big and that we should think about splitting it up into smaller classes (or units) that each solve a single subproblem.

11.3 Test one behavior at a time

As we've seen, there are often multiple behaviors that need to be tested for a given piece of code. In many cases, each of these behaviors requires a slightly different scenario to be set up in order to test it, meaning that the most natural thing to do is test each scenario (and its associated behavior) in its own test case. Sometimes, however, there may be a way to concoct a single scenario that tests multiple behaviors in one go. But just because this might be possible doesn't mean it's a good idea.

11.3.1 Testing multiple behaviors at once can lead to poor tests

Listing 11.11 shows the code for a function to filter a list of coupons down to only the valid ones. The function takes a list of candidate coupons and returns another list containing only the ones that meet a set of criteria for being valid. There are a number of important behaviors that this function exhibits:

- Only valid coupons are returned.
- A coupon is considered invalid if it has already been redeemed.
- A coupon is considered invalid if it has expired.
- A coupon is considered invalid if it was issued to a different customer than the one given in the function call.
- The returned list of coupons is sorted in descending order of value.

Listing 11.11 Code to get valid coupons

```
List<Coupon> getValidCoupons(
    List<Coupon> coupons, Customer customer) {
  return coupons
      .filter(coupon -> !coupon.alreadyRedeemed())
      .filter(coupon -> !coupon.hasExpired())
      .filter(coupon -> coupon.issuedTo() == customer)
      .sortBy(coupon -> coupon.getValue(), SortOrder.DESCENDING);
}
```

As we've already discussed, it's important that we test every behavior of a piece of code, and the `getValidCoupons()` function is no exception to this. One approach we might be tempted to take is to write one massive test case that tests all the function behaviors in one go. Listing 11.12 shows what this might look like. The first thing to notice is that it's quite hard to understand what exactly the test case is doing. The name `testGetValidCoupons_allBehaviors` is not very specific about what is being tested, and the amount of code in the test case makes it quite hard to follow. In chapter 10, we identified *understandable test code* as one of the key features of a good unit test. We can immediately see that testing all the behaviors in one go like this fails that criterion.

Listing 11.12 Testing everything at once

```
void testGetValidCoupons_allBehaviors() {
  Customer customer1 = new Customer("test customer 1");
  Customer customer2 = new Customer("test customer 2");
  Coupon redeemed = new Coupon(
      alreadyRedeemed: true, hasExpired: false,
      issuedTo: customer1, value: 100);
  Coupon expired = new Coupon(
      alreadyRedeemed: false, hasExpired: true,
      issuedTo: customer1, value: 100);
  Coupon issuedToSomeoneElse = new Coupon(
      alreadyRedeemed: false, hasExpired: false,
      issuedTo: customer2, value: 100);
  Coupon valid1 = new Coupon(
      alreadyRedeemed: false, hasExpired: false,
      issuedTo: customer1, value: 100);
  Coupon valid2 = new Coupon(
      alreadyRedeemed: false, hasExpired: false,
      issuedTo: customer1, value: 150);

  List<Coupon> validCoupons = getValidCoupons(
      [redeemed, expired, issuedToSomeoneElse, valid1, valid2],
      customer1);

  assertThat(validCoupons)
      .containsExactly(valid2, valid1)
      .inOrder();
}
```

Testing all the behaviors in one go also fails another of the criteria we identified in chapter 10: well-explained failures. To understand why, let's consider what happens if an engineer accidentally breaks one of the behaviors of the `getValidCoupons()` function by removing the logic to check that a coupon has not already been redeemed. The `testGetValidCoupons_allBehaviors()` test case will fail, which is good (because the code is broken), but the failure message will not be particularly helpful at explaining which behavior has been broken (figure 11.3).

Having test code that's hard to understand and failures that are ill explained not only wastes other engineers' time, but it can also increase the chance of bugs. As was discussed in chapter 10, if any engineer is intentionally changing one of the behaviors of the code, then we want to be sure that the other, seemingly unrelated behaviors are not accidentally affected too. A single test case that tests everything in one go tends to only tell us that something has changed, not exactly what has changed, so it's much

Because the test case tests all the behaviors, we can't identify which behavior is broken from looking at the test case name.

```
Test case testGetValidCoupons_allBehaviors failed:
Expected:
  [
    Coupon(redeemed: false, expired: false,
           issuedTo: test customer 1, value: 150),
    Coupon(redeemed: false, expired: false,
           issuedTo: test customer 1, value: 100)
  ]
But was actually:
  [
    Coupon(redeemed: false, expired: false,
           issuedTo: test customer 1, value: 150),
    Coupon(redeemed: true, expired: false,
           issuedTo: test customer 1, value: 100),
    Coupon(redeemed: false, expired: false,
           issuedTo: test customer 1, value: 100)
  ]
```

It's quite difficult to figure out which behavior is broken from the failure message.

Figure 11.3 Testing multiple behaviors in one go can result in poorly explained test failures.

harder to have confidence about exactly which behaviors an intentional change has and hasn't affected.

11.3.2 Solution: Test each behavior in its own test case

A much better approach is to test each behavior separately using a dedicated, well-named test case. Listing 11.13 shows what the test code might look like if we did this. We can see that the code inside each test case is now a lot simpler and easier to understand. We can identify from each test case name exactly which behavior is being tested, and it's relatively easy to follow the code to see how the test works. Judging by the criterion that unit tests should have understandable test code, the tests are now greatly improved.

Listing 11.13 Testing one thing at a time

```
void testGetValidCoupons_validCoupon_included() {      <-- Each behavior is
  Customer customer = new Customer("test customer");       tested in a dedicated
  Coupon valid = new Coupon(                               test case.
      alreadyRedeemed: false, hasExpired: false,
      issuedTo: customer, value: 100);

  List<Coupon> validCoupons = getValidCoupons([valid], customer);
```

```
  assertThat(validCoupons).containsExactly(valid);
}

void testGetValidCoupons_alreadyRedeemed_excluded() {
  Customer customer = new Customer("test customer");
  Coupon redeemed = new Coupon(
      alreadyRedeemed: true, hasExpired: false,
      issuedTo: customer, value: 100);

  List<Coupon> validCoupons =
      getValidCoupons([redeemed], customer);

  assertThat(validCoupons).isEmpty();
}

void testGetValidCoupons_expired_excluded() { ... }

void testGetValidCoupons_issuedToDifferentCustomer_excluded() { ... }

void testGetValidCoupons_returnedInDescendingValueOrder() { ... }
```

Each behavior is tested in a dedicated test case.

By testing each behavior separately and using an appropriate name for each test case, we now also achieve well-explained failures. Let's again consider the scenario where an engineer accidentally breaks the `getValidCoupons()` function by removing the logic to check that a coupon has not already been redeemed. This will result in the `testGetValidCoupons_alreadyRedeemed_excluded()` test case failing. The name of this test case makes it clear exactly which behavior has been broken, and the failure message (figure 11.4) is much easier to understand than the one we saw earlier.

Despite the benefits of testing one thing at a time, writing a separate test case function for each behavior can sometimes lead to a lot of code duplication. This can seem especially clunky when the values and setup used in each test case are almost identical except for some minor differences. One way to reduce this amount of code duplication is to use *parameterized tests*. The next subsection explores this.

The name of the test case makes it immediately clear which behavior is broken.

```
Test case testGetValidCoupons_alreadyRedeemed_excluded failed:
Expected:
  []
But was actually:
  [
    Coupon(redeemed: true, expired: false,
           issuedTo: test customer, value: 100)
  ]
```

The failure message is much easier to understand.

Figure 11.4 Testing one behavior at a time often results in well-explained test failures.

11.3.3 Parameterized tests

Some testing frameworks provide functionality for writing *parameterized tests*; this allows us to write a test case function once but then run it multiple times with different sets of values in order to test different scenarios. Listing 11.14 shows how we might use a parameterized test to test two of the behaviors of the `getValidCoupons()` function. The test case function is marked with multiple `TestCase` attributes. Each of these defines two Booleans and a test name. The `testGetValidCoupons_excludesInvalidCoupons()` function has two Boolean function parameters; these correspond to the two Booleans defined in the `TestCase` attributes. When the tests run, the test case will be run once for each of the set of parameter values defined in the `TestCase` attributes.

Listing 11.14 Parameterized test

```
[TestCase(true, false, TestName = "alreadyRedeemed")]
[TestCase(false, true, TestName = "expired")]
void testGetValidCoupons_excludesInvalidCoupons(
    Boolean alreadyRedeemed, Boolean hasExpired) {
  Customer customer = new Customer("test customer");
  Coupon coupon = new Coupon(
      alreadyRedeemed: alreadyRedeemed,
      hasExpired: hasExpired,
      issuedTo: customer, value: 100);

  List<Coupon> validCoupons =
      getValidCoupons([coupon], customer);

  assertThat(validCoupons).isEmpty();
}
```

The test case will be run once with each set of parameter values.

The test case accepts different values via function parameters.

The parameter values are used during test setup.

> **Ensure failures are well explained**
>
> In listing 11.14, each set of parameters has an associated `TestName`. This ensures that any test failures are well explained, because it will result in messages like `Test case testGetValidCoupons_excludesInvalidCoupons.alreadyRedeemed failed`. (Notice that the test case name is suffixed with the name of the set of parameters that resulted in the failure `alreadyRedeemed`.)
>
> Adding names for each set of parameters is usually optional when writing parameterized tests. But omitting them can result in poorly explained test failures, so it's good to think about what the test failures will look like when deciding if they're needed.

Parameterized tests can be a great tool for ensuring that we test all the behaviors one at a time without repeating lots of code. The syntax and way in which parameterized tests are set up can vary a lot between different testing frameworks. Configuring parameterized tests can also be incredibly verbose and clunky in some frameworks and scenarios, so it's worth researching what the options are for whatever language you're using and considering the pros and cons. Some options are as follows:

- For C#, the NUnit test framework provides the `TestCase` attribute (similar to the example in listing 11.14): http://mng.bz/qewE.
- For Java, JUnit provides support for parameterized tests: http://mng.bz/1Ayy.
- For JavaScript, with the Jasmine test framework it's relatively easy to write parameterized tests in a bespoke way, as described in this article: http://mng.bz/PaQg.

11.4 Use shared test setup appropriately

Test cases often require some amount of setup: constructing dependencies, populating values in a test data store, or initializing other kinds of state. This setup can sometimes be quite laborious or computationally expensive, and as such many testing frameworks provide functionality to make this easier to share between test cases. There are usually two distinct times at which shared setup code can be configured to run, distinguished by the following terms:

- `BeforeAll`—Setup code within a `BeforeAll` block will run once before any of the test cases are run. Some testing frameworks refer to this as `OneTimeSetUp` instead.
- `BeforeEach`—Setup code within a `BeforeEach` block will run once before each test case is run. Some testing frameworks refer to this as just `SetUp`.

In addition to providing ways to run setup code, frameworks also often provide ways to run teardown code. These are often useful for undoing any state that the setup code or test cases may have created. And again, there are usually two distinct times at with teardown code can be configured to run, distinguished by the following terms:

- `AfterAll`—Teardown code within an `AfterAll` block will run once after all the test cases have run. Some testing frameworks refer to this as `OneTimeTearDown` instead.
- `AfterEach`—Teardown code within an `AfterEach` block will run once after each test case is run. Some testing frameworks refer to this as just `TearDown`.

Figure 11.5 illustrates how these various pieces of setup and teardown might look in a piece of test code and the sequence in which they will run.

Using blocks of setup code like this results in setup being shared between different test cases. This can happen in two important, but distinct ways:

- *Sharing state*—If setup code is added to a `BeforeAll` block, it will run once before all test cases. This means that any state it sets up will be shared between all the test cases. This type of setup can be useful when setup is slow or expensive (e.g., starting a test server or creating a test instance of a database). But if the state that gets set up is mutable, then there is a real risk that test cases might have adverse effects on one another (we'll explore this more in a moment).

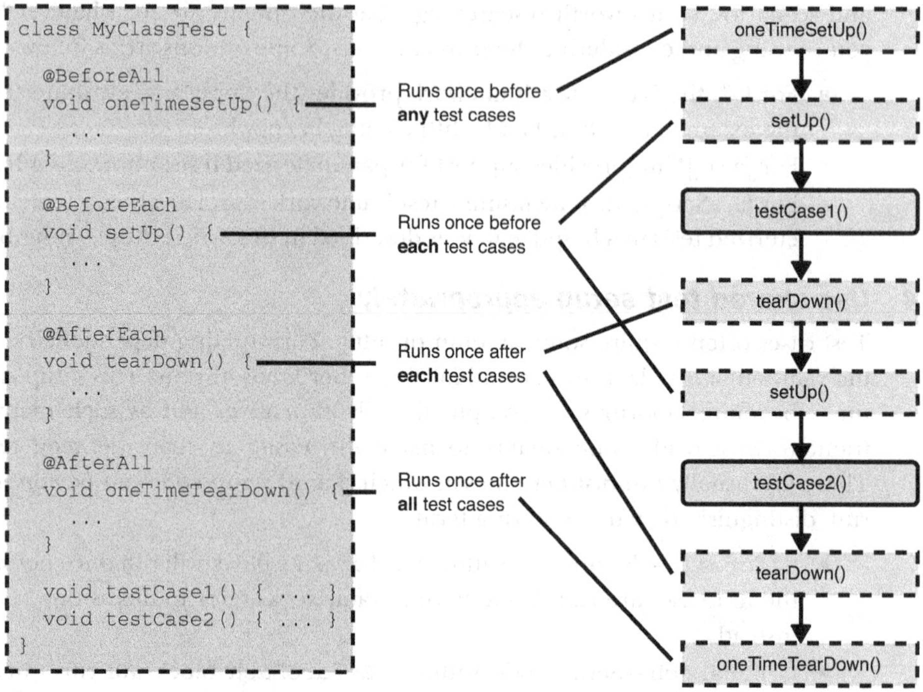

Figure 11.5 Testing frameworks often provide a way to run setup and teardown code at various times relative to the test cases.

- *Sharing configuration*—If setup code is added to a `BeforeEach` block, it will run before each test case, meaning the test cases all share whatever configuration the code sets up. If that setup code contains a certain value or configures a dependency in a certain way, then each test case will run with that given value or a dependency configured in that way. Because the setup runs before each test case, there is no state shared between test cases. But as we'll see in a moment (in section 11.4.3), sharing configuration can still be problematic.

If setting up some particular state or dependency is expensive, using shared setup can be a necessity. Even if this isn't the case, shared setup can be a useful way to simplify tests. If every test case requires a particular dependency, then it might be beneficial to configure it in a shared way rather than repeating a lot of boilerplate in every test case. But shared test setup can be a double-edged sword; using it in the wrong ways can lead to fragile and ineffective tests.

11.4.1 Shared state can be problematic

As a general rule, test cases should be isolated from one another, so any actions that one test case performs should not affect the outcome of other test cases. Sharing mutable state between test cases makes it very easy to inadvertently break this rule.

To demonstrate this, listing 11.15 shows part of a class and function for processing an order. The two behaviors that we'll concentrate on are the following:

- If an order contains an out-of-stock item, the order ID will be marked as delayed in the database.
- If payment for an order is not yet complete, the order ID will be marked as delayed in the database.

Listing 11.15 Code that writes to a database

```
class OrderManager {
  private final Database database;
  ...

  void processOrder(Order order) {
    if (order.containsOutOfStockItem() ||
        !order.isPaymentComplete()) {
      database.setOrderStatus(
          order.getId(), OrderStatus.DELAYED);
    }
    ...
  }
}
```

The unit tests should contain a test case for each of these behaviors (these are shown in listing 11.16). The `OrderManager` class depends on the `Database` class, so our tests need to set one of these up. Unfortunately, creating an instance of `Database` is computationally expensive and slow, so we create one in a `BeforeAll` block. This means that the same instance of database is shared between all the test cases (meaning the test cases share state). Unfortunately, this also makes the tests ineffective. To understand why, consider the sequence of events that happens when the tests run:

- The `BeforeAll` block will set up the database.
- The `testProcessOrder_outOfStockItem_orderDelayed()` test case will run. This results in the order ID being marked as delayed in the database.
- The `testProcessOrder_paymentNotComplete_orderDelayed()` test case then runs. Anything that previous test cases put in the database is still there (because the state is shared), so one of two things might happen:
  - The code under test is called, everything works correctly, and it marks the order ID as delayed. The test case passes.
  - The code under test is called, but it's broken. It doesn't save anything to the database to mark the order ID as delayed. Because the code is broken, we'd hope that the test case fails. But it instead passes because `database.getOrderStatus(orderId)` still returns `DELAYED`, because the previous test case saved that value to the database.

Listing 11.16 State shared between test cases

```
class OrderManagerTest {
  private Database database;

  @BeforeAll
  void oneTimeSetUp() {
    database = Database.createInstance();
    database.waitForReady();
  }

  void testProcessOrder_outOfStockItem_orderDelayed() {
    Int orderId = 12345;
    Order order = new Order(
        orderId: orderId,
        containsOutOfStockItem: true,
        isPaymentComplete: true);
    OrderManager orderManager = new OrderManager(database);

    orderManager.processOrder(order);

    assertThat(database.getOrderStatus(orderId))
        .isEqualTo(OrderStatus.DELAYED);
  }

  void testProcessOrder_paymentNotComplete_orderDelayed() {
    Int orderId = 12345;
    Order order = new Order(
        orderId: orderId,
        containsOutOfStockItem: false,
        isPaymentComplete: false);
    OrderManager orderManager = new OrderManager(database);

    orderManager.processOrder(order);

    assertThat(database.getOrderStatus(orderId))
        .isEqualTo(OrderStatus.DELAYED);
  }
  ...
}
```

The same instance of database is shared between all test cases.

OrderManager constructed with the shared database

Results in the order ID being marked as delayed in the database

OrderManager constructed with the shared database

May pass even if the code is broken, because the previous test case saved this value to the database

Sharing mutable state between different test cases can very easily lead to problems. If at all possible, it's usually best to avoid sharing state like this. But if it is necessary, we need to be very careful to ensure that the changes that one test case makes to the state don't affect other test cases.

11.4.2 Solution: Avoid sharing state or reset it

The most obvious solution to the problem of sharing mutable state is to just not share it in the first place. In the case of the `OrderManagerTest`, it would be more ideal if we didn't share the same instance of `Database` between test cases, so if setting up `Database` is less slow than we thought, then we might consider creating a new instance for each test case (either within the test cases or using a `BeforeEach` block).

Another potential way to avoid sharing mutable state is to use a test double (as discussed in chapter 10). If the team that maintains the `Database` class has also written a `FakeDatabase` class for use in testing, we could make use of this. Creating an instance of `FakeDatabase` is likely fast enough that we can create a new one for each test case, meaning no state is shared.

If creating an instance of `Database` really is prohibitively slow and expensive (and we can't use a fake), then sharing an instance of it between test cases might well be unavoidable. If this is the case, we should be very careful to ensure that the state is reset between each test case. This can often be achieved using an `AfterEach` block within the test code. As mentioned previously, this will run after each test case, so we can use it to ensure that the state is always reset before the next test case runs. The following listing shows what the `OrderManagerTest` test might look like if we use an `AfterEach` block to reset the database between test cases.

Listing 11.17 State reset between test cases

```
class OrderManagerTest {

  private Database database;

  @BeforeAll
  void oneTimeSetUp() {
    database = Database.createInstance();
    database.waitForReady();
  }

  @AfterEach
  void tearDown() {
    database.reset();
  }

  void testProcessOrder_outOfStockItem_orderDelayed() { ... }

  void testProcessOrder_paymentNotComplete_orderDelayed() { ... }
  ...
}
```

The database is reset after each test case.

Test cases will never be affected by values saved by other test cases.

> **NOTE: GLOBAL STATE** It's worth noting that the test code is not the only way state can be shared between test cases. If the code under test maintains any kind of global state, then we'll need to ensure that the test code resets this between test cases. Global state was discussed in chapter 9, and the conclusion was that it's usually best to avoid it. The impact that global state can have on the testability of code is yet another good reason for not using it.

Sharing mutable state between test cases is less than ideal. If it can be avoided this is usually preferable. If it can't be avoided, we should ensure that the state is reset between each test case. This ensures that test cases don't have adverse effects on one another.

11.4.3 Shared configuration can be problematic

Sharing configuration between test cases doesn't immediately seem as dangerous as sharing state, but it can still result in ineffective tests. Imagine that another part of our infrastructure for processing orders is a system that generates postage labels for packages. Listing 11.18 contains the function that generates the data object to represent a postage label for an order. There are a few important behaviors that we need to test, but the one we will concentrate on is whether the package is marked as large. The logic for this is quite simple: if the order contains more than two items, the package is considered large.

Listing 11.18 Postage label code

```
class OrderPostageManager {
  ...

  PostageLabel getPostageLabel(Order order) {
    return new PostageLabel(
      address: order.getCustomer().getAddress(),
      isLargePackage: order.getItems().size() > 2,
    );
  }
}
```

If the order contains more than two items, the package is marked as large.

If we concentrate on just the `isLargePackage` behavior, then we need test cases for at least two different scenarios:

- *An order containing two items.* This should result in the package not being marked as large.
- *An order containing three items.* This should result in the package being marked as large.

If anyone inadvertently changes the logic in the code for deciding how many items makes a package large, then one of these test cases should fail.

Let's now imagine that constructing a valid instance of the `Order` class is more laborious than in previous subsections: we need to supply instances of the `Item` class and an instance of the `Customer` class, which also means creating an instance of the `Address` class. To save ourselves from repeating this configuration code in every test case, we decide to construct an instance of `Order` in a `BeforeEach` block (which runs once before each test case). Listing 11.19 shows what this looks like. The test case that tests the scenario where there are three items in the order uses the instance of `Order` created by the shared configuration. The `testGetPostageLabel_threeItems_largePackage()` test case therefore relies on the fact that the shared configuration creates an order containing exactly three items.

Listing 11.19 Shared test configuration

```
class OrderPostageManagerTest {
  private Order testOrder;

  @BeforeEach
  void setUp() {
    testOrder = new Order(
      customer: new Customer(
        address: new Address("Test address"),
      ),
      items: [
        new Item(name: "Test item 1"),
        new Item(name: "Test item 2"),
        new Item(name: "Test item 3"),
      ]);
  }
  ...

  void testGetPostageLabel_threeItems_largePackage() {
    PostageManager postageManager = new PostageManager();

    PostageLabel label =
        postageManager.getPostageLabel(testOrder);

    assertThat(label.isLargePackage()).isTrue();
  }
  ...
}
```

Shared configuration (annotates `setUp()`)

The test case relies on the fact that the shared configuration adds exactly three items to the order.

This tests one of the behaviors that we care about and avoids the need to repeat a load of clunky code to create an `Order` in every test case. But, unfortunately, things might go wrong if other engineers ever need to modify the tests. Imagine that another engineer now needs to add a new piece of functionality to the `getPostageLabel()` function: if any of the items in the order are hazardous, the postage label needs to indicate that the package is hazardous. The engineer modifies the `getPostageLabel()` function to look like the following listing.

Listing 11.20 A new piece of functionality

```
class PostageManager {
  ...

  PostageLabel getPostageLabel(Order order) {
    return new PostageLabel(
        address: order.getCustomer().getAddress(),
        isLargePackage: order.getItems().size() > 2,
        isHazardous: containsHazardousItem(order.getItems()));
  }

  private static Boolean containsHazardousItem(List<Item> items) {
    return items.anyMatch(item -> item.isHazardous());
  }
}
```

New functionality to mark whether package is hazardous

The engineer has added a new behavior to the code, so they obviously need to add new test cases to test this. The engineer sees that there is an instance of `Order` constructed in the `BeforeEach` block and thinks, "Oh great. I can just add a hazardous item to that order and use that in one of my test cases." Listing 11.21 shows the test code after they do this. This has helped the engineer test their new behavior, but they have inadvertently ruined the `testGetPostageLabel_threeItems_largePackage()` test case. The whole point in that test case is that it tests what happens when there are exactly three items in the order, but it's now testing what happens when there are four items, so the test no longer fully protects against the code being broken.

Listing 11.21 Bad change to shared configuration

```
class OrderPostageManagerTest {
  private Order testOrder;

  @BeforeEach
  void setUp() {
    testOrder = new Order(
      customer: new Customer(
        address: new Address("Test address"),
      ),
      items: [
        new Item(name: "Test item 1"),
        new Item(name: "Test item 2"),
        new Item(name: "Test item 3"),
        new Item(name: "Hazardous item", isHazardous: true),     <-- Fourth item added to order in shared configuration
      ]);
  }
  ...

  void testGetPostageLabel_threeItems_largePackage() { ... }     <-- Now tests the case of four items rather than intended case of three items

  void testGetPostageLabel_hazardousItem_isHazardous() {     <-- New test case for testing that the label is marked with hazardous
    PostageManager postageManager = new PostageManager();

    PostageLabel label =
        postageManager.getPostageLabel(testOrder);

    assertThat(label.isHazardous()).isTrue();
  }
  ...
}
```

> **Shared test constants**
>
> A `BeforeEach` or `BeforeAll` block are not the only ways to create shared test configuration. Using a shared test constant can often achieve exactly the same thing and can suffer the same set of potential problems we just discussed. If `OrderPostageManagerTest` configured the test order in a shared constant instead of a `BeforeEach` block, it might look like the following snippet:
>
> ```
> class OrderPostageManagerTest {
>   private const Order TEST_ORDER = new Order(      <-- A shared test constant
>       customer: new Customer(
>         address: new Address("Test address"),
>       ),
>       items: [
>         new Item(name: "Test item 1"),
>         new Item(name: "Test item 2"),
>         new Item(name: "Test item 3"),
>         new Item(name: "Hazardous item", isHazardous: true),
>       ]);
>   ...
> }
> ```
>
> Technically, this also shares state between test cases, but it's good practice to only create constants using immutable data types, meaning no mutable state is shared. In this example, the `Order` class is immutable. If it were not immutable, then sharing an instance of `Order` in a shared constant would probably be even more of a bad idea (for the reasons discussed in section 11.4.1).

Shared configuration can be useful for preventing code repetition, but it's usually best not to use it to set up any values or state that specifically matter to test cases. It's very hard to keep track of exactly which test cases rely on which specific things in the shared configuration, and when changes are made in the future this can result in test cases no longer testing the thing they are intended to test.

11.4.4 Solution: Define important configuration within test cases

It can seem laborious to repeat configuration in every test case, but when a test case relies on specific values or state being set up, it's often safer. And we can usually make this less laborious by using helper functions so that we don't have to repeat lots of boilerplate code.

In the case of testing the `getPostageLabel()` function, creating an instance of the `Order` class seemed quite clunky, but creating it in shared configuration resulted in the problems we saw in the previous subsection. We can mostly avoid both these issues by defining a helper function for creating an instance of `Order`. Individual test cases can then call this function with the specific test values that they care about. This avoids lots of code repetition without having to use shared configuration and suffering the problems that can come with it. The following listing shows what the test code looks like with this approach.

Listing 11.22 Important configuration within test cases

```
class OrderPostageManagerTest {
  ...

  void testGetPostageLabel_threeItems_largePackage() {
    Order order = createOrderWithItems([
      new Item(name: "Test item 1"),
      new Item(name: "Test item 2"),
      new Item(name: "Test item 3"),
    ]);
    PostageManager postageManager = new PostageManager();

    PostageLabel label = postageManager.getPostageLabel(order);

    assertThat(label.isLargePackage()).isTrue();
  }

  void testGetPostageLabel_hazardousItem_isHazardous() {
    Order order = createOrderWithItems([
      new Item(name: "Hazardous item", isHazardous: true),
    ]);
    PostageManager postageManager = new PostageManager();

    PostageLabel label = postageManager.getPostageLabel(order);

    assertThat(label.isHazardous()).isTrue();
  }
  ...

  private static Order createOrderWithItems(List<Item> items) {
    return new Order(
      customer: new Customer(
        address: new Address("Test address"),
      ),
      items: items);
  }
}
```

Test cases perform their own setup for important things.

Helper function for creating an Order with specific items

When a piece of configuration directly matters to the outcome of a test case, it's usually best to keep it self-contained within that test case. This defends against future changes inadvertently ruining the tests, and it also makes the cause and effect within each test case clear (because everything that affects a test case in a meaningful way is there within the test case). Not every piece of configuration fits this description, however, and the next subsection discusses when shared configuration can be a good idea.

11.4.5 When shared configuration is appropriate

The previous subsections demonstrate why it's good to be cautious about the use of shared test configuration, but this doesn't mean that it's never a good idea to use it. Some pieces of configuration are necessary but don't directly affect the outcome of test cases. In scenarios like this, using shared configuration can be an excellent way to keep tests focused and understandable by avoiding unnecessary code repetition and boilerplate.

To demonstrate this, imagine that constructing an instance of the `Order` class also requires providing some metadata about the order. The `PostageManager` class ignores this metadata, so it's completely irrelevant to the outcome of the test cases in `OrderPostageManagerTest`. But it's still something that test cases need to configure, because an instance of the `Order` class can't be constructed without it. In a scenario like this, it makes a lot of sense to define the order metadata once as shared configuration. Listing 11.23 demonstrates this. An instance of `OrderMetadata` is placed into a shared constant called `ORDER_METADATA`. Test cases can then make use of this constant instead of having to repeatedly construct this required, but otherwise irrelevant, data.

Listing 11.23 Appropriate use of shared configuration

```
class OrderPostageManagerTest {
  private const OrderMetadata ORDER_METADATA =
      new OrderMetadata(
          timestamp: Instant.ofEpochSecond(0),
          serverIp: new IpAddress(0, 0, 0, 0));

  void testGetPostageLabel_threeItems_largePackage() { ... }
  void testGetPostageLabel_hazardousItem_isHazardous() { ... }
  ...

  void testGetPostageLabel_containsCustomerAddress() {
    Address address = new Address("Test customer address");
    Order order =  new Order(
      metadata: ORDER_METADATA,
      customer: new Customer(
        address: address,
      ), items: []);

    PostageLabel label = postageManager.getPostageLabel(order);

    assertThat(label.getAddress()).isEqualTo(address);
  }
  ...

  private static Order createOrderWithItems(List<Item> items) {
    return new Order(
      metadata: ORDER_METADATA,
      customer: new Customer(
        address: new Address("Test address"),
      ),
      items: items);
  }
}
```

An instance of OrderMetadata is created in a shared constant.

Shared OrderMetadata used in test cases

Functions should ideally take only what they need

Chapter 9 discussed how function parameters should ideally be focused, meaning that functions take only what they need. If the tests for a piece of code require configuring a lot of values that are required but otherwise irrelevant to the behavior of the code, then it might be a sign that the function (or constructor) parameters are not focused enough. For example, we might argue that the `PostageManager.getPostageLabel()` function should take just an instance of `Address` and a list of items instead of a complete instance of the `Order` class. If this were the case, then the tests would not need to create irrelevant things like an instance of `OrderMetadata`.

Shared test setup can be a bit of a double-edged sword. It can be very useful for preventing code repetition or repeatedly performing expensive setup, but it also runs the risk of making tests ineffective and hard to reason about. It's worth thinking carefully to ensure that it's used in an appropriate way.

11.5 Use appropriate assertion matchers

An *assertion matcher* is usually the thing in a test case that ultimately decides if the test has passed. The following snippet contains two examples of assertion matchers (`isEqualTo()` and `contains()`):

```
assertThat(someValue).isEqualTo("expected value");
assertThat(someList).contains("expected value");
```

If a test case fails, then the assertion matcher is also the thing that produces the failure message to explain why. Different assertion matchers produce different failure messages (depending on what they assert). In chapter 10 we identified *well-explained failures* as one of the key features of a good unit test, so ensuring that we chose the most appropriate assertion matcher is important.

11.5.1 Inappropriate matchers can lead to poorly explained failures

To demonstrate how the use of an inappropriate matcher can lead to poorly explained test failures, we'll concentrate on testing the code in listing 11.24. `TextWidget` is a component used in a web app UI to display text. In order to control the styling of the component, various class names can be added to it. Some of these class names are hard coded and other custom ones can be supplied via the constructor. The `getClassNames()` function returns a combined list of all class names. An important detail to note is that the documentation for the `getClassNames()` function states that the order of the returned class names is not guaranteed.

Listing 11.24 TextWidget code

```
class TextWidget {
  private const ImmutableList<String> STANDARD_CLASS_NAMES =
      ["text-widget", "selectable"];
  private final ImmutableList<String> customClassNames;

  TextWidget(List<String> customClassNames) {
    this.customClassNames = ImmutableList.copyOf(customClassNames);
  }

  /**
   * The class names for the component. The order of the class
   * names within the returned list is not guaranteed.
   */
  ImmutableList<String> getClassNames() {
    return STANDARD_CLASS_NAMES.concat(customClassNames);
  }

  ...
}
```

Hard-coded class names

Custom class names supplied via the constructor

Gets a list of all class names (hard-coded and custom)

As we saw earlier, we should ideally aim to test one behavior at a time. One of the behaviors that we need to test is that the list returned by `getClassNames()` contains the `customClassNames`. One approach we might be tempted to take to test this is to compare the returned list with an expected list of values. Listing 11.25 shows this. But there are a couple of problems with this approach, as follows:

- The test case is testing more than it's meant to. The name of the test case suggests that it's only testing that the result contains the custom class names. But it's in fact also testing that the result contains the standard class names.
- If the order in which the class names are returned ever changes, then this test will fail. The documentation for the `getClassNames()` function explicitly says that the order is not guaranteed, so we should not create a test that fails when it changes. This could lead to false alarms or flakey tests.

Listing 11.25 Over-constrained test assertion

```
void testGetClassNames_containsCustomClassNames() {
  TextWidget textWidget = new TextWidget(
      ["custom_class_1", "custom_class_2"]);

  assertThat(textWidget.getClassNames()).isEqualTo([
      "text-widget",
      "selectable",
      "custom_class_1",
      "custom_class_2",
  ]);
}
```

Let's consider another idea we might try. Instead of comparing the returned result to an expected list, we might individually check that the returned list contains the two values we care about: `custom_class_1` and `custom_class_2`. Listing 11.26 shows one way we might achieve this: asserting that `result.contains(...)` returns true. This has solved the two problems we just saw: the test now only tests what it's meant to and a change in order will not cause the test to fail. But we've introduced another problem: the test failures will not be well explained (figure 11.6).

Listing 11.26 Test assertion with poor explainability

```
void testGetClassNames_containsCustomClassNames() {
  TextWidget textWidget = new TextWidget(
      ["custom_class_1", "custom_class_2"]);

  ImmutableList<String> result = textWidget.getClassNames();

  assertThat(result.contains("custom_class_1")).isTrue();
  assertThat(result.contains("custom_class_2")).isTrue();
}
```

Figure 11.6 shows what the failure message looks like if the test case fails due to one of the custom classes being absent. It's not obvious from this failure message how the actual result differs from the expected one.

```
Test case testGetClassNames_containsCustomClassNames failed:
The subject was false, but was expected to be true
```

Failure message does little to explain the problem.

Figure 11.6 An inappropriate assertion matcher can result in a poorly explained test failure.

Ensuring that a test fails when something is broken is essential, but as we saw in chapter 10, it's not the only consideration. We also want to ensure that a test only fails when something is genuinely broken and that test failures are well explained. To achieve all these aims, we need to choose an appropriate assertion matcher.

11.5.2 *Solution: Use an appropriate matcher*

Most modern test assertion tools contain myriad different matchers than can be used in tests. One matcher on offer might be one that allows us to assert that a list contains at least a certain set of items in an unspecified order. Examples of such matchers are as follows:

- *In Java*—The `containsAtLeast()` matcher from the Truth library (https://truth.dev/).
- *In JavaScript*—The `jasmine.arrayContaining()` matcher from the Jasmine framework (https://jasmine.github.io/)

Listing 11.27 shows what our test case looks like if we use a `containsAtLeast()` matcher. The test case will fail if `getClassNames()` fails to return any of the custom class names. But it will not fail due to changes in other behaviors, such as the hard-coded class names being updated or the order changing.

Listing 11.27 Appropriate assertion matcher

```
testGetClassNames_containsCustomClassNames() {
  TextWidget textWidget = new TextWidget(
      ["custom_class_1", "custom_class_2"]);

  assertThat(textWidget.getClassNames())
      .containsAtLeast("custom_class_1", "custom_class_2");
}
```

If the test case fails, then the failure message will be well explained, as shown in figure 11.7.

```
Test case testGetClassNames_containsCustomClassNames failed:
Not true that
  [text-widget, selectable, custom_class_2]
contains at least
  [custom_class_1, custom_class_2]
-------
missing entry: custom_class_1
```

Failure message gives a clear explanation of how the actual and expected behaviors differed.

Figure 11.7 An appropriate assertion matcher will produce a well-explained test failure.

In addition to producing better explained failures, using an appropriate matcher often makes the test code slightly easier to understand. In the following snippet, the first line of code reads more like a real sentence than the second line:

```
assertThat(someList).contains("expected value");
assertThat(someList.contains("expected value")).isTrue();
```

In addition to ensuring that a test fails when the code is broken, it's important to think about how a test will fail. Using an appropriate assertion matcher can often make the difference between a well-explained test failure and a poorly explained one that will leave other engineers scratching their heads.

11.6 Use dependency injection to aid testability

Chapters 2, 8, and 9 provided examples where the use of dependency injection improved code. In addition to those examples, there's another very good reason to use dependency injection: it can make code considerably more testable.

In the previous chapter, we saw how tests often need to interact with some of the dependencies of the code under test. This occurs whenever a test needs to set up some initial values in a dependency or verify that a side effect has occurred in one. In addition to this, section 10.4 (chapter 10) explained how it's sometimes necessary to use a test double as a substitute for a real dependency. It's therefore clear that there are scenarios where a test will need to provide a specific instance of a dependency to the code under test. If there's no way for the test code to do this, it might well be impossible to test certain behaviors.

11.6.1 Hard-coded dependencies can make code impossible to test

To demonstrate this, listing 11.28 shows a class for sending invoice reminders to customers. The `InvoiceReminder` class doesn't use dependency injection and instead creates its own dependencies in its constructor. The `AddressBook` dependency is used by the class to lookup customers' email addresses, and the `EmailSender` dependency is used to send emails.

Listing 11.28 Class without dependency injection

```
class InvoiceReminder {
  private final AddressBook addressBook;
  private final EmailSender emailSender;

  InvoiceReminder() {
    this.addressBook = DataStore.getAddressBook();      // Dependencies are created
    this.emailSender = new EmailSenderImpl();           // in the constructor.
  }

  @CheckReturnValue
  Boolean sendReminder(Invoice invoice) {
    EmailAddress? address =
        addressBook.lookupEmailAddress(invoice.getCustomerId());   // Email address looked-up using addressBook
    if (address == null) {
      return false;
    }
    return emailSender.send(      // Email sent using emailSender
        address,
        InvoiceReminderTemplate.generate(invoice));
  }
}
```

There are a few behaviors that this class exhibits (such as the following), and we should ideally test each of them:

- That the `sendReminder()` function sends an email to a customer when their address is in the address book
- That the `sendReminder()` function returns true when an email reminder is sent
- That the `sendReminder()` function does not send an email when the customer's email address cannot be found
- That the `sendReminder()` function returns false when an email reminder is not sent

Unfortunately, it's quite difficult (and maybe even impossible) to test all these behaviors with the class in its current form, for the following reasons:

- The class constructs its own `AddressBook` by calling `DataStore.getAddressBook()`. When the code runs in real life, this creates an `AddressBook` that connects to the customer database to look up contact information. But it's not suitable to use this in tests, because using real customer data could lead to flakiness as the data changes over time. Another more fundamental problem is that the environment the test runs in probably doesn't have permission to access the real database, so during testing the returned `AddressBook` might not even work.
- The class constructs its own `EmailSenderImpl`. This means the test will have the real-world consequence of sending real emails. This is not a side effect that a test should be causing and is an example where we need to protect the outside world from the test (as discussed in chapter 10).

Normally, an easy solution to both these problems would be to use a test double for the `AddressBook` and the `EmailSender`. But in this scenario we can't do this because we have no way to construct an instance of the `InvoiceReminder` class with test doubles instead of real dependencies. The `InvoiceReminder` class has poor testability, and a likely consequence of this is that not all its behaviors will be tested properly, which obviously increases the chance of bugs in the code.

11.6.2 Solution: Use dependency injection

We can make the `InvoiceReminder` class a lot more testable and solve this problem by using dependency injection. Listing 11.29 shows what the class looks like if we modify it so its dependencies can be injected via the constructor. The class also includes a static factory function, so it's still easy for real users of the class to construct it without having to worry about dependencies.

Listing 11.29 Class with dependency injection

```
class InvoiceReminder {
  private final AddressBook addressBook;
  private final EmailSender emailSender;

  InvoiceReminder(
      AddressBook addressBook,
      EmailSender emailSender) {              // Dependencies injected via the constructor
    this.addressBook = addressBook;
    this.emailSender = emailSender;
  }

  static InvoiceReminder create() {
    return new InvoiceReminder(
        DataStore.getAddressBook(),           // Static factory function
        new EmailSenderImpl());
  }
```

```
  @CheckReturnValue
  Boolean sendReminder(Invoice invoice) {
    EmailAddress? address =
        addressBook.lookupEmailAddress(invoice.getCustomerId());
    if (address == null) {
      return false;
    }
    return emailSender.send(
        address,
        InvoiceReminderTemplate.generate(invoice));
  }
}
```

It's now very easy for tests to construct the `InvoiceReminder` class using test doubles (in this case a `FakeAddressBook` and a `FakeEmailSender`):

```
...
FakeAddressBook addressBook = new FakeAddressBook();
fakeAddressBook.addEntry(
    customerId: 123456,
    emailAddress: "test@example.com");
FakeEmailSender emailSender = new FakeEmailSender();

InvoiceReminder invoiceReminder =
    new InvoiceReminder(addressBook, emailSender);
...
```

As was mentioned in chapter 1, testability is heavily related to modularity. When different pieces of code are loosely coupled and reconfigurable, it tends to be much easier to test them. Dependency injection is an effective technique for making code more modular, and as such it's also an effective technique for making code more testable.

11.7 Some final words on testing

Software testing is a massive topic, and the things we've covered in these final two chapters are just the tip of a much bigger iceberg. These chapters have looked at unit testing, which is the level of testing that engineers usually encounter most frequently in their everyday work. As was discussed in chapter 1, two other levels of testing that you're very likely to come across (and make use of) are the following:

- *Integration tests*—A system is usually built up of multiple components, modules, or subsystems. The process of linking these components and subsystems together is known as *integration*. Integration tests try to ensure that these integrations work and stay working.
- *End-to-end tests*—These test typical journeys (or workflows) through a whole software system from start to finish. If the software in question were an online shopping store, then an example of an E2E test might be one that automatically drives a web browser to ensure that a user can go through the workflow of completing a purchase.

In addition to different levels of testing, there are many different types of testing. The definitions of these can sometimes overlap, and engineers don't always agree on exactly what they mean. A by no means exhaustive list of a few concepts that it's good to be aware of are as follows:

- *Regression testing*—Tests that are regularly run in order to ensure that the behavior or functionality of the software has not changed in an undesirable way. Unit tests are usually an important part of regression testing, but it can also include other levels of testing, such as integration tests.
- *Golden testing*—Sometimes referred to as *characterization testing*, these are usually based on a saved snapshot of the output from the code for a given set of inputs. If the observed output of the code ever changes, then the tests will fail. These can be useful for ensuring that nothing has changed, but when the tests do fail it can be difficult to determine the reason for the failure. These tests can also be incredibly fragile and flakey in some scenarios.
- *Fuzz testing*—This was discussed in chapter 3. Fuzz tests call the code with lots of random or "interesting" inputs and check that none of them cause the code to crash.

There is a wide and varied array of techniques that engineers can use to test software. Writing and maintaining software to a high standard often requires using a mixture of them. Although unit testing is probably the type of testing you will come across most, it's unlikely that it alone will fulfill all your testing needs, so it's well worth reading about different types and levels of testing and keeping up to date with any new tools and techniques.

Summary

- Concentrating on testing each function can easily lead to insufficient testing. It's usually more effective to identify all important behaviors and write a test case for each.
- Test the behaviors of the code that ultimately matter. Testing private functions is nearly always an indication that we're not testing the things that ultimately matter.
- Testing one thing at a time results in tests that are easier to understand, as well as better explained test failures.
- Shared test setup can be a double-edged sword. It can avoid the repetition of code or expensive setup, but it can also lead to ineffective or flakey tests when used inappropriately.
- The use of dependency injection can considerably increase the testability of code.
- Unit testing is the level of testing that engineers tend to deal with most often, but it's by no means the only one. Writing and maintaining software to a high standard often requires the use of multiple testing techniques.

You've made it to the end (and even read the chapters about testing)! I hope you've enjoyed the journey through this book and learned some useful things along the way. Now we're done with the 11 chapters of prelude, onto the most important part of the book: the readable version of that chocolate brownie recipe in appendix A.

appendix A
Chocolate brownie recipe

Chocolate Brownie Recipe

You will need the following:

100 g butter
185 g 70% dark chocolate
2 eggs
½ teaspoon vanilla essence
185 g caster sugar (or superfine sugar)
50 g flour
35 g cocoa powder
½ teaspoon salt
70 g chocolate chips

Method:

1. Preheat oven to 160°C (320°F).
2. Grease and line a small (6×6 inch) baking tin with baking paper.
3. Melt butter and dark chocolate in a bowl over a saucepan of hot water. Once melted, take off the heat and allow to cool.
4. Mix eggs, sugar, and vanilla essence in a bowl.
5. Add the melted butter and dark chocolate to the eggs and sugar and mix.
6. In a separate bowl, mix the flour, cocoa powder, and salt and then sieve into the eggs, sugar, butter, and chocolate. Mix just enough to fully combine.
7. Add chocolate chips and mix just enough to combine.
8. Place the mix into the baking tin and bake for 20 minutes.

Allow to cool for several hours.

appendix B
Null safety and optionals

B.1 Using null safety

If the language we're using supports null safety (and we've enabled it, should that be required), there will be a mechanism for annotating types to indicate that they can be null. This often involves a `?` character to indicate nullability. Code will often look something like the following:

```
Element? getFifthElement(List<Element> elements) {
  if (elements.size() < 5) {
    return null;
  }
  return elements[4];
}
```

The ? in Element? indicates that the return type can be null.

If an engineer using this code forgets to handle the scenario where `getFifthElement()` returns null, their code will not compile, as demonstrated in the following listing:

```
void displayElement(Element element) { ... }

void displayFifthElement(List<Element> elements) {
  Element? fifthElement = getFifthElement(elements);
  displayElement(fifthElement);
}
```

The parameter to this function is non-nullable (since the type is Element and not Element?).

The variable fifthElement is nullable, as its type is Element?.

A compiler error would occur at this line, since the function expected a non-nullable argument yet it's being called with a nullable value here.

To make the code compile, the engineer has to check that the value returned by `getFifthElement()` is not null before using it to call a function whose parameter is non-nullable. The compiler is able to deduce which code paths are only reachable when the value is non-null and thus determine if usage of the value is safe.

```
void displayFifthElement(List<Element> elements) {
  Element? fifthElement = getFifthElement(elements);
  if (fifthElement == null) {
    displayMessage("Fifth element doesn't exist");
    return;
  }
  displayElement(fifthElement);
}
```

This if-statement means that the function will return early if fifthElement is null.

The compiler can deduce that this line is only reachable if fifthElement is non-null.

NOTE: COMPILER WARNINGS VS ERRORS In C#, using a nullable value unsafely only results in a compiler warning and not a compiler error. If you're using C# and you've enabled null safety, it might be wise to configure your project to upgrade these warnings to errors to ensure they don't go unnoticed.

As we can see, with null safety we can use null values and the compiler will keep track of when a value logically can and cannot be null, and make sure a potentially null value is not used unsafely. This allows us to benefit from how useful null values are without suffering the dangers of null pointer exceptions (and alike).

B.1.1 Checking for nulls

Languages with null safety often provide a succinct syntax for checking if a value is null and only accessing a member function or property on it if it is not null. This can eliminate a lot of boilerplate, but the pseudocode convention in this book will stick with a more verbose form of checking for nulls to keep it analogous to a wider set of languages that don't offer this syntax.

Nonetheless, to show what is meant by this, imagine there's a function to look up an address that returns null if no address can be found:

```
Address? lookupAddress() {
  ...
  return null;
  ...
}
```

Some code that calls this function might need to check if the return value of `lookupAddress()` is null and only call a `getCity()` function on the address if it's not null. Code examples in this book will do this with a verbose if-statement to check for a null value:

```
City? getCity() {
  Address? address = lookupAddress();
  if (address == null) {
    return null;
  }
  return address.getCity();
}
```

But be aware that most languages that support null safety also provide more compact syntaxes for this kind of thing. For example, we would probably be able to write the code we just saw in a more succinct way using a *null conditional operator*:

```
City? getCity() {
  return lookupAddress()?.getCity();
}
```

As we can see, there are multiple benefits to utilizing null safety. Not only does it make our code less error prone, but it can also allow us to make use of other language features to make code a lot more succinct while still being readable.

B.2 Using optional

If the language we're using does not provide null safety, or if we can't use it for whatever reason, then returning null from a function might cause a surprise for a caller. To avoid this, we can instead use a type like `Optional` to force callers to be aware that the return value might not be present.

The code from the previous section looks like the following using an `Optional` type:

```
Optional<Element> getFifthElement(List<Element> elements) {
  if (elements.size() < 5) {
    return Optional.empty();
  }
  return Optional.of(elements[4]);
}
```

An engineer using this code could then write something like the following:

```
void displayFifthElement(List<Element> elements) {
  Optional<Element> fifthElement = getFifthElement(elements);
  if (fifthElement.isPresent()) {              <-- Checks that the optional value is present before using it
    displayElement(fifthElement.get())         <-- The value within the optional is accessed by calling the get() function on it.
    return;
  }
  displayMessage("Fifth element doesn't exist");
}
```

This is admittedly a little clunky, but `Optional` types typically provide various member functions that can make using them a lot more succinct in some scenarios. One example of this is an `ifPresentOrElse()` function (as seen in Java 9). If we rewrite the `displayFifthElement()` function to use `Optional.ifPresentOrElse()`, it would look like the following:

```
void displayFifthElement(List<Element> elements) {
  getFifthElement(elements).ifPresentOrElse(
      displayElement,                          <-- displayElement() is called with the element if it is present.
      () -> displayMessage("Fifth element doesn't exist"));   <-- The displayMessage() function is called if the element is not present.
}
```

Depending on our scenario, using an `Optional` type can be a little verbose and clunky, but the issue of unhandled null values can quickly become so pervasive that the cost of the extra verbosity and clunkiness usually more than pays for itself in terms of improved code robustness and reduced buginess.

Optional in C++

At the time of writing, the C++ standard library version of `optional` does not support references, meaning it can be hard to use it for returning class-like objects. A notable alternative is the Boost library version of `optional`, which does support references. There are pros and cons to each approach (which we won't go into here), but if you're considering using `optional` in your C++ code then it's worth reading about the subject:

- Standard library version of `optional`: http://mng.bz/n2pe
- Boost library version of `optional`: http://mng.bz/vem1

appendix C *Extra code examples*

C.1 The builder pattern

Chapter 7 contained a simplified implementation of the builder pattern. In reality engineers often make use of a number of techniques and language features when implementing the builder pattern. Listing C.1[1], demonstrates a more complete implementation of the builder pattern in Java. Some things to note in this implementation are as follows:

- The `TextOptions` class constructor is private to force other engineers to use the builder pattern.
- The `TextOptions` class constructor takes an instance of `Builder` as a parameter. This makes the code a little easier to read and maintain because it avoids very long lists of parameters and arguments.
- The `TextOptions` class provides a `toBuilder()` method that can be used to create a prepopulated instance of the `Builder` class from an instance of the `TextOptions` class.
- The `Builder` class is an inner class of the `TextOptions` class. This serves two purposes:
  - It makes the name spacing a little nicer, because the `Builder` can now be referred to using `TextOptions.Builder`.
  - In Java, this allows the `TextOptions` and `Builder` classes to have access to private member variables and methods on one another.

[1] Inspired by the forms of builder pattern seen in *Effective Java*, third edition, by Joshua Bloch (Addison-Wesley, 2017), as well as various codebases such as the Google Guava libraries.

Listing C.1 Builder pattern implementation

```
public final class TextOptions {
  private final Font font;
  private final OptionalDouble fontSize;
  private final Optional<Color> color;

  private TextOptions(Builder builder) {
    font = builder.font;
    fontSize = builder.fontSize;
    color = builder.color;
  }

  public Font getFont() {
    return font;
  }

  public OptionalDouble getFontSize() {
    return fontSize;
  }

  public Optional<Color> getColor() {
    return color;
  }

  public Builder toBuilder() {
    return new Builder(this);
  }

  public static final class Builder {
    private Font font;
    private OptionalDouble fontSize = OptionalDouble.empty();
    private Optional<Color> color = Optional.empty();

    public Builder(Font font) {
      this.font = font;
    }

    private Builder(TextOptions options) {
      font = options.font;
      fontSize = options.fontSize;
      color = options.color;
    }

    public Builder setFont(Font font) {
      this.font = font;
      return this;
    }

    public Builder setFontSize(double fontSize) {
      this.fontSize = OptionalDouble.of(fontSize);
      return this;
    }
```

Constructor private and accepts a Builder as a parameter

toBuilder() function allows creation of a pre-populated builder.

The Builder class is an inner class of TextOptions.

Private Builder constructor for copying from some TextOptions

```
    public Builder clearFontSize() {
      fontSize = OptionalDouble.empty();
      return this;
    }

    public Builder setColor(Color color) {
      this.color = Optional.of(color);
      return this;
    }

    public Builder clearColor() {
      color = Optional.empty();
      return this;
    }

    public TextOptions build() {
      return new TextOptions(this);
    }
  }
}
```

Some examples of how this code might be used are as follows:

```
TextOptions options1 = new TextOptions.Builder(Font.ARIAL)
    .setFontSize(12.0)
    .build();

TextOptions options2 = options1.toBuilder()
    .setColor(Color.BLUE)
    .clearFontSize()
    .build();

TextOptions options3 = options2.toBuilder()
    .setFont(Font.VERDANA)
    .setColor(Color.RED)
    .build();
```

index

A

B

C

F

M

N

S